UNHEALTHY WORK:
Causes, Consequences, Cures

Editors
Peter L. Schnall, Marnie Dobson,
and Ellen Rosskam

Associate Editors
Deborah R. Gordon, Paul A. Landsbergis,
and Dean Baker

Critical Approaches in the Health Social Sciences Series
Series Editor: RAY H. ELLING

Routledge
Taylor & Francis Group
LONDON AND NEW YORK

First published 2009 by Baywood Publishing Company, Inc.

2 Park Square, Milton Park, Abingdon, Oxon OX14 4RN
711 Third Avenue, New York, NY 10017, USA

Routledge is an imprint of the Taylor & Francis Group, an informa business

First issued in paperback 2017

Library of Congress Catalog Number: 2009008901
ISBN 13: 978-0-89503-335-2 (hbk)

Library of Congress Cataloging-in-Publication Data

Unhealthy work : causes, consequences, cures / editors, Peter L. Schnall, Marnie Dobson, and Ellen Rosskam ; associate editors, Deborah R. Gordon, Paul A. Landsbergis, and Dean Baker.
     p. ; cm. -- (Critical approaches in the health social sciences series)
   Includes bibliographical references and index.
   ISBN 978-0-89503-335-2 (cloth : alk. paper) 1. Industrial hygiene. 2. Public health.
3. Job stress. I. Schnall, Peter L. II. Dobson, Marnie, 1972- III. Rosskam, Ellen, 1960-
IV. Series: Critical approaches in the health social science series.
   [DNLM: 1. Occupational Health. 2. Occupational Diseases. 3. Occupational Medicine--methods. 4. Stress, Psychological. 5. Workload--psychology. 6. Workplace--psychology.
WA 400 U57 2009]

RC967.U513 2009
616.9'803--dc22

                                                          2009008901

Cover art: © Paul Chesley – Getty Images

ISBN 978-0-89503-335-2 (hbk)
ISBN 978-0-415-78469-6 (pbk)

Table of Contents

iii

CONCLUSION

Acknowledgments

This collected volume represents an array of work from researchers and scholars in various academic disciplines, including public health, epidemiology, sociology, anthropology, economics, and medicine, as well as from non-academics in the labor movement and from the business community. As editors we would like to thank all our contributors for their dedication to this project.

Much of this book evolved out of presentations made during a forum titled *The Way We Work and Its Impact on Our Health* held at the University of California, Los Angeles in April 2004. This forum was inspired by a small group of California researchers led by Dr. Julia Faucett, Dean of the School of Nursing at UC San Francisco. Dr. Faucett played a pivotal role in organizing this forum and advancing the project to where it is today. We would also like to thank the sponsors of the forum including: the Southern California Center for Occupational and Environmental Health (UCLA and UC Irvine); the Northern California Center for Occupational and Environmental Health (UC Berkeley, UC San Francisco, and UC Davis); the National Institute for Occupational Safety and Health (NIOSH); the Center for Social Epidemiology; as well as the Northern and Southern California Education and Research Centers, and, in particular, Dr. William Hinds, Director of the SC ERC.

Additionally the editors would like to acknowledge the ongoing support of this project by Dr. Dean Baker, Director of the UC Irvine COEH, and Dr. John Froines, Director of UCLA COEH. Also particularly important has been the funding and support generated by the Center for Social Epidemiology and, in particular, its sponsors Sherry and Jane Schnall, who have given generously to the Center.

Many people have helped along the way. The editors would like to acknowledge Dr. Karen Kendrick, Ms. Amanda Meaker, and Ms. Susan Holcomb, without whose efforts and support we could not have completed this project.

Co-editor Dr. Ellen Rosskam wishes to extend her gracious thanks to the Woodrow Wilson International Center for Scholars, Southeast Europe Project for allowing her the time and space to complete chapter revisions on this book.

The editors would like to acknowledge the two peer-reviewers who put significant time and effort into reviewing this substantial manuscript. Thanks to them and their insightful comments, the book was improved and reshaped considerably. We also thank Dr. Ray Elling as series editor at Baywood for his thoughtful input and commitment to this project.

Beyond the Individual: Connecting Work Environment and Health

Deborah R. Gordon and Peter L. Schnall

Work, so fundamental to basic survival and health, as well as to wealth, well-being, and positive social identity, has its darker and more costly side too.[1] Work can negatively affect our health, an impact that goes well beyond the usual counts of injuries, accidents, and illnesses from exposure to toxic chemicals. The *ways in which work is organized*—particularly its pace, intensity and the space it allows or *does not allow* for control over one's work process and for realizing a sense of self-efficacy, justice, and employment security—can be as toxic or benign to the health of workers over time as the chemicals they breathe in the workplace air. Certain ways in which work is organized have been found to be detrimental to mental and physical health and overall well-being, causing depression and burnout [1-2], as well as contributing to a range of serious and chronic physical health conditions, such as musculoskeletal disorders, hypertension, chronic back pain, heart disease, stroke, Type II diabetes, and even death [3-5]. Accordingly, many occupational health scientists refer to these particularly noxious characteristics of work as hazards or risk factors of the psychosocial work environment to which employees are exposed. Consider, for example, some of the following research findings linking work organization and health:

- Employees who remained at their jobs throughout a major downsizing at a factory in Sweden were twice as likely to die in the next 7-1/2 years from heart disease (and 30% more likely to die from all causes) as those who had no downsizing at their workplace [6];

---

[1] This introduction was in many ways a collective product of all the editors of this volume for which we are extremely grateful. We particularly acknowledge the invaluable and generous contribution of Dr. Marnie Dobson to its form and content.

- Men who experienced having little control over meeting the high demands of their jobs—what is called job strain—were three times more likely to have high blood pressure than those who experienced more control, even when all other risk factors were taken into account [7];
- Men and women employees who felt they were insufficiently rewarded for their efforts at work—what is called effort-reward imbalance—were twice as likely to suffer from cardiovascular disease, depression, or alcohol dependency compared to those who felt sufficiently rewarded for their efforts at work [8]; and
- Employees who felt that their boss was not fair-minded had almost a third more incidents of cardiovascular disease compared to employees who felt that their boss was fair-minded [9].

These studies show employees' experiences of job insecurity, intensified workload with little control, imbalanced reciprocity, and unfairness in the workplace can negatively affect their physical and mental health.

As we understand it today, a major pathway from these characteristics of the work environment to health or disease or injury is through the mechanism of *prolonged, chronic stress*. Stress is commonly thought of as a biological and psychological process located within the individual. The *sources* of stress, however, can be internal or external. Some occupational health researchers—including the editors of this volume—describe these sources of stress as "work stressors" as they arise in the work environment itself, specifically the social environment. Scientific evidence supports the conclusion that one connecting thread by which work stressors impact health is through the mechanism of *lack of control* over one's work environment or one's job. Low levels of control over work are closely related to and in fact part of the definition of being in positions of lower socioeconomic status, and importantly, people in these positions have a higher risk of developing more diseases and dying prematurely (see chapter 3). Ultimately, work stressors reflect an imbalance of power between employer and employee, an imbalance which is growing under the pressures of globalization, neoliberal policies [10], and economic competition. This imbalance is manifested in dwindling union membership [11], longer work days, decreasing vacation time, intensified work pace, greater work demands, and less employment and income security. Yet this social environment and its impact are often invisible, ignored, or overshadowed by the prevailing idea that locates the cause and cure of stress primarily in the individual, specifically the mind and emotions, and that considers stress at work essentially a psychological problem of individuals.

While the identification and elimination of physical health hazards at work continues to be a contested battleground for prevention and regulation in the United States [12-15], exposure to particular physical work environments, such as chemical toxins, radiation, noise, or needle sticks, *have* been recognized as legitimate work-related health hazards. Such widespread consensus, however, are still far off for hazards embedded in the way work is organized, leaving debate about how to control them even more distant.

This book grew from the conviction that a convincing international body of evidence *already exists* which demonstrates the negative health effects of particular types of work organization. In fact, stress in the workplace constitutes a "fast-growing literature" [16] and sociologists in the United Kingdom, where job stress is officially recognized, have already analyzed it in terms of "the making of a new epidemic" [17]. Yet this body of knowledge still has minimal circulation and impact in the United States, not only among employees, the group most directly affected by work risk factors, but also among employers, unions, physicians, government agencies, and other important stakeholders (see chapter 10).

This limited impact in the United States calls for inquiry and explanation, particularly as it sharply contrasts with other industrialized countries, particularly in Western Europe [18]. We believe it results not only from obvious and powerful political and economic forces [12] against identifying and limiting hazards related to work organization, but from less visible cultural forces as well, particularly the predominant value of individualism in the United States which manifests itself in the overwhelming tendency to locate the causes and responsibility for getting sick (disease etiology) and for getting better squarely on the shoulders of the individual. This focus makes it difficult to recognize the power of the social environment to influence disease or health, despite evidence to the contrary. In addition, dominant philosophical assumptions that sustain scientific preference for causal explanations that are measurable, material (biological), and close to a health outcome—for example, explaining heart disease by looking at high blood pressure as opposed to the workplace influences that can lead to both high blood pressure and heart disease—often make social explanations appear vague, as they are difficult to locate materially, invalid, as they are considered *immeasurable*, and of weak influence, as they are too far *upstream* from the real causative action. It is the synergistic combination of political, economic, cultural, and philosophical forces, we argue, that helps support and sustain a primary focus on individual rather than work or social environment causes of illness and that accounts for much of the limited response in the United States to the extensive research documenting hazards of the social-psychological work environment.

We begin this introduction with the premise that a good society must have as a moral basis the well-being of its working people. Five sections then follow that briefly address: 1) the political and economic context in which work has evolved into the current globalized system; 2) approaches to measuring and explaining sources of stress in the workplace and their impacts on health; 3) why a social approach to the workplace and health is so difficult in the United States; 4) a social approach to occupational health; and 5) the evolution and structure of this book.

A "GOOD SOCIETY" PROTECTS WORKERS FROM HARM AT WORK

As a society, we count our civility among a number of valued traits. High among them is our belief that people are entitled to work in conditions that are safe and not knowingly harmful to their health and to be fairly rewarded for their work. Since such conditions do not happen automatically or gratuitously, bitter struggles have been waged over the decades, often led by the collective power of organized labor, in order to pass laws to protect workers from unsafe working conditions that contradict basic human needs. Thus we place limits on age (such as prohibition of child labor), number of hours of work per day and week, and on how much a worker may carry. We institute rest breaks, lunch time, weekends, safety regulations, environmental protections and procedures, and minimum wage requirements. We require hard hats, masks, and other personal protections to limit exposure to known physical and chemical hazards. We view these hard-won protections as signs of our civility, community, and respect for each other, as progress from meaner Dickensian times to an ever more enlightened society, what we consider a good society.

Working conditions, most agree, should be safe from injury and avoidable illness or harm. Work should *not* make people ill in the process, and when it does, workers should be compensated accordingly. This understanding has become part of a basic, agreed-upon "social contract," in which the government is given some power to govern employers, employees, and the work environment. Our value for safe and healthy work was written into law in the Occupational Safety and Health Act (OSHA) of 1970.

The globalization of work and neoliberal practices of deregulation, however, are presenting serious challenges to established protections of worker health as well as posing new risks to health. As employment and work is continually reinvented in the United States, concern for the conditions of work is increasingly eclipsed by a growing attitude, "just be glad you have a job!"

GLOBALIZATION: THE CHANGING NATURE OF WORK AND CHALLENGES TO THE SOCIAL CONTRACT

Profound changes in the ways in which work is organized and carried out have taken place over the last 200 years, particularly in the Western world and more recently in the rapidly industrializing nations of Asia. Farming and craftwork, which predominated for many centuries, were largely replaced by the industrial revolution, and with it, skilled workers who had once exercised substantial control over their work processes were replaced by lower-skilled labor in new machine-based production technologies [19]. The introduction of Taylorism at the beginning of the 20th century—a new "scientific" approach to maximizing productivity— further reshaped the workplace by breaking down complex, traditional craft-based work processes into small, individual tasks to be performed in a specified amount of time, in a repetitive manner, and controlled by supervisors or mid-level management, leading to the birth of the assembly line. And while originally used for manufacturing, this lead to the assembly line mode of work organization has been transposed to service-sector and white-collar office jobs and to centralized multinational organizations which now divide up work tasks and processes often across national borders. The result of these and other 20th century developments: deskilled workers in many occupations with the power to control the production process increasingly concentrated in the hands of employers and management.

A second premise in this book, clearly influenced by globalization, is that the transformations in work and work organization that began 200 years ago are now accelerating so much as to even be considered another industrial revolution [20]. Globalization has included, among other things: outsourcing of labor to developing countries; feminization of the work force; increases in unemployment, underemployment, and employment insecurity; increases in temporary, part-time, flexible labor—"precarious work"; and a sharp increase in the economic gap between the rich and the poor (see chapter 2). In the 1998 Tokyo Declaration, occupational health experts from Europe, Japan, and the United States described this new world of work—"organization restructuring, mergers, acquisitions and downsizing, the frantic pace of work and life, the erosion of leisure time and/or the blending of work and home time" [21]—and the motor behind it: ". . . driven by economic and technological changes aiming at short-term productivity and profit gain" [21].

The social and economic forces brought about by global economic competition are determining the ways in which work is unhealthy, how noxious it is, and who are most exposed. In fact, these changes disproportionately affect people in lower socioeconomic positions, particularly women and immigrant ethnic minority groups, whose health is already more vulnerable. Women are becoming the poorest component of the workforce, and in turn, the most numerous, being employed in low-income service-sector and manufacturing jobs (see chapter 2). Migrant workers searching desperately for employment are being pulled into developed nations where they often become part of disadvantaged minority groups concentrated in the lowest-skilled work and marginal sectors of the economy that offer minimal or no benefits, such as health insurance.

In industrialized countries, this globalization of the economy over the last 30 years has led to a second round of new systems of work organization, such as lean production [22], and the intensification of work through increased work demands on a reduced workforce. Consider some of the following data:

- one-third or more major organizations broadly reduced their workforce in the 1990s and between January 1999 and December 2001;
- 9.9 million jobs were eliminated, and temporary employment multiplied six-fold to nearly three million between 1982-1998 [10, pp. 184-185];
- the average work year for working age couples in the United States has increased by nearly 700 hours in the last two decades of the twentieth century [23], more hours per year than any other industrialized country. Time away from home, due to commuting, has increased significantly while vacation time has decreased [24].

Although little addressed in the United States, these changing working conditions are negatively affecting worker health, indicating that the gains of "lean" production for employers come at a high cost to workers' health (see chapters 6 and 7). For example, in a 2007 U.S. survey, about three-quarters (74%) of workers at all occupational levels reported feeling stress from work [25]. And this stress proves very costly: disability reported as due to job stress in 1997 (23 days) was four times greater than the median for all other injuries and illnesses combined [26]. In a 1998 study of 46,000 workers, health care costs were nearly 50% greater for employees reporting high levels of stress in comparison to those who were "stress-free" [27].

While the causes of ill health may be in question, the spiraling costs of employee health—both due to work injuries and payment of health insurance—has moved health and work to front and center stage. Clearly, not all stakeholders (e.g., management, labor, employees, government) share the same interest in protecting worker health [12, 15], with many in management/business seeing it primarily as a cost and a drain on profits. More recently, however, efforts are being made to redefine worker health as an investment and source of profit. This book addresses how these social and economic processes are changing both work and the health of working populations.

Notwithstanding the abundant problems around work in developing countries, this book focuses mainly on the detrimental health effects experienced by working people in industrialized countries, particularly in the United States, albeit with the aim that this knowledge can be applied in developing countries as well.

PSYCHOSOCIAL STRESSORS AT WORK LEAD TO POOR HEALTH

By what mechanisms do social factors—from class differences to poverty to racism to work organization—become embodied in human experience? In other words, how does the social enter the body? In this book, we focus on stress as a fundamental pathway between the social world (the work environment) and the body. Although debate continues over exact definitions of the term *stress*, it is generally agreed that stress is best understood as a *process* originating in 1) environmental demands or stressors, which 2) if appraised (evaluated or experienced) as threatening, will trigger 3) acute (immediate) emotional and physiological reactions, which if repeated and prolonged, will give rise to 4) biological (for example, high blood pressure) and behavioral (for example, smoking or alcohol use) effects, which in turn can lead to 5) long-term health consequences, such as chronic disease (e.g., hypertension) and eventually death. Throughout the *stress process,* other factors, either within us or within the environment, 6) may protect or *buffer* people exposed to stress from its potentially adverse health impact [28].

The study of stress and work—variously referred to as work stress, job stress, and occupational stress—approaches an industry of publications in itself. Theories of work stress abound [29-32], each with its own important distinctions and specific technical languages. This book aims to translate and demystify those languages so that non-experts and researchers can better communicate and learn from each other. One main approach to work stress, and the one proposed throughout this book—a public health approach that originated in Scandinavia [19, 33, 34]—has focused on the links between work, stress, and cardiovascular disease (heart attacks and strokes) (see Chapter 6) and the determining power of the UK environment.

Another dominant approach to work stress considers the sources of stress as primarily an "interactional/transactional" relationship between the work environment *and* the individual worker, often referred to as person-environment fit [35]. This approach considers physiological response to stress (as indicated by biological arousal such as elevated blood pressure) as dependent upon a subject's perception (appraisal) of stress. In other words, stress is only registered if a person consciously experiences something as stressful. In contrast, the public health approach argues that work stressors are an *objective* part of the work environment. Regardless of whether environmental demand is actually experienced at any one time as stressful or not, *chronic* encounters or exposures with such situations will lead to a physiological arousal of stress in the body if not the mind of *most* people, at *most* times, and in *most* places [29, p. 3]. This argument is supported by recent research that confirms that physiological arousal (such as increased blood pressure or heart rate) can take place even when individuals do not report feeling "anxious" or "stressed," particularly when the situations they encounter are normal and routine, as in everyday work [28]. Importantly, then, stressors can apparently affect our health *even* if we are not always conscious of them or are feeling anxiety. In this way, the public health model expands the traditional occupational health approach of objective hazards and exposures to include a new type of environment neither chemical nor physical, but what is referred to as *psychosocial* or simply social.

To be sure, correctly understanding what chronic or repeated and prolonged exposure means is critical to identifying *unhealthy* levels of stressors. Some level of stress enhances performance in life situations, including work. However, the increasing consensus in the scientific community is that occupational stressors are a threat to human health, a burden *in and of themselves*, not only as they contribute to the risk of developing chronic diseases [28]. In this sense, stress is rarely referred to as something positive and good.

Thus, the key distinction for the public health approach is between stress and stressors—the distinction between *self-reported stress,* on the one hand, which is what most people think of or refer to when they talk about stress, and *exposure to psychosocial work stressors*, on the other. Hypertension, "the silent killer," exemplifies this process: infrequently associated with symptoms of stress or anxiety [36] but strongly associated with job stressors (such as job strain and effort-reward imbalance).

In turn, the survey questions used to measure and analyze these stressors aim primarily at evaluating *workplace conditions, not the emotions* of the people involved. Several particular job characteristics have been identified as hazardous. In the demand-control or job strain model [19], one of the most widely accepted models of work stress [29], strain (physical or mental distress) results from a combination of high psychological demands coupled with low control or decision latitude over carrying out the work tasks. Decision latitude is a technical term meant to combine both the authority to make decisions, e.g., having a say over how one organizes one's work tasks, with the chance to use and develop skills on the job (skill discretion). Together with social support at work, control helps us deal with, or *buffer,* the effects of work demands [37]. Workers exposed to high demands yet who have high levels of control over how the work is to be done—a common situation among managers and professionals, for example—evidence fewer stress-related health problems than those lacking control or social support at work [37].

A second model within the public health approach, referred to as the "effort-reward imbalance model" [35], locates the source of stress-related illness in a perceived imbalance between the effort one puts out on the job and the rewards one receives. In other words, a perceived lack of reciprocity or fairness (high effort plus low rewards) can lead to adverse health consequences for the people involved. This model assesses both the characteristics of work and the subjects' evaluation/ appraisal of the importance such characteristics have to them.

Research has consistently shown that workers in jobs with high demands and low control (job strain) are at increased risk of developing and dying from cardiovascular disease, *even* after taking into account known biomedical and behavioral risk factors, including high serum cholesterol, cigarette smoking, and high blood pressure [3, 7]. Thus, while the dominant approach to work stress and to cardiovascular disease in the United States focuses on getting individuals to change their individual behaviors (offering programs for weight loss, smoking cessation, and exercise, for example), evidence shows that even taking these factors into consideration, workers showing evidence of job strain are *still* at a greater risk of early death from cardiovascular disease than those who don't. Work stressors also have been regularly linked to an increased risk of musculoskeletal disorders (such as back pain and tendinitis) [4] and with psychological ill health [1, 38].

"Organization of work" (or work organization) is a term recently taken up by the National Institutes for Occupational Safety and Health (NIOSH), the U.S. government research agency concerned with work and health, to capture particular characteristics of the work environment [39]. The term was first used to refer to high demand, low control, high effort, and low reward characteristics, but gained additional meaning in the 1990s and beyond as major changes in the organization of work, such as lean production and precarious work, have spread around the world. Stress at work was recognized as a leading health and safety problem by NIOSH, and in 2002, "organization of work and occupational health and safety" was identified as one of 21 priority agenda items of the National Occupational Research Agenda (NORA) [39].

Together, these risk factors capture threats to workers' *social survival*, as opposed to their physical survival [40]. Such was the conclusion of medical anthropologist Bev Davenport in a recent study of hypertension among transit operators, based on the bus drivers' sense that "your job was on the line at all times, . . . someone was looking over your shoulder and you could get busted for almost any infraction and then lose your security" [40, p. 143]. Some experience of uncontrollability of the work environment or the job is echoed in the *constrained agency* experienced by many people on the bottom of unequal situations, which physician/anthropologist Paul Farmer and others refer to as "structural violence"[2] [41].

---

[2] The term "structural violence" refers to a form of violence embedded in the systematic ways a given social structure or social institution assaults human dignity and constrains human freedom, while at the same time slowly killing people by preventing them from meeting their basic needs. In *Mountains Beyond Mountains: Healing the World: The Quest of Dr. Paul Farmer* by Tracy Kidder, Random House, New York, 2004.

It is reasonable to conclude that one of the mechanisms by which social class contributes to ill health is through exposure to stressful working conditions. The current increase in social inequality—the unequal distribution of wealth and opportunity—in the United States (see chapter 3) undoubtedly means that greater proportions of the working population are and will be exposed to poor working conditions. Recognizing this threat is a fundamental task for those concerned with occupational health and population health.

POLITICAL, ECONOMIC, AND CULTURAL DIMENSIONS OF WORK-RELATED DISEASE ETIOLOGY

A third premise of this book is that political, economic, and cultural forces play major roles in how the work-health relationship is conceptualized, studied, diagnosed, and treated. As many historians have carefully documented, social forces such as politics and economics have much to say about what we know and do not know in science [42], much as they clearly influence what impact particular scientific findings will have. Similarly, some historians, social scientists, and analysts of medicine have long challenged the idea that disease categories and etiology reflect objective, natural states free from social and cultural influence. Sociologist Sylvia Tesh [43], for example, could have been thinking of contemporary approaches to work and health etiology and prevention in the United States and Scandinavian countries when she argued that embedded in approaches to illness prevention lie "hidden arguments" of a social, political, and economic nature. Which scientific knowledge and theories are used, which are ignored, are all affected by political struggles among diverse interests, which reflect different beliefs about the relative responsibilities of the *individual* or *the group (collective, community)* for people's health.

Arriving at the answers to these many questions involves debates and disagreements over data, evaluations of cause and effect, and battles over regulation and prevention that reflect assumptions, interests, and power well beyond the specific topics discussed. Objective scientific data constitute only one part of the picture and rarely provide simple or unambiguous answers. Rather, science is also a collective, social process in which consensus and authority are required in order for something to be legitimately identified as a "work-related illness." Political and economic forces fight to influence which scientific findings are produced and circulated, which diseases are recognized and officially designated as "work-related." In many developed countries such as Scandinavia, Canada, Italy where political and economic systems are oriented to the good of the collective—exemplified by universal policies of national health insurance, guaranteed paid vacation time for all workers, minimum pensions for all—and where not coincidentally the labor movement remains powerful, data connecting specific working conditions to health are routinely collected and the study of work and health significantly developed. In striking contrast, no national databases assessing working conditions and health of the same person even exist in the United States [23], making the scientific documentation of connections between workplace characteristics and health effects extremely difficult. In the United States, businesses might be subject to increased regulatory monitoring and loss of profit and control in the workplace if more common health problems (such as hypertension, cardiovascular disease, and depression) are recognized and defined as by-products of demanding, low control, and insecure work. In the absence of a national health plan in the United States, health costs are borne by businesses through the provision of health insurance and Workers' Compensation.

The tendency to ignore the potential impact of work on health is most strikingly demonstrated in the near complete absence of questions about work and working conditions in the routine medical history taken by physicians in the United States, whereas "job strain" is illegal in a number of European countries [18].

A final premise of this book is that one of the main "languages" in the United States is *individualism*: we think, talk, act, evaluate, explain, and blame first and foremost in terms of the individual rather than a community or a social context. We think of disease and illness in terms of risk factors or health habits or lifestyle or genes *of an individual*; we think of prevention as directed toward changing the individual—for example, through stress management techniques, more exercise, or healthy eating habits—rather than toward the workplace, community, economic, or political systems. The individual is considered responsible not only for his or her health but also for his or her achievement or failure at work, under the assumption of equal opportunity and meritocracy, a philosophy of, "you get what you deserve (or earn)" [44]. Those who fail, by being sick, unemployed, underemployed, or poor, are often considered second-class citizens.

The dominance *of individualism* shows up in our everyday and professional language in which social phenomena are often referred to in psychological and/or individual terms. For example, work stress researcher Cary L. Cooper writes about, "The new psychological contract and associated stressors," while asking: "How can organizations continue to demand more and more of their employees, including loyalty, while providing less and less job security and support? Is the *psychological* contract between employer and employee worth the metaphorical paper it is written on?" [27, p. 1, italics ours].

Disease risk factors, such as smoking, drinking, and exercise behaviors, are approached as if they were entirely individual when in fact they are strongly affected by social factors, including work stress and social class, in their genesis and reinforcement. Cigarette smoking, as an example, arose as a common behavior in the early 20th century with the mass production of cigarettes and their widespread dissemination and use among troops during World War I to cope with combat stress. Weight is affected by work that requires less physical labor, and by work stress, which can exhaust people and limit their ability to exercise—factors not entirely within the control of individuals. Similarly, the experience of stress itself is often approached as a matter of individual will, as many stress management programs teach that "it's up to you whether stress affects your health or not." This book will show why this standard stress management advice is only one side of the story; even if we put them out of our minds and "get used to them," chronic, everyday stressors in our work environment can still affect our health [28].

Final obstacles to greater recognition of social causes of illness lie in dominant approaches to knowledge in science in the United States. For example, social environmental conditions, such as social climate or a sense of powerlessness or job insecurity, which many people suspect affects their health, are readily dismissed as scientifically intangible and non-measurable, and thus receive little explanatory and preventive attention. Similarly, the fact of individual variation in response to environmental stressors is also used as support for individualist approaches. If response is varied, if not all people get equally stressed from the same situation, so the argument goes, the prime mover must be individual, not environmental. This approach to environmental toxins, including cigarettes, often reflects an ideology of survival of the fittest; rather than setting the bar to the threshold that protects the weakest so that everyone will be protected, the weakest individuals are "eliminated."

Finally, most chronic illnesses have no one single cause, but rather result from multiple influences, one of which may be work. Working conditions can cause, contribute to, accelerate, or trigger symptoms of ill health. Requiring evidence that work is the *only* cause of an illness raises the threshold criteria for labeling something work-related so high it discourages official recognition and prevention of the *contribution* of many working conditions to ill health and injury.

CONNECTING THE DOTS: WHAT NEEDS TO BE DONE?

One of the purposes of this book is to bring into awareness the connections between the political and social hierarchies in which we live and work and experiences of physical strain and distress [45]. It may seem easy, but *making the connections between social conditions and individual health is, not accidentally, quite difficult.*

While healthy work can **appear** expensive to employers in short-term and monetary terms, when one takes into account the social burdens on the health care system, or on families and increasing household debt and household bankruptcy due to the costs of ill health or unemployment due to ill health, the costs of disability payments or workers' compensation insurance for employers—prevention of disease **saves** money. But this way of thinking requires a shift from considering businesses as autonomous entities, fully responsible for all their costs themselves, to considering work and businesses as part of a larger collective which shares responsibility. The prevailing assumption is that if an illness is labeled "work-related," then the employers are responsible for cause, costs, and cure. This undoubtedly discourages interest in learning about the impact of work on health, much less preventing it. Nevertheless, while companies do bear some burden for rising health care costs and workers' compensation, most costs for occupational disease today are not paid by employers but by individuals and their families and the Social Security system [46].

In this global economy, U.S. companies must compete with prices world-wide, including those based on minimal worker protection. Hard-earned elements of our social contract are being altered, high among them the formation and power of labor unions, sometimes in plain sight, more often secretly, but most importantly, without the engagement, discussion, and agreement of working people. Thus, two fundamental problems, the changing nature of work and the costs of health and health care, move in parallel: the search for profit in an increasingly competitive global economy—where enough profit is becoming a contradiction in terms—through intensified and insecure work, on the one hand, and a chronic concern for people's health and the cost of it, on the other. It appears to be a zero-sum game.

By connecting some often invisible dots between work and health, this book presents a social approach to occupational health, one that focuses on unhealthy workplace practices and their health, human, and economic costs to workers and employers alike. The strongest appeal to employers is usually made by showing how worker health costs affect their bottom line. Yet this presents a societal challenge—the need for companies to survive and grow, which requires that work processes be efficient and competitive—while ensuring that work is sufficiently safe, humane, and financially rewarding to meet employees' needs. As a society, we must go beyond the bottom line as our ultimate justification. This book argues for embracing healthy practices and humane working conditions not only to save money and to increase economic productivity, but *"because that is what good societies do and what human beings need and deserve"* [47].

The work ethic appears to be very strong and dominant in the United States. However, as Lipscomb et al. write, "We live in a society that values work, yet this value does not always extend to the worker" [48, p. 42]. While working hard is a fundamental American cultural value, working ourselves to death—literally—or into chronically ill health, is not worthy of pride as a nation. Whereas labor unions and collectively bargained agreements limited workload and required employers to provide vacation, sick leave, and pensions, increasingly companies employ work-forces that are non-unionized with little or no protections and enforcement of existing laws. As individuals we must question the power of the employer to allow and even require unnecessary suffering at work and remember that suffering (or stress) will find its way into our bodies and have effects throughout our lives. The effects do not end with the shift.

OVERVIEW: FROM THE FORUM TO THE BOOK

The beginnings of this book are rooted in a forum organized in 2004 among various stakeholders in California, *The Way We Work and Its Impact on our Health,* aimed at finding a common ground and connecting the dots between work and health. The initiators of the Forum are university researchers in occupational health, committed to producing accurate scientific knowledge that is also understandable to all people and that leads to appropriate practices. The follow-up of the conference is partly to be found in this volume, which built upon the initial presentations of authors from various disciplines and backgrounds with input from the editors.

The book focuses on both problems and solutions related to noxious work environments and their health impacts. Part I presents the social context of work within the forces of globalization today and the important changes taking place in work in the United States and Canada; Part II presents scientific findings that link the globalization of work and particular modes of work organization with their consequences and costs of ill health and lowered productivity for employees, employers, taxpayers, and the broader society. And Part III asks, "what can and should be done to reduce and prevent these health consequences?," and offers some answers through actual case examples of strategies used by labor unions, researchers, and businesses.

REFERENCES

1. Rugulies, R., U. Bultmann, B. Aust, and H. Burr, Psychosocial Work Environment and Incidence of Severe Depressive Symptoms: Prospective Findings from a 5-Year Follow-up of the Danish Work Environment Cohort Study, *American Journal of Epidemiology,* 163:10, pp. 877-887, 2006.
2. Rafferty, Y., R. Friend, and P. Landsbergis, The Association between Job Skill Discretion, Decision Authority and Burnout, *Work and Stress,* 15:1, pp. 73-85, 2001.
3. Belkic, K., P. Landsbergis, P. Schnall, and D. Baker, Is Job Strain a Major Source of Cardiovascular Disease Risk?, *Scandinavian Journal of Work Environment and Health,* 30:2, pp. 85-128, 2004.
4. Krause, N., D. R. Ragland, B. A. Greiner, S. L. Syme, and J. M. Fisher, Psychosocial Job Factors Associated with Back and Neck Pain in Public Transit Operators, *Scandinavian Journal of Work Environment and Health,* 23:3, pp. 179-186, 1997.
5. Krause, N. and D. R. Ragland, Occupational Disability Due to Low Back Pain: A New Interdiscipline Classification Based on a Phase Model of Disability, *Spine,* 19:9, pp. 1011-1020, 1994.
6. Vahtera, J., M. Kivimäki, J. Pentti, A. Linna, M. Virtanen, P. Virtanen, and J. Ferrie, Organisational Downsizing, Sickness Absence, and Mortality: 10-Town Prospective Cohort Study, *British Medical Journal,* 328:7439, pp. 555, 2004.
7. Schnall, P. L., C. Pieper, J. E. Schwartz, R. A. Karasek, Y. Schlussel, R. B. Devereux, et al., The Relationship between "Job Strain," Workplace Diastolic Blood Pressure, and Left Ventricular Mass Index. Results of a Case-Control Study [Published Erratum Appears in JAMA 1992 Mar 4;267(9):1209], *Journal of the American Medical Association,* 263:14, pp. 1929-1935, 1990.
8. Siegrist, J., Social Reciprocity and Health: New Scientific Evidence and Policy Implications, *Psychoneuroendocrinology,* 30:10, pp. 1033-1038, 2005.
9. Kivimaki, M., M. Elovainio, J. Vahtera, and J. E. Ferrie, Organizational Justice and Health of Employees: Prospective Cohort Study, *Occupational and Environmental Medicine,* 60, pp. 27-34, 2003.
10. Navarro, V., Neoliberalism, Health Inequalities, and Quality of Life, *International Journal of Health Services,* 37:1, pp. 47-62, 2007.
11. Brown, M. P., Labor's Critical Role in Workplace Health and Safety in California and Beyond—as Labor Shifts Priorities, Where Will Health and Safety Sit?, *New Solutions,* 16:3, pp. 249-266, 2006.
12. Navarro, V. (ed.), *The Political and Social Context of Health,* Baywood, Amityville, NY, 2004.
13. Tweedale, G. and J. McCulloch, Science Is Not Sufficient: Irving J. Selikoff and the Asbestos Tragedy, *New Solutions,* 17:4, pp. 293-310, 2007.
14. Levenstein, C., Asbestos: Immoral Fiber, Licentious Interests, *New Solutions,* 17:4, pp. 275-278, 2007.
15. Rest, K., Silenced Science: Air Pollution Decision-Making at the EPA Threatens Public Health, *New Solutions,* 17:1-2, pp. 13-16, 2007.

16. Rossi, A. M., P. L. Perrewé, S. L. Sauter, and S. M. Jex, Foreword, in *Stress and Quality of Working Life: Current Perspectives in Occupational Health*, Rossi, A. M., P. L. Perrewé, and S. L. Sauter (eds.), IAP, Greenwich, CT, pp. ix-xi, 2005.
17. Wainwright, D. and M. Calnan, *Work Stress: The Making of a Modern Epidemic*, Open University Press, Buckingham, UK, 2002.
18. Levi, L., The European Commission's Guidance on Work-Related Stress and Related Initiatives: From Words to Action, in *Stress and Quality of Working Life: Current Perspectives in Occupational Health*, Rossi, A. M., P. L. Perrewé, and S. L. Sauter (eds.), IAP, Greenwich, CT, pp. 167-182, 2005.
19. Karasek, R. and T. Theorell, *Healthy Work: Stress, Productivity, and the Reconstruction of Working Life*, Basic Books, New York, 1990.
20. Cooper, C. (ed.), The Changing Nature of Work: The New Psychological Contract and Associated Stressors, in *Stress and Quality of Working Life: Current Perspectives in Occupational Health*, Rossi, A. M., P. L. Perrewé, and S. L. Sauter (eds.), IAP, Greenwich, CT, pp. 1-8, 2006.
21. The Tokyo Declaration, *Journal of the Tokyo Medical University*, 56:6, pp. 760-767, 1998.
22. Landsbergis, P. A., J. Cahill, and P. Schnall, The Impact of Lean Production and Related New Systems of Work Organization on Worker Health, *Journal of Occupational Health Psychology*, 4:2, pp. 108-130, 1999.
23. Sauter, S. and L. Murphy, Approaches to Job Stress in the United States, in *Stress and Quality of Working Life: Current Perspectives in Occupational Health*, Rossi, A. M., P. L. Perrewé, and S. L. Sauter (eds.), IAP, Greenwich, CT, pp. 183-197, 2006.
24. Gross, J., As Parents Age, Baby Boomers and Business Struggle to Cope, in *New York Times*, New York, p. 1, March 25, 2006.
25. APA, *Stress a Major Health Problem in the U.S. Warns APA: New Poll Shows Stress on the Rise, Affecting Health, Relationships and Work*, American Psychiatric Association, Washington, DC, 2007.
26. Webster, T. and B. Bergman, Occupational Stress: Counts and Rates, *Compensation and Working Conditions*, 4:3, pp. 38-41, 1999.
27. Goetzel, R., D. Anderson, R. W. Whitmer, R. J. Ozminkowski, R. L. Dunn, and, J. Wasserman, The Relationship between Modifiable Health Risks and Health Expenditure: An Analysis of Employer Hero Health Risk and Cost Databases, *Journal of Occupational and Environmental Medicine*, 40, pp. 843-854, 1998.
28. Johnson, J. V., Occupational Stress, in *Preventing Occupational Disease and Injury*, Weeks, J. L., B. S. Levy, and G. R. Wagner (eds.), American Public Health Association, Washington, DC, 2004.
29. Cooper, C. (ed.), *Theories of Organizational Stress*, Oxford University Press, Oxford, 1998.
30. Cooper, C., P. Dewe, and M. O'Driscoll, *Organizational Stress: A Review and Critique of Theory, Research, and Applications*, Sage, CA, 2001.
31. Dollard, M., Introduction. Costs, Theoretical Approaches, Research Designs, in *Occupational Stress in the Services Professions*, Dollard, M., A. Winefield, and H. Winefield (eds.), Taylor and Francis, London, pp. 1-43, 2003.
32. Peterson, C. L. (ed.), *Work Stress: Studies of the Context, Content, and Outcomes of Stress*, Baywood, Amityville, NY, 2003.
33. Johnson, J. V. and G. Johansson (eds.), *The Psychosocial Work Environment and Health: Work Organization, Democratization, and Health. Essays in Memory of Bertil Gardell*, Baywood, Amityville, NY, 1991.

34. Siegrist, J., Adverse Health Effects of High-Effort/Low-Reward Conditions, *Journal of Occupational Health Psychology*, 1, pp. 27-43, 1996.
35. Lazarus, R. S. and S. Folkman, *Stress, Appraisal and Coping*, Springer, New York, 1984.
36. Friedman, R., J. E. Schwartz, P. L. Schnall, et al., Psychological Variables in Hypertension: Relationship to Casual or Ambulatory Blood Pressure in Men, *Psychosomatic Medicine*, 63, pp. 19-31, 2001.
37. Johnson, J. V. and E. M. Hall, Job Strain, Workplace Social Support, and Cardiovascular Disease: A Cross-Sectional Study of a Random Sample of the Swedish Working Population, *American Journal of Public Health*, 78:10, pp. 1336-1342, 1988.
38. Van Der Doef, M. and S. Maes, The Job Demand-Control(-Support) Model and Psychological Well-Being: A Review of 20 Years of Empirical Research, *Work & Stress*, 13:2, pp. 87-114, 1999.
39. Sauter, S. L., W. S. Brightwell, M. J. Colligan, et al., *The Changing Organization of Work and Safety and Health of Working People: Knowledge Gaps and Research Directions*, NIOSH, CDC, Cincinatti, OH, 2002.
40. Davenport, B. A., *Driving Driven: Urban Transit Operators, Hypertension, and Stress (Ed) Management*, Unpublished Ph.D. dissertation in Medical Anthropology, UCSF/UCB, 2004.
41. Farmer, P., On Suffering and Structural Violence: A View from Below, *Daedelus*, 125:1, pp. 261-283, 1996.
42. Proctor, R., *Cancer Wars: How Politics Shapes What We Know and Don't Know About Cancer*, Basic Books, New York, 1995.
43. Tesh, S., *Hidden Arguments: Political Ideology and Disease Prevention Policy*, Rutgers University Press, New Brunswick, NJ, 1988.
44. Ehrenreich, B., *Bait and Switch*, Harper, New York, 2005.
45. Lock, M. and N. Scheper-Hughes, A Critical-Interpretive Approach in Medical Anthropology, in *Medical Anthropology: Contemporary Theory and Method*, Sargent, C. and T. M. Johnson (eds.), Praeger, Westport, CT, pp. 41-70, 1996.
46. Leigh, J. P. P. and J. A. Robbins, Occupational Disease and Workers Compensation: Coverage, Costs, and Consequences, *Milbank Quarterly*, 82:4, pp. 689-722, 2004.
47. Frank, J. W., Concluding Remarks California State Forum, in *The Way We Work and It's Impact on our Health*, University of California, Los Angeles, 2004.
48. Lipscomb, H. J., D. Loomis, M. A. McDonald, R. A. Argue, and S. Wing, A Conceptual Model of Work and Health Disparities in the U.S., *International Journal of Health Services*, 36:1, pp. 25-50, 2006.

PART I

The Changing Nature of Work

OVERVIEW

Work in advanced industrialized societies has undergone a continuous transformation over the last 200 years. As globalization proceeds, more people are drawn into its global processes. The end of the "cold war" and the relatively recent entry of Chinese, Indian, Russian, and other workers into the global economy have resulted in a doubling of the global workforce to more than three billion workers during the last 30 years. A debate has raged over the social consequences of these changes: whether they have benefitted or harmed working people. There has been a rising standard of living for many in Western societies paralleled by better health and longer life expectancies. Still, there are some bleak realities of life under capitalism which demand attention, not the least of which among them is the fact, according to the ILO,[1] that as of 2003 some 1.4 billion people work for less than U.S. $2/day and that 20% of the world's working people (600 million) earn less than U.S. $1/day which is well below the extreme poverty level. Concomitantly, 25,000 people die each day worldwide from hunger (more than nine million each year). One must inquire whether these are the consequences of globalization or has globalization acted to mitigate these outcomes?

The four chapters in this section attempt to capture the changes that have occurred worldwide, and particularly in the United States and Canada, during the last several decades, including the quantity and kind of work, the composition of the workforce, and changes in employment contracts. In her chapter "Economic Globalization and Its Effects on Labor," Chrisy Moutsatsos places current workplace conditions in a larger context of global economic changes since the 1970s. Many of these changes, she argues, have resulted from the economic philosophy and practices of neo-liberalism which have led to deregulation of labor markets, and "the dismantling of the social protections and redistributive policies of the earlier welfare state." This

[1] *World Employment Report 2004-05: Employment, productivity and poverty reduction*. Geneva, ILO 2005. ISBN 92-2-114813-0. For more information, please contact ILO Department of Communication and Public Information at communication@ilo.org

chapter explores why the American workplace has shifted from production to service provision, flexible labor, and outsourcing its jobs overseas. Changes in the U.S. workplace are placed in the context of changing economies around the world. Low-income workers in China and India are part of a growing global labor force, out-competing low-income workers in the United States and Europe. The key issues in this shift include structural adjustment, offshore manufacturing and free trade zones, manufacturing and service economies, lean production, flexible labor, the decline of unions, privatization, and the decline of welfare as well as the increase in gaps between the rich and the poor. She notes that the changes that have occurred over the last three decades in the composition of the workforce, the quantity and kind of work, and employment contracts are profound. The proportion of the employed population working both part-time and greater than full-time has increased. In addition, a much higher proportion of the working age population is now in the labor market than in 1970, principally because of the increase in numbers of working women. Among the employed population, while the length of the work week has changed little, the total work effort has increased dramatically, due to an increase in the number of weeks worked each year. Conversely, "private time" and "vacation time" have declined steeply, meaning less time to recover from work-related injury or fatigue. These changes in the numbers working and the increasing quantity of work have occurred in tandem with a shift away from manufacturing industries and occupations to service industries and occupations and a blurring of the traditional distinctions between salary and wage earners.

Historically, salaried workers were paid a fixed salary and provided some degree of job security to design or oversee production ("white-collar workers"); while the greater majority were paid hourly wages (hence the term "wage earners") to carry out production without job security ("blue-" or "pink-collar workers"). However, in recent years there has been a melding of working conditions, with blue-collar workers being asked to be involved in improving production processes, while white-collar workers are no longer provided the same levels of job security.

Paralleling the worldwide changes in work noted in the first chapter in this section have been the profound changes in socioeconomic status with increasing social inequality and unequal income distribution, particularly in the United States. In his chapter, Jeffrey Johnson describes and defines the varying definitions of social class as it is used to understand the ongoing association between socioeconomic status and health. He presents data on the relationships between social class, occupational grade, and cardiovascular disease and examines contemporary debates over the social mechanisms that allow income inequality to impact population health. Workers directly feel the cost of income inequality as they find themselves unable to find work at a living wage and increasingly find that they are priced out of health care insurance in the United States. Income inequality is being fueled by the larger global economy through increasing part-time work and underemployment. The intensification of work leads to more health problems, which results in higher costs to business, or if there is a lack of health insurance, the health problem may become more severe before being effectively treated in an emergency situation.

Smith and Frank take up the issue of the impact of globalization on job characteristics in Canada in their chapter "The Changing Nature of Work in Canada and
Other Developed Countries: What Do the Trends Over Time Tell Us?" In contrast
to the United States where there is a paucity of data on the nature and quality of
work, the Canadian Labor Market Survey demonstrates that it is possible to collect
such data nationally. They note that there have been a number of changes in the
Canadian labor force over the last 30 years. Underemployment and multiple
job holdings have both increased, although these patterns differed by gender
and level of education with women now generally more likely to be both underemployed and multiple job holders compared to men. The percentage of underemployed and unemployed labor force participants increases with lower levels of
education. They find wages are increasing in Canada but are unequally distributed
with low-wage, uneducated, unskilled workers reporting no real change in labor
market income in the last 20 years. The Canadian data show increases in service
work (with production decreasing; paid and unpaid overtime; dual-worker families,
and absenteeism due to family responsibilities; the proportion of highly skilled
or educated workers doing jobs that do not require their skills or education;
and part-time work, multiple job holding, temporary work, and contract labor).
Consequently, as work expands, private life contracts, with less time for family
and one's self.

Ed Yelin addresses in his chapter, "The Changing Nature of Work in the United
States," the impact of globalization on the U.S. workforce from two perspectives: 1)
changes in employment and 2) the distribution of jobs by occupation and industry.
With regard to employment, he notes that more people have entered the U.S.
workforce during the last 40 years mostly due to the fact that women now comprise
more than 50% of the workforce (the percentage of men working has actually fallen
slightly during this period with the largest decrease being among the 55- to
64-year-old age group). Stagnant wages for men may be one reason women are
leaving home to enter the workplace.

His findings include: 1) increased labor force participation among working age
adults, especially women; 2) increased numbers of people per family in the workforce; 3) increases in the number of weeks worked per year; 4) increases in part-time
work, nonstandard shifts, non-consecutive days off, and multiple job-holding; and
5) a decrease in blue-collar occupations (manufacturing and extractive industries),
and an increase in white-collar occupations. He draws on Paul Osterman's earlier
work on historical patterns of employment suggesting that there has been a flattening
of the occupational hierarchy consistent with a "democratization" of work tasks.
But democratization is not necessarily all positive, as it is accompanied by an
increase in contingent employment, job loss, and job insecurity. In sum, job demands
have increased significantly, while job security has decreased significantly. In
addition, he notes, as does Chrisy Moutsatsos in her chapter, that U.S. workers are
working more hours per year due mostly to working a greater number of weeks
per year (as opposed to hours per week). Changes in the nature of the type of jobs
in the United States appear similar to those noted in Canada by Peter Smith and
John Frank (authors of chapter 4) with manufacturing workers decreasing 25% while

service workers in the United States have increased 300%. These changes reflect the impact of off-shoring—the movement of production jobs from industrialized Western countries to the less developed countries in the periphery, such as in Asia.

Unfortunately, as these chapters document, many important questions about today's workforce remain unanswered with our current findings. Few studies and fewer governments collect information about the workforce to allow for recognition of the changing prevalence of work stressors and how these exposures relate to health outcomes. What is needed are institutionally supported surveillance systems that can identify high-risk populations early enough to allow for interventions prior to the manifestation of work-related epidemics of negative health outcomes.

CHAPTER 2

Economic Globalization and Its Effects on Labor

Chrisy Moutsatsos

This chapter examines contemporary labor trends in the United States and else-where as they are shaped by economic globalization. Globalization is a term currently used to refer to everything from international trade, migration, and tourism, to the distribution of American popular culture to the rest of the world. Globalization and the strong economic connections between various regions of the globe are not a new phenomenon. What is new is the fact that since the 1970s most preexisting economic, social, cultural, and political connections between various nations are intensifying as the movement of goods, services, capital, culture, and people across national boundaries is speeding up at an unprecedented rate [1, 2]. In other words, globalization at the moment is marked by unprecedented global interconnectivity, integration, and interdependence in all realms, including the economy, social life, technology and information, culture, politics, and ecology [3].

Some of the key features of economic globalization include: the development of international organizations such as the World Trade Organization (WTO), the World Bank, the International Monetary Fund (IMF), and the International Finance Corporation (IFC), all working to ensure the economic vitality of nation-states around the world; the majority of the world's economic activity orchestrated by transnational corporations and taking place in the regions of North America, Western Europe, Japan, and Southeast Asia; a dramatic increase in the number of capital investments and the rate by which they cross the globe; a great increase in the dependency of economically developing countries on industrialized countries; and the restructuring of labor markets in industrialized and industrializing regions [cf. 4, 5].

Economic globalization as it is experienced today is deeply seated in the political and economic philosophy and practices of neoliberalism which "emphasizes the primacy of markets over government, and which advocates policies that have led to the deregulation of labor markets, and the dismantling of the social protections and redistributive policies of the earlier welfare state" (see chapter 3, p. 41). Since the 1970s, neoliberal thinking has fueled the principal policy commitments proposed primarily by the American international financial institutions mentioned above as a "global model" that should be adopted by all countries wishing for economic growth and political stability. Also known as the "Washington Consensus," these policies strive to produce a global economic reality which operates with very little state intervention and regulation. Moreover, according to these policies, governing states are prompted to minimize the public sector and privatize all social services. Finally, labor markets should be "flexible," i.e., accommodate the fluctuating needs of various industries but without the safety net of long-term secure employment (the meaning of flexibility will be discussed in detail shortly) [6].

Neoliberal thought and the American-based economic policies it has inspired have steadily impacted the global economy, and especially the international division of labor. Since the 1970s, key changes in labor trends in the United States and Northern Europe have included a decline in manufacturing jobs, the loss of high-wage jobs in management, an increase in low-wage occupations in the service sector, and an overall increase in unemployment rates, especially in Europe [7, 8]. As American and Northern European wage earners have been struggling to stay in the labor market, new labor markets have been forming in the industrializing regions of the world.

Another important labor trend, and an outcome of neoliberal economic policies, has been a qualitative change of steady, unionized labor into "flexible" labor, i.e., more and more jobs, whether requiring skilled or unskilled labor[1] have been steadily transformed from long-term, contractual and with benefits and union representation, to contingent, part-time, and non-contractual [5, 6, 9]. This trend, in addition to the increase of women's participation in the labor force globally, has been identified as the "feminization" of the workforce [10, 11]. In addition to the increase of women's participation in the workforce worldwide, the feminization of labor also refers to the changing nature of jobs to have characteristics more closely associated with those typifying jobs historically performed by women [12, pp. 22-30].

Characteristics of women's work include low wages, low status, low levels of training, less stable work, less powerful jobs, emotional labor, and a lack of skills development or occupational development. Overall, the feminization of labor is directly associated with much greater social and economic *insecurity* [11, 12]. In other words, the feminization of labor also refers to the increase in part-time and temporary contractual work, lower wages, and lower skilled workers replacing more highly skilled workers [12].

These changes in global labor trends correspond to the shift toward flexible business practices employed by corporations and manufacturers and the decline of unionized workforces in industrialized countries since the 1970s. For instance,

---

[1] The term "unskilled" labor should be used critically, as there is really no job that doesn't require some level of skill. Framing a job as requiring "no skill" is one way for underpaying one's effort. For more on this discussion, see [9, 10].

such practices include off-shoring, outsourcing, and subcontracting. While off-shoring refers to the relocation of business processes such as production, manufacturing, or services from one country to another, outsourcing involves the assigning of selected company operations to an outside entity that specializes in the management of the outsourced operations often at a significantly reduced cost. Both off-shoring and outsourcing may involve subcontracting. Retailers such as Wal-Mart, Sears Roebuck, J. C. Penney, Nike, Reebok, and Liz Claiborne, while they design and market their brand-name products, they habitually use middlemen in regions such as Southeast Asia, China, and India to allocate the production of their goods [10].

Globalization is not a new phenomenon and its proponents have attributed to it the creation of wealth, improved health, as well as the global transference of democratic political structures, laws, social movements, international aid organizations, and the progression of new information technologies which have arguably had much positive impact throughout the world. However, the impact of economic globalization on labor trends, individual workers, communities, and nations is a subject of contentious debate. The proponents of economic globalization advocate that the moving of factory and other business operations around the globe has and will continue to create new work opportunities for the unemployed and will thus allow all regions of the world to develop economically, and decrease poverty, unemployment rates, disease, and gender inequality.[2] One famous proponent of this stance is American economist Jeffrey Sachs. In his best-selling book on how to end world poverty, Sachs advocates that the financial investing of developed countries in developing ones, and the subsequent creation of new jobs, is the necessary solution to pull all people out of poverty. Although he recognizes that many workers in these areas are suffering from a lack of governmental regulations and workplace rights, he sees this circumstance as a necessary evil that will eventually lead to growth for all [13].

However, many others see the new trends in the global labor market as deeply problematic. Despite the optimism of the globalization hopefuls, at the moment some three billion people—that is about half the number on the globe—live on under two dollars a day and 86% of the world's resources are still consumed by the world's wealthiest 20%.[3] Thus, critics of economic globalization argue that the last two decades of market growth on a global level have mainly assisted the growth of economies in the already industrialized countries rather than those of peripheral regions. While enabling transnational corporations to remain profitable, economic globalization is creating new global inequalities for individuals and communities along economic, racial, and gender lines [4, 14, 15]. According to The Institute of Management's *Flexible Patterns of Work* (1986), the new global labor market consists of a small core and ever-expanding peripheries. For the most part, the core

[2] See IMF "The Impact of Globalization on Workers and Their Trade Unions" (http://www.imf.org)
[3] http://www.globalissues.org/TradeRelated/FreeTrade/Neoliberalism.asp

is comprised of workers who are employed full-time and are important for the future of the corporation. This segment, which is constantly decreasing in all industrialized countries, also enjoys employment stability and retirement benefits. The first periphery is comprised of full-time workers with "easy-to-acquire-and-find" abilities and is marked by high turnover. The second periphery, which is the fastest growing labor segment at present, is comprised of workers who are part-time or temporary, for the most part have no collective representation, and have very little employment security or benefits [16].

The economic inequality that has resulted from this new international division of labor is also related to the significant wage differences that exist between workers in the industrialized world versus the industrializing ones. For instance, while in 1975 the highest average manufacturing wage was less than two and a half times the lowest average wage (Sweden, $7.18 per hour vs. Japan, $3.00), in 2002 the ratio between the highest wage and the lowest was 27 to 1 (Germany, $24.31 vs. China $0.90) [17].

In addition to the increase of global economic inequality and the steady replacement of secure employment with insecure and flexible labor, neoliberal economic and political policies and the global economic restructuring that has resulted from them have dangerously challenged workers' representational politics and voice worldwide [6]. Whereas union membership in the 1950s was about a third of the workforce, in 1983 it had fallen to 20%. Today, union membership has declined to about 12% of the workforce, because of job losses and despite recent gains in some industries and regions such as California.[4] As argued by Annycke, Bonnet, Dasgupta, Figueiredo, Khan, Rosskam, and Standing, in the 2004 ILO report *Economic Security for a Better World*, since the 1980s there has been a global decline in collective voice, particularly as it manifests itself in union membership. Collective voice is necessary for maintaining employment security and a check on company and other policies that undermine the welfare of workers. Nonetheless, all hope is not lost as there are a number of emerging forms of collective voice worldwide (for details, see [6]).

This chapter briefly examines first, the historical events that have led to contemporary patterns in economic globalization and global market trends; then it will explore the specific characteristics of the changes in labor in the industrialized and industrializing world, the rise of flexible labor worldwide, and the feminization of labor.

THE ECONOMIC CRISIS OF THE 1970S AND THE MOVE TO FLEXIBLE LABOR

The new flexible business strategies that are impacting the current state of the global division of labor, such as off-shoring and so forth, are the direct outcome of

---

[4] Zipperer, B. and John Schmitt. Union Rates Increase in 2007, January 25, 2008, http://www.cepr.net/content/view/1441/220/ accessed 2/08/2008.

changes in the global flow of capital since World War II. The U.S. effort to rebuild the war-destroyed economies of Western Europe and Japan aided its post-war boom with the expansion of U.S.-based corporations in these regions and elsewhere. However, by the mid-1960s as European and Japanese economies had recuperated and their markets had become saturated by products made in the United States, they were ready to establish export markets of their own. At this time, the United States was faced with the overproduction of mass produced standardized products that were not absorbed as readily in the international market as they had been previously. Additionally, the excess of U.S. governmental funds and the few opportunities for capital investment and growth abroad resulted in a period of economic recession. It was exacerbated by the oil crisis of the early 1970s brought on by the raising of oil prices by the Gulf States. The decision of the member states of OPEC (Organization of Oil-Exporting Countries) to restrict the production of oil resulted in the doubling of the previously inexpensive oil prices on which the U.S. economy depended. Since Japan, England, and France had developed more energy-efficient technologies, in contrast to the hard-hit U.S. economy, they were not affected as much [16, 18].

The U.S. economy responded to the culminating economic crisis of the 1970s with a 15-year period of intense economic, social, and political restructuring and economic readjustment. As a result, the existing model of capitalist production and accumulation, known to economists as Fordism, was succeeded by a new economic model called flexible accumulation.[5] As explained by cultural geographer David Harvey, unlike Fordism, flexible accumulation emphasizes "the emergence of entirely new sectors of production, new ways of providing financial services, new markets, and above all, greatly intensified rates of commercial, technological, and organizational innovation" [16]. The shift from Fordism to flexible accumulation has been the key force behind the contemporary restructuring of the new international labor trends [7].

As U.S., Northern European, and East Asian manufacturers have strived to produce affordable new commodity trends and innovative products to keep mostly North American and European consumers interested and always buying, they have been on a constant quest for locating cheaper and unregulated labor markets in other world regions, resorting to outsourcing manufacturing production and subcontracting practices. Former colonies of North America and Europe, in their effort to pay their economic development debts to the International Monetary Fund and the World Bank, have been identified as promising labor markets. Consequently, over the last 40 years they became the primary locales for the outsourcing of manufacturing by recruiting their young and mostly unskilled populations. For instance, countries such as the Philippines, Mexico, China, and India, to name a few, have established several industrial areas called Free Trade Zones (FTZ), also

---

[5] According to Regulation Theory, which is the most widely accepted theory of capitalist activity, Fordist accumulation and flexible accumulation are the two distinct periods of capitalist accumulation in the twentieth century. Similarly to other Marxist approaches, Regulation Theory views capitalist expansion as a "discontinuous process, one marked by expansion followed by crisis" [5].

known as Export Processing Zones. These are usually designated manufacturing territories of the host country located on the outside of large urban centers and when possible, on the banks of rivers.

FTZs have been very attractive to foreign investors because they are usually for the most part exempt from any existing government regulations regarding labor costs and contracts. Tax codes instituted in the United States have allowed many industrialists to avoid paying taxes on the profits they make overseas in these industrial zones. Since the 1970s, FTZs have been integral to the international division of labor. According to Millen, "by the mid-1990s, over 200 EPZs employed over two million workers in more than 50 countries. Around 80% of the workforce in EPZs are women, the majority of whom are single and between the ages of 18 and 25" [10, p. 188].

The off-shoring of manufacturing jobs has been succeeded by the off-shoring of service work. For instance, U.S. firms are steadily moving a variety of service jobs, such as programming, customer service call centers, and entry-level word-processing jobs to India, the Barbados, and other countries with lower wages than the United States, and an ample supply of what is considered "unspecialized labor." This trend of moving service jobs abroad has been enabled in part because of technological advances which allow information to move rapidly about the globe. Currently, occupations in the United States that are targeted for offshore service production include medical receptionists, diagnostic support services, paralegals, financial support, computer and math professionals, and office support [19].

CONTEMPORARY LABOR TRENDS

Job Loss in the United States and Other Industrial Regions

There have been two recent waves of job loss in the United States and other industrialized countries due to global economic restructuring: one among manufacturing workers in the 1980s, and the other among white-collar workers in manufacturing, wholesale, retail trade, and public and private services in the early 1990s [20]. While in 1970 manufacturing engaged 69.7 million workers in the United States, Australia, France, Italy, Sweden, Canada, Japan, Germany, The Netherlands, and England, by 1997 it employed only 63.7 million. The overall greatest loss of manufacturing jobs has occurred in England, from 8.5 million in 1970 to 4.9 million in 1992 [21]. In the United States, the loss of factory jobs has been continuous. Between 1991 and 1992, 5.5 million factory workers were laid off [21]. In the three-year period between 1999 and 2001, 1.3 million were terminated from their jobs [22] while in the 2003-2005 time period another 1.1 million factory workers were out of work, constituting the highest percentage of laid-off workers in U.S. history [23].

While all sectors of manufacturing have been downsized, certain sectors have been altered more due to the movement of factories to FTZs or elsewhere in the developing world. Beginning in the 1970s, American steel companies began changing their investment strategies and business operations resulting in the shrinking of this industry. By 1984, 20% of all steel companies' productive capacity was eliminated and 40% of all steelworkers were laid off. American rubber workers have faced the same fate. Whereas in the 1950s, American-based companies produced 75% of the country's tires and 50% of the country's other non-tire rubber goods, today half of U.S. tire manufacturing is conducted offshore. Also, while in the 1960s General Motors and Ford produced more than 50% of all the cars in the world, by 1992 their output accounted for only 20.9%, and in 2006 output was only 16%. Overall, within the last 30 years, employment in the U.S. car industry has declined by 25% [24], despite concerted efforts by the UAW and other unions to stem the tide of layoffs. As a result, union membership in manufacturing overall continues to fall, from 11.7% in 2006 to 11.3% in 2007, compared to small gains in the private health and education sectors from 8.3% to 8.8% between 2006 and 2007.[6]

According to the Office of Aerospace Automotive Industries, although jobs in the automotive industry increased by 8% between 1991 and 2005, looking at this trend alone "hides a significant and dramatic downturn that has decimated the industry since the year 2000. In that year, employment reached a peak of 1,313,600 workers, but the drop from that peak over the ensuing five years to 2005's level represents a *decline of 16%*, with a *total loss of 215,000 jobs*" [25].[7] Other manufacturing sectors that moved overseas include consumer electronics, the garment industry, and the semiconductor industry [24].

In the 1990s, white-collar workers, believing their jobs were safe and stable, also began losing their jobs to downsizing, off-shoring, and subcontracting. For instance, companies such as AT&T, Delta Airlines, and Eastman Kodak laid off thousands of middle management and higher-paid employees in order to remain profitable. Sears, Roebuck and Company let 50,000 employees go [20].

Facing Unemployment

The availability of cheaper labor costs abroad has resulted in unemployment and non-traditional work arrangements for U.S. and Northern European workers. In the 1990s the overall number of unemployed workers in all developed countries was measured at 36 million [26]. The rates of unemployment have been greater in Europe than, for instance, the United States and Japan. In 1996 unemployment in the countries that are part of the OECD (Organization for Economic Co-operation and Development) was 7.5% while in the European Union it was 11.3%, and in Eastern Europe it was 11.8%. In 1997 Eurostat reported an estimated 18 million unemployed E.U. citizens [26]. Ten years later, unemployment rates have decreased, in the European Union to 7.3% and in the OECD to 5.4% [27-29].

Unemployment in industrialized countries has been greater among women and the young than men. In the European Union in 1997, 12.6% of women and 21.1% of people under the age of 25 were unemployed. In contrast, the industrializing

---

[6] Union Members in 2007. Bureau of Labor Statistics: United States Dept. of Labor, Washington, DC. USDL 08-0092 (Jan. 25, 2008), http://www.bls.gov/news.release/pdf/union2.pdf
[7] http://www.ita.doc.gov/td/auto/domestic/staffreports/Jobloss.pdf

countries belonging to the APEC (Asia-Pacific Economic Cooperation), such as China, Hong Kong, Malaysia, Korea, Thailand, and Singapore, have had an overall unemployment rate of only 3% or lower. In 1996, the Philippines had the highest rate at 8.6% [26].

The material and psychological effects of losing one's job are varied and their severity cannot be underestimated. These effects can range from depression, the dissolution of personal relationships, alcohol and drug abuse, and even suicide [30]. When, in 1982, an RCA television cabinet-making factory in Indiana moved its operations overseas, 850 factory workers had to come to grips with unemployment and the realization that they had been "dumped" from the "middle class" [31]. As one laid-off employee stated:

> We are down to rock bottom and will probably have to sell the house to live or exist until I find a job here or somewhere else. I have been everywhere looking in Cass, White, and Carroll counties. We have had no help except when the electric company was going to shut off the utilities in March and the Trustee [County Welfare] paid that $141. My sister-in-law helps us sometimes with money she's saved back or with food she canned last summer [31, p. 64].

As reported by the U.S. Labor Department, only 26% of manufacturing workers in the United States who have lost their jobs have found new jobs paying the same or more than their previous one [26]. Overall, the reemployment rate for factory workers who have lost their jobs has been lower than that of workers displaced from other industries. During the 2003-2005 period the reemployment rate for manufacturing workers was 65% lower than the overall reemployment rate for all displaced laborers [23]. Currently, industrial jobs are being replaced by jobs in the service sector such as educational services, health care and social assistance, and professional and business services. According to the Bureau of Labor Statistics, these services represent the industry sectors with the strongest employment growth and are projected to grow more than twice as fast as the overall economy.[8]

The Development of New Labor Markets

As manufacturing and other jobs have been decreasing in the United States and other industrialized countries, new job markets have been forming and employing workers in industrializing regions of the world. American and Northern European consumer goods are now made all over the world in diverse localities such as Sri Lanka, Indonesia, the Philippines, Belarus, Moldova, Haiti, and the Marianna Islands. According to the United Nations Development Program's 1999 *Human Development Report,* the majority of transnational corporations invest in countries with an ample supply of what is often considered unskilled labor, loose work regulations, and with the most political stability. An example of such a top choice of countries at the moment is China.

---

[8] http://www.bls.gov/news.release/ecopro.nr0.htm

The Chinese government, anticipating foreign investment, began establishing "special economic zones" along its coastal regions in the 1980s. By the mid-1990s, Korean and Taiwanese investors preferred investing in China instead of their own countries, since it was viewed as a primary source of new pools of cheap labor. In 1995, the ratio of factory wages in China compared to South Korea, Taiwan, and Japan was approximately 1:30. Between 1985 and 1996, the portion of Chinese exports from foreign-owned plants grew 40%. During the 1990s, China took 45% of direct foreign investment in Asia. China now produces about half of the world's shoes and a proliferating array of electronic items, toys, and garments for the global economy [32].

In order to accommodate the new industrialization efforts of the government, farms and rice paddies became the grounds where new factories were built, thus resulting in the loss of the primary means of independent subsistence for large numbers of the rural population. Many local farmers now live off the rents from the factories, while literally millions of migrants from China's poorer rural areas have left their homes and families and have migrated to the new industrialized areas. Unlike factory workers in the United States who are still protected by labor laws and work an average 40 hours per week, China's factory workers often labor through 12-hour shifts, 7 days a week, under the disciplinary quota-watchful eye of foreign supervisors and managers [32].

In their discussion of the working conditions in 54 non-state-run Chinese footwear factories, Chan and Xiaoyang argue that "the management practices at workplaces in the PRC [People's Republic of China] are no less authoritarian, disciplinary, and punitive than their counterparts in England in the period of the Industrial Revolution" [33, p. 561]. The researchers found that workers were forced to work overtime in addition to the already long work hours they completed on a daily basis, had their bathroom visits monitored, and were even physically punished when management thought appropriate. While men workers were more likely to be fined for breaking factory rules such as not wearing an identification badge, wearing the wrong shoes, drinking water during production hours, talking while working, and so on, women were mostly penalized by having to work overtime [33]. On occasion, violating one of the factories' regulations would be punishable by docking one's pay for half a day to up to several days.

Extreme discipline is only one of the ongoing issues Chinese factory workers have to face. Ongoing sweatshop working conditions, the absence of necessary safety precautions, very low wages, and labor violations are constantly issues reported and monitored by China Labor Watch.[9] Being migrants from rural areas, most workers are also plagued with the alienation and hardship that comes from being removed from close-knit communities and kin [31, 34].

The Rise of Flexible Work

The trend toward "flexible labor" results partly from declines in union power and union membership. In the United States, union membership has declined considerably

[9] http://www.chinalaborwatch.org/index.htm

over the last 50 years, despite tiny gains in 2007, particularly in California which saw 200,000 more union members. The trend was in the opposite direction for manufacturing workers.[10] U.S. and Northern European manufacturing workers who have lost their jobs because of outsourcing, if not left unemployed, mostly have to settle for what are defined as non-traditional and flexible work arrangements, i.e., part-time, lower paying, non-unionized service jobs without benefits, and fixed-term contracts. As reported by the U.S. Labor Department, only 26% of manufacturing workers in the United States who have lost their jobs have found new jobs paying the same or more than their previous one [22] (see chapter 5).

The part-time employment numbers differ much from country to country. For instance, in 1996, countries with high levels of part-time employment were the Netherlands (36.5%), Ireland (27.9%), and Switzerland (27.4%), while part-time employment was relatively low in Hungary (4.9%), Greece (5%), and Italy (6.6%). In the European Union, 32% of the part-time labor market was dominated by women while only 5% was comprised by men. In the United States in 1997, 18% of all wage and salaried employees worked part-time, that is 22.0 million out of 119.5 million full-time workers. In 1995, part-time labor comprised two-fifths of the Canadian labor market and has been the growing type of labor in this country [35].

Automobile producers such as Toyota, Nissan, and Honda provide a clear picture of the fate of temporary workers. While hiring an average of 2,000 people to staff their production line, only 1,200 workers may enjoy permanent status at one time. The other 800 are categorized as temporary or contingent laborers who are hired by temporary work agencies such as Manpower. In the event of an economic downturn, the temporary workers are the first to go without ever receiving any type of compensation.

In 1996, one in four persons in the American labor force was a contingent, temporary, or part-time worker. According to the Bureau of Labor Statistics, in 2005 contingent workers accounted for 1.8 to 4.1% of all U.S. employment.[11] Such laborers included typists, secretaries, engineers, computer specialists, lawyers, or managers. Their salaries were paid by an employment agency and excluded any benefits packages [36].

Whether working for a factory or an office, temporary work takes a toll on individuals [8]. In her work, called "Just a Temp," Jackie Rogers notes how temporary workers in addition to receiving low wages and engaging in contingent employment, also experience alienation on multiple levels: first, in relation to the other more permanent workers; second, in relation to the work itself; and third, in terms of their sense of self-identity as valuable members of the workforce. Temps she interviewed referred to the work they had to do as "monotonous, mindless, and even robotic" [8, p. 205]. As one of her informants noted, "I worked in a bank and stuffed envelopes for five days straight. He delegated me these huge boxes to stuff,

---

[10] Zipperer, B. and John Schmitt. Union Rates Increase in 2007, January 25, 2008, http://www.cepr.net/content/view/1441/220/ accessed 2/08/2008.
[11] Bureau of Labor Statistics. Contingent and Alternative Employment Arrangements, February 2005, http://www.bls.gov/cps/USDL 05-1433

so like I would only have to go to him two days later. I'd just go to him when I ran out of stuff to stuff" [8, p. 206]. In terms of their alienation from other permanent workers, one informant puts it in perspective:

> And there was no Christmas present for you under the tree like the rest of the company would get. . . . There were some places where it was just blatant, just terribly blatant. Whenever there was going to be a company party or something, the temps had to stay and work. You know, cover the phones so the regular people got to go. You could tell where the second-class citizenship started [8, p. 208].

Temps also struggled with their identity as workers. Workers noted that they could not be themselves but instead they figured they had to "have a pretty strong personality so that you can be *adaptable* and you have to be *political* . . . be very *pliable* [and] *mold* to any situation . . ." [8, p. 21, emphasis in original].

The Feminization of Labor

The new trends shaping labor around the world have impacted all workers but have affected women laborers in specifically gendered and racialized ways. Women in industrialized countries are the main labor force for the growing service sector. In 1991, two-thirds of employed women in the United States worked as teachers, nurses, clerks in sales, and in other services. U.S. women workers on average make only 70% of what men make. There has been a solid increase in the ratio of women's income to men's income, but only because men's income has been on the decline.

While women in the United States and other industrialized countries are mainly working in service industries, Third World women workers have been incorporated in the international division of labor as workers in agriculture, large-scale manufacturing of goods such as handicrafts and food processing, and as workers in the sex and tourist industries [11]. Much of the world's 27 million laborers working in FTZs are young women. In Bangladesh, 80% of the garment workers are women. And while both men and women off-shore workers are considered cheap laborers by foreign investors, women fare even worse in terms of compensation than their fellow male laborers. Women workers living and working in the so-called "Third World" tend to get hired in the lower paying industries known as "light" industries, such as those manufacturing textiles, garments, food processing, cigarettes, toys, shoes, electronics, and data entry. Men in the same regions tend to be preferred as workers in the higher paying "heavy" industries of steel, automobile, chemical and petrochemical, aircraft and aerospace, shipbuilding, and machinery [37].

Women and more often young girls with minimal formal schooling are preferred as workers of the global assembly line because of dominant ideologies rooted in patriarchy. They tend to construct females as easier to discipline than men workers, and thus easier to control by a mostly male-dominated management. They are also the preferred work pool because as women, they are viewed as dependents of fathers, brothers, or husbands and as such, it is deemed justifiable that they get paid less than their male counterparts. For the most part, their work is constructed as temporary, unskilled, and easily replaceable [38].

Anthropologist Aihwa Ong's work on Malaysian women workers of the electronics industry is a case in point. Her ethnography of Malaysia's Free Trade Zones' employment practices shows that girls from the age of 16 were the main recruits for work producing electronics components. In this context, there are many gendered and racial assumptions shaping the preference of young women workers over local men laborers. For one, as Muslims these young women are perceived by foreign managers of the plants as "docile," "obedient," and thus easily controlled and directed. Their fingers are considered to be more "agile" and "nimble" than men's and thus "naturally suited" for the delicate handling of electronic components. Working only till the age of 24, these workers are regularly replaced with new young women workers because of serious burnout and persistent health issues, such as chronic fatigue, irreversible eyestrain, and poisoning due to overexposure to chemicals, and so forth [39].

Feminization of Work and Migration

Economic globalization has also impacted the trends of global migration. As argued by sociologist Saskia Sassen, "globalization has produced a new kind of migration, with new conditions and dynamic of its own" [40, p. 255]. Unlike the migrations of the past where it was mostly men laborers migrating in search of work, currently much of the migrating labor force is constituted by women. For instance, in "1946, women were fewer than 3% of the Algerians and Moroccans living in France; by 1990, they were more than 40%. Overall, half of the world's 120 million legal and illegal migrants are now believed to be women" [41, p. 5].

The new feminization of the migration of women from industrializing regions to industrialized ones has a direct correlation to the increase of the entrance into the paid labor market by North American and Northern European women. Unable to keep up with the double-shift of household work in addition to paid labor, many American and Northern European women have since the 1970s become more and more dependent on the domestic labor of migrant nannies, maids, and nurses from places such as the Philippines and Latin America, to name a few [41].

Living and working abroad, having often left their own children in the care of relatives, women migrant workers often face many challenges: adapting to new cultural demands, long and unregulated hours of work, and in many cases, abusive working conditions [42-45]. Regretfully, in addition to the women who migrate voluntarily to do mostly domestic work, there are also large numbers of women who find themselves unwillingly trafficked as sex workers and sex slaves. As this economic activity is part of the underground global economy there are no official figures on this type of migration, only speculation. According to Kevin Bales, president of Free the Slaves, America's largest anti-slavery organization, there are at least 30,000 to 50,000 sex slaves in captivity in the United States at any given time [46].

THINKING ABOUT HEALTH IN THE NEW
GLOBAL ECONOMY

As discussed, economic globalization, as it has been unfolding since the 1970s, has indeed impacted people's work experiences in the United States and elsewhere. An issue that needs to be addressed further is how the neoliberal economic policies and the actions of transnational corporations shaping economic globalization are impacting workers' health. As the contributors of this book show, among others, "globalization has a complex influence on health" [47, p. 834].

Critics of economic globalization argue that as transnational corporations reach all over the globe looking for new territories to set up shop, there is strong evidence that they play a great role in impacting the health of workers and communities around the globe—mostly in a negative way. Indirectly, because transnational corporations are involved in manufacturing, they impact the environment through the waste they discharge into lakes, rivers, oceans, ground, and the atmosphere. Furthermore, transnational corporations "can have a detrimental impact on health and well-being through their aggressive advertising and promotion of products such as infant formula, cigarettes, pesticides, pharmaceuticals, and weapons" [10, p. 178].

In industrializing regions, low wages that do not allow for regular access to health care, poor working conditions that often do not comply with safety regulations, noxious work organizations that create psychosocial stressors, long work hours without adequate rest, all have direct and negative impact on the health of millions of factory workers. The full impact of globalization in creating these deleterious working conditions that impact on the mental and physical well-being of working people has yet to be fully determined. Yet others see some promise in globalization improving the health of people around the globe. As argued by Cornia, "if properly managed, globalization can lead to important health gains" [47, p. 534]. In his work on the relationships between health and globalization, he argues that:

> In countries that have met most of the domestic conditions for opening up and have led access to international markets at fairly unconstrained conditions, a judicious mix of unorthodox domestic policies and managed globalization has contributed to rapid growth, a rise in living standards, and gains in health status, In this connection, the experiences of China, Costa Rica, the countries of the East Asian "tiger economies," India, Viet Nam, and a few other countries should be distilled and the related lessons learned [47, pp. 534-535].

Yet, even when optimistic, Cornia admits that, "the domestic and international conditions for successful globalization have been met in relatively few countries. In several countries, growth has been hindered and improvement in health has been slowed down by premature, unselective, and poorly sequenced globalization" [47, p. 535].

The growth of inequality and poverty around the world is bad for population health [28, 48]. While some health indicators are improving in developing countries, in countries like the United States which is experiencing growing inequality, the improvements in health are in fact reversing, as can be seen in the worsening of U.S.

infant mortality rates.[12] The goal of this chapter has been to orient the reader to the labor trends arising internationally as a consequence of neoliberal ideology and contemporary patterns of economic globalization. These trends are affecting workers worldwide in adverse ways, and, as the chapters following suggest, they are also having an influence "locally" in terms of promoting greater inequality within the United States, as well as on the organization of work and its effects on the health of American workers.

REFERENCES

1. Appadurai, A., Disjuncture and Difference in the Global Cultural Economy, *Public Culture,* 2:2, pp. 1-24, 1990.
2. Ellwood, W., *The No-Nonsense Guide to Globalization,* Verso, London, UK, 2002.
3. Raskin, P., T. Banuri, G. Gallopin, et al., *The Great Transition: The Promise and the Lure of the Times Ahead,* Tellus Institute, Boston, MA, 2002.
4. Spiegel, J. M., R. Labonte, and A. S. Ostry, Understanding "Globalization" as a Determinant of Health Determinants: A Critical Perspective, *International Journal of Occupational and Environmental Health,* 10, pp. 360-367, 2004.
5. Quinlan, M., Labour Market Restructuring in Industrialised Societies: An Overview, *Economic Labor Relations Review,* 9, pp. 1-30, 1998.
6. Annycke, P., F. Bonnet, S. Dasgupta, et al., *Economic Security for a Better World,* International Labour Office, Geneva, Switzerland, 2004.
7. Knudsen, D. C., T. Koh, and J. S. Boggs, Assessing the Regulationist View of History: An Analysis of Employment Change in America, 1940-1989, *Economic Geography,* 73:4, pp. 371-389, 1997.
8. Rogers, J., Just a Temp, in *The Transformation of Work in the New Economy: Sociological Readings,* Perruci, R. and C. C. Perruci (eds.), Roxbury Publishing Company, Los Angeles, CA, pp. 199-219, 2007.
9. Ostry, A. S. and J. M. Spiegel, Labor Markets and Employment Insecurity: Impacts of Globalization on Service and Healthcare-Sector Workforces, *International Journal of Occupational and Environmental Health,* 10, pp. 368-374, 2004.
10. Millen, J. V., T. H. Holtz, D. Fallows, and R. Rosenbaum, Dying for Growth, Part I: Transnational Corporations and the Health of the Poor, in *Dying for Growth: Global Inequality and the Health of the Poor,* Kim, J. Y., J. V. Millen, A. Irwin, and J. Gershman (eds.), Common Courage Press, Monroe, ME, pp. 177-224, 2000.
11. Mies, M., *Patriarchy and Accumulation on a World Scale : Women in the International Division of Labour,* Third World Books, Zed Books, London and Atlantic Highlands, NJ, 1986.
12. Rosskam, E., *Excess Baggage: Leveling the Load and Changing the Workplace,* Baywood, Amityville, NY, 2007.
13. Sachs, J. D., *The End of Poverty: Economic Possibilities for Our Time,* Penguin, New York, 2005.
14. Rodrik, D., *The New Global Economy and Developing Countries: Making Openness Work,* Johns Hopkins University Press, Baltimore, MD, 1999.

[12] Infant Mortality Tables 1946-2002, National Center for Health Statistics, U.S. Department of Health and Human Resources, Washington, DC, 2004.

15. Rodriguez, F. and D. Rodrik, *Trade Policy and Economic Growth: A Skeptic's Guide to the Cross-National Evidence*, Centre for Economic Policy Research, London, UK, 2000.
16. Harvey, D., *The Condition of Postmodernity: An Enquiry into the Origins of Cultural Change*, Basil Blackwell, Oxford, 1989.
17. Anderson, S., J. Cavanagh, T. Lee, and The Institute of Policy Politics Studies, *Field Guide to the Global Economy*, The New Press, New York, 2005.
18. Amott, T., *Caught in the Crisis: Women and the U.S. Economy Today*, Monthly Review Press, New York, 1993.
19. Freeman, C., *High Tech and High Heels in the Global Economy: Women, Work, and Pink-Collar Identities*, Duke University Press, Durham, NC and London, 2000.
20. Uchitelle, L. and N. R. Kleinfield, The Price of Jobs Lost, in *The Transformation of Work in the New Economy: Sociological Readings*, Perruci, R. and C. C. Perruci (eds.), Roxbury Publishing Company, Los Angeles, CA, pp. 83-92, 2007.
21. Gardner, J. M., Worker Displacement: A Decade of Change, *Monthly Labor Review*, pp. 45-57, April 1995.
22. Factory Workers Have Highest Risk of Displacement, *Monthly Labor Review*, U.S. Department of Labor, Bureau of Labor Statistics, Washington, DC, 2002.
23. Displaced Workers Summary, *Monthly Labor Review*, U.S. Department of Labor, Bureau of Labor Statistics, Washington, DC, 2006.
24. Phillips, B., *Global Production and Domestic Decay: Plant Closings in the U.S.*, Garland Publishing, Inc., New York and London, 1998.
25. U.S. Automotive Industry Employment Trends, United States Department of Commerce, Office of Aerospace and Automotive Industries, March 30, 2005. Prepared by ITA/MAS/MFG/OAAI/03-30-06.
26. Merllié, D. and P. D. Paoli, *Labour Market Trends and Globalization's Impact on Them*, International Labour Organization, Geneva, Switzerland, 2004.
27. Eurostat, Euro Area Unemployment Down to 7.3%, 2007. Eurostat Press Office. Luxembourg, Germany.
28. Navarro, V. and C. Muntaner (eds.), *Political and Economic Determinants of Population Health and Well-Being: Controversies and Developments*, Baywood, Amityville, NY, 2004.
29. Organization for Economic Co-Operation and Development (OECD), Standardized Unemployment Rates, 2007.
30. Ehrenreich, B., *Bait and Switch: The (Futile) Pursuit of the American Dream*, Metropolitan Books, New York, 2005.
31. Solinger, D. J., The Creation of a New Underclass in China and Its Implications, in *POSRI International Forum on China's Development: Key Challenges for China's Sustained Growth*, Seoul, Korea, 2004. Conference paper.
32. McMichael, P., *Development and Social Change: A Global Perspective*, Pine Forge Press, Thousand Oaks, CA, 2004.
33. Chan, A. and Z. Xiaoyang, Disciplinary Labor Regimes in Chinese Factories, *Critical Asian Studies*, 35:4, pp. 559-584, 2003.
34. Sassen, S., *Globalization and Its Discontents*, The New Press, New York, 1998.
35. Broad, D., Globalization Versus Labor, *Monthly Review*, 47:7, pp. 20-32, 1995.
36. Perrucci, R. and E. Wysong, Global Economy and Privileged Class, in *The Transformation of Work in the New Economy*, Perrucci, R. and C. C. Perruci (eds.), Roxbury Publishing Company, Los Angeles, pp. 63-82, 2007.
37. Enloe, C., *Bananas, Beaches, and Bases: Making Feminist Sense of International*, University of California Press, Berkeley, CA, 1989.

38. Mohanty, C. T., Women Workers and Capitalist Scripts: Ideologies of Domination, Common Interests, and the Politics of Solidarity, in *Feminist Genealogies, Colonial Legacies, Democratic Features*, Alexander, J. M. and Chandra Talpade Mohanty (eds.), Routledge, New York and London, pp. 3-29, 1997.
39. Ong, A., *Spirits of Resistance and Capitalist Discipline: Factory Women in Malaysia*, SUNY Press, Albany, NY, 1987.
40. Sassen, S., Global Cities and Survival Circuits, in *Global Woman: Nannies, Maids, and Sex Workers in the New Economy*, Ehrenreich, B. and A. R. Hochschild (eds.), Granta, London, UK, pp. 254-274, 2003.
41. Ehrenreich, B. and A. Hochschild, Introduction, in *Global Woman: Nannies, Maids and Sex Workers in the New Economy*, Ehrenreich, B. and A. Hochschild (eds.), Granta Books, London, UK, pp. 1-14, 2003.
42. Rivas, L. M., Invisible Labors: Caring for the Independent Person, in *Global Woman: Nannies, Maids and Sex Workers in the New Economy*, Ehrenreich, B. and A. R. Hochschild (eds.), Granta, London, UK, pp. 70-84, 2003.
43. Anderson, B., Just Another Job? The Commodification of Domestic Labor, in *Global Woman: Nannies, Maids and Sex Workers in the New Economy*, Ehrenreich, B. and A. R. Hochschild (eds.), Granta, London, pp. 104-114, 2003.
44. Constable, N., Filipina Workers in Hong Kong Homes: Household Rules and Relations, in *Global Woman: Nannies, Maids and Sex Workers in the New Economy*, Ehrenreich, B. and A. R. Hochschild (eds.), Granta, London, UK, pp. 115-141, 2003.
45. Zarembka, J., America's Dirty Work: Migrant Maids and Modern-Day Slavery, in *Global Woman: Nannies, Maids and Sex Workers in the New Economy*, Ehrenreich, B. and A. R. Hochschild (eds.), Granta, London, UK, pp. 142-153, 2003.
46. Landesman, P., The Girls Next Door (How Sex Trafficking Works), January 25, 2004. Available from: nytimes.com
47. Cornia, G. A., Globalization and Health: Results and Options, *World Health Organization*, 79:9, pp. 834-841, 2001.
48. Navarro, V. (ed.), *The Political and Social Context of Health*, Baywood, Amityville, NY, 2004.

CHAPTER 3

The Growing Imbalance: Class, Work, and Health in an Era of Increasing Inequality

Jeffrey V. Johnson

WHY STUDY SOCIAL CLASS?

Social class position is a powerful predictor of illness and death from many forms of both chronic and infectious disease [1]. Those in the upper class live longer and are healthier while those in lower classes die at a younger age and are considerably less healthy over their entire life course [2]. Moreover, numerous studies have found that a "gradient" exists along the social class continuum—with increasingly higher class position, health improves, and with descending class position, health deteriorates [3, 4]. Although there continues to be a considerable debate as to what explains this class gradient, there is an emerging consensus that social class is a "fundamental determinant" of population health [5]. Some of the pathways linking lower social class position to ill health include economic deprivation, lack of educational opportunities, and adverse exposures associated with differences in geographic and community environmental characteristics such as exposure to violence and to toxic substances like lead and carbon monoxide [3, 6]. Other pathways involve class differences in consumption patterns including unhealthy foods, cigarettes, alcohol, and illicit drug usage [7]. Social class position is also strongly associated with access (or lack thereof) to social and public resources, quality health care, informal social networks, institutional resources, and inter-generational resources [8]. Still another pathway involves differences in the nature of the social and work environments, and includes the class differences in stress from adverse labor market experiences, including unemployment, underemployment, and chronic exposure to stressful work organizations. These specific pathways linking social class to health may change over time. New causal paths might emerge, others might be removed, yet as long as the society continues to have a social class structure, it is almost certain there will continue to be health "disparities" between classes—this is what is meant when we say class is a "fundamental determinant" of health [5].

Social class is much more than just a property of individuals—it is an expression of macro-societal forces that "produce" stratified hierarchies within modern societies. Together with race and gender, class constitutes a core social structure [8]. As a societal structure, social class is associated with enormous inequalities that we observe in nearly every aspect of human existence across the entire life course. Social class is also intimately bound up with work and the labor process [9]. It is through our work, and the work of our parents, that we enter into the life chances and circumstances of a particular social class [10]. In this chapter, we will introduce and explore some of the critical themes that have emerged in research examining the relationship between class, work, and health. We start by identifying several distinct and in some ways contradictory "understandings" of what social class is. We'll then examine how work organization exposure varies by social class and will address the question: "To what extent does the psychosocial work environment— specifically those models discussed elsewhere in this book: job strain and effort- reward imbalance—serve as a pathway between social class and adverse health outcomes?" Finally, we turn to an examination of the growing wealth and power imbalance between social classes and why social inequality between classes is increasing in the United States and in many other countries around the world.

WHAT IS SOCIAL CLASS AND HOW DOES IT WORK?

There are two fundamentally different ways to understand and examine the concept of social class: *Positional measures* of class are based on incremental changes in skill, income, or prestige across a social continuum and reflect one's position in the division of labor [11]. *Relational measures* are based on social structure and the fundamental property and power relations that exist between classes—such as the ownership and control of capital assets [11, 12]. The most widely used definition of class in social epidemiology is one that emphasizes one's social position and is derived from the work of Max Weber, a German sociologist who worked in the period just before and after World War I and who is most widely known for his work on the formation of bureaucracies [13]. Weber's concept of class emphasizes the importance of an individual's differential access to material and social resources—what he refers to as one's "life chances" [13]. According to Weber: "'Class situation' is, in this sense, ultimately 'market situation'" [13]. From this perspective, social classes can be understood as groups in the population that develop a common sense of identity because of their relative bargaining power on the market and their differential ability to acquire material resources or other assets (e.g., education) [3, 11, 14]. Social class position may be inherited and passed on to one's children in the form of the wealth that improves one's "life chances." In practice, Weber's view of social class has been conceptualized as a system of hierarchical stratification where some socially valued element such as status, prestige, wealth, education, income, or skill is distributed along a continuum of graded ranks. In this view, one's position in the stratification system is determined by how much one may "have" of a valued social asset or assets

[11, 13, 15]. Examples include ranking systems based on years of education, amount of household income, or personal ownership of assets such as homes or cars. One's occupation can also be used to assign an individual to a position within a stratification continuum based on the degree of skill, prestige, or status associated with a particular job [16]. Information from income, education, and occupation may be combined into a single score or category which is often referred to as socioeconomic status (SES) or socioeconomic position (SEP) [3, 16]. Although not originally intended as such, SES or SEP measured in this way becomes more like an individual characteristic than an aspect of social structure to which the individual may belong [14].

One of the most commonly used "common-sense" positional stratification schemas consists of six classes, based on a graded hierarchy of access to material resources [17]:

1. Upper class
2. Upper middle class
3. Middle class
4. Lower middle class
5. Lower class
6. Under class

Another widely used social class scale was developed in the United Kingdom and is based on six occupational groups. Developed by Registrar General Stevenson in 1913, it conceptualizes occupations as a measure of what he termed "standing within the community" or "culture"—a measure of the prestige or social status that each occupation has in the society [16]. It was later revised to more clearly reflect the level of skill required at each occupational class level. This system consists of six class groups:

1. Social Class I (professional)
2. Social Class II (intermediate)
3. Social Class IIINM (skilled non-manual)
4. Social Class IIIM (skilled manual)
5. Social Class IV (partly skilled)
6. Social Class V (unskilled)

Critics have pointed out a number of problems with this way of measuring social class. Some have suggested that the degree to which work has become routine today is a more meaningful distinguishing characteristic than skill. Others argue that the degree of control over the work process is the most important underlying element of social class [18]. More recent formulations of the United Kingdom classification system have incorporated these criticisms in the current National Statistics Socio-Economic Classification system where classes are defined by prospects of promotion, whether they are paid an hourly wage or a salary, and levels of job autonomy [16]. This newer system is only now being used in epidemiological research. (See Galobardes [16] and Lynch and Kaplan [3] for a more extended discussion of social class measurement.)

There are a number of problems with measuring social class using a finely graded stratification system, particularly when they consist of combinations of income, education, and occupation. This fact was cogently pointed out by Parkin [14] some years ago:

> In place of a model of structured inequality a picture emerged of a highly fragmented and inchoate social order comprised of loose aggregates of individuals having nothing in common other than a similar score in the measurement of ranked indices. Each individual was thus conceived of as a summation of his high and low statuses, rather as if these were separate items on a personal balance sheet which could be totted up to record the state of his moral and social credit in the Great Ledger of Society [p. 202].

A markedly different understanding of class comes to us from the Marxian tradition [11, 19-24]. Marx emphasized the economic and political *relationship* between dominant and subordinate class groups. In contrast to Weber's emphasis on differential access to the "life chances" of individuals and groups, Marx pinpoints the exploitation of the working class ("labor") by the employing class ("capital") as the key to the understanding of how class formations come into being [11, 17, 25]. Marx also emphasized the centrality of work as a key determinant of class, because it is the specific nature of exploitation in the workplace that most clearly expresses the character of the relationship between classes [9, 11, 24, 26]. For Marx, the labor process "determines the relation of domination and servitude, as it emerges directly out of production itself and in turn reacts upon production" [23]. Marx argued that exploitation forms the basis of the class system, and upon it is "founded the entire structure of the economic community, which grows up out of the conditions of production itself. . . . It is always the direct relation between the masters of the conditions of production and the direct producers which reveals the innermost secret, the hidden foundation of the entire social edifice . . ." [23].

Marx's theory of class and work has had considerable influence on occupational health research [9, 26-28]. Research on the impact of control over the work process on health, for instance, has been greatly influenced by Braverman's [24] application of the Marxist theory of the labor process. Yet until quite recently this relational perspective has not often been used to measure the social class variable itself. This is beginning to change; for example, Muntaner and his colleagues have applied a relational theory of class developed by E. O. Wright in a number of recent studies [29]. Wright, one of the most influential scholars of social class in the United States, has formulated a class matrix of 12 categories by applying the following three underlying dimensions of ownership, skill, and power [17]:

- Ownership of capital assets,
- Control of organizational assets, and
- Possession of skill or credential assets

According to Wright, the intersection of these three dimensions does not create a linear gradient as do the Weberian positional schema. He identifies an upper class consisting of those who own and control organizational assets and a working class of wage laborers who have relatively little control over organizational assets [12]. Between these two classes are individuals, who, according to Wright, are in "contradictory class locations" for they are both exploited and exploiters [12]. They may be exploiters in the sense that they exercise power and control over the work of others as would be the case, for example, of a middle level manager or supervisor, but yet they are also exploited since they are subject to the decisions of owners and upper level executives. In their application of this model, Muntaner, Borrell, Benach, Pasarin, and Fernandez [29] have shown that low-level supervisors are at higher risk of depression and anxiety disorders than upper management or non-supervisory workers. They note that traditional measures of SES would have predicted supervisors to be at lower levels of risk because they have more prestige and pay than non-managerial workers [29].

One of the most provocative and important aspects of a relational class perspective is that it focuses attention on the very small group in the society who form an economic elite by virtue of their wealth and power and their commanding influence over the economic and political life of the society [11, 30, 31]. The social class framework introduced by Clement and Myles [32], for example, is even more strongly relational than that of Wright's theory and gives much greater attention to this elite group. Clement and Myles refer to this group as the capitalist-executive class. According to these authors, the elite class may be defined by its possession of: 1) real economic ownership; 2) power to direct production to specific purposes; 3) power to dispose of products; and 4) command over strategic decision-making [32]. This group is rarely studied in social epidemiology because it is virtually invisible demographically, consisting of less than 0.1% of the population. Who are they? For one thing, they are the beneficiaries of the growing income inequality. The economist Paul Krugman, quoting data from the U.S. Congressional Budget Office, notes that between 1973 and 2000 the incomes of 90% of average Americans fell by 7%, while the income of the top 0.1% grew by 343% and that of the top 0.01% rose by 599% [33].

There is a growing interest among social class theorists in the rising economic and political power of ruling elites and their historical role in promoting the ascendancy of "*neoliberalism*," the political and economic philosophy and practice that emphasizes the primacy of markets over government, and which advocates policies that have led to the deregulation of labor markets, and the dismantling of the social protections and redistributive policies of the earlier welfare state [27, 30, 34, 35]. (This term can be deceptive for readers in the United States. It does *not* mean "liberal" as we normally use the term; rather, it refers to the idea that the *market* should be liberated from any restraints advocated by conservative economists such as Milton Friedman.) For example, the influential social theorist David Harvey suggests that: "Though it has been effectively disguised, we have lived through a whole generation of sophisticated strategizing on the part of ruling elites to restore, enhance, or, as in China and Russia, to construct an overwhelming class power" [30].

While positional stratification systems describe gradational differences in access to material and social resources, a relational framework considers the historical movement of class forces and their power in relation to each other. From this perspective, the seemingly "old fashioned" view of a polarization of class interests between "capital" and "labor" may still be relevant, particularly if we include E. O. Wright's insights. The simplest relational schema therefore, and the one we will apply later in this chapter, would define three basic social classes: 1) an economic elite class made up of the most wealthy and powerful members of the society who own and control large corporations and other powerful institutions; 2) an increasingly large working class whose members are engaged in direct productive or reproductive (human service) work; and 3) a third class made up of managers and professionals who share some of the characteristics of both the elite class and the working class and hence are said to occupy a "contradictory class location" in that their work involves administering bureaucratic organizations in the interests of the elite, yet their personal history, work experience, and professional training and ethics may lead them to identify at times with the working class [12, 36].

SOCIAL CLASS AND WORK EXPOSURE: DO WORKERS IN LOWER SOCIAL CLASS POSITIONS HAVE MORE ADVERSE WORK ENVIRONMENT EXPOSURES THAN THOSE IN HIGHER CLASS POSITIONS?

Research has shown that hazardous work organization exposures such as piece-rate payment systems, monotonous and repetitive work, long working hours, and low levels of work control—factors which may also increase risk of illness—are differentially distributed along class lines [6, 9, 37-39]. Individuals in lower socio-economic positions, particularly unskilled manual and lower level service occupations, are much more likely to be exposed to these kinds of risk factors than those in professional and managerial jobs [40]. This differential work exposure across social class categories may be an important part of the explanation for the class gradient in cardiovascular disease (CVD) risk [41].

Recent research has shown that there are marked differences in a number of work organization characteristics across the different social class groups [42, 43]. For example, the proportional distributions of work control, low variety, and low social support among men and women in the United Kingdom, are shown in Table 1 [42]. Clearly, there are pronounced differences in work exposures across the class continuum. The most marked differences can be observed when comparing the proportion of male workers who report low control over their work: managerial and professional workers (class groups I and II) have 6% with low control compared to partly skilled and unskilled manual workers (class groups IV and V) where 40% or more report low control. Skilled lower level white-collar and service-sector employees report intermediate levels of control. Rather than a step-wise decline in the quality of work with declining class rank, this data indicates that these two important job characteristics are similar in three broad class categories: managers and professionals, skilled service and manual workers, and less skilled manual workers. By contrast, severe lack of social support does appear to follow a stepwise decline with descending social class position. A roughly similar trend can be observed for women, though their jobs appear substantially worse in some respects (more than 92% of unskilled manual female workers report low variety at work, for example).

Table 1. Low Control and Variety at Work and Severe Lack of Social Support in Relation to Gender and Social Class[a]

	Class I	Class II	Class IIINM	Class IIIM	Class IV	Class V
Men						
Low control	6	6	21	22	40	47
Low variety	9	18	35	35	62	66
Low support	10	12	16	18	21	26
Women						
Low control	14	10	36	31	50	46
Low variety	8	22	56	52	74	92
Low support	6	9	12	13	14	15

[a]Values are percentages for all British men and women in each social class (British Surgeon General's system) who are aged 16 or older (from Marmot and Wilkinson, used with permission) [42].

In our own research on large representative samples of the Swedish labor force (see Table 2), we have found that the degree of control at work is strongly associated with social class position [40]. Social support at work, by contrast, is only weakly (but positively) associated with social class. We have found that other exposures tend to be much more present in certain class groups than others. Hazardous work exposures and heavy physical job demands are often present in lower level service and manual groups while being almost non-existent in managerial and professional class groups [40]. When examining patterns of multiple exposures across social class groups, it becomes evident that the lower-level office and service workers are much more like manual workers than they are like managerial and professional workers. The managerial and professional class tends to have high psychological job demands, high levels of work control, and very low levels of physical demands and low levels of hazardous exposure. Other research has shown that they work longer hours and their jobs require considerable flexibility [9]. Lower-level clerical, service, and manual jobs (e.g., working class jobs), by contrast, have much less control, are more routinized, and have fewer psychological job demands and considerable monotony. Working class jobs also have much higher physical demands and more hazardous exposures [6, 9, 40].

HOW DO THE TWO MOST WIDELY USED CONCEPTUAL MODELS OF OCCUPATIONAL STRESS— THE DEMAND-CONTROL AND THE EFFORT-REWARD IMBALANCE MODEL—VARY BY SOCIAL CLASS?

Some authors have argued that the job strain dimension of the demand-control model is "orthogonal" or not related to social class [44]. This is because psychological job demands, as we've noted above, are more likely to be present in upper social class groups (managers and professionals), a finding that has been noted

Table 2. Age-Adjusted Work Environment Means (0-10) for Swedish Men
by Social Class from a Random Sample of the Employed
Swedish Population by *Statistics Sweden* [40]

Class	Control	Support	Psych	Physical	Hazard	N
Managers and professionals	6.93	9.25	6.29	1.43	1.34	535
Middle level white collar	6.43	9.40	5.89	2.03	2.09	707
Lower level white collar	5.76	9.02	4.99	2.61	2.10	347
Skilled manual	4.60	8.97	3.66	5.78	4.72	901
Unskilled manual	3.83	8.24	3.87	5.19	4.06	913
Total						3,403

in other studies as well [43, 45]. The pattern for job decision latitude (work control) is the reverse—low levels are more likely to be found in lower social class groups. What about the combination of high demands and low control—job strain itself? Choi, Karasek, Ostergren, Ferrario, and DeSmet [44] have recently reported findings from the multi-center JACE study performed in Europe that show that the job strain diagonal (the high demand-low control combination) does not increase or decrease in association with the class gradient. (The results of this study are shown in Table 3.) The investigators have used a simplified three-level indicator of class where class I are managerial and professional workers, class II are technical, service, and sales workers; and class 3 are manual workers. As the investigators suggest, these results do not provide strong evidence for a class gradient [44] (although there is some indication that the proportion of high strain varies by class for women in Table 3). For both men and women, class I managers and professionals are much less likely to have high job strain than class II and III office, service workers, and manual workers. Only 8% of male managerial and professional workers report high strain while nearly 20% of class II and III workers report high strain. This difference is even higher in women—with 37.6% of class III and 25% of class II workers reporting high strain compared to only 10.6% of class I employees. These patterns are more indicative of a polarization of class characteristics between a managerial professional class and a working class of lower-level service, clerical, sales, and manual workers. It's also important to draw attention to the gradient that does exist for both men and women. Along the other dimension of the demand-control model, the activity-passivity diagonal, the pattern in Table 3 suggests that with increasing class position the proportion of active workers increases and the proportion of passive workers decreases.

Although Karasek's original intent in formulating the demand-control model was to examine both the strain and the activity dimensions, passive work has generally not been examined as a risk factor. At least conceptually, however, it is plausible to suggest that passive jobs may also be associated with risk for distress and adverse health behavior. Therefore, a more accurate indicator of relative "class burden" would be to examine the proportion of individuals in each class strata who are exposed to either high strain or passive working conditions. The result of this analysis of the JACE study is shown in Table 4. For both men and women, there is a clearly increasing proportion of workers exposed to adverse work organization characteristics (e.g., either strain or passivity) with decreasing social class position.

The pattern of results in Table 4 also suggests that a meaningful interaction may exist between gender, class position, and adverse work organization exposure. Women are substantially more likely to be in an adverse exposure condition at each level of occupational class compared to men, and also demonstrate a more marked gradient across the class continuum. It is particularly significant that more than 80% of women in manual occupations (class III) are in either high strain or passive jobs. For both men and women, those in class II and class III are much more likely to be in an adverse exposure condition than are those in class I. These findings suggest that if we focus only on the strain dimension of the demand-control model we may

Table 3. Percent of Males and Females Within Each Quadrant of the Demand-Control Model from the JACE Study [44]

Social class	Low strain	Active	Passive	High strain
Males				
I	27.6	57.5	6.9	8.0
II	27.5	28.7	25.8	18.1
III	29.9	16.8	33.8	19.5
Females				
I	37.0	39.2	13.1	10.6
II	22.2	21.7	30.8	25.3
III	8.3	7.3	46.7	37.6

Table 4. Percent of Males and Females in the JACE Study Who are in Either High Strain or Passive Jobs [44]

Social class	% of males in either high strain or passive jobs	% of females in either high strain or passive jobs
Class I	14.9	23.7
Class II	43.9	56.1
Class III	53.3	84.3

be underestimating the degree to which adverse work organization exposure actually varies by social class position. The other major model of occupational stress, the effort-reward imbalance model [46], also has a somewhat inconsistent relationship with social class. It is probably because the "effort" component of the model increases with higher class position, while the "reward" component decreases [47]. Recent findings from the Whitehall study of British civil servants indicates that those in higher occupational grades have a greater probability of reducing their effort-reward imbalance over time compared to workers in lower grades [47].

DOES THE IMPACT OF WORK ORGANIZATION EXPOSURE VARY BY SOCIAL CLASS?

The impact of adverse work organization exposure also varies markedly by social class. Recent findings from the European Science Foundation's Study on Social Variation in Health Expectancy strongly suggest that workers in lower social class positions are more vulnerable to the impact of both job strain and effort/reward imbalance [37]. A number of studies have shown that the impact of job strain and iso-strain (high demand, low control, and low social support jobs) is significantly greater for individuals in manual occupations compared to those in non-manual jobs [48-51]. Hallqvist, Diderichsen, Theorell, Reuterwall, Ahlbom, and Group [51], for example, have shown that Swedish men working in manual occupations exposed to high levels of job strain have a relative risk of 10.00 (95% CI 2.6-38.4) for non-fatal myocardial infarction. By contrast, non-manual workers with high levels of job strain had a substantially lower relative risk of 1.5 (0.6-3.5). Johnson and Hall [50] report a similar pattern of findings in another Swedish study. When social support is added to the demand-control model, manual male workers with high iso-strain (high demands, low control, and low social support) have an odds ratio of 7.22 (95% CI 1.60-7.39) for cardiovascular disease prevalence compared to non-manual workers with high iso-strain who have an odds ratio of 2.44 (95% CI 0.95-6.28) [50]. Landsbergis and his colleagues also have found pronounced class differences on the impact of job strain [48, 52]. They studied how the impact of improvements in job strain over time varied in upper and lower income groups. Workers with higher income levels showed no significant improvement in blood pressure when their jobs improved (high strain at time one but not at time two). Lower income workers, however, showed a significant decline of 5.5 mm Hg in ambulatory blood pressure between time one to time two when their jobs improved [48].

Kupper, Singh-Manoux, Siegrist, and Marmot [53] have examined the impact of the effort-reward imbalance ratio among different employment grades in the Whitehall study of British civil servants and found greater vulnerability for the lowest employment grades. Those in the lowest employment grade, clerical, with the high effort-low reward condition were found to have a statistically significant relative risk of 1.56 compared to clericals with low effort-high reward. By contrast, neither administrators nor professionals with high effort-reward imbalance were found to have statistically significant excess risk, though the odds ratios were elevated above 1.00 for both groups [53].

DOES WORK EXPOSURE HELP EXPLAIN THE
SOCIAL CLASS GRADIENT IN HEALTH?

An increasing number of research findings suggest that class differences in adverse work organization exposure (particularly in job control, or lack thereof) may be an important causal pathway that accounts for a significant proportion of the relationship between social class position and health [1, 41, 47, 54, 55]. The most thorough investigation of this mediating relationship has been the Whitehall study of British civil servants performed by Marmot and his colleagues who have found that much of the inverse social gradient in coronary heart disease can be explained by differences in the psychosocial work environment [1, 4, 41, 42, 56]. They report that the largest contribution to the class gradient in CHD can be attributed to differences in control at work [41]. More recently, research on the Whitehall cohort has shown that the social gradient in angina is partially explained by longitudinal changes in effort-reward imbalance (ERI) [47]. Men who reduced their ERI over time were found to have less risk for angina and it was the men in higher grades who were more likely to have a decrease in their ERI over time compared to those in lower grades [47]. A growing number of studies have reported similar findings:

- In Denmark, a large prospective study found that about two-thirds of the social gradient in self-reported health (SRH) status could be explained by a combination of work environment and lifestyle factors with the largest contribution coming from the work factors [57].
- Another Danish study by Anderson examined the mediating effects of decision authority, skill discretion, and job demands on the social class gradient in myocardial infarction and found that only skill discretion showed a clear mediating effect [58].
- In Holland, psychosocial work environment characteristics were also found to explain a substantial proportion of the social class gradient which was attributed to the differential distribution of low job control and hazardous work conditions across occupational classes [59].
- In Sweden, approximately 25% of the income gradient in SRH in men and 29% in women can be explained by a combination of ergonomic exposure as well as differences in decision authority and skill discretion. The authors note that psychological job demands did not contribute to explaining inequalities as they were found to be more common in higher income jobs [45].
- In Canada, researchers used the National Population Health Survey to examine the social class gradient in the change in SRH over time and found that the decline in health status was moderately reduced after adjusting for both health behaviors and psychosocial work exposures [60].
- In the United States, recent cross-sectional findings also suggest that physical and psychosocial work environment characteristics play an important mediating role in the SES and health relationship and explain some, though not all, of the gradient [61].

- In France, research findings from the Gazel Study indicate that approximately 20% of the class gradient in sickness absence can be attributed to both physical and psychosocial exposure. There was a specificity of effect with psychosocial exposure explaining a portion of the gradient for psychiatric and musculoskeletal-related absences while physical exposures explained injury-related absences [62].
- In Finland, research from the Helsinki Health Study showed that a substantial proportion of the social class gradient in SRH can be accounted for by job control. The investigators also noted that when psychological job demands were controlled for, the relationship between social class and SRH was reinforced [63].

Although there is considerable and increasing evidence that psychosocial work environment characteristics do explain a meaningful proportion—though by no means all—of the social class gradient in health, there continues to be some debate concerning the interpretation of these findings. An alternative explanation is that it is material disadvantages rather than psychosocial factors that are the more likely explanations of the social class gradient in health [64]. According to this view, since adverse psychosocial factors and material disadvantages are so strongly correlated, it is difficult to ascertain which set of factors are truly causally related to class differences in health [64]. These authors conclude that work stress is not a plausible explanation for the class gradient and the observed associations are probably spurious and are more likely due to unmeasured confounding and reporting bias [64]. Though these authors provide a valuable corrective to the tendency to "psychologize" social reality, in their critique they suggest that the psychosocial work environment can be reduced exclusively to a question of the feelings one may have about, for example, work control or lack thereof. This prompts us to ask the question: What is truly important to health? Is it one's feeling or "sense of control" over the work process or is it the reality of actually being able to control one's own pace and methods of work? We would argue that the reality of having or not having control over one's daily life at work constitutes a material reality. As we will discuss in the next section, control over the work process has historically been a contested terrain between the economic elite and the working class. In this sense, the power to control the work process is very real and lies at the heart of managerial strategies to intensify production which have become embodied in the principles of scientific management and lean production.

GROWING INEQUALITY AND THE CHANGING BALANCE OF POWER BETWEEN CLASSES

Although social and occupational class systems based on access to social resources and/or levels of skill or prestige are useful in describing the distribution and the impact of adverse work organization exposures, they tell us little about why class systems exist in the first place or whether the balance of power between classes influences health. In this concluding section, we use the *relational* perspective on social class introduced previously to examine recent changes in the work process and in the growing level of inequality between social classes. A relational theory of class begins its analysis by identifying the elite or ruling class whose interests predominate within the society and whose continued well-being involves the continued exploitation of a subordinate or working class. Clearly, there are great structural differences between classes in terms of the ownership of wealth and control over workplace institutions. The class structure of modern society is an expression of dynamic political and economic forces operating over time at macro-societal and increasingly global levels [27, 65]. Although social classes have been present since the agricultural revolution and early urban settlement, their present form emerged with the industrial revolution and the growing centrality of capitalism and the market as the major determinant of class structure. In capitalist economies, the most powerful class consists of those who own and control the most productive assets in the society—the corporations. As mentioned previously in this chapter, Clement and Myles [32] refer to this elite group as the capitalist-executive class which they define by their economic ownership of corporate firms and their power to direct production and command strategic decision-making in the society as a whole. This class constitutes what Coburn [66] calls "the business classes," what Wright [17] describes as "capitalists," and what Harvey [30] suggests is a ruling class made up of an elite whose interests involve "liberating corporate and business power and re-establishing market freedoms" [30]. We will use the term "economic elite class."

In a capitalist society, the interests of this elite class and the form these interests take in relation to other class groups, particularly the working class, is irrevocably bound up with their ownership and control of large corporations. In order to survive in dynamic and competitive capitalist environments, corporations must continue to invest in order to improve efficiencies and reduce costs while at the same time increasing the rate at which profits are generated. Competition between corporations has historically led to an increase in size as firms struggle to obtain a greater market share while at the same time making the capital investments necessary to cut costs and improve efficiency. As the size of the firm increases, however, it becomes ever more challenging to increase the rate of return on invested capital. As Moody notes: "It is as though a rising surf of profits is overwhelmed and buried beneath a tidal wave of accumulated capital" [27, p. 47]. In different historical periods corporate elites have pursued markedly different strategies for capital accumulation. The strategy for the current period, which Harvey suggests began in 1980, emphasizes, according to him, the global flexibility and movement of financial capital and the neoliberal strategy of "accumulation by dispossession" [30]. This global strategy of accumulation will be discussed shortly. During much of the twentieth century, however, the dominant capital accumulation strategy focused on improving productive efficiencies by transforming the labor process through managerial and technological innovations. Historically, one important way in which this occurred was by increasing productivity—often by changes in work organization designed to reduce labor costs. "Scientific Management" or "Taylorism" is perhaps the most well known example of how this process can lead to a transformation in how work is organized [24]. In the late nineteenth and early twentieth centuries, F. W. Taylor advocated a radical program of removing planning and decision-making authority from skilled workers on the shop floor, while at the same time centralizing mental and conceptual work in the hands of a new managerial class [24, 67]. By fragmenting the work process into its simplest possible components, the proponents of "scientific management" hoped to both reduce labor costs by employing fewer skilled workers and to increase productivity through their newly won control over the pace, speed, and intensity of the production process itself. Work environments that have been designed in this way implicitly embody class relations [68, 69]. To the extent that work is fragmented and deskilled for the working class, it becomes more manageable for the economic elite and managerial classes [24, 27, 69]. The control over pace and intensity of work performance has historically been transferred from workers to owners and managers for the purpose of increasing the profitability of the enterprise [24]. The technical aspects of this work transformation have been implemented by the managerial/professional class; indeed scientific management techniques became the bedrock of industrial engineering, and they continue to dominate the ways in which jobs are designed even today [67]. The work organizations created by "scientific management" are highly stressful [9, 70]. These workplaces produce high levels of job strain because they have very high demands for performance and productivity and, at the same time, very low levels of control over meaningful decisions about how the work is to be performed. More recently, "lean production" methods have led to an even more intensified form of scientific management, referred to by some observers as a kind of "management by stress" [27].

In the later two decades of the twentieth century, this earlier accumulation strategy, although never abandoned, has been displaced in emphasis by what Harvey refers to as "accumulation by dispossession" [30]. According to Harvey: "Accumulation by dispossession entails a very different set of practices from accumulation through the expansion of wage labor in industry and agriculture" [30]. If the earlier accumulation strategy emphasized maximizing productive forces within an industrial economy, accumulation by dispossession involves the increasing primacy of globalized financial capital, and the pivotal role played by speculative practices—either in the stock market and through the global buying and selling of currencies, or through the massive use of debt financing to fuel continued consumption. This transition was driven by the prolonged economic crises of the 1970s and the failure of the earlier capital accumulation strategy to maintain and generate continued economic growth. Coburn describes the political character of this transition into what has become an increasingly global form of capitalism:

> Economic globalization, as a real force, and as ideology, brought the re-emergence of business on national and international levels to a dominant class position from the previous phase of nationally focused monopoly capitalism in which capital and labor had arrived at various forms of accommodation. Contemporary business dominance, and its accompanying neo-liberal ideology and policies led to attacks on working class rights in the market (e.g., by undermining unions) and to citizenship rights . . . [66, p. 44].

For the last 25 years, the relative strength of the working class in modern industrial societies has been diminishing compared to that of the economic elite. In addition to the rise in the power of financial capital, it has been driven by increasing global competition between transnational corporations and by the international and domestic political "success" of market fundamentalism (e.g., neoliberalism) promulgated by the economic elite which has resulted in a weakening of social protections and a decline in the strength of the labor movement [27, 30, 34, 66]. The decline in working class power has come about as a consequence of the deliberate assault on the trade union movement by the economic elite [27, 30]. McCall [71] describes how this process occurred in the United States:

> . . . employers mobilized: they expanded operations in non-union locations more than in unionized locations; they fought union certification elections with more gusto and more success than in earlier periods; they formed the Business Roundtable in 1972 to legislatively curtail the power of unions; they successfully and surprisingly fought major pro-labor law and pro-consumer protection legislation in the late 1970s; they took advantage of new entrants to the workforce that were traditionally less organized, such as women and immigrants; and they created new human resource departments and policies that sought to improve working conditions in non-union workplaces as a way to thwart interest in unions. Corporate political action committees also ramped up considerably over the course of the decade, overwhelmingly favoring Republicans by the end of the decade [71, p. 20].

Another significant aspect of accumulation by dispossession has involved the destruction of the welfare state and the privatization and commercialization of public services such as education and health care [30, 35, 66]. Freed of the regulatory and redistributive policies of the welfare state, the modern labor process is increasingly one of flexibilization: involving the functional flexibilization of the workplace (lean production) and the numeric flexibility of the labor force (precarious employment) [72]. In addition, a polarized and segmented global architecture of production is emerging with a dwindling core of skill-flexible workers and a growing number of time-flexible workers who perform the more hazardous and labor intensive operations [27]. In the United States, these changes have been accompanied by an increasing polarization of income and wealth—with the greatest gains going to the top 0.1% of the population [33, 73]. The globalization of work and the labor process has also taken on a class character. The transfer of many jobs to low-wage countries—and the threat that this transfer might occur—has severed much of the social contract that existed in the United States between classes in the post-World War II era. In many ways, we have returned to the starker realities of the nineteenth century social landscape with an increasing polarization between society's "winners" and "losers." Third World workers have also become victims of a "downward leveling"—a "race to the bottom"—where we see the working conditions for most of the working class being pulled in the direction of the most desperate and least empowered [74]. These changes have brought with them a remarkable increase in both class and regional inequality within countries and globally between countries [75, 76].

During the last two decades, income inequality in the United States has grown dramatically [33, 73]. The United States has the most unequal distribution of adjusted household income among any of the advanced industrialized (Organisation for Economic Co-operation and Development (OECD)) countries [77]. The gap between the top income strata and the lower strata has been increasing to such an extent that by the late 1990s the top 1% of the U.S. population owned 40% of American wealth while the lowest 40% controlled less than half of 1% of total wealth [78]. As former Labor Secretary Robert Reich [79] summarizes: ". . . today the gap is greater than at any time in living memory. All the rungs on the economic ladder are farther apart than they were a generation ago, and the space between them continues to spread." Rising inequality is a direct consequence of the neoliberal policies put in place by governments supported by and favorable to the economic elite [30, 34]. Prior to the adoption of neoliberal tax and social policies in the 1980s, income inequality had dramatically declined following the post-World War II period as a consequence of the redistributive tax policies and social programs implemented by the New Deal [30, 66].

Much of the current inequality is due to the very low wages and poor living standards of lower-income working class families and is exacerbated by the decreasing levels of social spending by a government that has increasingly embraced neoliberalism [30, 66]. Low-income Americans are markedly worse off than those in comparable economic situations in other advanced industrial (OECD) countries where the lower-income population continues to receive substantial social and economic support from their governments [80]. Recent data from the United Nations Development Report shows that the United States spends less on public social expenditures in general and significantly less on education, welfare, public health, and unemployment support than do most of the other OECD countries [36]. It is worthwhile emphasizing that there is a marked variation in inequality and poverty across developed countries [65, 66, 81]. This is due to the continued existence of welfare policies in some countries, for example, those in Scandinavia, which continue to provide social programs that alleviate the impact of poverty and dramatically shorten its duration [65, 66, 81]. The marked contrast in the degree of social protections across countries is, according to the work of Huber and Stephens, a direct consequence of the degree to which the working class has been able to mobilize and maintain political power: "The struggle over welfare states is a struggle over distribution, and thus the organizational power of those standing to benefit from redistribution, the working and lower middle classes, is crucial" [81]. Navarro and Shi have also shown that those societies with the highest proportion of unionized workers and where social democratic parties have maintained political power continue to have the strongest welfare states and the lowest levels of poverty and inequality [65].

As income disparities within a society increase, so does the number of people living in poverty [78, 82]. For example, a study of 16 industrial nations demonstrated that the degree of income inequality within a nation is strongly associated with the proportion of children living in poverty—with the United States having both the greatest level of income inequality and the largest proportion of children living in poverty of any of these nations [77]. Poverty is a major determinant of population health (see Raphael [78] for an excellent overview). The combination of adverse psychosocial and environmental exposure, severe material deprivation associated with poor nutrition, and the lack of access to education, health care, and other cultural and material assets of the society available to those in upper income strata, all combine to increase the likelihood that lower income populations will suffer from and prematurely die of many diseases and conditions at every stage of the life cycle [78].

In addition to the findings on the impact of poverty, there is also a significant body of research that suggests that societies with higher income inequality have higher mortality rates [1, 75, 76]—irrespective of the absolute deprivation associated with poverty. Although recent studies outside the United States have challenged the view that the degree of income inequality—in and of itself—is associated with poor health in all industrialized societies [82], there is still considerable evidence that growing economic inequality has led to decrements in population health at the national, state, and local levels within the United States [76]. Studies have shown that the degree of income inequality within each of the 50 states is more strongly associated with total mortality and general social well-being than average income within a state [83]. In a recent review, Subramanian and Kawachi [76] note that most studies which have shown an association between income inequality and poor health have been performed in the United States, whereas those studies which have not shown an association have come from countries that have much more egalitarian income distributions as well as much stronger social programs in place [76].

A number of different social mechanisms have been proposed to explain the contextual impact of income inequality on population health. Wilkinson [75] has suggested that societies with greater income inequality have a rigid class hierarchy that contributes to the atrophy of social relations and the formation of a "culture of inequality" that is characterized by hostility between members, lack of trust, lack of reciprocity, and increasing rates of violence and other signs of social disintegration. Kawachi [83] has suggested that high levels of income inequality lead to a decline in social cohesion, trust, and the willingness of social members to act jointly to solve collective problems. He suggests that greater equality in income creates the conditions for more "social capital" defined as the resources available to individuals and to society by the presence of strong networks of cohesive social relationships within a community, state, or society [83].

By contrast, Lynch, Smith, Kaplan, and House emphasize the importance of political and material explanations [82]. These take two forms: first, material deprivation associated with lower income contributes to chronic negative exposures and lack of resources over the life-course which has a powerful impact on health. Secondly, these researchers [82] and others [34, 66, 84] emphasize the importance of under-investment in human and social infrastructure that occurs in many societies with high levels of income inequality. In the United States, higher income inequality has been found to be strongly associated with reductions in social infrastructure such as unemployment insurance, social welfare, work disability, education and medical expenditures, environmental controls, and occupational health regulations. Based on recent evidence, Subramanian and Kawachi [76] have also begun to integrate this perspective into their own by noting that the most consistent association between income inequality and health in the United States occurs at the state level and suggesting that economic polarization may lead to political polarization which would influence the pattern of spending by state legislatures on health care, education, and welfare which, in turn, would have a direct influence on the health of the poor and working class in that state.

CONCLUSION

As we have seen, however one measures it, social class has an enormous influence on the way the work environment influences health. We have examined two very different ways of thinking about class. Socioeconomic and occupational position is useful in describing differences in exposure characteristics and in identifying which strata are most vulnerable to psychosocial risk factors—such as low work control. In addition, as we have seen, differences in psychosocial work environment exposures also serve to explain a significant portion of the social class gradient in health in a number of different societies. By contrast, a relational perspective on class emphasizes the historical shift in power between class groups, specifically the current ascendancy of the economic elite class. The economic policies of neoliberalism have benefited the elite class and have resulted in profound changes in the workplace as well as growing inequalities in both health and wealth in many different countries. The United States has the greatest income inequality of any Western industrialized country. Our social infrastructure is one of the weakest. We have increasingly moved away from a concern with equality toward a social and political structure that seems most effective in generating wealth for the economic elite. Hopefully, research on the class determinants of health inequalities may serve to challenge the legitimacy of those who have benefited materially and who continue to dominate the public discourse about what represents "the possible." Until the elite economic class ideology of neoliberalism and market supremacy has been thoroughly discredited, it is unlikely that any meaningful progress toward improving social inequalities will occur. Specifying the impact of neoliberal market-oriented reforms on the work environment and upon social inequality will be a critically important focus for future inquiry. For, as David Harvey has so movingly pointed out:

> The more neoliberalism is recognized as a failed utopian rhetoric masking a successful project for the restoration of ruling-class power, the more the basis is laid for a resurgence of mass movements voicing egalitarian political demands and seeking economic justice, fair trade, and greater economic security [30, pp. 203-204].

REFERENCES

1. Marmot, M., *The Status Syndrome: How Social Standing Affects Our Health and Longevity*, Henry Holt, New York, 2004.
2. Evans, R. G., Introduction, in *Why Are Some People Healthy and Others Not? The Determinants of Health in Populations*, Evans, R. G., M. L. Barer, and T. R. Marmor (eds.), Aldine de Gruyter, New York, pp. 3-26, 1994.
3. Lynch, J. and G. Kaplan, Socioeconomic Position, in *Social Epidemiology*, Berkman, L. F. and I. Kawachi (eds.), Oxford University Press, New York, pp. 13-35, 2000.
4. Marmot, M. G., G. Rose, M. Shipley, and P. J. Hamilton, Employment Grade and Coronary Heart Disease in British Civil Servants, *Journal of Epidemiology and Community Health*, 32, pp. 244-249, 1998.
5. Link, B. G. and J. C. Phelan, Social Conditions as Fundamental Causes of Disease, *Journal of Health and Social Behavior*, 35:Extra Issue, pp. 80-94, 1995.
6. Evans, G. W. and E. Kantrowitz, Socioeconomic Status and Health: The Potential Role of Environmental Risk Exposure, *Annual Review of Public Health*, 23, pp. 303-331, 2002.
7. Cockerham, W. C., The Sociology of Health Behavior and Health Lifestyles, in *Handbook of Medical Sociology*, Bird, C. E., P. Conrad, and A. M. Fremont (eds.), Prentice Hall, Upper Saddle River, NJ, pp. 159-172, 2000.
8. House, J. S. and D. R. Williams, Understanding and Reducing Socioeconomic and Racial/Ethnic Disparities in Health, in *Health and Social Justice*, Hofrichter, R. (ed.), Jossey-Bass, San Francisco, CA, pp. 89-101, 2003.
9. Johnson, J. V. and E. M. Hall, Class, Work, and Health, in *Society and Health*, Amick, B. C., S. Levine, A. R. Tarlov, and D. C. Walsh (eds.), Oxford University Press, New York, pp. 247-271, 1995.
10. Giddens, A., Positivism and Its Critics, in *A History of Sociological Analysis*, Bottomore, T. and R. Nisbet (eds.), Basic Books, New York, pp. 237-286, 1978.
11. Therborn, G., What Does the Ruling Class Do When It Rules? Some Reflections on Different Approaches to the Study of Power in Society, in *Classes, Power, and Conflict*, Giddens, A. and D. Held (eds.), University of California Press, Berkeley, CA, pp. 224-248, 1982.
12. Wright, E. O., *Classes*, Verso, London, UK, 1985.
13. Weber, M., Wirtschaft Und Gesellschaft, in *From Max Weber*, Gerth, H. and C. W. Mills (eds.), Oxford University Press, New York, pp. 180-195, 1958.
14. Parkin, F., Social Stratification, in *A History of Sociological Analysis*, Bottomore, T. and R. Nisbet (eds.), Basic Books, New York, pp. 599-632, 1978.
15. Wright, E. O. (ed.), *The Debate on Classes*, Verso, London, UK, 1989.
16. Galobardes, B., M. Shaw, D. A. Lawlor, G. D. Smith, and J. Lynch, Indicators of Socioeconomic Position, in *Methods in Social Epidemiology*, Oakes, J. M. and J. S. Kaufman (eds.), Jossey-Bass, San Francisco, CA, pp. 47-85, 2006.
17. Wright, E. O., *Class Counts*, Cambridge University Press, Cambridge, MA, 1997.
18. Bartley, M., D. Blane, and G. Davey Smith (eds.), *The Sociology of Health Inequalities*, Blackwell, Oxford, 1998.
19. Wright, E. O. and L. Perrone, Marxist Class Categories and Income Inequality, *American Sociological Review*, 42, pp. 32-55, 1977.
20. Wright, E. O., Varieties of Marxist Conceptions of Class Structure, *Politics and Society*, 9, p. 339, 1980.

21. Soderfeldt, B., Inequality in Health: A Comparative Methodological Analysis of a New Way to Measure Social Classes, in *Department of Social Medicine*, Karolinska Institute, Stockholm, Sweden, Sundbyberg and Orebro, p. 183, 1988.
22. Navarro, V. (ed.), *The Political Economy of Social Inequalities: Consequences for Health and Quality of Life*, Baywood, Amityville, NY, 2002.
23. Marx, K., *Selected Writings in Sociology and Social Philosophy*, Bottomore, T. and M. Rubel (ed.), Watts and Co., London, UK, 1956.
24. Braverman, H., *Labor and Monopoly Capital, Monthly Review Press*, New York, 1974.
25. Roemer, J., *A General Theory of Exploitation and Class*, Harvard University Press, Cambridge, MA, 1983.
26. Muntaner, C. and V. Navarro, Conclusion: Political, Economic and Cultural Determinants of Population Health—A Research Agenda, in *Political and Economic Determinants of Population Health and Well-Being*, Navarro, V. and C. Muntaner (eds.), Baywood, Amityville, NY, pp. 551-556, 2004.
27. Moody, K., *Workers in a Lean World*, The Haymarket Series, Davis, M. and M. Sprinker (ed.), Verso, London, UK, 1997.
28. Bartley, M. and M. Marmot, Social Class and Power Relations in the Workplace, *Occupational Medicine: State of the Art Reviews*, 15:1, pp. 73-78, 2000.
29. Muntaner, C., C. Borrell, J. Benach, M. I. Pasarin, and E. Fernandez, The Associations of Social Class and Social Stratification with Patterns of General and Mental Health in a Spanish Population, *International Journal of Epidemiology*, 32, pp. 950-958, 2003.
30. Harvey, D., *A Brief History of Neoliberalism*, Oxford University Press, Oxford, NY, 2005.
31. Bourdieu, P., *Firing Back: Against the Tyranny of the Market 2*, The New Press, New York, 2003.
32. Clement, W. and J. Myles, *Relations of Ruling: Class and Gender in Post-Industrial Societies*, McGill-Queens University Press, Montreal, Canada, 1997.
33. Krugman, P., The Death of Horatio Alger, in *The Nation*, January 5, 2004, pp. 16-17, 2004.
34. Navarro, V., Neoliberalism, "Globalization," Unemployment, Inequalities, and the Welfare State, in *The Political Economy of Social Inequalities: Consequences for Health and the Quality of Life*, Navarro, V. (ed.), Baywood, Amityville, NY, pp. 33-108, 2002.
35. Bourdieu, P., *The Essency of Neoliberalism: Utopia of Endless Exploitation*, Le Monde Diplomatique, France, 1998.
36. United-Nations-Development-Program, *Human Development Report, 2001: Making New Technologies Work for Human Development*, United Nations Development Program, Geneva, Switzerland, 2001.
37. Siegrist, J. and M. G. Marmot, Health Inequalities and the Psychosocial Environment—Two Scientific Challenges, *Social Science and Medicine*, 58:8, pp. 1463-1473, 2004.
38. Marmot, M. G. and T. Theorell, Social Class and Cardiovascular Disease: The Contribution of Work, *International Journal of Health Services*, 18, pp. 659-674, 1988.
39. Engels, F., *The Condition of the Working-Class in England*, Granada Publishing Limited, London, UK, 1981.
40. Johnson, J. V. and E. M. Hall, Towards an Understanding of the Interconnectedness of Class, Work and Health, in *Working Conference on Society and Health*, Harvard University, Boston, MA, 1992.
41. Marmot, M. G., H. Bosma, H. Hemingway, E. Brunner, and S. Stansfeld, Contribution of Job Control and Other Risk Factors to Social Variations in Coronary Heart Disease Incidence, *Lancet*, 350, pp. 235-239, 1997.

42. Marmot, M. and R. G. Wilkinson, Psychosocial and Material Pathways in the Relation between Income and Health: A Response to Lynch, et al., *British Medical Journal*, 322, pp. 1233-1236, 2001.

43. Kristensen, T. S., V. Borg, and H. Hannerz, Socioeconomic Status and Psychosocial Work Environment: Results from a Danish National Study, *Scandinavian Journal of Public Health*, 59:Supplement, pp. 41-48, 2002.

44. Choi, B., R. Karasek, P.-O. Ostergren, M. Ferrario, and P. DeSmet, An Orthogonal Relationship between Social Class Gradient and Job Strain Axis of the Demand-Control Model, in *4th ICOH*, 2005.

45. Hemstrom, O., Does High Income Buffer the Association Between Adverse Working Conditions and Ill Health?, *Scandinavian Journal of Public Health*, 33:2, pp. 131-137, 2005.

46. Siegrist, J., D. Starke, T. Chandola, et al., The Measurement of Effort-Reward Imbalance at Work: European Comparisons, *Social Science & Medicine*, 58, pp. 1483-1499, 2004.

47. Chandola, T., J. Siegrist, and M. Marmot, Do Changes in Effort-Reward Imbalance at Work Contribute to an Explanation of the Social Gradient in Angina?, *Occupational and Environmental Medicine*, 62, pp. 223-230, 2005.

48. Landsbergis, P. A., P. L. Schnall, K. Warren, T. G. Pickering, and J. E. Schwartz, The Effect of Job Strain on Ambulatory Blood Pressure in Men: Does It Vary by Socioeconomic Status?, *Annals of New York Academy of Science*, 896, pp. 414-416, 1999.

49. Johnson, J. V., E. M. Hall, and T. Theorell, Combined Effects of Job Strain and Social Isolation on Cardiovascular Disease Morbidity and Mortality in a Random Sample of the Swedish Male Working Population, *Scandinavian Journal of Work Environment and Health*, 15, pp. 271-279, 1989.

50. Johnson, J. V. and E. M. Hall, Job Strain, Workplace Social Support, and Cardiovascular Disease: A Cross-Sectional Study of a Random Sample of the Swedish Working Population, *American Journal of Public Health*, 78:10, pp. 1336-1342, 1988.

51. Hallqvist, J., F. Diderichsen, T. Theorell, C. Reuterwall, A. Ahlbom, and S. S. Group, Is the Effect of Job Strain on Myocardial Infarction Risk Due to Interaction between High Psychological Demands and Low Decision Latitude? Results from Stockholm Heart Epidemiology Program (Sheep) I, *Social Science & Medicine*, 46, pp. 1405-1415, 1998.

52. Landsbergis, P., P. Schnall, T. Pickering, K. Warren, and J. Schwartz, Lower Socioeconomic Status among Men in Relation to the Association between Job Strain and Blood Pressure, *Scandinavian Journal of Work, Environment and Health*, 29:3, pp. 206-215, 2003.

53. Kupper, H., A. Singh-Manoux, J. Siegrist, and M. Marmot, When Reciprocity Fails: Effort Reward Imbalance in Relation to Coronary Heart Disease and Health Functioning within Whitehall II Study, *Occupational and Environmental Medicine*, 59, pp. 777-784, 2002.

54. Albertsen, K., H. Hannerz, V. Borg, and H. Burr, The Effect of Work Environment and Heavy Smoking on the Social Inequalities in Smoking Cessation, *Public Health*, 117, pp. 383-388, 2003.

55. Ala-Mursula, L., J. Vahtera, J. Pentti, and M. Kivima, Effect of Employee Worktime Control on Health: A Prospective Cohort Study, *Occupational and Environmental Medicine*, 61, pp. 254-261, 2004.

56. Marmot, M. G. and M. Bartley, Social Class and Coronary Heart Disease, in *Stress and the Heart*, BMJ Books, London, UK, pp. 5-19, 2002.

57. Borg, V. and T. S. Kristensen, Social class and self-rated health: Can the gradient be explained by differences in life style or work environment, *Social Science and Medicine,* 51, pp. 1019-1030, 2000.
58. Andersen, I., H. Burr, T. S. Kristensen, et al., Do Factors in the Psychosocial Work Environment Mediate the Effect of Socioeconomic Position on the Risk of Myocardial Infarction? Study from the Copenhagen Centre for Prospective Population Studies, *Occupational and Environmental Medicine,* 61, pp. 886-892, 2004.
59. Schrijvers, C. T. M., H. VandeMhen, K. Stronks, and J. P. Mackenbach, Socioeconomic Inequalities in Health in the Working Population: The Contribution of Working Conditions, *International Journal of Epidemiology,* 27, pp. 1011-1018, 1998.
60. Mustard, C. A., M. Vermeulena, and J. N. Lavis, Is Position in the Occupational Hierarchy a Determinant of Decline in Perceived Health Status?, *Social Science & Medicine,* 57, pp. 2291-2303, 2003.
61. Warren, J. R., P. Hoonakkerb, P. Carayonb, and J. Brand, Job Characteristics as Mediators in SES-Health Relationships, *Social Science & Medicine,* 59, pp. 1367-1378, 2004.
62. Melchior, M., N. Krieger, I. Kawachi, L. F. Berkman, I. Niedhammer, and M. Goidberg, Work Factors and Occupational Class Disparities in Sickness Absence: Findings from the Gazel Cohort Study I, *American Journal of Public Health,* 95, pp. 1206-1212, 2005.
63. Rahkonen, O., M. Laaksonen, P. Martikainen, E. Roos, and E. Lahelma, Job Control, Job Demands, or Social Class? The Impact of Working Conditions on the Relation between Social Class and Health, *Journal of Epidemiology and Community Health,* 60, pp. 50-54, 2006.
64. Macleod, J. and G. D. Smith, Psychosocial Factors and Public Health: A Suitable Case for Treatment?, *Journal of Epidemiology and Community Health,* 57, pp. 565-570, 2003.
65. Navarro, V. and L. Shi, The Political Context of Social Inequalities and Health, in *Political Economy of Social Inequalities,* Navarro, V. (ed.), Baywood, Amityville, NY, pp. 403-418, 2002.
66. Coburn, D., Beyond the Income Inequality Hypothesis: Class, Neo-Liberalism, and Health Inequalities, *Social Science & Medicine,* 58, pp. 41-56, 2004.
67. Kanigel, R., *The One Best Way: Frederick Winslow Taylor and the Enigma of Efficiency,* Viking, New York, 1997.
68. Noble, D. F., *Forces of Production,* Alfred A. Knopf, New York, 1984.
69. Noble, D. F., *America by Design,* Oxford University Press, New York, 1977.
70. Johnson, J. V., *Work Fragmentation, Human Degradation and Occupational Stress,* U.S. Department of Labor, Occupational Health and Safety Administration, Washington, DC, 1980.
71. McCall, L., *How New Corporate Practices Redistribute Income to the Top,* Demos, New York, 2004.
72. Scott, H., Reconceptualizing the Nature and Health Consequences of Work-Related Insecurity for the New Economy: The Decline of Worker's Power in the Flexibility Regime, *International Journal of Health Services,* 34, pp. 143-153, 2004.
73. Krugman, P., Left Behind Economics, in *New York Times,* Opinion, p. 14, July 14, 2006.
74. Brecher, J. and T. Costello, *Global Village or Global Pillage,* South End Press, Boston, MA, 1994.
75. Wilkinson, R. G., *Unhealthy Societies: The Applications of Inequality,* Routledge, New York, 1996.
76. Subramanian, S. V. and I. Kawachi, Income Inequality and Health: What Have We Learned So Far?, *Epidemiology Reviews,* 26, pp. 78-91, 2004.

77. Raphael, D., From Increasing Poverty to Societal Disintegration: How Economic Inequality Affects the Health of Individuals and Communities, in *Unhealthy Times: The Political Economy of Health and Care in Canada,* Armstrong, H., P. Armstrong, and D. Coburn (eds.), Oxford University Press, Toronto, 2001.

78. Raphael, D., A Society in Decline, in *Health and Social Justice: Politics, Ideology, and Inequity in the Distribution of Disease,* Hofrichter, R. (ed.), Jossey-Bass, San Francisco, CA, pp. 55-88, 2003.

79. Reich, R. B., T. I. P. I., The Inequality Paradox, in *The Inequality Paradox: Growth of Income Disparity,* Auerbach, J. A. and R. Belous (eds.), National Policy Association, Washington, DC, 1998.

80. Smeeding, T. M., U.S. Income Inequality in a Cross-National Perspective: Why Are We So Different?, in *The Inequality Paradox: Growth of Income Disparity,* Auerbach, J. A. and R. Belous (eds.), National Policy Association, Washington, DC, 1998.

81. Huber, E. and J. D. Stephens, *Development and Crisis of the Welfare State: Parties and Policies in Global Markets,* The University of Chicago Press, Chicago, IL, 2001.

82. Lynch, J. W., G. D. Smith, G. A. Kaplan, and J. S. House, Income Inequality and Mortality, in *Health and Social Justice: Politics, Ideology, and Inequity in the Distribution of Disease,* Hofrichter, R. (ed.), Jossey-Bass, San Francisco, CA, pp. 217-227, 2003.

83. Kawachi, I., B. P. Kennedy, and A. R. Tarlov (eds.), *The Society and Population Health Reader, Vol. 1: Income Inequality and Health,* New Press, New York, 1999.

84. Muntaner, C., J. W. Lynch, and G. D. Smith, Social Capital, Disorganized Communities, and the Third Way: Understanding the Retreat from Structural Inequalities in Epidemiology and Public Health, in *Political and Economic Determinants of Population Health and Well-Being,* Navarro, V. and C. Muntaner (eds.), Baywood, Amityville, NY, pp. 427-450, 2004.

CHAPTER 4

The Changing Nature of Work in Canada and Other Developed Countries: What Do the Trends Over Time Tell Us?

Peter Smith and John Frank

The goal of this chapter is to describe changes in various dimensions of work in Canada and around the world. While there appears to be a general consensus that both the nature of work and the availability of work have changed over the last 30 years in all developed countries, there does not appear to be similar consensus concerning precisely which working conditions have changed, to what extent, and whether these changes have had an overall positive or negative impact on the health of labor market participants.

To help answer some of these questions, we have divided this chapter into two sections. The first section will present *changes in the nature of work* using data from the Canadian Labor Force Survey (LFS), from the years 1976 through to 2003. The LFS is a monthly survey, conducted by Statistics Canada, using a complex, rotating panel sample, designed to efficiently estimate month-to-month changes in the Canadian labor force participation in the civilian, non-institutionalized population aged 15 years or more. Residents of the Yukon, Northwest Territories, and Nunavut, persons living on Indian reserves, and full-time members of the Canadian armed forces are excluded from coverage. The number of households sampled has changed slightly over time given varying levels of funding and improvements in survey design. Since 1995, the sample size has been approximately 54,000 households. Each household remains in the survey for a period of 6 months. At any one time, six representative sub-samples are included in the survey. Each month, one sub-sample is removed from the survey (at the completion of its 6 months) and is replaced by a new sub-sample from a similar area [1]. For the purpose of the analyses presented in this chapter, monthly labor force estimates have been averaged, providing an annual estimate.

While it was originally designed to measure characteristics such as industrial participation and unemployment statistics, a number of other questions are asked of participants in the LFS, enabling us to describe some changes in the labor market conditions of various population sub-groups. While the trends we have presented in this section are all Canadian, there is no reason to believe that the Canadian labor market is significantly different from the U.S. labor market or other labor markets in developed economies around the world. Where possible, we have presented similar information from U.S. sources.

The second section of this chapter will review the research examining *changes in the self-reported psychosocial work characteristics* (e.g., self-reported job security, job satisfaction, or job control) of labor force participants across a number of countries.

1. CHANGES IN THE NATURE OF WORK OF THE CANADIAN LABOR FORCE

Setting the Context

Figure 1 describes the general patterns of unemployment, underemployment, and multiple job holdings in the Canadian labor force between 1976 and 2003 (definitions of terms used in this chapter, such as "underemployment," are listed in Appendix 1). While patterns in multiple job holdings were consistently rising throughout this time period, both unemployment and underemployment showed major fluctuations, in line with two economic shocks. The first occurred at the start of the 1980s and the second was at the start of the 1990s.

However, the patterns described above differed by gender. Between 1976 and 2003, the percentage of the male labor force working multiple jobs rose from 2.5% to 4.3% in 1975, peaking at 4.7% in 1990. In contrast, the percentage of women working multiple jobs rose from 1.4% in 1976 to 5.8% in 2003, surpassing men. Similarly, women were more likely to be underemployed over this time period. Between 1990 and 1994, during the second economic shock, the percentage of women who were underemployed rose from 5.5% to 9.2%, while the percentage of men who were underemployed rose from 1.9% to 3.6%. A similar pattern was observed during the first economic shock between 1981 and 1984.

We also see differences when comparing underemployment and multiple jobs across level of education. Table 1 presents the percentage of unemployed and

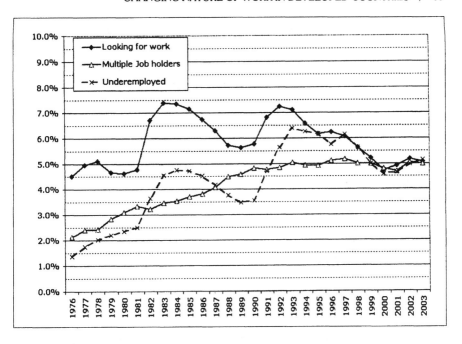

Figure 1. Changes in unemployment, underemployment, and multiple job holding. Canada 1976-2003. Canadian Labor Force Survey.

underemployed labor force participants by level of education in 1990,[1] in 1993 at the height of the second economic shock, and in 2003. Across all years, respondents with less than secondary education had the highest percentage of underemployment and unemployment and participants with university degrees had the lowest percentage. When examining the percentage of labor force participants working multiple jobs by education level, there was no increase between 1990 and 2003. Further, respondents with university degrees were the most likely to be working multiple jobs (5.9% in 1990 and 5.7% in 2003), and respondents with less the secondary education the least (3.6% in 1990 and 3.5% in 2003).

[1] Labor Force Survey questions assessing respondent's level of education changed between 1976 and 2003, making comparisons over this time period problematic. In 1990, the education questions changed to allow people who had not completed secondary education to report on other education they had received (e.g., trade certificates or a 5-day word processing course). The impact of these changes in wording predominantly affected the number of respondents with some post-secondary education and those who had completed secondary schooling. A comparison of the years 1989 and 1990 demonstrated that the number of participants with no post-secondary training decreased (12%), while the number of non-university certificates and diplomas rose 64%. Respondents with university degrees are the only group not affected by the changes in wording in the Labor Force Survey questionnaire [2].

Table 1. Changes in Unemployment and Underemployment by
Education Level, 1990 to 2003

	1990 (%)	1993 (%)	2003 (%)	Change 1990-1993 (%)	Change 1993-2003 (%)
Unemployment (%)					
No secondary school	6.3	7.2	5.9	0.9	−1.3
Secondary school	6.2	8.0	5.5	1.8	−2.5
Some post-secondary	5.2	7.1	4.6	1.8	−2.5
University degree	3.1	4.4	3.6	1.3	−0.9
Underemployment (%)					
No secondary school	4.7	7.9	6.3	3.2	−1.6
Secondary school	3.7	7.3	6.1	3.6	−1.2
Some post-secondary	3.1	5.8	4.7	2.7	−1.1
University degree	2.0	3.6	3.6	1.6	0.0

Figure 2 presents the trend in average weekly labor market income, from three different time series, using the Survey of Employment, Payrolls, and Hours, between 1961 and 2004. Between 1976 and 2003, the time period for other labor market trends presented in this chapter, the average weekly wage rose from $228 to $690, an absolute increase of 203%. It should be noted that after adjusting wages for changes in the cost of living (using the consumer price index), the actual change in median and average hourly wages for full-time workers between 1981 and 2004 was approximately 5%, while wages for part-time workers decreased by approximately 14% [3].

Further, it does not appear that these changes have been equally distributed across labor market participants. Data from the Survey of Labor and Income Dynamics, not adjusted for changes in the cost of living, demonstrate that the average wage increase for unskilled workers between 1993 and 2003 was 13.5% for men and −0.5% for women compared to 85.7% for men and 75.9% for women in senior management occupations. The increases in salaries also followed a gradient throughout the hierarchy of occupational skill requirements (for full details see Table 2). In addition, previous reports that have adjusted for changes in the cost of living have suggested the wage rates for low-paid workers (full-time employees earning less than $10 per hour, in year 2000 dollars) did not improve between 1980 and 2000, and may have actually decreased [3, 4]. Further, as can be seen in Table 2, wage rates for women within similar occupational skill groups are substantially less than for men, even after adjustment for a variety of other workplace factors [5].

Findings from the United States on changes in wage rates describe a similar story of inequality in the benefits across different levels of the labor market over time. Information from the U.S. Congressional Budget Office shows that over the 18-year

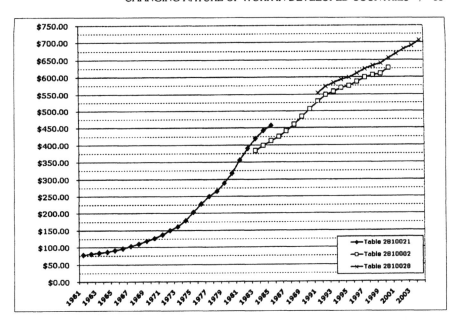

Figure 2. Individual average weekly earnings. All industries.
Canada 1961 to 2004. Survey of Employment Payrolls and Hours.

period between 1979 and 1997, the second lowest fifth and the lowest fifth of the U.S. labor market reported changes in their average after-tax income of 6% and –1% respectively. Over the same time period, participants in the 81st to 95th percentile of earnings reported changes of 28%. Participants in the next 4% reported changes of 46%, while the top percent of the labor market had an after-tax income increase of 157% [6] and (see chapter 3).

Who is Working?

The last 27 years have seen three major compositional changes in the type of participants in the Canadian labor force: 1) there has been an increase in the number of women employed; 2) there has been a decrease in the number of young adults (less than 25 years), and 25 to 34 year olds, who are employed, with a concurrent increase in employment in the 35- to 55-year age group; and 3) there has been an increase in the number of labor force participants who have educational levels at or above university bachelor degrees. Figure 3 presents these changes in the Canadian labor force between 1976 and 2003.

The increasing number of women who are employed has had a major impact on the labor force participation of couples with children. Figure 4 describes these changes in the labor force participation rates for couples with children less than 5 years of age. In 1976, only 20% of couples with children less than 5 years old were both working, while 64% of couples had only one person working, with the

Table 2. Adjusted Mean[a] Salaries in 1993 and 2003 by Gender
and Skill Requirements of Job (N for All Years = 155,808)

Training required based on National Occupational Classification	1993	2003	% increase	$ increase
Senior Management				
Men	$48,019	$89,157	85.7	$41,138
Women[b]	$29,387	$51,704	75.9	$22,317
Middle Management				
Men	$46,561	$63,969	37.4	$17,408
Women	$37,137	$50,766	36.7	$13,630
University education				
Men	$44,306	$58,857	32.8	$14,550
Women	$36,373	$46,358	27.5	$9,985
Apprenticeship or certificate				
Men	$38,223	$45,863	20.0	$7,640
Women	$30,727	$36,224	17.9	$5,497
Secondary school				
Men	$31,663	$38,367	21.2	$6,704
Women	$24,711	$29,310	18.6	$4,599
No training required				
Men	$27,868	$31,624	13.5	$3,757
Women	$24,210	$24,085	−0.5	−$125

[a]Adjusted for age (grouped), industry, workplace size, and sector (public versus private).
[b]Mean salaries for women in senior management positions had large variations across study years given the relatively small number of women in this occupational category in any given year (N for each year ranged from 20 to 46 observations).
Source: Survey of Labour and Income Dynamics

other being a non-labor force participant. By 1989, the percentage of one-participant labor force couples and two full-time labor force participant couples was the same. In 2003, the number of dual full-time couples had increased to 46% of all couples with children less than 5 years old, while one-labor-force-participant couples had reduced further to 28%.

However, although the labor force participation of women has increased, they still face many structural barriers in the workplace. Women suffer a disproportionate burden of chronic musculoskeletal injuries [7]. Contributing to this problem is workplace equipment being designed for average male dimensions, as well as questionably gender-appropriate job assignments, even under the same job title [8, 9]. Further, the frequency and causes of women's work-related health problems are not well understood, as the majority of research in this area is conducted on

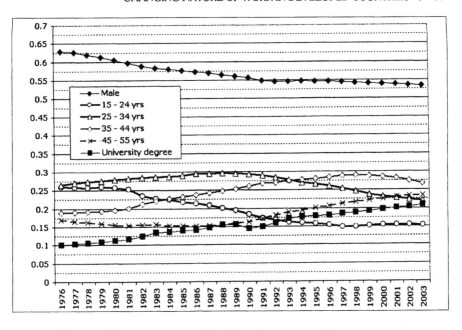

Figure 3. The percentage of the labor force by gender, age group, and university qualifications, 1976 to 2003.

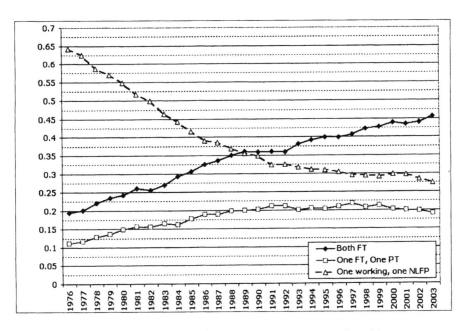

Figure 4. Changes in labor force participation for couples with one or more children aged less than 5 years, 1976 to 2003.

male population groups. This extends to research on most work-stress models, such as the demand-control and effort-reward imbalance models.

Further, it would appear that within the household, women still undertake many of their traditional housekeeping roles, even though they are working, leading to tension between work and family roles [10]. Figure 5 shows that the percentage of women who take time off work due to family responsibilities has increased from 2% to 4% between 1976 and 2003, and exceeds men in similar positions.

The changes in the age distribution of the labor force are primarily due to the general ageing of the Canadian population between 1976 and 2003. In 1976, 15- to 24-year-olds comprised 26% of the population and 26% of the labor force. In 2003, they made up 16.5% of the population and 15% of the labor force. Similarly, 25- to 34-year-olds comprised 21% of the population and 26% of the labor force. In 2003, they comprised 15% of the population and 22% of the labor force. As the Canadian population has aged, so has the labor force, with the declining percentage of younger workers in the labor market redistributed into an increasing percent of workers aged 35-55 years. In 1976, 35- to 55-year-olds comprised 29% of the population and 36% of the labor force. In 2003, they comprised 39% of the population and half of the labor force.

The increasing educational level of labor force participants is also likely to have impacts on the health of labor force participants into the future. Increasing numbers of Canadian students are pursing university education as opposed to working in

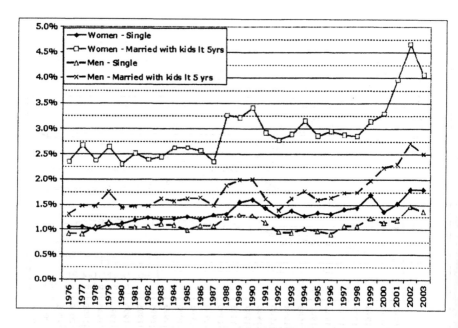

Figure 5. Comparing the percent of labor force absence due to family responsibilities for couples with children under 5 years of age, and single labor force participants.

trades or apprenticeships or going directly from school to work [11]. However, it does not appear that the number of skilled occupations in the labor force has increased to the same extent. Recent research using the Canadian National Population Health Survey and the Survey of Labor and Income Dynamics shows that not only is there an increasing percentage of Canadian labor force participants who have educational qualifications above what is required for their current job, but for respondents with university education, being overqualified for their job is associated with increased probability of declining self-rated health status over the next 4 years [12].

Further, although the educational qualifications of Canadian labor force participants have increased, the percentage working in low-wage jobs has not. Data from the Canadian Census shows the percentage of the Canadian labor force aged 15-64 years of age who are low paid workers[2] did not substantially change between 1980 and 2000, moving from 15% to 16% [4].

Changes in Industries and Occupations

Another key shift in the Canadian labor market over the last 25 years is the change in the industrial composition of the labor market (see Figure 6). The 1980s saw a decline in the percentage of employment in both the manufacturing and construction industries, along with an increase in community services (education and health and welfare services). The mid-1990s saw a slight rebound for the manufacturing industry; however, since the start of 2000, it has steadily declined and the percentage of employees in manufacturing is nearing its lowest point in the last 27 years [13].

Figure 7 presents the changes in the percentage of the labor force employed in the public sector and the percentage of the labor force who are self-employed. The percentage of employment in the public sector has decreased from 24% in 1976 to 19% in 2003. This decrease has almost entirely been picked up by an increase in self-employment from 11% of the labor force in 1976 to a peak of 16.7% in 1998 and remained at 15.1% in 2003. In contrast, employment in the private sector has remained relatively steady, moving from 64.1% of the labor force in 1976 to 65.6% in 2003. Compared to the employment in the public sector, self-employment is commonly associated with lower levels of worker protection, such as higher levels of unpaid overtime, lower job security, fewer pensions, and less compensation for workplace injuries. Further, increases in job insecurity as a result of increases in self-employment, both through the fear of job loss and the fear of not being able to find future work, have been associated with lower levels of health [14].

Changes in the Number of Hours Worked
(Usual versus Actual and Families with Children)

The last 27 years also have seen changes in the number of hours worked by individuals and in particular couples with children, both within the United States,

---

[2] Earning less than $375 CDN per week in year 2000 dollars.

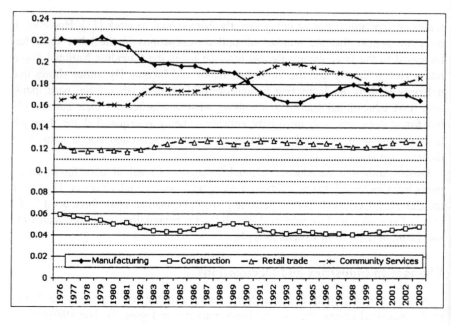

Figure 6. Changes in manufacturing, construction, community services, and retail trade as a percentage of the labor force.

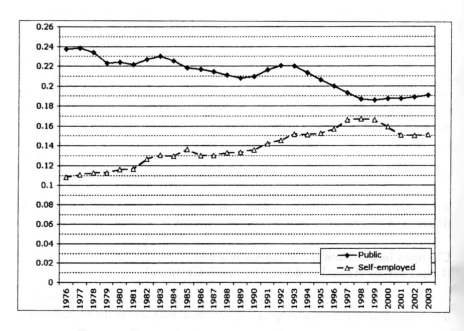

Figure 7. Changes in the percentage of workers in the public sector and self-employment.

Canada, and most other developed countries [15]. Movement away from goods-producing industries into service-related industries has resulted in the need for different measures of productivity by management. Production value per worker in manufacturing plants, and other blue-collar industries, is easily measured and monitored. However, within white-collar, non-manual industries, such as education and management, the measurement of productivity per worker is more ambiguous. Some researchers suggest one of the only ways to assess productivity in white-collar industries is the use of "face time" [16]. That is, workers demonstrate their productivity and commitment to a firm by being the first to arrive in the morning and the last to leave in the evening [17].

In spite of these fears, the trends in the usual hours worked by Canadians have not increased. The usual number of hours worked per week reported by full-time, non-self-employed, labor force participants in Canada has declined minimally from 41.9 hours per week for men, and 38.8 hours per week for women in 1976, to 41.2 hours per week for men and 38.4 hours per week for women in 2003. However, one may question what respondents report when asked about their usual work hours. For example, do they include unpaid (or paid) extra hours worked on a semi-regular basis? To help clarify these questions, in 1997 the Labor Force Survey changed its question on usual working hours, asking respondents only to report their normal paid hours, not counting overtime. While this change in question did not make a large difference to reports of usual hours per week, it allowed an examination of extra hours worked by Canadian labor force participants.

Figure 8 presents the average percentage of full-time, non-self-employed labor force participants whose actual hours worked in the previous week were greater than the hours they usually work. In 2003, almost a quarter of full-time, non-self-employed men (and a similar proportion of Canadian women), were required to work more hours in the previous week than they were paid for. It is important to note these are monthly averages, which account for fluctuations throughout the year in accordance with the business cycle. Non-self-employed males, who are employed full-time, worked an extra 2.4 hours, on average, per week (women worked 1.5 extra hours per week). Of these extra hours, responses from the 2003 Labor Force Survey estimated that 54% are unpaid. In other words, it is estimated that in the year 2003 the Canadian labor force put in up to 624 million extra unpaid hours of work[3]. While it is not possible to estimate the amount of unpaid work in 1976 because of question changes in the Labor Force Survey, the total number of unpaid extra hours in 1997 (the first time this question was asked) was 512 million (a 22% increase in unpaid extra hours between 1997 and 2003).

Further, examination of working hours at the level of the individual does not consider the changes in labor force participation by couples in Canada, in particular those couples with children under 5 years of age. Between 1976 and 2003, the usual

---

[3] This estimate is based on the assumption that extra hours worked in the survey week in a given month were the same as the rest of the weeks in that survey month. If we assume that no other unpaid overtime was worked in each survey month, the unpaid overtime worked in 2003 totals 144 million extra hours.

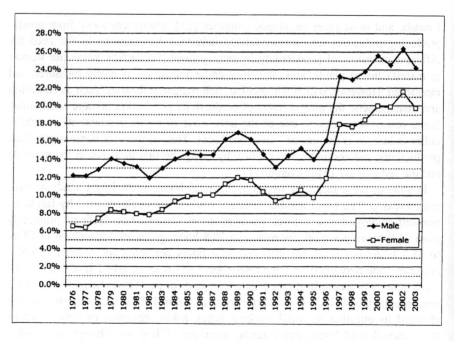

Figure 8. Percentage of full-time, non-self-employed labor force
participants whose actual hours of work are greater
than their usual hours of work.
Note: The question on usual working hours per week changed in 1997.
Pre-1997 respondents were asked to report the hours they usually worked
in a typical week, regardless of whether they were paid. Beginning in
January 1997, respondents were asked to report the normal paid
or contract hours, not counting paid or unpaid overtime.

number of hours worked by couples with children less than 5 years old increased
from 53 to 64 hours per week. Research from Australia suggests that more than
one in five mothers is back at work by the time her child is 6 months old [18]. More
research is needed to examine the effect that greater working hours have on family
environments and its subsequent impact on childhood health measures, such as
childhood self-esteem and obesity levels.

As the percentage of workers who are required to work extra hours increases,
we would expect the measurement error concerning the usual number of hours
worked per week to increase. Researchers examining working hours must consider this issue when monitoring trends in working hours over time. Further,
given that working extra hours is likely linked to perceptions of commitment to
a company, more research is needed to examine the effects of being unable to
work extra hours (e.g., mothers may be unable to work extra hours regularly due
to family commitments and we would expect this tendency to be greater for
single mothers) with commensurate effects on career progression and subsequent
health outcomes.

In conclusion, there have been a number of changes in the Canadian labor force over the last 27 years. Underemployment and multiple job holdings have both increased, although these patterns differed by gender and level of education. Women are now generally more likely to be both underemployed and multiple job holders compared to men. The percentage of underemployed and unemployed labor force participants increases with lower levels of education. The opposite pattern is observed for multiple job holding. Wages are increasing. However, the increases are not equally distributed across the labor market; low-wage, uneducated, unskilled workers reported no real change in labor market income during the last 20 years. The labor force in 2003 is on average older than it was in 1976. A greater proportion of women are now working, although their average wage rate is still lower than males' overall. Further, it would appear that women are still undertaking a majority of traditional roles in the household. The labor force of today is better educated than in previous years, although better education has not led to wage increases for low-paid workers or increases in the proportion of skilled occupations. Finally, changes in industrial composition may have led to a greater number of work-hours per week. This finding seems to be true both for individuals, as measured by extra hours of work per week, and for the total number of usual hours worked by couples with children.

2. CHANGES IN SELF-REPORTED PSYCHOSOCIAL WORK CHARACTERISTICS

In the second part of this chapter, we will focus on changes in psychosocial working conditions. It has been argued that new systems of work arrangements, such as lean production and flexible work arrangements, have had certain unforeseen impacts on the psychosocial working conditions of labor market participants. Those working under these new arrangements have reported decreased feelings of job control and job security and higher levels of job demands [19-21].

However, while the measurement of many aspects of work—such as those described in the previous section—are routinely measured in most labor market surveys, psychosocial characteristics, such as self-perceived job demands and job control, are not. Very little information exists, particularly within North America, to help us answer certain key questions [19]. For example, are job characteristics changing across the entire labor force? If changes are occurring, are they consistent across different socioeconomic groups?

Moreover, researchers who are interested in surveying work characteristics face a basic challenge: what should they measure and how should they measure it? Inconsistencies still exist in the measurement of job control, job support, and job demands. Some authors prefer analyses using tertiles, others use quartiles, and others choose to keep the dimensions of each scale continuous [22-24]. Further, for the measurement of increasing job demands, current scales do not distinguish between increases in working pace, and increases in working hours, which may have differential effects on the health of workers [25]. Similar problems exist in the measurement of job strain [26]. Such basic measurement issues must be resolved if we are to make the best use of surveillance data on job characteristics collected in the future.

In addition to a lack of data collection, the measurement of changes in psychosocial working conditions is hampered by concurrent confounding changes in the labor market. For example, the amount of control one has over his or her job is related to the position in the occupational hierarchy [27]. If the number of skilled occupations increased over a 10-year period, we would expect concurrent increases in the level of job control, as skill level is related to perceptions of job control. Therefore, there is a need for researchers measuring changes in psychosocial working conditions to make sure they account for compositional changes in the labor market between the two (or more) time points that they are measuring.

Data from the European Union [28] suggests that between 1990 and 1995, levels of work intensity increased, while levels of job control decreased. During the next 5 years, work intensity continued to increase, while learning opportunities on the job decreased, as did the percentage of monotonous jobs. At the same time, levels of job control and the complexity of work remained steady.

It is important to note that differences in both the direction and strength of these changes varied across different industrial sectors [29] and between men and women [30]. Concurrent data specific to the labor force in Denmark reported no changes in job control, although decreases in job insecurity were observed over the same 10-year period, after adjusting for compositional changes in the labor force over time [31].

U.S. researchers have been able to extract some North American data by comparing the Quality of Employment Survey (1977) and the National Study of the Changing Workforce [32]. This comparison suggests that employees are required to work faster, harder, and have less time to get things done on the job than they did 20 years ago. However, these findings should be interpreted with caution, given a number of methodological limitations related to the comparison of these two surveys [19].

Another paper focusing on changes in the United States labor market, using the General Social Survey, has reported that workers' perceptions of the overall quality of their jobs (measured by one question on job satisfaction) remained relatively stable during the period 1989 to 1998. However, during the same period the percentage of workers who reported that their "job was secure" decreased, as did the proportion of workers who described their jobs as "interesting" [33].

In conclusion, in relation to changes in psychosocial working conditions, there appears to be some evidence that some working conditions are changing, although the quality of information in the European Union is greater than that presently available in North America. Greater emphasis on the measurement of different psychosocial work dimensions, as well as integration of the surveillance of these working characteristics into population-based surveys, so that measurement can be stratified across specific labor market groups (such as occupation and industry, gender and education) would add greatly to our understanding of the changing nature of work in North America.

APPENDIX ONE
Definitions from the Canadian Labor Force Survey

Unemployment: Percentage of population who report they are actively looking for work.

Underemployment: Percentage of non-self-employed labor force who are working part-time because there is no full-time work available.

Multiple Jobs: The percentage of the total labor force (excluding the unemployed) who report working two or more jobs concurrently.

Self-Employment: Percentage of the labor force who are not salaried workers. Includes incorporated and unincorporated businesses with and without employees, but excludes unpaid family workers.

Absence from Work Due to Family Responsibilities: The percentage of the non-self-employed labor force who reported a part-week absence from work due to family responsibilities. Full-week absences were only included for respondents with children over the age of 3 years, as maternity leave is included as a full-week absence.

REFERENCES

1. Statistics Canada, *A Guide to the Labour Force Survey,* 71-543-GIE, pp. 1-38, 2003.
2. Gower, D., *The Impact of the 1990 Changes to the Education Questions on the Labour Force Survey*, Statistics Canada, Ottawa, pp. 1-16, 1993.
3. Morissette, R. and G. Picot, *Low-Paid Work and Economically Vulnerable Families over the Last Two Decades*, Business and Labour Market Analysis Division, Statistics Canada, Ottawa, pp. 1-40, 2005.
4. Chung, L., Low Paid Workers: How Many Live in Low-Income Families?, *Perspectives on Labour & Income*, 5:10, pp. 5-14, 2004.
5. Drolet, M., *The Persistent Gap: New Evidence on the Canadian Gender Gap*, Statistics Canada, Ottawa, 2002.
6. Johnson, J. V., *The Growing Imbalance: Class Inequalities in Work and Health in an Era of Flexibilization*, unpublished presentation, 2005.
7. Smith, P. M. and C. A. Mustard, Examining the Associations between Physical Work Demands and Work Injury Rates between Men and Women in Ontario, 1990-2000, *Occupational and Environmental Medicine*, 61, pp. 750-756, 2004.
8. Messing, K., Are Women Biologically Fit for Jobs? Are Jobs Fit for Women?, in *One-Eyed Science: Occupational Health and Women Workers*, Temple University Press, Philadelphia, PA, pp. 23-40, 1998.
9. Messing, K., Women Workers and Their Working Conditions, in *One-Eyed Science: Occupational Health and Women Workers*, Temple University Press, Philadelphia, PA, pp. 1-11, 1998.
10. Duxbury, L. and C. Higgins, *Work-Life Balance in the New Millennium. Where Are We? Where Do We Need to Go?*, Canadian Policy Research Network, Ottawa, pp. 1-92, 2001.
11. Corak, M., G. Lipps, and J. Zhao, *Family Income and Participation in Post-Secondary Education*, Statistics Canada, Ottawa, pp. 1-36, 2003.
12. Smith, P. M. and J. W. Frank, When Aspirations and Achievements Don't Meet. A Longitudinal Examination of the Differential Effect of Education and Occupational

Attainment on Declines in Self-Rated Health among Canadian Labour Force Participants, *International Journal of Epidemiology*, 34:4, pp. 827-834, 2005.

13. Cross, P., Recent Changes in the Labour Market, *Canadian Economic Observer*, March, pp. 3.1-3.10, 2005.

14. Sverke, M., J. Hellgren, and K. Naswall, No Security: A Meta-Analysis and Review of Job Insecurity and Its Consequences, *Journal of Occupational Health Psychology*, 7:3, pp. 242-264, 2002.

15. Jacobs, J. A. and K. Gerson, Overworked Individuals or Overworked Families?, *Work and Occupations*, 28:1, pp. 40-63, 2001.

16. Maume Jr, D. J. and P. Houston, Job Segregation and Gender Differences in Work-Family Spillover among White-Collar Workers, *Journal of Family and Economic Issues*, 22:2, pp. 171-189, 2001.

17. Fried, M., Taking Time: Parental Leave Policy and Corporate Culture, in *Women in the Political Economy*, Steinberg, R. J. (ed.), Temple University Press, Philadelphia, PA, 1998.

18. Australian Institute of Family Studies, *Growing Up in Australia: The Longitudinal Study of Australian Children*, Commonwealth of Australia, Melbourne, pp. 1-29, 2005.

19. Landsbergis, P., The Changing Organization of Work and the Safety and Health of Working People: A Commentary, *Journal of Occupational & Environmental Medicine*, 45:1, pp. 61-72, 2003.

20. Smith, V., New Forms of Work Organization, *Annual Review of Sociology*, 23, pp. 315-339, 1997.

21. Smith, V., Crossing the Great Divide: Negotiating Uncertainty, Risk and Opportunity, in *Crossing the Great Divide: Worker Risk and Opportunity in the New Economy*, ILR Press, Ithaca, NY, pp. 157-179, 2001.

22. Landsbergis, P. and T. Theorell, Measurement of Psychosocial Workplace Exposure Variables, *Occupational Medicine: State of the Art Reviews*, 15:1, pp. 163-171, 2002.

23. de Lange, A. H., T. W. Taris, M. A. Kompier, I. Houtman, and P. Bongers, "The Very Best of the Millennium": Longitudinal Research and the Demand-Control-(Support) Model, *Journal of Occupational Health Psychology*, 8:4, pp. 282-305, 2003.

24. Hammar, N., L. Alfredsson, and J. V. Johnson, Job Strain, Social Support at Work, and Incidence of Myocardial Infarction, *Occupational and Environmental Medicine*, 55, pp. 548-553, 1998.

25. Kristensen, T. S., J. B. Bjorner, K. B. Christensen, and V. Borg, The Distinction between Work Pace and Working Hours in the Measurement of Quantitative Demands at Work, *Work and Stress*, 18:4, pp. 305-322, 2004.

26. Wall, T. D., P. R. Jackson, S. Mullarkey, and S. K. Parker, The Demands-Control Model of Job Strain: A More Specific Test, *Journal of Occupational and Organizational Psychology*, 69, pp. 153-166, 1996.

27. Mustard, C. A., M. Vermeulen, and J. N. Lavis, Is Position in the Occupational Hierarchy a Determinant of Decline in Perceived Health Status?, *Social Science and Medicine*, 57, pp. 2291-2303, 2003.

28. Paoli, P. and D. Merllie, *Third European Survey on Working Conditions 2000*, European Foundation for the Improvement of Living and Working Conditions, Dublin, Ireland, pp. 1-72, 2001.

29. Houtman, I., F. Andries, R. van den Berg, and S. Dhondt, *Sectoral Profiles of Working Conditions*, European Foundation for the Improvement of Living and Working Conditions, Dublin, Ireland, pp. 1-70, 2002.

30. Fagan, C. and B. Burchell, *Gender, Jobs and Working Conditions in the European Union*, European Foundation for the Improvement of Living and Working Conditions, Dublin, Ireland, pp. 1-91, 2002.
31. Burr, H., J. Bjorner, T. Kristensen, F. Tuchsen, and E. Bach, Trends in the Danish Work Environment in 1990-2000 and Their Associations with Labour-Force Changes, *Scandinavian Journal of Work, Environment and Health*, 29:4, pp. 270-279, 2003.
32. Bond, J. T., E. Galinksy, and J. E. Swanberg, *The National Study of the Changing Workforce*, Families and Work Institute, New York, pp. 1-176, 1998.
33. Handel, M. J., Trends in Perceived Job Quality, 1989 to 1998, *Work and Occupations*, 32:1, pp. 66-94, 2005.

CHAPTER 5

The Changing Nature of Work in the United States

Edward Yelin

Labor market analysts frequently divide into those focused on changes in the quantity of work, those focused on changes in the distribution of occupations and industries, and those focused on the nature of the employment contract across sectors of the economy. Even among those analyzing changes in the quantity of work, some focus on the growth of part-time employment, while others focus on the increase in the average overall hours of employment among American workers. Such divisions obscure the scope of the changes in employment and preclude an understanding of why those changes are occurring. In this chapter, I review the evidence for each of these kinds of changes in employment, and then provide a quick summary of the research which attempts to tie the changes together into a comprehensive view of the emerging labor market.

QUANTITY OF EMPLOYMENT

The principal change in the quantity of employment over the last several decades has been the increase in the proportion of the working age population that is in the labor force (Figure 1). In 1965, 58.9% of the working age population was in the labor force, but by 2000, 67.2% were, an increase of 14.1% in relative terms [1]. This overall increase is the result of a 7.4% decrease among men (most pronounced among men 55-64 (Figure 2), and a 53.2% increase among women, which is consistent across age groups (Figure 3). Thus, the overall increase has been accompanied by increased feminization of the labor force.

During this time, average hours worked per week among U.S. workers have stayed relatively constant [2], while weeks worked per year have increased, resulting in a net increase in the amount of time worked per year [3]. Concomitantly, there has been an increase in the proportion working greater than full-time, which is more than 40 hours per week [4], and non-standard shifts [5].

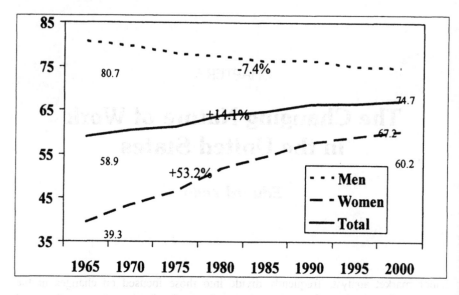

Figure 1. Labor force participation rate, by gender, U.S., 1965-2000.
Source: Jacobs, 1998, pp. 23-32; BLS, 1999.

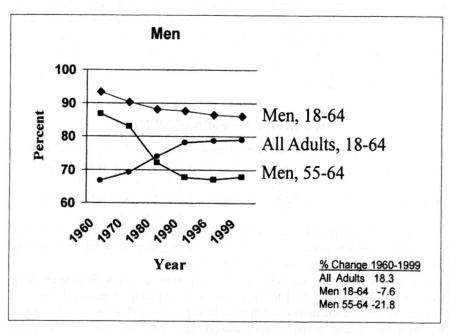

Figure 2. Labor force participation rates among men, by age,
U.S., 1960-1999.
Source: Jacobs, 1998, pp. 23-32; BLS, 1999.

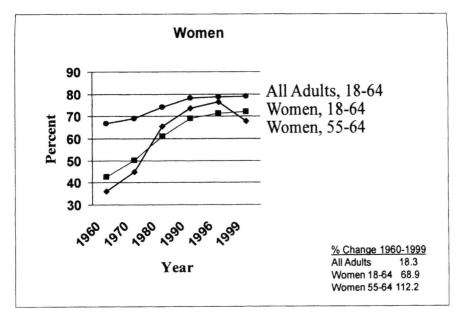

Figure 3. Labor force participation rates among women, by age,
U.S., 1960-1999.
Source: Jacobs, 1998, pp. 23-32; BLS, 1999.

Overall, a greater proportion of the working age population is employed, the average worker is putting in more hours per year, and fewer are working a standard full-time work week (more work greater than full-time and have non-standard shifts).

DISTRIBUTION OF JOBS, BY OCCUPATIONS AND INDUSTRIES

Between 1960 and 2000, the number of non-farm workers increased from 54.2 to 131.8 million, almost two and a half times [1-6]. During this time, the number of workers in goods-producing sectors of the economy rose by only about a quarter, while the number in the services sectors increased more than three-fold. As a result, workers in goods-production were 38% of the workforce in 1960, but less than 25% by 2000 (Table 1).

The data concerning the distribution of workers by occupation are consistent with the industry trends [7, 8]. In 1960, only 43% of workers were in white-collar occupations, while 36 and 12% were in blue-collar and service work occupations, respectively (Table 2). By 2000, white-collar workers constituted about 60% of all workers, service workers were 14%, while blue-collar workers were only 25%. Within the white-collar category, the share of jobs in professional specialty occupations increased by about a quarter in relative terms (to 16%), the share in managerial

Table 1. Distribution of Industries, 1960 and 2000

Major industry	1960	2000
Goods production	37.7%	24.7%
Services industries	62.3%	75.3%

Source: Statistical Abstract of US, 1993, 2001.

Table 2. Distribution of Occupations, 1960 and 2000

Major occupation	1960	2000
White collar	43.4%	59.4%
Blue collar	36.6%	24.6%
Service	12.2%	13.5%
Farm, mining	7.9%	2.5%

Source: Statistical Abstract of US, 1981, 2001.

occupations increased by almost three-fold (to 31%), while the share in administrative support (clerical) occupations declined by about 12% (data on share of jobs in various white-collar occupations not in figures). Of course, these figures for relative changes in the share of jobs mask the fact that there has been an absolute change in most categories, including over the very long term, occupations associated with manufacturing.

Thus, in the United States in the most recent four decades, there has been a shift away from goods production and the blue-collar occupations associated with that kind of work to service industries and the white-collar occupations associated with those sectors. Of great importance, and contrary to the predictions of pessimistic analysts from the early 1970s who thought that there would be a fundamental deskilling of jobs [9], there has been a shift within white-collar occupations to professional and managerial positions and a slight decrease in the proportion in clerical occupations, no doubt due to the computerization of the office. Clearly, this discussion is limited to the United States and other developed nations, since much production occurs outside the developed world.

SHIFTING NATURE OF EMPLOYMENT CONTRACT

Throughout much of the post-war period, the U.S. labor market was divided into two distinct spheres [10, 11]. White-collar workers were paid to design work processes and then supervise their implementation. They were provided security of employment and paid on a salaried basis. Blue-collar workers were paid hourly wages to implement the processes designed by others. Although they were not provided the same kinds of security, in practice, lay-offs occurred infrequently due to the success of the U.S. economy in general and the manufacturing sector in particular.

In the last decade or so, there has been a melding of the working conditions of the two sets of workers. On the one hand, white-collar workers are no longer afforded the same levels of job security, while on the other hand, blue-collar workers have been asked to be involved in the design and implementation of work processes. In many industries, hierarchies have been flattened, usually with a reduction in the number of middle managers [12]. In many cases, but certainly not all, blue-collar and white-collar workers alike have been asked to take on a more demanding set of tasks. The principal change is that now white-collar workers have seen their primary perk—security—eroded.

In addition to the foregoing changes within workplaces, firms are increasingly maintaining a smaller core of workers hired on a permanent basis. Instead, firms bring in workers to do specific projects, often hiring them as independent contractors rather than as employees [13, 14]. Often, the permanent employees of a firm work beside the workers brought on to complete specific projects. At other times, many of the functions formerly performed by permanent workers on-site have been farmed out to contractors; increasingly these contractors may be located overseas. In recent years, there has been a shift in the kinds of jobs performed by outside contractors [15]. Initially, day-to-day production activities were performed outside the firm, whether the manufacturing of goods or the provision of services (for example, call centers, routine accounting work, or data management). Subsequently, some of the higher level design functions such as computer programming were shifted outside the firm. More recently, there is evidence that even some managerial functions are being shifted as well.

Thus, firms are asking a greater proportion of workers to be involved in the design and improvement of production processes while retaining a smaller core of workers on a permanent basis and using non-permanent staff (frequently off-site) to do an increasing share of work. Because of these changes, a decreasing share of workers is hired long-term and provided health and pension benefits.

As a result of international competition, in many industries there has been significant downward pressure on wages, while for other workers with skills that remain in demand, real wages have been rising substantially. Indeed, there has been relative growth in the number of both low- and high-wage workers, with a "hollowing" out of the middle of the earnings distribution [3] (Table 3). But many of the employment practices described above would appear to apply to increasing fractions of low- and high-wage labor. For workers in occupations that are in demand, the growth of contingent forms of labor may work quite well, allowing them to move among jobs quickly and to intersperse periods of work and leisure. For a far greater number of workers, the combination of higher demands on the job and lower levels of job security and declining real wages make the current labor market extremely stressful [16].

Table 3. Share of Income Accruing to Various Income Levels
in Constant $s, U.S., 1970-1999

	< 10k	25-35k	> 75k
1970	12.9%	15.2%	10.1%
1980	11.6%	13.9%	13.1%
1990	11.0%	13.7%	17.6%
1999	9.2%	12.7%	22.6%
% Change	−29%	−17%	+124%

SUMMARIZING THE CHANGES

Job demands, including the raw work hours per year as well as the increased intellectual and psychological demands associated with more active involvement in the design, implementation, and monitoring of work processes, have increased over the last several decades. The increase in work time and the increasing involvement in how work is done as well as in the actual production has been accompanied by a loosening of ties between workers and firms, with fewer workers afforded job security and health and pension benefits. Thus, the core of workers with jobs with high demands on the one hand, but providing high levels of pay and benefits, and high levels of security has been reduced. No doubt the combination of high demands and lower security is increasing levels of stress.

REFERENCES

1. U.S. Bureau of the Census, *Statistical Abstract of the United States*, U.S. Bureau of the Census, Washington, DC, pp. 367, 392, 2002.
2. International Labour Office, *Key Indicators of the Labour Market 2001-2002*, International Labour Office, Geneva, Switzerland, 2001.
3. Mishel, L., J. Bernstein, and J. Schmitt, *The State of Working America 2000/2001*, Cornell University Press, Ithaca, NY, 2001.
4. Rones, P. L., R. E. Ilg, and J. M. Gardner, Trends in Hours of Work since the Mid-1970s, *Monthly Labor Review*, pp. 3-14, April 1997.
5. Hamermesh, D., *Workdays, Workhours, and Work Schedules: Evidence for the United States and Germany*, Upjohn Institute, Kalamazoo, MI, 1996.
6. U.S. Bureau of the Census, *Statistical Abstract of the United States*, U.S. Bureau of the Census, Washington, DC, p. 417, 1993.
7. U.S. Bureau of the Census, *Statistical Abstract of the United States*, U.S. Bureau of the Census, Washington, DC, p. 401, 1981.
8. U.S. Bureau of the Census, *Statistical Abstract of the United States*, U.S. Bureau of the Census, Washington, DC, pp. 380-382, 2001.
9. Braverman, H., Labor and Monopoly Capital: The Degradation of Work in the Twentieth Century, *Monthly Review Press*, New York, 1974.

10. Osterman, P., *Employment Futures: Reorganization, Dislocation, and Public Policy,* Oxford University Press, New York, 1988.
11. Osterman, P., *Securing Prosperity: The American Labor Market: How It Has Changed and What to Do About It,* Princeton University Press, Princeton, NJ, 1999.
12. Yelin, E. and L. Trupin, Disability and the Characteristics of Employment, *Monthly Labor Review,* 126, pp. 20-31, 2003.
13. Belous, R., *The Contingent Economy: The Growth of the Contemporary, Part-Time, and Subcontracted Workforce,* National Planning Association, Washington, DC, 1989.
14. Benner, C., *Work in the New Economy: Flexible Labor Markets in Silicon Valley,* Blackwell Publishers, New York, 2002.
15. Uchitelle, L., A Missing Statistic: U.S. Jobs That Went Overseas, in *New York Times,* New York, October 5, 2003.
16. Benner, C., B. Brownstein, and A. Dean, *Walking the Lifelong Tightrope: Negotiating Work in the New Economy,* Working Partnerships, San Jose, CA, 1999.

Editors Note
Trends in Working Conditions: Some Additional Data

Data from European Union surveys, collected every 5 years since 1990, provide excellent information on trends in the labor market and in job characteristics. They show increases in part-time and temporary ("contingent" or "precarious") work and increases in work intensity and job demands between 1990 and 2005. However, decreases in job control have occurred since 1995 [1], suggesting an increase in "job strain" (high demand-low control jobs). Little data is available to determine whether these trends vary by social class. However, data from annual Swedish surveys indicate that "hectic plus monotonous" work, a proxy measure for high demands and low control, has increased since 1992 to a greater extent for blue-collar workers than for white-collar workers [2].

The proportion of workers whose work is electronically monitored is increasing [3-5], with 45% of U.S. employers using such methods in 1999 [5]. Computer operators and directory assistance/customer service operators are monitored through their computers, while more mobile workers, such as package delivery and truck drivers and utility workers, are being monitored through GPS devices attached to their vehicles or cell phones [3-5]. Monitoring tends to lower job control, creating an emphasis on quantity and speed over quality, deadline pressure and threat of reprimand [3, 6], that is, increases in job stress.

In many developed countries between 1970 and 2000 there was a decline in the proportion of the workforce who are members of labor unions. Thus, workers have had less "voice" and resources to address the changing nature of work. The Scandinavian countries are exceptions to this trend, with high and increasing proportions of the workforce unionized during this period [7]. Between 2000-2007, there appears to be a reversal of the decline—an increase in national union federation membership worldwide [8], including a slight increase in the United States between 2006-2007 [9].

Total hours worked per year (by members of the paid labor force) have changed little in the past 25 years in the United States and Canada, in sharp contrast to Europe and Japan [10], where the benefits of increasing productivity have been translated into shorter work hours. Workers in the United States and Canada work 200-300 more hours per year than those in France, Germany, or Sweden [10]. One reason for this disparity is that the United States is the only developed country that provides no legal minimum paid vacation days or holidays, compared to a minimum of 20 paid vacation days per year in many European countries [11]. And, in the United States, as more women have entered the workforce, the total number of family hours worked per year (middle-income husbands and wives with children, age 25-54) increased 16.2% between 1979-2002 [12], very similar to the 20.8% increase in family work hours for Canada between 1976-2003 reported in Chapter 4 of this volume—testaments to the increased stress that working parents and families are facing.

REFERENCES

1. *Fifteen Years of Working Conditions in the EU: Charting the Trends.* European Foundation, Dublin, Ireland, 2006.
2. Joachim, V., Statistics Sweden, Stockholm.
3. Office of Technology Assessment, U.S. Congress, *The Electronic Supervisor: New Technology, New Tensions,* Washington, DC, 1987.
4. Gruber, J., *Labor and Employment Law,* Summer 2005.
5. *Electronic Monitoring: A Poor Solution to Management Problems,* The National Workrights Institute, 2007:
   http://www.workrights.org/issue_electronic/em_article.html
6. Smith, M. J., B. C. Amick, Electronic Monitoring at the Workplace, in *Job Control and Worker Health,* Sauter S. L., J. J. Hurrell Jr., and C. L. Cooper (eds.), Wiley, New York, pp. 275-289, 1989.
7. Kwon, H. Y. and J. Pontusson, *Globalization, Union Decline and the Politics of Social Spending Growth in OECD Countries, 1962-2000,* Yale University, New Haven, CT, November 2006.
8. Hall-Jones, P., *Painting Unionism by Numbers.* www.newunionism.net. October 22, 2007 (based on data from 174 national labor federations in 106 countries).
9. *New York Times,* January 26, 2008.
10. *Key Indicators of the Labour Market* (KILM), Geneva, Switzerland, International Labour Office, 2007.
11. Ray, R., J. Schmitt, *No-Vacation Nation.* Center for Economic and Policy Research, Washington, DC, 2007
12. *The State of Working America 2004-05,* Figure 1T, Economic Policy Institute, Washington, DC, 2005.

PART II

The Health and Economic Costs of "Unhealthy" Work

OVERVIEW

Given the widespread impact of workplace stressors on working people's health, the substantial health and economic costs—in absenteeism and decreased productivity—should not be a surprise. The chapters in this section address the consequences ·
and the costs of psychosocial factors in the workplace on the various stakeholders concerned with workplace health and safety—workers, employers, and society as a whole. That ill health is a consequence of the way work is organized has generated a sizeable scientific research literature since the 1970s. Researchers in the field of occupational health and social epidemiology have developed models of psychosocial stressors that measure the complex ways in which the organization of work impacts the health of working populations. The building of a scientific knowledge base around occupational stress highlights the ways in which the "social," particularly work organization, is related to the prevalence of both physical health problems in working populations (including cardiovascular disease and hypertension) and mental health problems (including psychological distress, anxiety, burnout, and depression). The key measures of work organization related to health include job characteristics such as job strain (the combination of high psychological demands and low decision latitude or control), social support, and effort-reward imbalance; as well as work hours, shift work, and the influence of downsizing, outsourcing, and flexible labor patterns.

In chapter 6, Paul Landsbergis, Peter Schnall, and Marnie Dobson present an overview of the research showing a strong relationship between psychosocial stressor exposures (e.g., job strain or high demand/low control work) and cardiovascular disease and hypertension. Following on, Marnie Dobson and Peter Schnall (chapter 7) offer a summary review of the literature on the effects of job strain, effort-reward imbalance, emotional labor, and long working hours, and fatigue on reported rates of psychological distress, anxiety, burnout, and depression.

The relationship between work and health is partly explained through the mechanism of social class, usually measured by income, education, or occupational status. Those lower on the social class ladder are more vulnerable to illness and die younger than people at higher rungs. As a key indicator of social class, work plays a complex and important role in the health of working populations, as discussed by Jeff Johnson (chapter 3) in part I. Adding to this complexity is how the combination of having a lower income and being a member of an ethnic minority group leads to greater disparities in health through differential exposures to noxious workplace stressors. On average, as social groups, ethnic minority workers are more likely to work in jobs lower on the occupational ladder often with noxious psychosocial working conditions, especially job strain.

Haiou Yang's chapter introduces race/ethnicity as another dimension of social inequality and health disparity. Ethnic minority groups in California, as in other parts of the United States, when compared to socially and economically dominant white Americans, have disproportionately higher percentages of their communities in the lowest socioeconomic strata. Responding to global trends in the economy, many minority workers are immigrants pulled from the "periphery" into core nations like the United States only to be exposed to noxious physical and psychosocial working environments. Yang presents data from the 2000 California Health Interview Survey (CHIS) showing an important relationship between existing health disparities in obesity, diabetes, and hypertension rates among African-American and Latino workers and the distribution of these workers in unskilled and clerical or semi-skilled occupational categories. The costs of poor working conditions and ill health are borne by some of the most socially vulnerable populations, many without health insurance. Yang concludes it is important for those in occupational health to combine work/industry and ethnicity perspectives in addressing these epidemics.

While the costs of stressful working conditions are eventually experienced in the bodies of chronically stressed workers, these costs are not just an individual problem with individual solutions. While all workers exposed to unhealthy working conditions should have access to workers' compensation and health insurance to deal with the consequences of work-related injury or illness, employers and business must have a vested interest in preventing work from damaging the health and well-being of their employees. In chapter 9, Maritza Jauregui and Peter Schnall highlight the very real and extraordinarily high costs to business of work-related stressors and occupational injuries and illness. Employee illness and injury cost employers money and time. Besides the direct costs of health care and workers' compensation, more hidden costs include absenteeism, presenteeism or diminished productivity, and employee turnover.

The changing nature of work affects work organization and exposes millions of workers to work-related stressors which have powerful "consequences" on the health and well-being of individuals, while at the same time representing enormous hidden costs to employers and society as a whole. While these chapters give a "snapshot" of the knowledge produced by scientific researchers in occupational health, the chapters that follow in part III of this book offer case examples of strategies and actions that challenge this social problem as one requiring social solutions.

CHAPTER 6

The Workplace and Cardiovascular Disease

Paul A. Landsbergis, Peter L. Schnall, and Marnie Dobson

Cardiovascular disease (CVD), including heart disease and stroke, is the major cause of disease and death in the industrialized world and is projected to become the most common cause of death worldwide by the year 2020. CVD and hypertension (high blood pressure) appear to be epidemics of recent historical origin, developing along with industrialization and urbanization, and now increasing in the context of economic globalization. Modern medicine focuses on individual risk factors for hypertension and CVD, often ignoring the important role that social factors, such as social class, work organization, and work-related psychosocial stressors, play in the development of hypertension and CVD. Social factors need to be fully integrated into explanations of disease development.

Increased CVD risk has been associated with job characteristics such as long work hours, shift work, "job strain" (a combination of high psychological work demands and low job decision latitude, or job control), high job efforts combined with low job rewards, injustice, job insecurity, and work that involves maintaining a high level of vigilance in order to avoid disaster, such as loss of human life. Sources of stress on the job (job stressors), besides acting directly on the human nervous system, may increase the risk of hypertension and CVD through a variety of mechanisms, including inhibiting healthy behaviors such as smoking cessation and exercise, or by producing psychological distress, such as anxiety and depression. Public health strategies are needed to address the pandemic of CVD, including worksite surveillance, development of the field of occupational cardiology, integration of health promotion with occupational health approaches, and job redesign.

THE SOCIAL-HISTORICAL CONTEXT

CVD, including heart disease and stroke, is the major cause of disease and death in the industrialized world, and is projected to become the most common cause of death worldwide by 2020 [1, 2]. In 2003, CVD caused 29.2% of all global deaths and 80% of all CVD deaths worldwide took place in developing, low- and middle-income countries [1].

Modern medical science has identified a number of individual risk factors for CVD including cigarette smoking, total and low density lipoprotein cholesterol, hypertension, fibrinogen, overweight, diabetes, and sedentary behavior (lack of exercise) [3]. However, essential hypertension, the leading cause of CVD worldwide [4], is considered by many to be an unexplained disease (hence the name "essential"). Essential hypertension, as well as smoking, sedentary behavior, and diabetes, have been linked to work stressors. Thus, much remains to be learned about the role of work in the development of CVD.

CVD and hypertension appear to be epidemics of recent historical origin [5, 6]. A major cross-cultural study found virtually no rise in blood pressure (BP) with age and no hypertension among hunter-gatherers, herders, or traditional family farmers [6]. In contrast, men and women in urban industrial societies have steady rises of blood pressure (BP) with age and hypertension is common [5, 6] (see Figure 1). This study also found large and significant correlations between BP and involvement in a money economy even after controlling for salt consumption and, for men, after controlling for body mass index (a measure of body weight) [6].

CVD, as a major cause of death, also developed at the same time as industrialization and urbanization [2, 7, 8], raising the question, what is it about industrialization and urbanization that leads to hypertension and CVD? Evidence suggests that one important factor is the transformation of working life during the last 100-200 years in developed countries, away from agricultural work and relatively autonomous craft-based work toward machine-based (including computer-based) labor, based on the principles of the assembly line [9, 10]. Key features of the assembly-line approach to job design, whether in factories or offices, are high workload demands combined with low employee control or autonomy (known as "job strain") [11], and, during periods of economic growth, long work hours.

The Social Patterning of CVD:
Social Class and Working Conditions

Extensive research has documented that CVD is more common not only among people facing work stressors [11, 12], but also among people of lower social class or socioeconomic position (SEP), for example, lower levels of education, income, or occupational status (see chapter 3). One possible explanation for the social class differences in CVD is greater exposure to unhealthy working conditions among lower SEP groups. For example, job control was "the biggest factor contributing to the socioeconomic gradient" in heart disease "risk across civil service employment grade" in a major study of British civil servants [14, 15] (see Figure 2). The higher CVD risk among men and women in lower SEP groups, for example, blue-collar workers, began to appear in the 1950s [16-18] and has risen progressively since then [19]. Among U.S. men aged 25-64, in 1969-70, low SEP men had a 30% greater risk of dying of CVD than high SEP men *of the same age*. However, it had

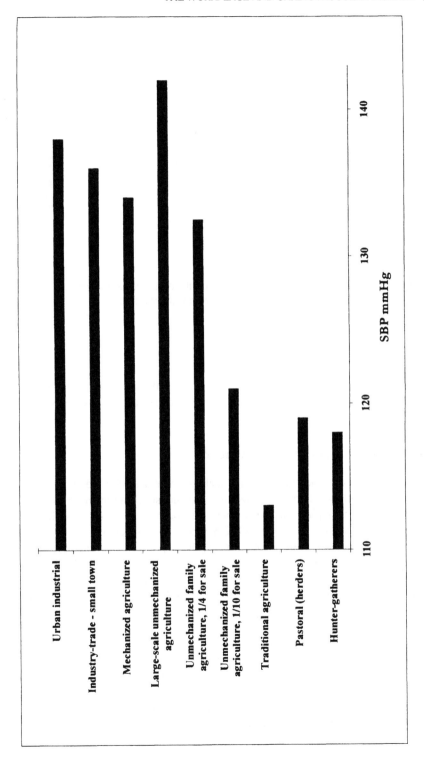

Figure 1. Cross-cultural variation in average systolic blood pressure (mm Hg), men aged 50-60.
Source: Data reported in [6].

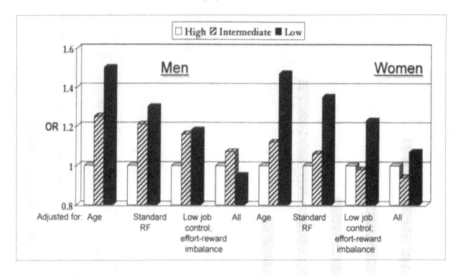

Figure 2. Association between occupational status and new coronary
heart disease (British Civil Servants). **Source**: [15].

increased to an 80% greater risk by 1997-98 [19]. Differences between higher
and lower SEP groups in new cases of CVD, whether fatal or not, are also increasing
[20, 21].

Current Economic and Workplace Trends

The development of hypertension as a global epidemic has occurred at the same
time as economic globalization, urbanization, and industrialization in developing
countries [2]. In developing countries, there has been a rapid increase in the
prevalence of (percentage of the population who have) hypertension, while in
developed countries, such as the United States, the prevalence of hypertension is
no longer decreasing, but actually increasing [22].

Current economic and workplace trends, driven by competition in the global
economy, may be having dramatic effects on workers' health (for example, CVD
rates are rising rapidly in developing countries, and in developed countries the
decline in CVD death rates is slowing and the gap between high- and low-income
workers is increasing). These trends in working conditions include offshoring,
outsourcing, downsizing, deregulation of health and safety, part-time and temporary
work, "teleworking," new management systems such as "lean production" which
contribute to intensification of work [23], and in the United States stagnant or falling
real income for a majority of the work force [24]. At the same time, substantial
changes in job characteristics have been occurring. Working to "tight deadlines" or
"at very high speed" (workload demands) increased in Europe between 1990-2005

[25], and in the United States, increases between 1977-1997 were reported for "never enough time to get everything done on my job" (from 40% to 60%) [26]. However, job control or autonomy, which can help workers better deal with job demands, showed a small decline between 1995 and 2005 in European surveys [25] suggesting an increase in overall job stressors. U.S. workers' average weekly work hours are now the longest in the developed world [27], working in jobs that are more stressful than in the past. One reason for this is that the United States is the only advanced economy in the world that does not guarantee its workers paid vacation. European countries establish legal rights to at least 20 days of paid vacation per year, and some guarantee 30 or more days. In the absence of government standards, almost one in four Americans have no paid vacation and no paid holidays [28].

These trends may affect the working conditions of lower SEP workers more severely. For example, the prevalence of "hectic plus monotonous work" in Sweden increased from 8.6% to 11% from 1992-2000 for the whole work force. However, for blue-collar workers, the increase in prevalence was much greater, from 12.6% to 20% [29].

CVD Mortality and Incidence Trends

Despite large declines in CVD death rates over the last 40 years in the United States , there have been small or no declines, at least in the last 20 years, in new cases of CVD whether fatal or not [31-34]. While smoking prevalence and cholesterol levels have dropped, there have been increases in rates of diabetes [35], overweight [36], and hypertension [37], and increasing recognition that psychosocial stressors may be contributing to these trends [38].

WORK ORGANIZATION AND CVD

Most people spend the majority of their waking hours at work and commuting to and from work. The *way* work is organized—the number of hours spent working, what hours of the day we work, the pace and intensity of work, how we feel about our jobs (e.g., whether we have or do not have employment security, whether our jobs provide us opportunities for skills development and growth), our social relationships at work—can affect our health.

Work Hours and Schedules

People working evening, night, or rotating shifts have a slightly higher risk of heart disease [39]. Research on long work hours (overtime work) point to a wide variety of health effects, including increases in work accidents and injuries, musculoskeletal disorders, fatigue, psychological symptoms, unhealthy behaviors (such as smoking or alcohol use), cardiovascular risk factors (such as high blood pressure), and CVD [40-43]. Prolonged exposure to work may act to increase fatigue thereby increasing heart disease risk while rest breaks, days off, and vacations all provide relief and lower risk. The stress of returning to work after a weekend off increases risk as increased heart disease deaths have been reported for Mondays compared to other days of the week [44].

Beginning in 1958, research has suggested that long working hours may increase risk of heart disease [45-50]. Much research has been conducted in Asia, beginning with the interest in Japan about *Karoshi*—"sudden death from overwork" [51]. The impact of overtime on health may be greater for workers in stressful jobs, such as professional drivers [52], shift workers [43], and older workers [41, 53].

Work-Related Psychosocial Stressors

Researchers have thought about and measured work stressors in various ways over the last 30 years [54-57]. The most highly studied type of work stressor is "job strain," that is, work which combines high psychological job demands with low job decision latitude or job control [11]. A more recently developed and important way of describing job stress is "effort-reward imbalance," a "mismatch between high workload (high demand) and low control over long-term rewards" [58, p. 1128]. Low reward includes low "esteem reward" (respect and support), low income, and low "status control" (poor promotion prospects, employment insecurity, and status inconsistency). Another stressor, "organizational injustice," has been defined in three ways: a) distributive injustice—is one unfairly rewarded at work?; b) procedural injustice—do decision-making procedures at work fail to provide for input from affected parties, useful feedback, and the possibility of appeal, and are they not applied fairly, consistently, and without bias?; c) relational injustice— do supervisors fail to treat workers with fairness, politeness, and consideration [59]? In addition, research studies have examined "threat-avoidant" vigilant work, i.e., work that involves continuously maintaining a high level of vigilance in order to avoid disaster, such as loss of human life [56]. This is a feature of a number of occupations at high risk for CVD, e.g., truck drivers, air traffic controllers, and sea pilots. More recently, researchers have been investigating the health effects of employment insecurity and "downsizing" [60].

JOB STRESSORS AND CVD

Job Strain, Return to Work, and CVD

A majority of studies of job strain and CVD, published between 1981 and 2002, showed that workers facing job strain had higher rates of CVD [57].

In addition to studies demonstrating that exposure to job strain plays a role in the original development of coronary artery disease, there have been three studies examining the impact of continued exposure to job strain after someone returns to work following a first heart attack. A study by Theorell and colleagues among 79 Swedish men who had survived a first heart attack before the age of 45 found that return to work at a high-strain job was a significant independent predictor of death due to coronary artery disease after five years of follow-up [61]. A study by Orth-Gomer and colleagues in 2000 involving 279 Swedish women found that marital stress predicted a second heart attack but that work stress did not [62].

However, a study published in 2007 of Canadian men and women, which measured job strain both after return to work and two years later, found that people exposed to job strain at both interviews (chronic job strain) were more than twice as likely to have a second heart attack compared with people who faced no job strain or job strain during only one of the measurement periods [63]. Dr. Orth-Gomer commented in an accompanying editorial that "Patients and physicians may benefit from widening the medical framework to include job strain evaluation" [64]. Currently, cardiologists assess post-heart attack patients only for physical workload capacity in determining the feasibility of returning to work. These findings clearly support the proposal that the patient's psychosocial work environment should be included in the return-to-work assessment and lend further credibility to the role of job strain in promoting coronary artery disease.

Effort-Reward Imbalance and CVD

A number of studies among men [58, 65-70], have found that workers facing effort-reward imbalance had higher rates of CVD. For example, a study of Finnish industrial workers found that those in the top third of effort-reward imbalance had 2.4 times the risk of death due to heart disease compared to the bottom third, over a follow-up period of 25 years, taking into account other risk factors for CVD [70].

Organizational Injustice and CVD

British civil servants reporting high relational injustice (low supervisor support) were 41% more likely to develop heart disease over a follow-up period of 8.7 years [71]. Similarly, Finnish factory workers reporting low supervisor support were 64% more likely to develop heart disease over 25 years [72]. These increased risks were seen after adjusting for age, gender, standard risk factors such as cholesterol, high blood pressure, and smoking, and job strain and effort-reward imbalance.

Threat-Avoidant Vigilant Work and CVD

Only a few studies have specifically examined threat-avoidant vigilant work and CVD [47, 73-75]. The strongest evidence for this risk factor comes from studies of single occupations, where professional drivers, particularly urban bus and taxi drivers, are the occupations with the most consistent increased risk of heart disease [76, 66] and hypertension [78].

Downsizing and CVD

Workforce reductions ("downsizing") were associated with a doubling of the risk of CVD mortality [60] among Finnish public employees who kept their jobs. After downsizing, those employees faced higher levels of physical work demands and job insecurity and lower levels of skill use and participation on the job [79].

Interaction between Job Stressors and Low Socioeconomic Position

Among men, the impact of job strain on CVD is more consistent and stronger among blue-collar workers (e.g., [80-82]), than among men in jobs with higher SEP. A similar interaction with SEP was seen for effort-reward imbalance among British civil servants [83]. The effect of job strain on blood pressure was also higher for lower SEP men working in New York City [84], and lower SEP men and women in Framingham, Massachusetts [85].

Most studies find connections between job stressors and CVD after taking into account adult SEP. Lower SEP in childhood also predicts future CVD, and this is not always accounted for in research studies. However, several studies have shown that the effects of work stress exist even after taking into account childhood SEP [86, 87].

What Proportion of CVD is Due to Job Stressors?

Researchers can calculate the "population attributable risk" (PAR) to determine the percentage of a particular disease that would be prevented if a particular exposure was eliminated. Some conservative estimates have been 7-16% of CVD due to job strain for men in Sweden [11], and 6% for men and 14% for women for monotonous high-paced work (a conservative proxy measure for job strain) in Denmark [55]. However, few studies have looked at the combined or synergistic effect of workplace stressors, which would increase estimates of the proportion of CVD due to work. One Swedish study [69] did find that the combined effects of job strain and effort-reward imbalance on CVD were much stronger than the separate effects of each job stressor.

WORK ORGANIZATION AND HYPERTENSION

Effect of Blood Pressure Measurement Techniques

Is the increased risk of CVD due to job strain a result of the fact that job strain increases blood pressure (BP)? Job strain is not strongly related to BP, when BP is measured in a clinic setting [54, 56, 88]. However, strong evidence of a job strain-BP relationship is found in studies where BP is measured by an ambulatory (portable) monitor [56]. This difference occurs because ambulatory monitors measure BP (as opposed to measurements in a clinic) during a person's normal daily activities and while exposed to the daily stressors that are the real causes of persistent increases in BP. On the other hand, relaxation can occur when people are away from work resulting in lower BP in the clinic setting. Ambulatory (ABP) monitoring involves wearing an automatic monitor on your arm throughout the work day, which records BP at preset intervals, such as every 30 minutes [89]. As ABP is a better measure than clinic BP of your true daily BP average, it is a better predictor of damage to the heart, such as increases in the size of the heart's left ventricle [90] and future CVD [91].

Long Work Hours and Blood Pressure

While studies are not always consistent, several Japanese studies have found a positive association between long work hours and hypertension. One Japanese study showed that ABP measurements of workers (taken with a portable monitor during normal daily activities) with 88 hours of overtime per month were significantly higher than those of persons who worked only 25 hours of overtime per month. In addition, the diastolic ambulatory blood pressure of workers with 88 hours of overtime in a busy season was significantly higher than that of the same group of workers during a less busy comparison season [92].

In another Japanese study, salesmen aged 50-60 who spent 61 or more hours per week commuting and working had higher systolic blood pressure than those who spent 57 hours or less [53]. A recent analysis of data from the California Health Information Survey (CHIS) demonstrated that as work hours per week increased so did the percentage of working people in California reporting hypertension [93] (see Figure 3).

Job Strain and Blood Pressure

In a review conducted in 2000, a majority of the 11 cross-sectional studies of job strain (or its components) and ABP among men found a relationship between job strain and higher work ABP [56]. In the five studies where ABP measurements were also made outside of work, men with job strain also had higher non-work systolic ABP, showing that the impact of job strain on ABP occurred across the whole day and night. Of the six cross-sectional studies of job strain and ABP among women published by 2000, four showed that women with job strain had higher work systolic

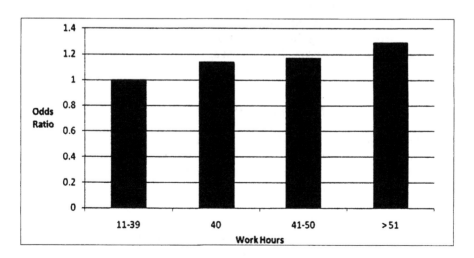

Figure 3. Risk of self-reported hypertension by hours worked per week California Health Interview Survey 2001 (CHIS).
Source: Data reported in [93].

ABP [94]. Workers with job strain typically have about 4-8 mm Hg higher work systolic ABP than those without job strain.

The only longitudinal (long-term) study of job strain and ABP, the New York City Work Site Blood Pressure Study (WSBPS), began in 1985. At the first round of data collection (Time 1), men with job strain showed increases in the size of their heart's left ventricle, a sign of damage to the heart [95], and had higher levels of work, home, and sleep ABP, after taking into account other risk factors, such as age, race, and weight, than men without job strain [96, 97]. These findings were recently replicated by the Belgian Job Stress Project [98].

Since the study participants returned 3 years later (Time 2), had their BP measured, and completed questionnaires about their jobs, it was possible to create a measure of chronic or longer-term exposure to job strain. Men facing job strain at both Time 1 and Time 2 (longer-term exposure) had an 11-12 mm Hg higher systolic and 6-9 mm Hg higher diastolic work ABP than men not facing job strain at either time. This difference is substantial, more than twice the difference between African Americans and whites in this sample and more than the effect on BP in this study sample of aging 25 years or gaining 50 pounds in weight [99]. To give an idea of the potential benefit of leaving a situation of job strain, those men reporting job strain at Time 1 but no job strain at Time 2 showed a drop in blood pressure 5.3 mm Hg systolic ABP at work and 4.7 mm Hg systolic ABP at home [99].

Other Job Stressors and Blood Pressure

Several studies have shown higher BP in men facing high efforts/low rewards at work [100-102], and one study also showed this relationship in women [102]. In a study of San Francisco transit operators, drivers with higher job barriers and time pressure (rated by experts)were at increased risk of having hypertension (defined as ≥160/95 mm Hg clinic blood pressure or currently taking medication for high blood pressure) after taking into account age, gender, and seniority [78].

MASKED HYPERTENSION

ABP monitoring allows us to identify "masked hypertension," that is, individuals with high ABP while working or over 24 hours, but normal BP in a clinic or doctor's office. Masked hypertension has not often been studied, but it has major clinical and public health significance. People with masked hypertension have heart damage, such as increases in the size of the heart's left ventricle [103, 104], atherosclerosis, as measured by the level of plaque in the carotid artery, the artery that carries blood to your brain [103, 105], or risk of heart disease and stroke [91, 106-108] similar to people who have been diagnosed with hypertension and much higher than people with normal blood pressure. In studies of people from the general population, 10-30% of people with normal clinic blood pressure had high ambulatory blood pressure, that is, masked hypertension [9].

Of all the published studies of masked hypertension, only one has looked at work-related risk factors. Among women workers in Ohio, masked hypertension (based on systolic BP) was more common in blue-collar and clerical workers than among higher status white-collar workers; however, such a pattern was not seen for diastolic BP [109].

In a preliminary analysis of data from men in the New York City Work Site BP Study, job strain was 54% more common among men with masked hypertension (at entry into the study) and more than five times more common (at the 3-year follow-up measurement period), taking into account other risk factors for high blood pressure such as age, race, weight, education, smoking, and alcohol use. In another preliminary analysis of data from a study of (primarily female) New York City health care workers, increased risk of masked hypertension was seen for workers facing job strain, effort-reward imbalance, shift work, and having only a high school education. These results are consistent with earlier research that job strain causes blood pressure to rise at work and throughout the day.

People with masked hypertension and no previous diagnosis of hypertension require counseling, possibly treatment, and measurement of their work stressors, but rarely receive them because their blood pressure in the doctor's office appears normal.

OTHER MECHANISMS BY WHICH WORK ORGANIZATION CAN LEAD TO CVD

Impact of Work Stressors on Traditional Risk Factors

Job Strain

Studies have shown that workers facing job strain (or its components—high job demands and low job control) smoke more (if they are smokers) or have greater difficulty quitting smoking [110-113]. In some studies, workers with job strain are heavier and exercise less [110, 114, 115]. Workers with low job control have higher levels of plasma fibrinogen, a chemical in the blood that contributes to atherosclerosis, that is, hardening of the arteries [116, 117]. And workers with low job control or job strain, in some studies, show greater atherosclerosis in the arteries in the heart or the arteries going to the brain [118-121]. High blood pressure also contributes to atherosclerosis [122].

In the United States, more than 120,000 people die each year suddenly and without warning from a sudden cardiac catastrophe. One possible reason is reduced heart rate variability, which is an important predictor of heart disease, as well as death from arrhythmias (heart rate rhythm disturbances) following a heart attack. A healthy heart will show lots of variation in heart rate over the course of a day, as the body responds to various demands and challenges. One study has shown a connection between job strain and reduced heart rate variability [123]. Other workplace stressors related to reduced heart rate variability are heavy mental workload, long work hours, or shift work [124].

Effort-Reward Imbalance

Finnish factory workers with effort-reward imbalance were heavier than those without effort-reward imbalance in one study [70]. Another study showed that Finnish public employees with effort-reward imbalance were more likely to have several risk factors for heart disease: overweight, smoking, heavy alcohol use, and lack of exercise [125]. Male British civil servants with effort-reward imbalance had an increased risk of developing Type 2 diabetes, although this pattern was not seen among female civil servants [126]. Finally, several studies have shown that workers with effort-reward imbalance had higher levels of cholesterol [102, 127, 128].

Long Work Hours

Overtime work was associated with unhealthy weight gain in two studies, increased alcohol use in two of three studies, and increased smoking in one of two studies, but it was not related to exercise or drug abuse [43]. One [129] of two [129, 130] Japanese studies found a relationship between work hours and adult onset (Type 2) diabetes.

WORK AND SOCIAL PSYCHOLOGICAL MECHANISMS

Modern medical science has tended to view behavioral/psychological factors in isolation, ignoring their relationship to objective stressors in the work environment and elsewhere. Emotions, behavior, and personality can be seen as the results of social conditions and may be some of the ways that social stressors increase the risk of heart disease and stroke. Many emotions "are responses to power and status differentials embedded within social situations" [131, p. 55].

Hypertension

Some studies have shown that high blood pressure is related to internalized aggression [132] and to anxiety [133, 134], although other studies have not found these connections [133-135]. Rarely have researchers looked at the possible interaction between work stressors and personality in the development of hypertension. In one study, hypertension was more common in male hourly workers with suppressed anger, but *only among those reporting job stress* [136]. Other studies have shown that study participants with hypertension [137], as well as those with normal BP but with a family history of hypertension [138], express fewer emotions and have a non-complaining attitude [11]. Such personality characteristics may result in part from a stressful work environment that "enforces a no-complaining attitude and prevents development of active emotional coping" [138].

Psychological Distress, Which May Increase the Risk of Heart Disease

Studies have found that workers facing job stressors have higher levels of anxiety [139-141], burnout [142-144], depression [139, 145-147], and hostility [148, 149]. Depression has been shown to be a risk factor for heart disease [150]. Therefore, this may be one way in which job stressors increase risk of heart disease (see chapter 7).

CONCLUSION

The important role that social mechanisms, such as work stressors and socio-economic position, play in the development of hypertension and CVD has not yet been integrated into traditional medical theories. Traditional medicine tends to focus on individual risk factors, while ignoring their social basis. A number of underutilized public health strategies that reflect our current broader understanding of the social causes of CVD are needed to adequately address the growing pandemic of CVD. The work-related causes of CVD need to be addressed in the United States and in the rest of the developed world, where the decline in CVD death rates is slowing and CVD risk factors such as hypertension, diabetes, and obesity are increasing; and in industrializing countries, such as China and India, where CVD death rates and risk factors are increasing rapidly and resources for public health and disease prevention are more limited [2, 22]. Efforts such as worksite surveillance, development of the field of occupational cardiology, integration of health promotion with occupational health approaches, and the use of job redesign are all sorely needed (see chapter 11). While some of these groundbreaking changes are taking place in Western Europe and Japan, they are lagging in the United States. As the world's largest economy continues to grow and spread its influence worldwide, the United States must also lead the way in advocating to its global partners the need for stronger protections for workplace health and safety.

ACKNOWLEDGMENTS

Some of the research findings in this chapter were supported in part by grants HL18232, HL30605, HL55165, and HL47540 from the National Heart, Lung and Blood Institute, Bethesda, MD, and grant OH07577 from the National Institute for Occupational Safety and Health, Cincinnati, OH.

REFERENCES

1. World Health Organization, *The Atlas of Heart Disease and Stroke,* World Health Organization, Geneva, Switzerland, 2004.
2. Graziano, J., Global Burden of Cardiovascular Disease, in *Heart Disease,* Zipes, D., P. Libby, R. Bonow, and E. Braunwald (eds.), Elsevier, London, UK, pp. 1-19, 2004.
3. Kannel, W. B., *The Framingham Experience, in Coronary Heart Disease Epidemiology,* Marmot, M. and P. Elliott (eds.), Oxford University Press, Oxford, NY, pp. 67-82, 1992.

4. Lawes, C., S. Vander Hoorn, M. Law, P. Elliott, S. MacMahon, and A. Rodgers, Blood Pressure and the Burden of Coronary Heart Disease, in *Coronary Heart Disease Epidemiology*, Marmot, M. and P. Elliott (eds.), Oxford University Press, Oxford, NY, pp. 152-173, 2005.

5. Schnall, P. L. and R. Kern, Hypertension in American Society: An Introduction to Historical Materialist Epidemiology, in *The Sociology of Health and Illness: Critical Perspectives*, Conrad, P. and R. Kern (eds.), St. Martin's Press, New York, pp. 97-122, 1981.

6. Waldron, I., M. Nowatarski, M. Freimer, J. P. Henry, N. Post, and C. Witten, Cross-Cultural Variation in Blood Pressure: A Qualitative Analysis of the Relationship of Blood Pressure to Cultural Characteristics, Salt Consumption and Body Weight, *Social Science and Medicine*, 16, pp. 419-430, 1982.

7. Mackinnin, A., The Origin of the Modern Epidemic of Coronary Artery Disease in England, *Journal of the Royal College of General Practitioners*, 37, pp. 174-176, 1987.

8. Faergeman, O., The Societal Context of Coronary Artery Disease, *European Heart Journal*, 7:Supplement A, pp. A5-A11, 2005.

9. Landsbergis, P., P. Schnall, K. Belkic, J. Schwartz, D. Baker, and T. Pickering, Working Conditions and Masked (Hidden) Hypertension: Insights into the Global Epidemic of Hypertension, *Scandinavian Journal of Work Environment and Health*, Suppl (6), pp. 41-51, 2008.

10. Schnall, P., K. Belkic, P. A. Landsbergis, and D. Baker, Why the Workplace and Cardiovascular Disease?, *Occupational Medicine: State-of-the-Art Reviews*, 15:1, pp. 1-5, 2000c.

11. Karasek, R. and T. Theorell, *Healthy Work: Stress, Productivity, and the Reconstruction of Working Life*, Basic Books, New York, 1990.

12. Schnall, P., K. Belkic, P. A. Landsbergis, and D. E. Baker, The Workplace and Cardio-vascular Disease, in *Occupational Medicine: State-of-the-Art Reviews*, Hanley and Belfus, Philadelphia, PA, 2000a.

13. Kaplan, G. A. and J. E. Keil, Socioeconomic Factors and Cardiovascular Disease: A Review of the Literature, *Circulation*, 88:4 Pt 1, pp. 1973-1998, 1993.

14. Kawachi, I. and M. Marmot, What Can We Learn from Studies of Occupational Class and Cardiovascular Disease?, *American Journal of Epidemiology*, 148, pp. 160-163, 1998.

15. Marmot, M. G., H. Bosma, H. Hemingway, E. Brunner, and S. Stansfeld, Contribution of Job Control and Other Risk Factors to Social Variations in Coronary Heart Disease Incidence, *Lancet*, 350, pp. 235-239, 1997.

16. Gonzalez, M. A., F. R. Artalejo, and J. R. Calero, Relationship between Socioeconomic Status and Ischaemic Heart Disease in Cohort and Case-Control Studies: 1960-1993, *International Journal of Epidemiology*, 27:3, pp. 350-358, 1998.

17. Marmot, M., A. M. Adelstein, N. Robinson, et al., Changing Social Class Distribution of Heart Disease, *British Medical Journal*, 2, pp. 1109-1112, 1978.

18. Wing, S., P. Dargent-Molina, M. Casper, W. Riggan, C. G. Hayes, and H. A. Tyroler, Changing Association between Community Structure and Ischaemic Heart Disease Mortality in the United States, *Lancet*, 2:8567, pp. 1067-1070, 1987.

19. Singh, G. K. and M. Siahpush, Increasing Inequalities in All-Cause and Cardiovascular Mortality among US Adults Aged 25-64 Years by Area Socioeconomic Status, 1969-1998, *International Journal of Epidemiology*, 31, pp. 600-613, 2002.

20. Hallqvist, J., M. Lundberg, F. Diderichsen, and A. Ahlbom, Socioeconomic Differences in Risk of Myocardial Infarction 1971-1994 in Sweden: Time Trends, Relative Risks and Population Attributable Risks, *International Journal of Epidemiology*, 27, pp. 410-415, 1998.
21. Tuchsen, F. and L. A. Endahl, Increasing Inequality in Ischaemic Heart Disease Morbidity among Employed Men in Denmark 1981-1993: The Need for a New Preventive Policy, *International Journal of Epidemiology*, 28, pp. 640-644, 1999.
22. Hajjar, I., J. Kotchen, and T. Kotchen, Hypertension: Trends in Prevalence, Incidence, and Control, *Annual Review of Public Health*, 27, pp. 465-490, 2006.
23. Landsbergis, P. A., J. Cahill, and P. Schnall, The Impact of Lean Production and Related New Systems of Work Organization on Worker Health, *Journal of Occupational Health Psychology*, 4:2, pp. 108-130, 1999.
24. Mishel, L., J. Bernstein, and H. Boushey, *The State of Working America 2002/2003*, Cornell University Press, New York, 2003.
25. European Foundation, *Fifteen Years of Working Conditions in the EU: Charting the Trends*, European Foundation for the Improvement of Living and Working Conditions, Dublin, Ireland, 2006.
26. Bond, J. T., E. Galinsky, and J. E. Swanberg, *The 1997 National Study of the Changing Workforce*, Families and Work Institute, New York, 1998.
27. International Labour Office, *Key Indicators of the Labour Market 2001-2002*, International Labour Office, Geneva, Switzerland, 2001.
28. Ray, R. and J. Schmitt, *No-Vacation Nation*, Center for Economic and Policy Research, Washington, DC, 2007.
29. Vogel, J., *Swedish Level of Living Survey Data*, Landsbergis, P. (ed.), Statistics Sweden, Stockholm, 2002.
30. Liao, Y. and R. S. Cooper, Continued Adverse Trends in Coronary Heart Disease Mortality among Blacks, 1980-91, *Public Health Reports*, 110, pp. 572-579, 1995.
31. Rosamond, W. D., L. E. Chanbless, A. R. Folsom, et al., Trends in the Incidence of Myocardial Infarction and in Mortality Due to Coronary Heart Disease, 1987 to 1994 [Abstract], *The New England Journal of Medicine*, 339, pp. 861-867, 1998.
32. Goldberg, R. J., J. Yarzebski, D. Lessard, and J. M. Gore, A Two-Decades (1975 to 1995) Long Experience in the Incidence, In-Hospital and Long-Term Case-Fatality Rates of Acute Myocardial Infarction: A Community-Wide Perspective, *Journal of the American College of Cardiology*, 33:6, pp. 1533-1539, 1999.
33. McGovern, P. G., J. Jacobs, D. R., E. Shahar, et al., Trends in Acute Coronary Heart Disease Mortality, Morbidity, and Medical Care from 1985 through 1997: The Minnesota Heart Survey, *Circulation*, 104, pp. 19-24, 2001.
34. Rosamond, W. D., A. R. Folsom, L. E. Chambless, and C.-H. Wang, Coronary Heart Disease Trends in Four United States Communities. The Atherosclerosis Risk in Communities (Aric) Study 1987-1996, *International Journal of Epidemiology*, 30, pp. S17-S22, 2001.
35. Harris, M. I., K. M. Flegal, C. C. Cowie, et al., Prevalence of Diabetes, Impaired Fasting Glucose, and Impaired Glucose Tolerance in US Adults—The Third National Health and Nutrition Examination Survey, 1988-1994, *Diabetes Care*, 21:N4, pp. 518-524, April 1998.
36. Kuczmarski, R. J., K. M. Flegal, S. M. Campbell, and C. L. Johnson, Increasing Prevalence of Overweight among US Adults, *Journal of the American Medical Association*, 272, pp. 205-211, 1994.

104 / UNHEALTHY WORK

37. Hajjar, I. and T. Kotchen, Trends in Prevalence, Awareness, Treatment, and Control of Hypertension in the United States, 1988-2000, *Journal of the American Medical Association,* 290:2, pp. 199-206, 2003.
38. Gornel, D. L., Rates of Death from Coronary Heart Disease: Letter to the Editor, *New England Journal of Medicine,* 340:9, pp. 730-732, 1999.
39. Steenland, K., Shift Work, Long Hours, and CVD: A Review, *Occupational Medicine: State-of-the-Art Reviews,* 15:1, pp. 7-17, 2000.
40. Spurgeon, A., J. M. Harrington, and C. L. Cooper, Health and Safety Problems Associated with Long Working Hours: A Review of the Current Position, *Occupational and Environmental Medicine,* 54:6, pp. 367-375, 1997.
41. Sparks, K., C. Cooper, Y. Fried, and A. Shirom, The Effects of Hours of Work on Health: A Meta-Analytic Review, *Journal of Occupational and Organizational Psychology,* 70, pp. 391-408, 1997.
42. van der Hulst, M., Long Workhours and Health, *Scandinavian Journal of Work Environment and Health,* 29:3, pp. 171-188, 2003.
43. Caruso, C., E. Hitchcock, R. Dick, J. Russo, and J. Schmit, *Overtime and Extended Work Shifts: Recent Findings on Illnesses, Injuries, and Health Behaviors,* NIOSH, Cincinnati, OH, pp. 1-49, 2004.
44. Barnett, A. and A. Dobson, Excess in Cardiovascular Events on Mondays: A Meta-Analysis and Prospective Study, *Journal of Epidemiology and Community Health,* 59:2, pp. 109-114, 2005.
45. Russek, H. I. and B. L. Zohman, Relative Significance of Heredity, Diet, and Occupational Stress in Coronary Heart Disease of Young Adults, *American Journal of Medical Science,* 235, pp. 266-275, 1958.
46. Theorell, T. and R. H. Rahe, Behavior and Life Satisfactions of Swedish Subjects with Myocardial Infarction, *Journal of Chronic Disease,* 25, pp. 139-147, 1972.
47. Alfredsson, L., C. Spetz, and T. Theorell, Type of Occupation and Near-Future Hospitalization for Myocardial Infarction and Some Other Diagnoses, *International Journal of Epidemiology,* 14, pp. 378-388, 1985.
48. Falger, P. R. J. and E. G. W. Schouten, Exhaustion, Psychologic Stress in the Work Environment and Acute Myocardial Infarction in Adult Men, *Journal of Psychosomatic Research,* 36, pp. 777-786, 1992.
49. Liu, Y. and H. Tanaka, Overtime Work, Insufficient Sleep, and Risk of Nonfatal Acute Myocardial Infarction in Japanese Men (the Fukuoka Heart Study Group), *Occupational and Environmental Medicine,* 59, pp. 447-451, 2002.
50. Sokejima, S. and S. Kagamimori, Working Hours as a Risk Factor for Acute Myocardial Infarction in Japan: Case-Control Study, *British Medical Journal,* 317, pp. 775-780, 1998.
51. Nishiyama, K. and J. V. Johnson, Karoshi—Death from Overwork: Occupational Health Consequences of Japanese Production Management, *International Journal of Health Services,* 27:4, pp. 625-641, 1997.
52. Raggatt, P., Work Stress among Long-Distance Coach Drivers: A Survey and Correlational Study, *Journal of Organizational Behavior,* 12, pp. 565-579, 1991.
53. Iwasaki, K., T. Sasaki, T. Oka, and N. Hisanaga, Effect of Working Hours on Biological Functions Related to Cardiovascular System among Salesmen in a Machinery Manufacturing Company, *Industrial Health,* 36, pp. 361-367, 1998.
54. Schnall, P. L., P. A. Landsbergis, and D. Baker, Job Strain and Cardiovascular Disease, *Annual Review of Public Health,* 15, pp. 381-411, 1994.

55. Kristensen, T. S., M. Kronitzer, and L. Alfedsson, *Social Factors, Work, Stress and Cardiovascular Disease Prevention*, The European Heart Network, Brussels, Belgium, 1998.

56. Belkic, K., P. A. Landsbergis, P. Schnall, et al., Psychosocial Factors: Review of the Empirical Data among Men, in *The Workplace and Cardiovascular Disease Occupational Medicine: State of the Art Reviews*, Schnall, P., K. Belkic, P. A. Landsbergis, and D. Baker (eds.), Hanley and Belfus, Philadelphia, PA, pp. 24-46, 2000.

57. Belkic, K., P. Landsbergis, P. Schnall, and D. Baker, Is Job Strain a Major Source of Cardiovascular Disease Risk?, *Scandinavian Journal of Work Environment and Health*, 30:2, pp. 85-128, 2004.

58. Siegrist, J., R. Peter, A. Junge, P. Cremer, and D. Seidel, Low Status Control, High Effort at Work and Ischemic Heart Disease: Prospective Evidence from Blue Collar Men, *Social Science and Medicine*, 31, pp. 1127-1134, 1990.

59. Kivimaki, M., M. Virtanen, M. Elovainio, A. Kouvonen, A. Vaananen, and J. Vahtera, Work Stress in the Etiology of Coronary Heart Disease—A Meta-Analysis, *Scandinavian Journal of Work Environment and Health*, 32:6(Special Issue), pp. 431-442, 2006.

60. Vahtera, J., M. Kivimaki, J. Pentti, et al., Organisational Downsizing, Sickness Absence, and Mortality: 10-Town Prospective Cohort Study, *British Medical Journal*, 328:7439, p. 555, 2004.

61. Theorell, T., A. Perski, K. Orth-Gomer, A. Hamsten, and U. de Faire, The Effects of the Strain of Returning to Work on the Risk of Cardiac Death After a First Myocardial Infarction Before Age 45, *International Journal of Cardiology*, 30, pp. 61-67, 1991.

62. Orth-Gomer, K., S. P. Wamala, M. Horsten, K. Schenck-Gustafsson, N. Schneiderman, and M. A. Mittleman, Marital Stress Worsens Prognosis in Women with Coronary Heart Disease, *Journal of the American Medical Association*, 284:23, pp. 3008-3014, 2000.

63. Aboa-Éboulé, C., C. Brisson, E. Maunsell, et al., Job Strain and Risk of Acute Recurrent Coronary Heart Disease Events, *Journal of the American Medical Association*, 298, pp. 1652-1660, 2007.

64. Orth-Gomer, K., Job Strain and Risk of Recurrent Coronary Events, *Journal of the American Medical Association*, 298:14, pp. 1693-1694, 2007.

65. Siegrist, J., Adverse Health Effects of High-Effort/Low-Reward Conditions, *Journal of Occupational Health Psychology*, 1, pp. 27-43, 1996.

66. Bosma, H., R. Peter, J. Siegrist, and M. Marmot, Two Alternative Job Stress Models and the Risk of Coronary Heart Disease, *American Journal of Public Health*, 88, pp. 68-74, 1998.

67. Lynch, J., N. Krause, G. A. Kaplan, J. Tuomilehto, and J. T. Salonen, Work Place Conditions, Socioeconomic Status, and the Risk of Mortality and Acute Myocardial Infarction: The Kuopio Ischemic Heart Disease Risk Factor Study, *American Journal of Public Health*, 87, pp. 617-622, 1997.

68. Lynch, J., N. Krause, G. A. Kaplan, R. Salonen, and J. T. Salonen, Workplace Demands, Economic Reward and Progression of Carotid Atherosclerosis, *Circulation*, 96:1, pp. 302-307, 1997.

69. Peter, R., J. Hallqvist, C. Reuterwall, J. Siegrist, T. Theorell, and The SHEEP Study Group, *Psychosocial Work Environment and Myocardial Infarction: Improving Risk Prediction by Combining Two Complementary Job Stress Models*, (submitted), 1999.

70. Kivimaki, M., P. Leino-Arjas, R. Luukkonen, H. Riihimaki, J. Vahtera, and J. Kirjonen, Work Stress and Risk of Cardiovascular Mortality: Prospective Cohort Study of Industrial Employees, *British Medical Journal*, 325, p. 857, 2002.

71. Kivimaki, M., J. Ferrie, E. Brunner, et al., Justice at Work and Reduced Risk of Coronary Heart Disease among Employees: The Whitehall II Study, *Archives of Internal Medicine*, 165, pp. 2245-2251, 2005.
72. Elovainio, M., P. Leino-Arjas, J. Vahtera, and M. Kivimaki, Justice at Work and Cardiovascular Mortality: A Prospective Cohort Study, *Journal of Psychosomatic Research*, 61 pp. 271-274, 2006.
73. Menotti, A. and F. Seccareccia, Physical Activity at Work and Job Responsibility as Risk Factors for Fatal Coronary Heart Disease and Other Causes of Death, *Journal of Epidemiology and Community Health*, 39, pp. 325-329, 1985.
74. Murphy, L. R., Job Dimensions Associated with Severe Disability Due to Cardiovascular Disease, *Journal of Clinical Epidemiology*, 44:2, pp. 155-166, 1991.
75. Suurnakki, T., J. Ilmarinen, G. Wagar, E. Jarvinen, and K. Landau, Municipal Employees' Cardiovascular Diseases and Occupational Stress Factors in Finland, *International Archives of Occupational and Environmental Health*, 59:2, pp. 107-114, 1987.
76. Belkic, K., R. Emdad, and T. Theorell, Occupational Profile and Cardiac Risk: Possible Mechanisms and Implications for Professional Drivers, *International Journal of Occupational Medicine and Environmental Health*, 11, pp. 37-57, 1998.
77. Tuchsen, F., High-Risk Occupations for Cardiovascular Disease, in *The Workplace and Cardiovascular Disease*, Schnall, P., K. Belkic, P. Landsbergis, and D. Baker (eds.), Hanley & Belfus, Philadelphia, PA, pp. 57-60, 2000.
78. Greiner, B., N. Krause, D. Ragland, and J. Fisher, Occupational Stressors and Hypertension: A Multi-Method Study Using Observer-Based Job Analysis and Self-Reports in Urban Transit Operators, *Social Science and Medicine*, 59, pp. 1081-1094, 2004.
79. Kivimaki, M., J. Vahtera, J. Pentti, and J. E. Ferrie, Factors Underlying the Effect of Organisational Downsizing on Health of Employees: Longitudinal Cohort Study, *British Medical Journal*, 320:7240, pp. 971-975, 2000.
80. Johnson, J. V. and E. M. Hall, Job Strain, Workplace Social Support, and Cardiovascular Disease: A Cross-Sectional Study of a Random Sample of the Swedish Working Population, *American Journal of Public Health*, 78:10, pp. 1336-1342, 1988.
81. Theorell, T., A. Tsutsumi, J. Hallqvist, et al., Decision Latitude, Job Strain and Myocardial Infarction: A Study of Working Men in Stockholm, *American Journal of Public Health*, 88, pp. 382-388, 1998.
82. Hallqvist, J., F. Diderichsen, T. Theorell, C. Reuterwall, A. Ahlbom, and The SHEEP Study Group, Is the Effect of Job Strain on Myocardial Infarction Due to Interaction between High Psychological Demands and Low Decision Latitude? Results from Stockholm Heart Epidemiology Program (SHEEP), *Social Science and Medicine*, 46:11, pp. 1405-1415, 1998.
83. Kuper, H., A. Singh-Manoux, J. Siegrist, and M. Marmot, When Reciprocity Fails: Effort-Reward Imbalance in Relation to Coronary Heart Disease and Health Functioning in the Whitehall II Study, *Occupational and Environmental Medicine*, 59, pp. 777-784, 2002.
84. Landsbergis, P., P. Schnall, T. Pickering, K. Warren, and J. Schwartz, Lower Socioeconomic Status among Men in Relation to the Association between Job Strain and Blood Pressure, *Scandinavian Journal of Work, Environment and Health*, 29:3, pp. 206-215, 2003.
85. Landsbergis, P., P. Schnall, R. Chace, L. Sullivan, and R. D'Agostino, *Psychosocial Job Stressors and Cardiovascular Disease in the Framingham Offspring Study: A Prospective Analysis* (poster), in 4th ICOH Conference on Work Environment and Cardiovascular Disease, Newport Beach, CA, 2005.

86. Brunner, E., M. Kivimäki, J. Siegrist, et al., Is the Effect of Work Stress Confounded by Socio-Economic Factors in the Valmet Study?, *Journal of Epidemiology and Community Health*, 58, pp. 1019-1020, 2004.

87. Kivimäki, M., M. Hintsanen, L. Keltikangas-Järvinen, et al., Early Risk Factors, Job Strain, and Atherosclerosis among Men in Their 30s: The Cardiovascular Risk in Young Finns Study, *American Journal of Public Health*, 97, pp. 450-452, 2007.

88. Guimont, C., C. Brisson, G. Dagenais, et al., Effects of Job Strain on Blood Pressure: A Prospective Study of Male and Female White-Collar Workers, *American Journal of Public Health*, 96:8, pp. 1436-1443, 2006.

89. Pickering, T., D. Shimbo, and D. Haas, Ambulatory Blood Pressure Monitoring, *The New England Journal of Medicine*, 354, pp. 2368-2374, 2006.

90. Verdecchia, P., D. Clement, R. Fagard, P. Palatini, and G. Parati, Task Force III: Target-Organ Damage, Morbidity and Mortality, *Blood Pressure Monitoring*, 4, pp. 303-317, 1999.

91. Pierdomenico, S., D. Lapenna, A. Bucci, et al., Cardiovascular Outcome in Treated Hypertensive Patients with Responder, Masked, False Resistant, and True Resistant Hypertension, *American Journal of Hypertension*, 18, pp. 1422-1428, 2005.

92. Hayashi, T., Y. Kobayashi, K. Yamaoka, and E. Yano, Effect of Overtime Work on 24-Hour Ambulatory Blood Pressure, *Journal of Occupational and Environmental Medicine*, 38:10, pp. 1007-1011, 1996.

93. Yang, H., P. Schnall, M. Jauregui, T. Su, and D. Baker, Work Hours and Self-Reported Hypertension among Working People in California, *Hypertension*, 48:4, pp. 744-750, 2006.

94. Brisson, C., Women, Work and Cardiovascular Disease, in *The Workplace and Cardiovascular Disease Occupational Medicine: State of the Art Reviews*, Schnall, P., K. Belkic, P. A. Landsbergis, and D. E. Baker (eds.), Hanley and Belfus, Philadelphia, pp. 49-57, 2000.

95. Schnall, P. L., C. Pieper, J. E. Schwartz, et al., The Relationship between 'Job Strain,' Workplace Diastolic Blood Pressure, and Left Ventricular Mass Index. Results of a Case-Control Study [published erratum appears in JAMA 1992 Mar 4;267(9):1209], *Journal of the American Medical Association*, 263:14, pp. 1929-1935, 1990.

96. Landsbergis, P. A., P. L. Schnall, K. Warren, T. G. Pickering, and J. E. Schwartz, Association between Ambulatory Blood Pressure and Alternative Formulations of Job Strain, *Scandinavian Journal of Work, Environment and Health*, 20:5, pp. 349-363, 1994.

97. Schnall, P. L., J. E. Schwartz, P. A. Landsbergis, K. Warren, and T. G. Pickering, Relation between Job Strain, Alcohol, and Ambulatory Blood Pressure, *Hypertension*, 19, pp. 488-494, 1992.

98. Clays, E., F. Leynen, D. De Bacquer, et al., High Job Strain and Ambulatory Blood Pressure in Middle-Aged Men and Women from the Belgian Job Stress Study, *Journal of Occupational and Environmental Medicine*, 49, pp. 360-367, 2007.

99. Schnall, P. L., P. A. Landsbergis, J. Schwartz, K. Warren, and T. G. Pickering, A Longitudinal Study of Job Strain and Ambulatory Blood Pressure: Results from a Three-Year Follow-Up, *Psychosomatic Medicine*, 60, pp. 697-706, 1998.

100. Vrijkotte, T. G., L. J. van Doornen, and E. J. de Geus, Effects of Work Stress on Ambulatory Blood Pressure, Heart Rate, and Heart Rate Variability, *Hypertension*, 35:4, pp. 880-886, 2000.

101. Peter, R. and J. Siegrist, Chronic Work Stress, Sickness Absence, and Hypertension in Middle Managers: General or Specific Sociological Explanations?, *Social Science and Medicine*, 45, pp. 1111-1120, 1997.

102. Peter, R., L. Alfredsson, N. Hammar, J. Siegrist, T. Theorell, and P. Westerholm, High Effort, Low Reward, and Cardiovascular Risk Factors in Employed Swedish Men and Women: Baseline Results from the Wolf Study, *Journal of Epidemiology and Community Health,* 52:9, pp. 540-547, 1998.

103. Liu, J. E., M. J. Roman, R. Pini, J. E. Schwartz, T. G. Pickering, and R. B. Devereux, Cardiac and Arterial Target Organ Damage in Adults with Elevated Ambulatory and Normal Office Blood Pressure [see Comments], *Annals of Internal Medicine,* 131:8, pp. 564-572, 1999.

104. Sega, R., G. Trocino, A. Lanzarotti, et al., Alterations of Cardiac Structure in Patients with Isolated Office, Ambulatory, or Home Hypertension: Data from the General Population, Pressione Arteriose Monitorate E Loro Associazioni (Pamela) Study, *Circulation,* 104:12, pp. 1385-1392, 2001.

105. Hara, A., T. Ohkubo, M. Kikuya, et al., Detection of Carotid Atherosclerosis in Subjects with Masked Hypertension and Whitecoat Hypertension by Self-Measured Blood Pressure at Home: The Ohasama Study, *Journal of Hypertension,* 25, pp. 321-327, 2007.

106. Bobrie, G., G. Chatellier, N. Genes, et al., Cardiovascular Prognosis Of "Masked Hypertension" Detected by Blood Pressure Self-Measurement in Elderly Treated Hypertensive Patients, *Journal of the American Medical Association,* 291, pp. 1342-1349, 2004.

107. Björklund, K., L. Lind, B. Zethelius, B. Andrén, and H. Lithell, Isolated Ambulatory Hypertension Predicts Cardiovascular Morbidity in Elderly Men, *Circulation,* 107, pp. 1297-1302, 2003.

108. Ohkubo, T., M. Kikuya, H. Metoki, et al., Prognosis of Masked Hypertension and White Coat Hypertension Detected by 24-H Ambulatory Blood Pressure Monitoring, *Journal of the American College of Cardiology,* 46, pp. 508-515, 2005.

109. Gallo, L. C., L. M. Bogart, A. M. Vranceanu, and L. C. Walt, Job Characteristics, Occupational Status, and Ambulatory Cardiovascular Activity in Women, *Annals of Behavioral Medicine,* 28:1, pp. 62-73, 2004.

110. Hellerstedt, W. L. and R. W. Jeffery, The Association of Job Strain and Health Behaviours in Men and Women, *International Journal of Epidemiology,* 26:3, pp. 575-583, 1997.

111. Kawakami, N., T. Haratani, and S. Araki, Job Strain and Arterial Blood Pressure, Serum Cholesterol, and Smoking as Risk Factors for Coronary Heart Disease in Japan, *International Archives of Occupational and Environmental Health,* 71:6, pp. 429-432, 1998.

112. Green, K. L. and J. V. Johnson, The Effects of Psychosocial Work Organization on Patterns of Cigarette Smoking among Male Chemical Plant Employees, *American Journal of Public Health,* 80, pp. 1368-1371, 1990.

113. Landsbergis, P. A., P. L. Schnall, D. K. Deitz, K. Warren, T. G. Pickering, and J. E. Schwartz, Job Strain and Health Behaviors: Results of a Prospective Study, *American Journal of Health Promotion,* 12:4, pp. 237-245, 1998.

114. Siegrist, J. and A. Rodel, Work Stress and Health Risk Behavior, *Scandinavian Journal of Work Environment and Health,* 32:6, pp. 473-481, 2006.

115. Johansson, G., J. V. Johnson, and E. M. Hall, Smoking and Sedentary Behavior as Related to Work Organization, *Social Science and Medicine,* 32, pp. 837-846, 1991.

116. Markowe, H. L., M. G. Marmot, M. J. Shipley, et al., Fibrinogen: A Possible Link between Social Class and Coronary Heart Disease, *British Medical Journal,* 291, pp. 1312-1314, 1985.

117. Brunner, E. J., G. D. Smith, M. G. Marmot, R. Canner, M. Beksinska, and J. O'Brien, Childhood Social Circumstances and Psychosocial and Behavioral Factors as Determinants of Plasma Fibrinogen, *Lancet*, 347, pp. 1008-1013, 1996.
118. Langosch, W., B. Brodner, and M. Borcherding, Psychosocial and Vocational Long-Term Outcomes of Cardiac Rehabilitation with Postinfarction Patients under the Age of Forty, *Psychosomatic Medicine*, 40, pp. 115-128, 1983.
119. Muntaner, C., F. J. Nieto, L. Cooper, J. Meyer, M. Szklo, and H. A. Tyroler, Work Organization and Atherosclerosis: Findings from the Aric Study. Atherosclerosis Risk in Communities, *American Journal of Preventive Medicine*, 14, pp. 9-18, 1998.
120. Hintsanen, M., M. Kivimaki, M. Elovainio, et al., Job Strain and Early Atherosclerosis: The Cardiovascular Risk in Young Finns Study, *Psychosomatic Medicine*, 67:5, pp. 740-747, 2005.
121. Rosvall, M., P. O. Ostergren, B. Hedblad, S. O. Isacsson, L. Janzon, and G. Berglund, Work-Related Psychosocial Factors and Carotid Atherosclerosis, *International Journal of Epidemiology*, 31:6, pp. 1169-1178, 2002.
122. Steptoe, A. and M. Marmot, Atherogenesis, Coagulation and Stress Mechanisms, *Occupational Medicine: State of the Art Reviews*, 15:1, pp. 136-138, 2000.
123. Collins, S. M., R. A. Karasek, and K. Costas, Job Strain and Autonomic Indices of Cardiovascular Disease Risk, *American Journal of Industrial Medicine*, 48, pp. 182-193, 2005.
124. Belkic, K., Cardiac Electrical Stability and Environmental Stress, *Occupational Medicine: State of the Art Reviews*, 15:1, pp. 117-120, 2000.
125. Kouvonen, A., M. Kivimäki, M. Virtanen, et al., Effort-Reward Imbalance at Work and the Co-Occurrence of Lifestyle Risk Factors: Cross-Sectional Survey in a Sample of 36,127 Public Sector Employees, *BMC Public Health*, 6, p. 24, 2006.
126. Kumari, M., J. Head, and M. Marmot, Prospective Study of Social and Other Risk Factors for Incidence of Type 2 Diabetes in the Whitehall II Study, *Archives of Internal Medicine*, 164, pp. 1873-1880, 2004.
127. Siegrist, J., H. Matschinger, P. Cremer, and D. Seidel, Atherogenic Risk in Men Suffering from Occupational Stress, *Atherosclerosis*, 69, pp. 211-218, 1988.
128. Siegrist, J., R. Peter, W. Georg, P. Cremer, and D. Seidel, Psychosocial and Biobehavioral Characteristics of Hypertensive Men with Elevated Atherogenic Lipids, *Atherosclerosis*, 86, pp. 211-218, 1991.
129. Kawakami, N., S. Araki, N. Takatsuka, H. Shimizu, and H. Ishibashi, Overtime, Psychosocial Working Conditions, and Occurrence of Non-Insulin Dependent Diabetes Mellitus in Japanese Men, *Journal of Epidemiology and Community Health*, 53:6, pp. 359-363, 1999.
130. Nakanishi, N., H. Yoshida, K. Nagano, H. Kawashimo, K. Nakamura, and K. Tatara, Long Working Hours and Risk for Hypertension in Japanese Male White Collar Workers, *Journal of Epidemiology and Community Health*, 55:5, pp. 316-322, 2001.
131. Kubzansky, L. D., I. Kawachi, S. Weiss, and D. Sparrow, Anxiety and Coronary Heart Disease: A Synthesis of Epidemiological, Psychological, and Experimental Evidence, *Annals of Behavioral Medicine*, 20:2, pp. 47-58, 1998.
132. Perini, C., F. B. Muller, U. Rauchfleisch, R. Battegay, V. Hobi, and F. R. Buhler, Psychosomatic Factors in Borderline Hypertensive Subjects and Offspring of Hypertensive Parents, *Hypertension*, 16, pp. 627-634, 1990.
133. Markovitz, J., K. A. Matthews, W. B. Kannel, J. L. Cobb, and J. B. D'Agostino, Psychological Predictors of Hypertension in the Framingham Study: Is There Tension in

Hypertension, *Journal of the American Medical Association,* 270:20, pp. 2439-2443, 1993.

134. Jonas, B. S., P. Franks, and D. D. Ingram, Are Symptoms of Anxiety and Depression Risk Factors for Hypertension? Longitudinal Evidence from the National Health and Nutrition Examination Survey I Epidemiologic Follow-Up Study, *Archives of Family Medicine,* 6, pp. 43-51, 1997.

135. Sparrow, D., A. J. Garvey, B. Rosner, and H. E. Thomas, Factors in Predicting Blood Pressure Change, *Circulation,* 65, pp. 789-794, 1982.

136. Cottington, E. M., K. A. Matthews, E. Talbott, and L. H. Kuller, Occupational Stress, Suppressed Anger, and Hypertension, *Psychosomatic Medicine,* 48, pp. 249-260, 1986.

137. Knox, S., J. Svensson, D. Waller, and T. Theorell, Emotional Coping and the Psychophysiological Substrates of Elevated Blood Pressure, *Behavioral Medicine,* 2, pp. 52-58, 1988.

138. Theorell, T., Family History of Hypertension—An Individual Trait Interacting with Spontaneously Occurring Job Stressors, *Scandinavian Journal of Work, Environment and Health,* 16(Suppl 1), pp. 74-79, 1990.

139. Stansfeld, S. A., F. M. North, I. White, and M. G. Marmot, Work Characteristics and Psychiatric Disorder in Civil Servants in London, *Journal of Epidemiology and Community Health,* 49, pp. 48-53, 1995.

140. Bourbonnais, R., C. Brisson, J. Moisan, and M. Vezina, Job Strain and Psychological Distress in White-Collar Workers, *Scandinavian Journal of Work, Environment and Health,* 22, pp. 139-145, 1996.

141. Bourbonnais, R., M. Comeau, and M. Vezina, Job Strain and Evolution of Mental Health among Nurses, *Journal of Occupational Health Psychology,* 4, pp. 95-107, 1999.

142. Landsbergis, P. A., Occupational Stress Faced by Health Care Workers: A Test of the Job Demand-Control Model, *Journal of Organizational Behavior,* 9, pp. 217-239, 1988.

143. Borritz, M., U. Bültmann, R. Rugulies, K. Christensen, E. Villadsen, and T. Kristensen, Psychosocial Work Environment Factors as Predictors for Burnout: Prospective Findings from 3-Year Follow-Up of the Puma Study, *Journal of Occupational and Environmental Medicine,* 47:10, pp. 1015-1025, 2005.

144. Ahola, K., T. Honkonen, M. Kivimaki, et al., Contribution of Burnout to the Association between Job Strain and Depression: The Health 2000 Study, *Journal of Occupational and Environmental Medicine,* 48:10, pp. 1023-1030, 2006.

145. Lennon, M. C., Sex Differences in Distress: The Impact of Gender and Work Roles, *Journal of Health and Social Behavior,* 28, pp. 290-305, 1987.

146. Karasek, R. A., Job Demands, Job Decision Latitude and Mental Strain: Implications for Job Redesign, *Administrative Science Quarterly,* 24, pp. 285-308, 1979.

147. Mausner-Dorsch, H. and W. Eaton, Psychosocial Work Environment and Depression: Epidemiologic Assessment of the Demand-Control Model, *American Journal of Public Health,* 90, pp. 1765-1770, 2000.

148. Bosma, H., S. A. Stansfeld, and M. G. Marmot, Job Control, Personal Characteristics, and Heart Disease, *Journal of Occupational Health Psychology,* 3:4, pp. 402-409, 1998.

149. Landsbergis, P. A., P. L. Schnall, D. Deitz, R. Friedman, and T. Pickering, The Patterning of Psychological Attributes and Distress by "Job Strain" and Social Support in a Sample of Working Men, *Journal of Behavioral Medicine,* 15:4, pp. 379-405, 1992.

150. Rugulies, R., Depression as a Predictor for Coronary Heart Disease: A Review and Meta-Analysis, *American Journal of Preventive Medicine,* 23:1, pp. 51-61, 2002.

CHAPTER 7

From Stress to Distress:
The Impact of Work on Mental Health

Marnie Dobson and Peter L. Schnall

When stress becomes a prolonged or chronic experience, it can result in psychological *distress,* including generalized anxiety, burnout, and depressive symptoms. Work-related stress can also be a factor in exacerbating pre-existing mental illnesses and may even precipitate clinically diagnosable symptoms of depression. A growing body of empirical evidence in the occupational health field is making connections between the way work is organized and burnout, as well as more long-term adverse psychological health outcomes such as chronic anxiety and clinical depression. In turn, psychological distress has been linked to absenteeism, "presenteeism," job dissatisfaction, and turnover [1-3].

The wear and tear of long working hours and physical harm to the body motivated the social reforms of the early years of industrialization, including the 8-hour work day and the 40-hour work week. Laws were established to allow for physical and mental recovery time from work; they are now seriously compromised to the detriment of the psychological (and physical) well-being of workers. Not only should the psychological effects of work stress be a concern for individuals, but also for employers, labor unions, and society as a whole.

STRESS: THE AMBIGUOUS THREAT

Anxiety, fatigue, burnout, and depression are familiar examples of "distress" and evidence has demonstrated that they are associated with prolonged exposure to stressful work. Stress, as a biological and psychological process, in and of itself is a "normal" human experience, one that can motivate in the short term but exhaust us in the long term. The work environment is filled with challenges that provoke "stress" and engage our adaptive coping abilities. While the stress response can be cognitive (e.g., mentally appraising an event as a threat or harmful), it is also a biological process (for example, increasing blood pressure, heart rate, or breathing rate) by which individuals respond to challenges or "stressors" in the environment. During

113

the many years of stress research, competing models have evolved, positing the causes of stress as environmental, psychological, and/or biological/physiological. Many stress researchers, however, now envision stress as an integrated phenomenon. It can be defined as a process by which "environmental demands that tax or exceed the adaptive capacity of the individual lead to psychological and biological changes which may place the individual at risk of disease" [4, 5]. Complicating matters, stressors may elicit a physiological stress response regardless of whether someone feels "stressed out" or anxious at a particular point in time. For example, people with high blood pressure (the "silent killer"), which can be caused by chronic job stressors, are not more likely to report anxiety than people without high blood pressure (see chapter 6) [6, 7].

Individuals are exposed to many different stressors in the social environment, including at work. The stressors can range from traumatic or significant life events, such as loss of a loved one, losing a job, or divorce; daily hassles, e.g., being stuck in a traffic jam; to chronic stressors, e.g., having a difficult boss or co-worker or rising credit card debt. The distribution of exposure to stressors and stress and access to social support and coping resources varies based on one's life circumstances, which are partly defined by gender, socioeconomic status, and marital status [8]. As argued elsewhere in this book by Jeff Johnson (see chapter 3), one's life circumstances may account for variation in exposure to stressful circumstances and to the resources available to cope [9]. Individuals are exposed to different kinds of stressors based on the type of work they do. While both the corporate Chief Executive Officer (CEO) and those in lower paid, low skilled jobs may experience highly demanding work and some of the biological effects of *stress,* the CEO has more control over the organization of his/her work and access to many more resources to deal with his/her stress.

Chronic exposure to psychosocial stressors in the work environment (e.g., high demands plus low control, high efforts plus low rewards, or long work hours) can be as noxious to your health as physical demands and chemical toxins. Prolonged exposure to stressors causes a chronic stress response, eventually exhausting an individual's capacity to "cope" with normal loads of stress. Over time, it can result in psychological distress (e.g., fatigue, burnout) and even major illnesses such as depression, hypertension, and cardiovascular disease.

DEPRESSION, ANXIETY, AND BURNOUT

Depression is a serious health condition that impacts the thoughts, feelings, and everyday lives of those that suffer from it, as well as significantly affecting relationships and work performance. While there are little differences in the rates of serious mental disorders by gender and race/ethnicity, women tend to experience minor depression and psychological distress in greater proportions than men and are almost twice as likely to experience episodes of depression [10, 11]. Such research findings may be due in part to exposure to greater stress as part of traditional gender roles, taking care of children, parents, and the household as well as work. It could also be related to socialization into stereotypical gender roles; women tend to be socialized into passivity and "learned helplessness" more than men. The National Institute for Mental Health estimates that approximately 10% of American adults in a year, about 19 million people 18 years and older, experience some form of depression [12], other studies have found a 5% 12-month prevalence and a 13% lifetime incidence [11]. Some of the symptoms of depression include a persistent sadness, feelings of hopelessness, loss of interest, decreased energy, difficulty concentrating, and restlessness and irritability. Depression has multiple causes, ranging from genetic or family history, personality traits (e.g., "neuroticism"), the impact of significant life events, such as loss of loved ones, or exposure to traumatic events, such as natural disasters or childhood trauma. Depression may also be caused by exposure to chronic stress, including stressors individuals might be exposed to in their work environment, such as high workload demands and a lack of autonomy.

Anxiety is commonly defined as an emotional state with physiological signs, such as increased blood pressure and heart rate, sweating, dryness of mouth, irregular breathing, muscle tension and tremors, and distinguishable from anger or sadness by its qualities, such as feelings of tension, nervousness, worry, and apprehension. Chronic anxiety can also be a personality trait, that is, a more stable individual difference. Those who have high "trait" anxiety are more likely to perceive situations as stressful or threatening and to respond with "state" anxiety [13]. The relationship between demanding work factors and anxiety would seem to be common sense; however, research shows mixed results, particularly whether high strain work environments are likely to be anxiety-provoking or whether those with trait-anxiety are more likely to perceive the work environment as stressful. The subject will be addressed later.

In the United States, *burnout* is not considered a clinical disorder. It is a syndrome fundamentally linked to the workplace and, in the popular culture, to parenting and athletic performance. There is a lack of U.S. national data on burnout, but some studies of single occupations show that the prevalence of burnout in the work context is particularly high within human service occupations. Figures range from 9% among nurses [14] to as high as 45% among medical students [15]. Burnout is the result of prolonged exposure to chronic job stressors [16]. Christina Maslach developed an instrument to measure burnout which consists of three parts: emotional exhaustion, depersonalization or cynicism, and lack of professional efficacy or personal accomplishment [17]. Emotional exhaustion is considered to be the main component of the syndrome, referring to a feeling of depleted energy or emotional resources [16]. Depersonalization or cynicism refers to negative feelings and distancing from others at work and is the "interpersonal" component of the syndrome. Reduced personal accomplishment is a lowered sense of productivity and self-efficacy and represents the "self-evaluation" aspect of burnout.

Anxiety, burnout, and depression can all be present in the same individuals. Mechanisms explaining the relationship between these outcomes and work stress are not well understood [18] and, while undoubtedly related to each other, they may have different physiological effects:

During its early stages, burnout may occur concomitantly with a high level of anxiety because of the active coping behaviors that usually entail a high level of arousal. When and if these coping behaviors prove ineffective, the individual may give up and engage in emotional detachment and defensive behaviors that may lead to depressive symptoms [19, p. 356].

Anxiety is often seen as a core component of depression and some studies have demonstrated a high co-morbidity rate between depression and anxiety [20, 21]. One recent study has shown that anxiety precedes the development of depressive disorders [22]. However, another recent experimental study compared patients suffering from depression and panic disorder and suggested that even though dysregulation of the hypothalamic-pituitary-adrenocortical (HPA) system (part of our endocrine system regulating stress hormones) is similar in the two patient populations (since both are stress-related conditions), the biological mechanisms of this dysregulation might be different [16]. Burnout is considered more closely related to chronic stress at work while depression is considered to be more pervasive and caused by a multiplicity of factors from family/genetic history, personality, and past and present exposure to stressful life events [23, 24], as well as chronic work stressors.

Many employed people quietly struggle with the effects of depression that may stem from non-work factors. However, many others may find that their working conditions exacerbate depression symptoms or lead to depressive episodes, spending endless weekends and evenings at work dealing with the feeling of being rushed to meet a deadline and being micro-managed by an overly demanding supervisor. A recent study demonstrated a strong association between burnout and depression, where those with burnout were eight times more likely to also suffer from depressive symptoms and five times more likely to experience depression [25]. Either way, depression in the workplace, whether caused by work-related stressors or by personal experiences with traumatic events, is a significant issue for those affected by it and can be a significant cost to employers in lost productivity, rising health care costs, and sick leaves or absences.

THE ORGANIZATION OF WORK AND MENTAL HEALTH

Locating responsibility for psychological illness within the work environment is a difficult enterprise. As union membership declines and antiunion government and employer sentiment grows, more immediate demands such as layoffs, budget cuts, and rising health care costs take precedence for unions over working conditions. Moreover, some in the labor movement argue that preventing layoffs and maintaining job security is a most important stress reducer. Nevertheless, workers' compensation systems throughout the United States are in turmoil. With businesses clamoring to be relieved of the obligation to meet rising health care costs, fewer claims are being considered, and fewer and lower benefits than ever are being paid out [26]. Workers suffering from psychological illness are being left "high and dry," as the case of Oregon suggests:

In 1987, there were 930,000 workers in Oregon; 196 stress claims were accepted that year. Ten years later, in 1997, the work force had grown by 40%, to 1.55 million; 66 stress claims, representing 0.000043% of employees, were accepted (cf. Oregon Department of Consumer and Business Services, 1999, pp. 1, 17) [26, p. 457].

Prior to 1986, Oregon was one of the most liberal states in the country when it came to its workers' compensation system, but in response to employers' financial concerns over premiums, a legislative act set new legal standards for proving work-related mental illness but not for physical claims. The two legal standards by which "causes" of work-related illness were judged were: 1) "material contributing cause," applied if a medical condition resulted from a discrete incident; and 2) "major contributing cause," applied when a medical condition was a result of repeated exposure to adverse work activities over time. After the 1990 legislation, only physical accidents could be defined by both 1 and 2, whereas mental claims could only be found under 2 and were subjected to four additional legal restrictions regarding standards of evidence. For example, the standards on mental claims shifted from "preponderance of evidence" which requires 51% certainty, to "clear and convincing evidence" which demands 75% certainty [26], thus making it even more difficult than ever for workers to prove their mental illness workers' compensation cases.

While workers in Oregon are facing a difficult fight to win benefits for work-related mental health conditions, the research evidence showing strong associations between certain detrimental forms of work organization and psychological distress and mental illness is growing. Job stressors, such as workload or job demands, low decision latitude (the extent to which you can decide on your own work tasks), low autonomy, under-reward, interpersonal or organizational conflict, are some of the leading features of the organization of work that can impact an individual's mental and physical health. The main psychosocial constructs of job strain [27] and effort-reward imbalance [28, 29] have been studied widely in relationship to psychological outcomes, including anxiety, burnout, and depression.

As well, new areas of psychosocial stress at work are being identified and integrated into empirical research on the effects on worker health. For example, *emotional labor,* first developed as a concept by sociologist Arlie Hochschild [30], assesses the effects of work that involves emotional interactions with clients or customers, typically performed by human service professionals and sales and service workers, a rapidly growing sector of developed economies. The possible effects of emotional labor on the mental health of employees have only just begun to be studied, particularly in terms of an increased risk of burnout [31, 32].

Most studies explore the hypothesis that stressful job characteristics cause or are associated with lack of psychological well-being, rather than the reverse, that psychological well-being or illness influence an individual's experience of job characteristics. One longitudinal study did investigate whether the psychological well-being of health care professionals influenced their perceptions of job demands or control. They found only weak evidence that emotional exhaustion at the first time point predicted reporting of higher job demands at Time 2 [33]. Mostly, they found empirical support for job characteristics such as demands, control, or support causing psychological well-being or illness, rather than the reverse.

Job Strain and Mental Health

Robert Karasek's job strain model (see Figure 1) assesses a range of jobs that vary by demands and control. Jobs categorized as high strain, i.e., "job strain" have been extensively studied in relationship to many health outcomes, particularly cardiovascular disease (CVD) risk, musculoskeletal disorders, and psychological outcomes [27]. In 1988, the job strain model was expanded to include the dimension of social support, which is associated with reduced strain and can also "buffer" or moderate the harmful effects of job strain [34].

There is a very large and growing body of research that links work stressors to anxiety, depressive disorders, depressive symptoms, and burnout (see Figure 2) [35], even after taking into account personality factors [36]. In a review of prospective studies, Tennant et al. suggested that most studies showed that "occupational stressors remain as independent predictors of depression" even after controlling for personality variables [36, p. 702]. Some personality factors may have an effect on the development of psychological problems, such as being prone to negative thinking and feelings (i.e., negative affectivity) or having Type A behavioral characteristics (e.g., high achieving workaholics, who often exhibit irritability and hostility especially around time delays), although there is also some evidence that work experience can shape personality factors [37, 38].

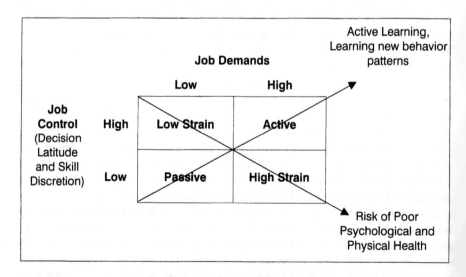

Figure 1. Karasek job strain model [27].

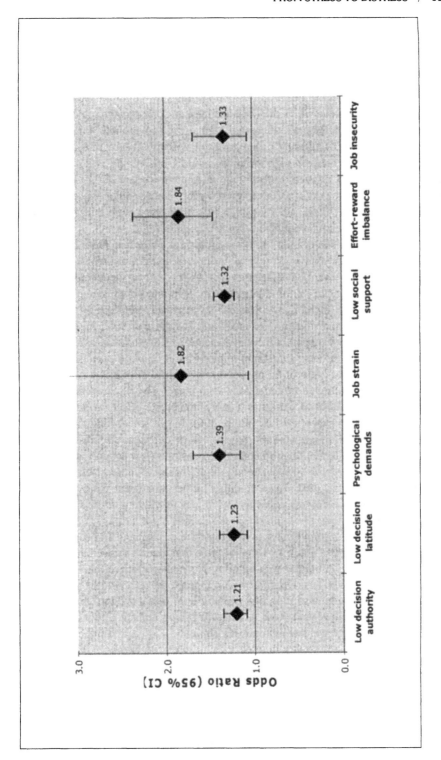

Figure 2. Meta-analysis of the association of work stressors and common mental disorders.

Many studies have shown an association between job strain and some form of psychological distress [25, 39-46]. Studies measuring components of Karasek's job-demand/control model have generally shown that high demands, low social support at work, and low decision-making authority predict depression [47-49]. Trait anxiety was not associated with job strain in the New York City blood pressure study, but was correlated with the separate measures of demands and decision-making latitude [39]. Several other studies that have measured job strain and anxiety, often as part of a battery of "psychological distress" domains, have shown a positive correlation between high job strain and anxiety [40-43]. In a recent study of more than 1,000 employed professionals in Australia, after taking into account gender, marital status, education level, employment status, major life events, and "negative affectivity," those reporting high job strain were more than three times more likely to experience anxiety [43].

In the classic Whitehall Study, an epidemiological study that followed middle-aged British civil servants over several years, researchers found that high job demands and effort-reward imbalance as well as low social support at work and low decision authority (e.g., job control) were associated with increased risk of psychiatric morbidity (including depression), even after controlling for psychiatric disorder at baseline, and adjusting for mood and "negative affectivity" [45]. While job demands and social support at the first stage of the study had a consistent impact on mental health at the next two time points (Phases 2 and 3), decision-making authority or control had less of an impact on psychiatric disorder at the last stage of the study than during the middle follow-up stage. The researchers suggest it might be because control at work has a more immediate effect on future mental health than other job characteristics [45, p. 306]. In the recent longitudinal study of more than 2,800 Belgian workers free from high depression scores at Time 1, exposure to high job strain, low job control, or isostrain (low support and high job strain) increased the risk of developing high levels of depression symptoms more than 6 years later [46]. These findings further strengthen the evidence that job stressors can cause depressive symptoms in people without pre-existing depressive symptoms.

Four cross-sectional studies have investigated the job demand and control model in relationship to burnout [44, 50]. Three of these four studies showed that demands and low control were associated with burnout. The non-supportive fourth study was of construction workers where burnout is not found to be as prevalent as in human service work. One study also investigated the role of social support among female social workers and found that those workers with high demands, low control, and low support were at greater risk of burnout [44].

Burnout might be a pathway through which those with highly demanding jobs and with little control over the work environment develop depression. A recent study of more than 3,000 Finnish employees looked at the association between job strain, burnout, and depression [25]. They found that those with high job strain were 7.4 times more likely than those with low job strain to have burnout and that those with job strain had a 3.8 times higher risk for depressive symptoms. However, they also found that the increased risk for depressive symptoms and for depression as a disorder due to high job strain was reduced by 69% after adjusting for burnout. These findings suggest there may be multiple pathways leading to work-related depression (see Figure 3). However, because it was a cross-sectional study, alternate explanations of the results are possible; for example, there may be individuals in the study whose depression started before they were exposed to job strain and thus was caused by other risk factors.

Effort Reward Imbalance and Mental Health

The idea of social reciprocity underpins the social contract of worker and employer—we should receive comparable reward for effort expended. When we work, our employer can expect our best efforts at performing our duties, and in return we can expect a comparable level of reward, including financial reward, job security, promotional opportunities, and respect. The concept of effort-reward imbalance (ERI) was developed by Johannes Siegrist to study lack of reciprocity (low rewards relative to high effort) and its association over a sustained period of time with the development of stress-related disorders [29]. The ERI model (see Figure 4) also encompasses the idea of having an "over-commitment" to work, meaning that some people may be more likely to expend a large amount of effort for low reward because of an "intrinsic" or personal over-commitment to their job [51].

In a review of longitudinal epidemiological studies, Siegrist found that "people who experience failed reciprocity at work are twice as likely to suffer from incident cardiovascular disease, depression, or alcohol dependence compared to those who are not exposed" [29, p. 1033]. ERI is considered better suited than job strain to assess work stress in occupations dealing in "person-based" interactions common to service and professional work [52]. In a study of 1,089 staff from the National Health Service in Great Britain, both job strain and ERI models were shown to predict mental distress and job satisfaction [53]. In a review of effort-reward imbalance in studies of the Japanese working population, one study of 604 nurses showed nurses with ERI, after controlling for job demands and control,

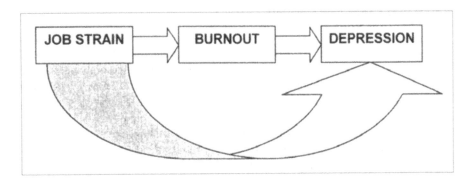

Figure 3. Relationship between job strain, burnout, and depression.

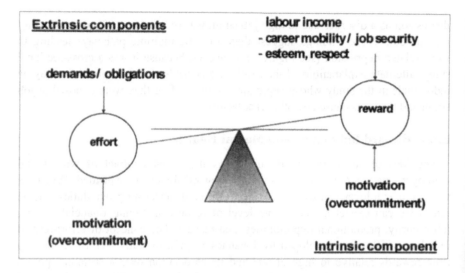

Figure 4. The model of effort-reward imbalance.
Modified from: Siegrist J (2002) [51].

had a four-fold higher risk for tension-anxiety (OR[1] = 4.1, 95% CI 2.9-5.9), as well as depression (OR = 3.9, 95% CI 2.7-5.6), fatigue (OR = 4.2, 95% CI 2.9-6.0), and burnout (OR = 4.9, 95% CI 3.7-7.0) [54].

In a comprehensive review of 45 studies on effort-reward imbalance, the authors found that the "extrinsic" ERI hypothesis, that high effort and low rewards increase the risk of poor health, is well supported by empirical evidence [55]. There are more inconsistent results for the "intrinsic" ERI hypothesis, which is that over-commitment will increase poor health. Five studies were identified showing that individuals with high effort and low reward job situations had elevated risks for emotional exhaustion, a key component of burnout. There was more limited support for ERI and depersonalization. ERI is more likely to cause emotional exhaustion, but not necessarily less job satisfaction or less work motivation.

Emotional Labor and Burnout

When the retail worker smiles and welcomes you into a clothing store or the check-out worker in the supermarket asks you if you found everything you needed, it is the often invisible labor required of many employees in the growing service sector of the economy. Emotional labor can generally be defined as a particular kind of emotion work that employees are paid to perform as part of their job. Sociologist Arlie Hochschild developed the concept of emotional labor in the mid-1980s to describe the "management of human feeling" in human service-oriented work, such as the work performed by flight attendants. Emotional labor requires workers to "create a publicly observable facial and bodily display," one that

---

[1] OR = odds ratio.

provokes positive responses in customers or clients [30]. It is the "relational" part of work found primarily, but not exclusively, in the service sector of the economy and, although not exclusively, often practiced in female-dominated occupations [56]. Emotional labor has been associated in several studies with negative health consequences such as burnout [31, 32, 57]. However, it has not yet been widely integrated into occupational health research as a psychosocial work stressor.

Most work on emotional labor has been theoretical and has given rise to two branches of study: job-focused emotional labor and employee focused emotional labor. *Job-focused emotional labor* is typically measured by the "frequency, duration, variety, and intensity" of interactions with customers or clients [57]. *Employee-focused emotional labor* involves the regulation of "natural" or authentic emotion in order to meet work demands, either expressing required positive emotions that are not in accordance with one's true inner feelings or suppressing negative emotions. For example, the call center worker responding to an irate customer might have to suppress their personal feelings of irritation or "upset" despite being yelled at and must remain pleasant and "reasonable" as the front-line "voice" representing the company. Many of these calls are "monitored for training purposes" as we are often informed when we call.

Ten years ago, researchers began finding positive associations between the frequency, intensity, and variety of emotions experienced and burnout [57]. However, since then, other researchers have begun to show, as in the above example, that *emotional dissonance,* a difference between the truly experienced emotion and the emotion that is required to be performed (e.g., "pleasantness") more consistently leads to negative health outcomes such as burnout [31, 32]. Being required to display positive emotion or suppress negative emotion may be a greater predictor for reduced psychological well-being than just the intensity or variety of emotions experienced on the job.

Some research suggests that the exigencies of human service work may require assessment of demands and job control that go beyond the classic "task level" Karasek demand/control model to include specific questions about emotional demands and management of clients [32, 58]. A parallel to Karasek's demand/control model has been developed which looks at emotional demands and emotional control or the "perception of the amount of control one has over the display of their emotions" [32]. In this research on human-service workers, Brotheridge and Grandey found that the frequency and duration of service interactions, and the intensity and variety of expression during those interactions, was *not* associated with emotional exhaustion or depersonalization. In fact, the "amount" of emotional labor performed was related to high personal accomplishment. In other words, having an emotionally demanding job, in and of itself, may actually be a positive experience. It was the requirement to hide negative emotions or display positive emotions which was significantly related to emotional exhaustion and depersonalization. However, the display rule to show positive emotion was related only to high personal accomplishment, suggesting that showing positive emotions may be more health-protective than having to hide negative emotion. Hiding negative emotions was the strongest predictor of burnout but disappeared when controlling for "negative affectivity" in this study [32]. This finding suggests that those who have a negative perspective in general may be more likely to experience negative emotions which they are required to suppress in their work. However, there is evidence that personality factors can be shaped by work experiences [37, 38]. For example, "trait" anxiety, a measure of "negative affectivity," was associated with lower job decision latitude and lower social support at work in the New York City Work Site Blood Pressure Study [39]. Thus, a history of exposure to work stressors may lead more quickly to burnout when hiding negative emotions is required.

In a Swedish study of 2,255 employees of an insurance organization, both quantitative work demands and emotional demands were assessed over a 1-year period [59]. This study found that the emotional demands of the job increased the risk of burnout more than quantitative demands. The authors concluded that it is important to include measures of emotion work when investigating the demand-control model's effects on burnout in human service workers.

The expanding service sector in the United States and throughout the industrialized world is giving rise to more emotional labor. Individuals must fake emotions oftentimes in order to keep their customers/clients happy, to keep the service interaction running smoothly, and to keep their jobs. In chapter 17, Stephen Smith explores the component parts of emotional labor, how we all "benefit" or "consume" emotional labor, and how reform and training could allow for a more "civil" society where emotional laborers as well as their customers/clients are not detrimentally affected by emotional labor gone awry.

Long Work Hours, Job Insecurity, and Mental Health

Increasing job insecurity and workloads in developed countries are resulting in longer working hours and more days worked a year in the United States [60, 61]. Ten- to twelve-hour work days are common in many occupational sectors, from the medical resident being trained to deal with round-the-clock demands to truck drivers barely able to restrict their work days to 15 hours, although work-hour limits are slowly being implemented in occupations affecting human health or safety. Among white-collar workers, the 9 to 5 work day appears to be a thing of the past. As downsizing is implemented and layoffs increase, work gets redistributed among remaining employees, increasing their workload and requiring longer hours to complete tasks. The threat of joining the ranks of the unemployed leads individuals to "choose" to work on the weekends and to stay late at night or arrive early in the morning. To be seen performing "above and beyond" is now a survival instinct.

The number of hours we work have increased, with the United States and Great Britain working the highest number of hours in comparison to Western European countries, and now higher than Japan [62, 63]. Working long hours can cause poorer physical and mental health and has been associated with smoking, poor diet, and a sedentary lifestyle [64]. In addition, working long hours means a greater exposure to noxious stressors in the work environment, including job strain and the negative aspects of emotional labor. See chapters 6 and 8 for research linking long working hours and high blood pressure and cardiovascular disease [65].

The consequences of downsizing in a company or organization can have direct effects on worker health because of the prevailing threat to job security as well as potentially leading to increased work demands and/or work hours. In a recent Finnish study of the effects of downsizing on the mental health of employees, researchers found that those who kept their jobs had a very high risk of being prescribed psychotropic medications (including anti-depressants) compared to those who did not experience downsizing [66]. The authors concluded that the managerial strategy of downsizing may pose excessive mental health risks to remaining employees.

Long working hours, including mandatory overtime or a "compressed work-week," which includes 12-hour days, can over-tire individuals and lead to sleep deprivation and fatigue. Fatigue is a potent risk factor in itself for lowered productivity and sickness absences as well as for poor mental and physical health. In Japan, concerns over long working hours and "karoshi," or death from overwork, prompted much research in the 1990s into the relationship between long hours and health [67]. Since then hours of work have dropped considerably in Japan, and now the United States leads developed countries in number of hours worked and is the only industrialized nation yet to institute government regulations on long working hours or paid vacations.

A large prospective epidemiological study of the prevalence and effects of prolonged fatigue was conducted by Dutch researchers beginning in 1998. The Maastricht Cohort Study was established to define and model the relationship between work factors and fatigue among a diverse population of working people in the Netherlands and found nearly 22% of the population reporting fatigue. There were also significant associations between the incidence of fatigue and burnout (which occurred in 13.7% of the sample) and psychological distress (in 22.9% of the sample) suggesting that fatigue may be a pathway to burnout and other forms of psychological distress [68].

Organizational Justice and Mental Health

Another way of looking at work stress is to measure justice at work. "Relational" justice is about whether supervisors treat their employees with respect and fair-ness (similar to social support) and "procedural" justice is about the fairness of formal decision-making procedures [69, p. 641]. Several studies have shown links between these measures of justice and mental health. For example, male and female British civil servants exposed to low "relational" justice at the start of the study were at higher risk of mental ill health (GHQ-30, mostly depression and anxiety disorders) 3 to 5 years later [70]. In a study of Finnish public employees, both "relational" and "procedural" injustice were related to symptoms of mental ill health (GHQ-12) and doctor-diagnosed depression 2 to 4 years later, in addition to the effects of effort-reward imbalance on mental ill health [71].

CONCLUSION:
PREVENTING DISTRESS BY CHANGING WORK

While it seems common sense that working conditions influence the mental well-being of workers, there is a serious disconnect between the growing evidence that this is the case and strategies to address the problem in the United States. A number of large companies took on the growing problem of stress in the workplace throughout the 1990s by instituting corporate "wellness" programs as part of Employee Assistance Programs (EAPs), introducing stress management techniques, including sometimes allowing employees to take "naps" during breaks or to practice meditation. While these practices may help to relieve individual symptoms of fatigue before employees become "burnt out" or depressed, this approach places the burden of solving the problem squarely on the shoulders of the individual worker, ignoring the structural problems in the organization of work.

If the way work is organized in many workplaces remains highly demanding and workers are continuously exposed to many work-related stressors (e.g., job strain and ERI) individually aimed solutions may not relieve the on-going and oftentimes invisible physiological and psychological effects this type of work produces in working populations. The sense that the level of effort that is expected from you as an employee is not being fairly rewarded with a comparable level of respect and a monthly salary that pays the bills can grind away at an individual's psychological health. Job security may be a thing of the past, although for some contract workers, other rewards might compensate for that. Yet, for many workers, temporary work is a significant stressor leading them to work longer hours, weekends, and forego vacations with the family in order to be seen to be performing "above and beyond the call of duty." As Quinlan describes it, "Apparent task control vanishes when overriding economic pressures . . . effectively mean the only choice is working harder and longer" [72, p. 352]. In a study of grocery warehouse workers, "Desperate to achieve performance targets that would secure further work and the prospects of a permanent job, temporary workers fulfilled the role of rate busters, undermining the resistance of permanent workers to serious work intensification and setting performance levels that two National Institute for Occupational Safety and Health studies later found to be unsustainable" [72, p. 354].

The working conditions of blue-collar work have traditionally been protected in industrialized societies by unionization and collective bargaining agreements. Rest breaks, work hour rules, and safety precautions are still areas of work that are bargained collectively. However, while the overwhelming majority of white-collar workers in the United States are not unionized, several big unions including the Communications Workers of America (CWA) and the United Auto Workers turned in the early 1990s to organizing in the growing service sector where work stressors were the predominant workplace hazards. Some unions have organized around reducing occupational stress and its causes in the work environment, including conducting stress education among members, establishing stress committees which inform collective bargaining, and conducting stress surveys in collaboration with researchers [73] (for more examples see Part III of this book). Instead of reinforcing the message that their members are getting from management that stress is a personal issue, unions such as the CWA, the American Federation of State, County, and Municipal Employees, and the Service Employees International Union focus on both educating individuals on coping styles as well as highlighting workplace causes of stress, validating employees' feelings while understanding that these feelings are shared by others in the workforce. However, focusing on reducing the health effects of stress often takes a back seat for many unions given membership decline, anti-union government and employers, and the immediate threats of layoffs, wage freezes, budget cuts, and rising health care costs.

Increasingly, service workers are required to paint a smile on their faces despite being asked to stand up all day behind a check-out counter, to respond with reasonableness to customers who are rude or even abusive to them, and to suppress negative emotions (including feelings of depression or fatigue) in order to maintain the image of the organization. While the work of emotional labor in and of itself can be a normal, fulfilling part of a job, sometimes it can negatively affect the health of workers, leading to high rates of burnout and an even more difficult struggle to perform emotional labor. What can be done to prevent the negative psychological effects of some aspects of emotional labor has barely begun to be addressed by researchers. Stephen Smith explores some possibilities for reform (see chapter 17).

Ultimately, the consequences of psychosocial stressors at work, including job strain, effort-reward imbalance, and emotional labor, come at an increasing cost to the mental health of working people and to society as a whole as we struggle to pay steadily rising health insurance premiums. Responsibility for psychological illness has typically been placed on the individual as part of the dominant ideology of "self-sufficiency"—that we should all be able to handle stressors, no matter how severe they are. Holding workplaces and employers accountable for their part in causing or worsening psychological distress or illness is an on-going struggle which often runs counter to this ideology. However, acting collectively to reduce sources of stress through local action, collective bargaining, or passing laws and regulations, can be empowering and health promoting.

Responsibility for changing the work-related aspects of psychological illness must be addressed at multiple levels. Individual workers need to be able to voice their experiences of fatigue, burnout, and depression and label them as reflections not of personal weakness but unhealthy work environments. Unions need to continue to encourage workers to speak up, to use their collective voice to improve working conditions. As part of this effort, unions can work with researchers to carry out workplace surveillance and document the associations between work organization and health. Business and government must also do their part. Employers need to recognize that these illnesses (and their costs) may be caused by their own business practices. Intervention efforts in workplaces need to take seriously the effects of work on the mental health of employees and go beyond simple *secondary* intervention programs of stress management, which locate the solution within the individual, to adjust the way work is organized and to focus on *primary* prevention instead. When and where necessary government must pass legislation regulating exposure to the worst workplace psychosocial hazards.

REFERENCES

1. Osterman, P., Thomas A. Kochan, Richard M. Locke, and M. J. Piore, *Working in America: A Blueprint for the New Labor Market*, MIT Press, Cambridge, MA, 2001.
2. Marchand, A., A. Demers, and P. Durand, Does Work Really Cause Distress? The Contribution of Occupational Structure and Work Organization to the Experience of Psychological Distress, *Social Science and Medicine*, 61, pp. 1-14, 2005.
3. Sanderson, K. and G. Andrews, Common Mental Disorders in the Workforce: Recent Findings from Descriptive and Social Epidemiology, *Canadian Journal of Psychiatry*, 51:2, 2006.
4. Cohen, S. and R. C. Kessler (eds.), *Measuring Stress: A Guide for Health and Social Scientists*, Oxford University Press, London, UK, 1997.
5. Lazarus, R. S., *Stress and Emotion: A New Synthesis*, Springer, New York, 1999.
6. Johnson, J. V., Occupational Stress, in *Preventing Occupational Disease and Injury*, Weeks, J. L., B. S. Levy, and G. R. Wagner (eds.), American Public Health Association, Washington, DC, pp. 464-473, 2004.
7. Friedman, R., P. A. Landsbergis, P. L. Schnall, et al., Psychological Variables in Hypertension: Relationship to Casual or Ambulatory Blood Pressure in Men, *Psychosomatic Medicine*, 63, pp. 19-31, 2001.
8. Pearlin, L. I., The Sociological Study of Stress, *Journal of Health and Social Behavior*, 30, pp. 241-256, 1989.
9. Turner, R. J., The Pursuit of Socially Modifiable Contingencies in Mental Health, *Journal of Health and Social Behavior*, 44:1, pp. 1-17, 2003.
10. Blehar, M. C. and D. A. Oren, Gender Differences in Depression, *Medscape Women's Health*, 2, pp. 3-4, 1997.
11. Hasin, D. S., R. D. Goodwin, F. S. Stinson, and B. F. Grant, Epidemiology of Major Depressive Disorder: Results from the National Epidemiological Survey on Alcoholism and Related Conditions, *Archives of General Psychiatry*, 62:10, pp. 1097-1106, 2005.
12. Regier, D. A., W. E. Narrow, and D. S. Rae, The De Facto Mental and Addictive Disorders Service System. Epidemiologic Catchment Area Prospective 1-Year Prevalence Rates of Disorders and Service, *Archives of General Psychiatry*, 50:2, pp. 85-94, 1993.
13. Spielberger, C. D. and R. L. Rickman, Assessment of State and Trait Anxiety in Cardiovascular Disorders, in *Anxiety and the Heart*, Byrne, D. G. and R. H. Rosenman (eds.), Hemisphere Publishing Corporation, New York, pp. 73-92, 1990.
14. Melchior, M., H. Philipsen, H. Abu-Saad, R. Halfens, A. Van Der Berg, and P. Gassman, The Effectiveness of Primary Nursing on Burnout among Psychiatric Nurses in Long-Stay Settings, *Journal of Advances in Nursing*, 24, pp. 694-702, 1996.
15. Guthrie, E., D. Black, H. Bagalkote, C. Shaw, M. Campbell, and F. Creed, Psychological Stress and Burnout in Medical Students: A Five-Year Prospective Longitudinal Study, *Journal of the Royal Society of Medicine*, 91, pp. 237-243, 1998.
16. Melamed, S., A. Shirom, S. Toker, S. Berliner, and I. Shapira, Burnout and Risk of Cardiovascular Disease: Evidence, Possible Casual Paths, and Promising Research Directions, *Psychological Bulletin*, 132:3, pp. 327-353, 2006.
17. Maslach, C., S. E. Jackson, and M. P. Leiter, *Maslach Burnout Inventory Manual*, Consulting Psychologist Press, Palo Alto, CA, pp. 19-26, 1996.
18. Glass, D. C. and J. D. McKnight, Perceived Control, Depressive Symptomatology, and Professional Burnout: A Review of the Evidence, *Psychology and Health*, 11, pp. 23-48, 1996.

19. Toker, S., A. Shirom, I. Shapira, et al., The Association between Burnout, Depression, Anxiety, and Inflammation Biomarkers: C-Reactive Protein and Fibrinogen in Men and Women, *Journal of Occupational Health Psychology*, 10:4, pp. 344-362, 2005.

20. Gorman, J. M. and J. D. Coplan, Comorbidity of Depression and Panic Disorder, *Journal Clinical Psychiatry*, 57:(Suppl 10), pp. 34-43, 2000.

21. Hettema, J. M., M. C. Neale, and K. S. Kendler, A Review and metaanalysis of the Genetic Epidemiology of Anxiety Disorders, *American Journal of Psychiatry*, 158, pp. 1568-1578, 2001.

22. Goodwin, R. D., R. Lieb, M. Hoefler, et al., Panic Attack as a Risk Factor for Severe Psychopathology, *American Journal Psychiatry*, 161, pp. 2207-2214, 2004.

23. Kendler, K. S., C. O. Gardner, and C. A. Prescott, Toward a Comprehensive Developmental Model for Major Depression in Women, *American Journal of Psychiatry*, 159, pp. 1133-1145, 2002.

24. Kendler, K. S., C. O. Gardner, and C. A. Prescott, Toward a Comprehensive Developmental Model for Major Depression in Men, *American Journal of Psychiatry*, 163, pp. 115-124, 2006.

25. Ahola, K., T. Honkonen, M. Kivimaki, et al., Contribution of Burnout to the Association between Job Strain and Depression: The Health 2000 Study, *Journal of Occupational and Environmental Medicine*, 48:10, pp. 1023-1030, 2006

26. U'Ren, R. and M. U'Ren, Workers' Compensation, Mental Health Claims and Political Economy, *International Journal of Law and Psychiatry*, 22:5-6, pp. 451-471, 1999.

27. Karasek, R. A., Job Demands, Job Decision Latitude and Mental Strain: Implications for Job Redesign, *Administrative Science Quarterly*, 24, pp. 285-308, 1979.

28. Siegrist, J., K. Siegrist, and I. Weber, Sociological Concepts in the Etiology of Chronic Disease: The Case of Ischemic Heart Disease, *Social Science and Medicine*, 22:2, pp. 247-253, 1986.

29. Siegrist, J., Social Reciprocity and Health: New Scientific Evidence and Policy Implications *Psychoneuroendocrinology*, 30:10, pp. 1033-1038, 2005.

30. Hochschild, A., *The Managed Heart: The Commercialization of Human Feeling*, University of California Press, Berkeley, 1983.

31. Liu, Y., P. L. Perrewé, W. A. Hochwarter, and C. J. Kacmar, Dispositional Antecedents and Consequences of Emotional Labor at Work, *Journal of Leadership & Organizational Studies*, 10:4, pp. 12-26, 2004.

32. Brotheridge, C. and A. Grandey, Emotional Labor and Burnout: Comparing Two Perspectives of "People Work," *Journal of Vocational Behavior*, 60, pp. 17-39, 2002.

33. de Jonge, J., C. Dormann, P. P. M. Janssen, M. F. Dollard, J. A. Landeweerd, and F. J. N. Nijhuis, Testing Reciprocal Relationships between Job Characteristics and Psychological Well-Being: A Cross-Lagged Structural Equation Model, *Journal of Occupational and Organizational Psychology*, 74, pp. 29-46, 2001.

34. Johnson, J. V. and E. M. Hall, Job Strain, Workplace Social Support, and Cardiovascular Disease: A Cross-Sectional Study of a Random Sample of the Swedish Working Population, *American Journal of Public Health*, 78:10, pp. 1336-1342, 1988.

35. Standfeld, S. L. and B. Candy, Meta-Analysis of the Association of Work Stressors and Common Mental Disorders, *Scandinavian Journal of Work, Environment, & Health*, 32:6, pp. 443-462.

36. Tennant, C., Work-Related Stress and Depressive Disorders, *Journal of Psychosomatic Research*, 51, pp. 697-704, 2001.

37. Kohn, M. L. and C. Schooler, Job Conditions and Personality: A Longitudinal Assessment of Their Reciprocal Effects, *American Journal of Sociology*, 87, pp. 1257-1286, 1982.
38. Matthews, K. A. and S. G. Haynes, Type a Behavior Pattern and Coronary Disease Risk: Update and Critical Evaluation, *American Journal of Epidemiology*, 123:6, pp. 923-960, 1986.
39. Landsbergis, P. A., P. L. Schnall, D. Deitz, R. Friedman, and T. Pickering, The Patterning of Psychological Attributes and Distress by "Job Strain" And Social Support in a Sample of Working Men, *Journal of Behavioral Medicine*, 15:4, pp. 379-405, 1992.
40. Bourbonnais, R., C. Brisson, J. Moisan, and M. Vezina, Job Strain and Psychological Distress in White-Collar Workers, *Scandinavian Journal of Work, Environment and Health*, 22, pp. 139-145, 1996.
41. Cropley, M., A. Steptoe, and K. Joekes, Job Strain and Psychiatric Morbidity, *Psychological Medicine*, 29, pp. 1411-1416, 1999.
42. Williams, R. B., J. C. Barefoot, J. A. Blumenthal, et al., Psychosocial Correlates of Job Strain in a Sample of Working Women, *Archives of General Psychiatry*, 54:6, pp. 543-548, 1997.
43. D'Souza, R. M., L. Strazdins, L. L. Y. Lim, D. H. Broom, and B. Rodgers, Work and Health in a Contemporary Society: Demands, Control, and Insecurity, *Journal of Epidemiology and Community Health*, 57, pp. 849-854, 2003.
44. Van Der Doef, M. and S. Maes, The Job Demand-Control(-Support) Model and Psychological Well-Being: A Review of 20 Years of Empirical Research, *Work & Stress*, 13:2, pp. 87-114, 1999.
45. Stansfeld, S., R. Fuhrer, M. Shipley, and M. Marmot, Work Characteristics Predict Psychiatric Disorders: Prospective Results from the Whitehall II Study, *Occupation and Environmental Medicine*, 56, pp. 302-307, 1999.
46. Clays, E., D. De Bacquer, F. Leynen, M. Kornitzer, F. Kittel, and G. De Backer, Job Stress and Depression Symptoms in Middle-Aged Workers—Prospective Results from the Belstress Study, *Scandinavian Journal of Work Environment and Health*, 33:4, pp. 252-259, 2007.
47. Wang, J., Work Stress as a Risk Factor for Major Depressive Episode(s), *Psychological Medicine*, 35, pp. 865-871, 2005.
48. Rugulies, R., U. Bultmann, B. Aust, and H. Burr, Psychosocial Work Environment and Incidence of Severe Depressive Symptoms: Prospective Findings from a 5-Year Follow-Up of the Danish Work Environment Cohort Study, *American Journal of Epidemiology*, 163:10, pp. 877-887, 2006.
49. Paterniti, S., I. Niedhammer, T. Lang, and S. M. Consoli, Psychosocial Factors at Work, Personality Traits and Depressive Symptoms: Longitudinal Results from Gazel Study, *British Journal of Psychiatry*, 181, pp. 111-117, 2002.
50. Schaufeli, W. B. and D. Enzmann, *The Burnout Companion to Study and Practice: A Critical Analysis*, Taylor & Francis, London, UK, 1998.
51. Siegrist, J. Effort-Reward Imbalance at Work and Health, in *Historical and Current Perspectives on Stress and Health*, Perrewé, P. and D. Ganster (eds.), JAI Elsevier, New York, pp. 261-291, 2002.
52. Marmot, M. G., J. Siegrist, and T. Theorell, Health and the Psycho-Social Environment at Work, in *Social Determinants of Health*, Marmot, M. G. and J. Siegrist (eds.), Oxford University Press, Oxford, NY, pp. 105-131, 1999.
53. Calnan, M., D. Wainwright, and S. Almond, Effort-Reward Imbalance and Mental Distress: A Study of Occupations in General Medical Practice, *Work and Stress*, 14:4, pp. 297-311, 2000.

54. Tsutsumi, A., K. Kayaba, M. Nagami, et al., The Effort Reward Imbalance and Mental Distress: Experience in Japanese Working Population, *Journal of Occupational Health*, 44, pp. 398-407, 2002.

55. van Vegchel, N., J. de Jonge, H. Bosma, and W. Schaufeli, Reviewing the Effort-Reward Imbalance Model: Drawing up the Balance of 45 Empirical Studies, *Social Science & Medicine*, 60, pp. 1117-1131, 2005.

56. Wharton, A., *Emotional Labor in the Service Economy: Emotional Labor, Its Measurement and Repercussions: The Psychosocial Consequences of Emotional Labor*, The Annals of The American Academy of Political and Social Science, January 1999.

57. Morris, J. A. and D. C. Feldman, The Dimensions, Antecedents, and Consequences of Emotional Labor, *Academy of Management Review*, 21, pp. 986-1010, 1996.

58. Borritz, M., U. Bültmann, R. Rugulies, K. Christensen, E. Villadsen, and T. Kristensen, Psychosocial Work Environment Factors as Predictors for Burnout: Prospective Findings from 3-Year Follow-Up of the Puma Study, *Journal of Occupational and Environmental Medicine*, 47:10, pp. 1015-1025, 2005.

59. Van Vegchel, N., J. De Jonge, M. Soderfeldt, C. Dormann, and W. B. Schaufeli, Quantitative Versus Emotional Demands among Swedish Human Service Employees: Moderating Effects of Job Control and Social Support, *International Journal of Stress Management*, 11:1, pp. 21-40, 2004.

60. Sparks, K., C. Cooper, Y. Fried, and A. Shirom, The Effects of Hours of Work on Health: A Meta-Analytic Review, *Journal of Occupational and Organizational Psychology*, 70, pp. 391-408, 1997.

61. Lee, S., D. McCann, and J. C. Messenger, *Working Time Around the World: Trends in Working Hours, Laws, and Policies in a Global Comparative Perspective*, Routledge and ILO, London and Geneva, 2007.

62. Caruso, C., E. Hitchcock, R. Dick, J. Russo, and J. Schmit, *Overtime and Extended Work Shifts: Recent Findings on Illnesses, Injuries, and Health Behaviors*, NIOSH, Cincinnati, OH, pp. 1-49, 2004.

63. International Labour Office, *Key Indicators of the Labour Market, 2005*, cited, Available from: http://www.ilo.org/public/english/employment/strat/kilm/kilm06.htm

64. Maruyama, S. and K. Morimoto, Effects of Long Working Hours on Lifestyles, Stress, and Quality of Life among Intermediate Japanese Managers, *Scandinavian Journal of Work Environment and Health*, 22, pp. 353-359, 1996.

65. Yang, H., P. Schnall, M. Jauregui, T. Su, and D. Baker, Work Hours and Self-Reported Hypertension among Working People in California, *Hypertension*, 48:4, pp. 744-750, 2006.

66. Kivimaki, M., T. Honkonen, K. Wahlbeck, et al., Organizational Downsizing and Increased Use of Psychotropic Drugs in Employees Who Remain in Employment, *Journal of Epidemiology and Community Health*, 61, pp. 154-158, 2007.

67. Shimomitsu, T. and L. Levi, Recent Working Life Changes in Japan, *European Journal of Public Health*, 2, pp. 76-86, 1992.

68. Kant, I. J., U. Bultmann, K. A. P. Schroer, A. J. H. M. Beurskens, and L. J. P. M. Van Amelsvoort, An Epidemiological Approach to Studying Fatigue in the Working Population: The Maastricht Cohort Study, *Occupational and Environmental Medicine*, 60, pp. 32-39, 2003.

69. Bourbonnais, R., Are Job Stress Models Capturing Important Dimensions of the Psycho-social Work Environment?, *Occupational and Environmental Medicine*, 64, pp. 640-641, 2007.

70. Ferrie, J., J. Head, M. Shipley, J. Vahtera, M. Marmot, and M. Kivimaki, Injustice at Work and Incidence of Psychiatric Morbidity: The Whitehall II Study, *Occupational and Environmental Medicine*, 63, pp. 443-450, 2006.
71. Kivimäki, M., J. Vahtera, M. Elovainio, M. Virtanen, and J. Siegrist, Effort-Reward Imbalance, Procedural Injustice and Relational Injustice as Psychosocial Predictors of Health: Complementary or Redundant Models?, *Occupational and Environmental Medicine*, 64, pp. 659-665, 2007.
72. Quinlan, M., C. Mayhew, and P. Bohle, The Global Expansion of Precarious Employment, Work Disorganization, and Consequences for Occupational Health: A Review of Recent Research, *International Journal of Health Services*, 31:2, pp. 335-414, 2001.
73. Landsbergis, P. A. and J. Cahill, Labor Union Programs to Reduce or Prevent Occupational Stress in the United States, *International Journal of Health Services*, 24, pp. 105-129, 1994.

CHAPTER 8

Work, Ethnicity, and Health in California

Haiou Yang

A workforce can be looked at in many different ways, for example, by demographics (age, gender, ethnic and racial make-up), legal status (permanent residents, immigrants, or illegal/undocumented workers), skill levels, educational attainment, employment status (part-time, full-time, temporary), wage level, type of occupation, medical coverage, and disability. Research investigating differences among these subgroups has found increased risk of disease and illness due to various environmental and work-related exposures and/or unique susceptibilities [1]. The U.S. workforce has witnessed a rapid increase in racial and ethnic diversity during the last two decades. This development is reflected in the increasing heterogeneity and inequality in the workforce, which has deep and profound ramifications for the incidence and prevalence of both diseases and injuries. California, in particular, has the highest proportion of ethnic minority populations in the United States. In 2000, California's population was 31% Latino, 12% Asian/Pacific Islander, 7% African American, 50% White Americans, and 1% Native American Indians. It is projected that by 2040, the proportion of Latinos in the total population of California will increase to nearly 50%, while only slightly more than 30% of the population will be White Americans [2].

These categories are generally understood to be socially constructed, not reflective of inherent biological traits, and aggregate important socio-cultural differences within groups. Being "Latino" is a personal political identity which may be voluntary or ascribed but may not fully capture the biographical or socioeconomic differences between being a second-generation Cuban-American, or a first-generation Mexican immigrant in the South-West. Aggregate data on race/ethnicity, however, serves as a useful proxy to understand how social inequality disproportionately affects the health of certain groups lower on the social hierarchy than others. Most minority groups in the United States are found disproportionately in lower

133

socioeconomic positions compared to Whites and often have a higher incidence of certain illnesses and diseases. These illnesses and diseases result in part from the conditions of poverty, including lack of access to health care, and in part from increased environmental exposures, in particular to poor work organization and psychosocial workplace exposures. Racial and ethnic health disparities among the working age population are, therefore, important issues in the research agenda of occupational health [2].

In addition to these changing demographic trends, workers in the United States have been impacted by the changing nature of work as the U.S. economy is becoming increasingly globalized (see chapter 2). Downsizing and lean production have emerged as new features of work organization in the United States. Subsequently, employment insecurity, job instability, increases in part-time work, lower pay, temporary work, contract work, long work hours, and shift work all have become common characteristics of work in America today [3]. There is little doubt that the changing nature of work organization is having serious adverse effects on workers' health and may be particularly detrimental for the population health of some racial/ethnic minority groups already experiencing higher prevalence rates of disease or injury.

This chapter, therefore, examines the racial and ethnic variations found in three major health outcomes: hypertension, diabetes, and obesity, among the working age population in California. Although a comprehensive investigation of demographic dynamics and the changing nature of work and their implications for racial and ethnic health disparities is beyond the scope of this chapter, this research explores work-related risk factors and racial/ethnic differences in hypertension, diabetes, and obesity among the working age population in California. This study is an expansion of our previous research with the same data set, which focuses on the association between long work hours and hypertension [4].

WHY FOCUS ON HYPERTENSION, OBESITY, AND DIABETES?

There are several reasons to focus on these three conditions. First, epidemiological evidence demonstrates that across the population, the percentage of hypertension, obesity, and diabetes increased substantially in the United States in the 1990s [5-8]. These three conditions are inter-related; the presence of all three illnesses is called the "metabolic syndrome" and can result in substantial cardiovascular morbidity and mortality [9-12]. Hypertension, obesity, and diabetes are related to work-related psychosocial stressors (see chapter 6), while obesity is a major contributor to both diabetes and hypertension. Moreover, existing research indicates marked racial and ethnic differences in the prevalence of hypertension, obesity, and diabetes, with an excess of all three conditions found among African Americans [13, 14] and a higher prevalence of diabetes found among Latino Americans [11, 15].

WHICH APPROACH TO USE:
INDUSTRY-BASED OR ETHNICITY-SPECIFIC?

Historically, ethnic health disparities and occupational health have been divided in two different domains of study. Over the last two decades, much of the research on racial and ethnic health disparities has been either industry-based or ethnicity-specific. Industry-based research tends to examine the racial and ethnic composition by different occupational health and safety indicators. Previous research from this field indicates that African Americans, Asian Americans, and Latino American workers on average have been concentrated in occupations with low pay, low skill requirements, low prestige, and they have been more adversely affected by work environment-related health problems and injuries [16]. Much of the ethnicity-specific research, however, focused mainly on comparing the prevalence of different health indicators for various racial and ethnic groups although some studies did go further to explore behavioral and socioeconomic risk factors associated with increased morbidity and mortality. For example, strong inverse relationships between socioeconomic status and cardiovascular disease among African Americans and White Americans have been well documented [17-20].

Less is known about Asian Americans and Latino Americans with respect to the relationship between socioeconomic status and cardiovascular disease. There exists a frequently disputed "model minority myth," that Asian Americans have "assimilated" more successfully than other minority groups and that this is reflected in their higher socioeconomic status and better health [21, 22]. Asian American health researchers have argued against this myth, showing that in reality Asian Americans and Pacific Islanders, like the other racial groupings in the United States, are heterogeneous groups composed of more than 50 ethnic and language subgroups, a spectrum of disparate socioeconomic statuses, and multiple generations of immigrants [21, 22]. Another debate has emerged involving what has been termed the "Hispanic Epidemiological Paradox" relating to Latino American health. Latino American health researchers are often puzzled by the tendency for Latino American people to have lower than average rates of infant mortality and some chronic illnesses despite the fact that many of them live in relatively lower socio-economic conditions [23-25].

It is important to go beyond the industry-specific or the ethnicity-specific approaches to look for new ways to examine racial and ethnic health disparities, particularly in relationship to work factors. Research on socioeconomic status and cardiovascular disease in the last decade has shed light on this area of research by pointing out two major pathways linking socioeconomic status and cardiovascular diseases. The first pathway is related to lifestyle and biomedical risk factors, focusing on individual behaviors such as smoking, unhealthy diet, and sedentary lifestyle, while another pathway is work-related, focusing on exposure to psychosocial factors (such as high demand and low control jobs or effort-reward-imbalance), access to health care, employment and income instability, and unemployment [26, 27]. Guided by this new perspective on health disparities, we examine the influence of work on health.

A NEW PERSPECTIVE ON HEALTH DISPARITIES:
THE INFLUENCE OF WORK

In general, adults working full time spend more than half of their waking lives at work and the demands and pressure of work frequently affect their health. The demands and pressure from work have become more intense in recent decades as the economy becomes increasingly globalized. Under globalization, U.S. manufacturers have faced increasing competition and consequent pressure to lower costs and improve technology. Downsizing and lean production have emerged as new forms of work organization. The consequences of downsizing and lean production for workers include more non-union work, employment insecurity, job instability, increases in part time work, lower pay, temporary work, contract work, long work hours, and shift work [3]. With advancement in technologies, both service and blue-collar workers have experienced an increase in cognitive complexities at work [3]. Racial and ethnic differences in incidence and prevalence of diseases and injuries may also be shaped by globalization of the economy and changes in work-related technologies. For example, many Latino immigrants moving into the U.S. economy are concentrated in the lowest paid service jobs and unskilled work, and as telecommunication technology advances, call centers "off-shore" to labor markets in India where wages are lower and working conditions less regulated. During the last decade, more research on workers' health has started to focus on risk factors at work that are linked to globalization of the economy and the changing nature of work.

PAST DATA SHORTAGES AND NEW
DATA SOURCES

A major obstacle to investigating the role of work in contributing to race/ethnic health disparities is a severe shortage of large-scale data sets that collect information on socioeconomic and demographic factors, occupation, work environment, as well as health data of workers from various ethnic backgrounds. The California Health Interview Survey (CHIS) is one of the few large-scale surveys that collect statewide information on demographic characteristics, work characteristics, ethnicity classifications, biological and health behavioral-related risk factors, and health conditions. However, the data set has limits if the goal is to examine the racial and ethnic disparities in a working age population for a number of reasons: a) its research design is cross-sectional which impacts determinations of causality; b) data on work characteristics are incomplete and do not include information on psychosocial factors at work and; c) health conditions are self-reported in nature [28].

The 2001 CHIS covered 55,000 households and was conducted in English and a number of other languages, including Spanish, Chinese, Vietnamese, Korean, and Khmer [29]. The respondents represented a population of approximately 1,588,000 workers in California who met the age range and work hours criteria (working 11 hours and over). The CHIS 2001 Public Use File provided useful information to explore issues related to racial and ethnic disparities and work. Specifically, five general areas of information were used for our analysis: a) health outcome information; b) demographic characteristics (gender, age, and ethnicity); c) work related characteristics (occupation and number of work hours per week); d) biological and health behavioral-related risk factors (tobacco consumption status and sedentary lifestyle); and e) socioeconomic status (education and household income).

In this chapter, we present data that provide evidence of a strong association between the three health outcomes and work-related variables, and racial and ethnic variations in these health conditions. This association is estimated with odds ratios (OR) and a 95% confidence interval (CI) using logistic regression analysis, controlling for relevant demographic factors, biological risk factors, and socioeconomic status variables. In epidemiological studies, an odds-ratio is a widely used and easy-to-interpret statistical indicator which compares the likelihood of exposure to risk factors.

WORK CHARACTERISTICS, HYPERTENSION, OBESITY, AND DIABETES

Work hours per week and occupation were the two work-related variables used in the analysis. We divided hours of work per week into four categories: a) 11 to 39; b) 40; c) 41 to 50; and d) 51 and over. Individuals with fewer than 11 hours of work per week were excluded from the analysis to avoid a possible bias due to the fact that those who work fewer hours per week (10 or less) may be more likely to have serious health conditions, including hypertension and cardiovascular diseases. The reference group used for work hours per week in the analysis was 11-39 hours. Also included in the analysis were eight occupational subgroups: a) executives, administrators, and managers; b) professionals and specialists; c) sales workers; d) administrative support workers; e) service workers; f) skilled workers; g) semi-skilled workers; and h) unskilled workers. The reference group used was the group of professionals and specialists.

Long Work Hours

Driven by the forces of globalization and the changing nature of work, Americans work longer hours than workers in most European countries, including the United Kingdom, Sweden, and Germany. The average American's work hours even exceeded Japanese workers in recent years [30]. Long work hours have been shown to be a risk factor for work-related health outcomes [31-33] and are associated with increased injury rates [34, 35], increased mortality [36, 37], and an adverse impact on a number of health conditions, including cardiovascular disease [38-40], diabetes [41, 42], hypertension [4, 33, 43-46], and unhealthy weight gain [47]. Research on the health effects of long work hours in the U.S. population has been limited. The data presented in this chapter begin to fill this research gap by exploring the association between number of work hours per week and three self-reported health conditions.

In terms of work hours per week, 23% worked less than 40 hours, 42% of
California workers worked 40 hours, 22% worked 41 to 50 hours, and 14% worked
more than 51 hours. There were significant differences in work hours between the
racial and ethnic groups in California (Table 1). More than 40% of Whites worked
41 hours and longer a week and had the highest proportion out of all the ethnic
groups working more than 51 hours a week (15%). More Latinos, African
Americans, and Asian Americans (48%) worked a conventional 40-hour work week,
compared to 35% of Whites. This interesting pattern may be due to the concentration
of minority workers in blue-collar and white-collar occupations that tend to be
traditional 40-hour-a-week jobs or part-time work (less than 40 hours a week).

A strong association between number of work hours per week and hypertension
was evident in the CHIS data reported in our recent study [4]. As indicated in
Table 2, a linear pattern between work hours and self-reported hypertension was
observed. Individuals who worked 40 (OR = 1.14, 95% CI = 1.01, 1.28) or 41 to
50 hours per week (OR = 1.17, CI = 1.04, 1.33) were at intermediate risk of
hypertension, compared with those who worked 11 to 39 hours. Individuals who
worked 51 or more hours per week were 1.29 times (OR = 1.29, CI = 1.10, 1.52)
as likely to have self-reported hypertension as individuals who worked 11 to 39
hours per week. A similar pattern between work hours and obesity was observed.
Compared with those who worked 11 to 39 hours per week, those who work 41
to 50 hours per week were 21% (OR = 1.21, CI = 1.03, 1.43) more likely to be
obese, and those who worked 51 hours or more were 31% (OR = 1.31; CI =
1.09,1.58) more likely to be obese. No relationship between number of work hours
and self-reported diabetes was observed.

Long work hours may increase the risk of developing hypertension and obesity
through several pathways [4, 32]. First, working longer hours implies shorter time
available for recovery from work and other activities, and insufficient time for sleep,
which is thought to be associated with disruption of physiological processes that
are linked to hypertension and obesity [48-52]. Second, long work hours are thought
to be linked to a risk for hypertension and obesity through unhealthy lifestyles and
behaviors, including smoking, unhealthy diet, and sedentary lifestyle. Furthermore,
long work hours expose workers for longer periods of time to noxious psychosocial
factors in the work environment, such as job strain and effort-reward imbalance,
which are believed to be associated with biological arousal and subsequent elevated
blood pressure. These risk factors may in turn lead to permanent physiological
changes, resulting in hypertension and obesity [32]. It has been reported that the
risk of obesity increases in high-demand and low-control work environments and
for those who work long hours [47].

Several longitudinal studies demonstrate a positive association between long work
hours and diabetes [41, 53, 54]. This study, however, finds no association between
number of work hours and self-reported diabetes. This could be attributed to the
limitation of the cross-sectional design of this survey in revealing the association
between long work hours and diabetes. Another reason for not observing an association between long work hours and diabetes in a cross-sectional study like CHIS
is that, unlike hypertension and obesity which are asymptomatic, diabetes involves a

lot of disabling conditions, such as neuropathic pain in feet, legs, hands, or arms, increased fatigue, and blurry vision [55, 56] which may contribute to selection bias whereby workers may cut back their work hours when they start to suffer these symptoms of diabetes.

Occupational Variation

There were dramatic and significant differences among race and ethnic groups in terms of occupational distribution (Table 1). More than 70% of Latinos in California were concentrated in the blue-collar and service sector, compared to 40% of African Americans, 35% of Asian Americans, and 32% of European Americans. Latino-Americans were least represented among professional and managerial groups (9%) in comparison to African Americans (30%), Asian Americans (39%), and European Americans (40%).

A significant pattern of occupational variation in hypertension was also observed (Table 2). Regardless of race and ethnicity, demographic characteristics, socioeconomic status, and other biological risk factors, when compared to professionals, unskilled workers were the most likely to have self-reported hypertension (OR = 1.50, 95% CI = 1.00, 2.25), followed by clerical workers (OR = 1.23, CI = 1.00, 1.51). Similar occupational variations in obesity were also observed; when compared to professionals, service workers (19%), semiskilled workers (21%), clerical workers (28%), and unskilled workers (46%) were more likely to be obese. However, no occupational variations in self-reported diabetes were observed.

It is not difficult to speculate about the mechanisms of these occupational variations. This pattern of clerical and unskilled workers having a higher prevalence of hypertension is consistent with research on job strain, where low control over work tasks tends to be more common in these occupations, and where low job control is a risk factor for hypertension [57-59]. Research on occupation [60] indicates that with mass customization of work processes associated with globalization of the economy, the nature of clerical and service work has shifted from unsystematic and labor intensive work to more routinized work with increased specialization, information processing, and cognitive complexity. With advancements in technologies and introduction of lean production, some researchers argue that blue-collar workers are also required to have higher cognitive and interactive skills. Others note that there has been a reduction in skill requirements and control over the production process among blue-collar workers.

RACE/ETHNICITY HEALTH DISPARITIES

In the analysis for this chapter, we define and analyze race and ethnicity using four aggregate categories: a) European Americans or White Americans (Non-Hispanic White); b) African Americans (Non-Hispanic Black); c) Latino Americans (including Mexican and Latinos or South and Central Americans); and d) Asian Americans (Non-Hispanic Asians and Pacific Islanders). White Americans were used as the reference group for comparisons. Native Americans were excluded from analysis in

Table 1. Ethnicity by Demographic, Socioeconomic, Work Characteristics, Health Risk Factors, 2001, California

	European Americans	African Americans	Latino Americans	Asian Americans	Average	P
Age group						< 0.0001
18 to 35	34.33	42.35	55.75	41.88	42.41	
36 to 50	41.98	41.97	34.53	41.42	39.58	
51 to 64	23.69	15.68	9.73	16.71	18.00	
Gender						<0.0001
Female	44.94	50.99	37.74	46.63	42.26	
Male	55.06	49.01	62.26	53.37	56.74	
Education						< 0.0001
Less than high school	4.72	5.77	44.39	7.74	17.47	
High school	21.41	25.85	25.98	16.14	22.47	
Some college	29.96	39.01	19.72	19.97	26.14	
College and higher	43.91	29.38	9.12	56.16	33.93	
Household income						< 0.0001
0-99% Federal Poverty Level	3.61	14.60	26.26	6.62	11.72	
100-199% Federal Poverty Level	9.93	18.53	31.44	14.88	17.66	
200-299% Federal Poverty Level	11.52	16.47	15.79	15.32	13.61	
300% + Federal Poverty Level	75.15	50.40	26.51	63.17	57.01	

						p
Occupation						< 0.0001
Professional	21.69	15.65	4.54	24.04	16.09	
Manager	18.78	14.11	5.35	15.24	13.75	
Clerical worker	12.71	18.54	9.43	12.36	11.90	
Sales worker	15.32	10.87	9.64	13.59	13.04	
Service worker	7.39	15.21	16.24	8.11	10.75	
Skilled worker	14.00	10.32	16.46	15.22	14.76	
Semiskilled worker	7.50	11.24	26.50	9.90	14.16	
Unskilled worker	2.61	4.05	11.82	1.54	5.55	
Work hours per week						< 0.001
11 to 39	24.27	23.00	21.89	20.66	23.02	
40	35.32	48.15	47.66	48.92	41.58	
41 to 50	24.51	17.11	18.84	19.81	21.73	
51 or more	15.90	11.74	11.61	10.61	13.67	
Biological and behavioral risk factors						
Self-reported hypertension	16.59	22.10	12.46	13.04	15.21	< 0.0001
Obesity	17.60	26.83	22.19	5.55	18.16	< 0.0001
Self-reported diabetes	3.07	5.34	4.41	2.63	3.57	< 0.0001
Smoking status						< 0.0001
Non-smokers	52.53	61.99	64.74	69.62	58.96	
Past smokers	27.06	16.68	18.08	13.76	22.03	
Current smokers	20.41	21.33	17.18	16.62	19.01	
Sedentary lifestyle	43.54	34.73	19.59	45.69	35.76	< 0.0001

Table 2. Multivariate Logistic Regression of Self-Reported Hypertension, Obesity, and Diabetes

Characteristics	Hypertension			Obesity			Diabetes		
	OR	95% CI*	p-Value	OR	95% CI	p-Value	OR	95% CI	p-Value
Age group									
18 to 35	1.00			1.00			1.00		
36 to 50	2.53	2.18, 2.94	< 0.0001	1.52	1.34, 1.72	< 0.0001	3.72	2.78, 4.97	< 0.0001
51 to 64	5.71	4.93, 6.62	< 0.0001	1.76	1.52, 2.03	< 0.0001	8.89	6.61, 11.96	< 0.0001
Gender									
Female	1.00			1.00			1.00		
Male	1.24	1.11, 1.39	< 0.0001	1.23	1.10, 1.36	< 0.0001	1.42	1.11, 1.83	0.007
Race/ethnicity									
European Americans	1.00			1.00			1.00		
African Americans	1.65	1.34, 2.03	< 0.0001	1.63	1.34, 1.99	< 0.0001	1.29	0.96, 1.74	0.09
Latino Americans	0.85	0.73, 0.98	0.03	1.08	0.94, 1.24	0.28	1.77	1.39, 2.26	< 0.0001
Asian Americans	0.89	0.77, 1.02	0.10	0.32	0.24, 0.42	< 0.0001	1.15	0.77, 1.72	0.49
Education									
Less than high school	1.00			1.00			1.00		
High school	0.95	0.78, 1.16	0.58	0.88	0.74, 1.05	0.14	0.89	0.67, 1.18	0.41
Some college	1.03	0.84, 1.25	0.79	0.89	0.73, 1.08	0.23	1.09	0.80, 1.49	0.57
College and higher	0.81	0.67, 0.98	0.03	0.48	0.38, 0.59	< 0.0001	0.72	0.51, 1.01	0.05

	OR	95% CI	P	OR	95% CI	P	OR	95% CI	P
Household income									
0-99% Federal Poverty Level	1.00			1.00			1.00		
100-199% Federal Poverty Level	0.81	0.36, 1.04	0.10	1.01	0.83, 1.23	0.91	0.77	0.54, 1.09	0.14
200-299% Federal Poverty Level	0.84	0.62, 1.14	0.27	0.98	0.79, 1.22	0.87	0.73	0.47, 1.12	0.15
300% + Federal Poverty Level	0.77	0.60, 0.98	0.04	0.82	0.68, 0.99	0.04	0.74	0.51, 1.07	0.11
Smoking									
Non-smokers	1.00			1.00			1.00		
Past smokers	1.26	1.13, 1.42	< 0.0001	1.16	1.04, 1.31	0.01	1.07	0.84, 1.36	0.59
Current smokers	1.16	1.01, 1.32	0.03	0.90	0.78, 1.03	0.11	0.94	0.73, 1.50	0.59
Sedentary lifestyle	1.10	0.99, 1.21	0.07	1.46	1.31, 1.64	< 0.0001	1.02	0.83, 1.24	0.87
Self-reported diabetes	2.66	2.23, 3.19	< 0.0001	3.17	2.60, 3.85	< 0.0001	3.18	2.61, 3.88	< 0.0001
Obesity									
Occupation									
Professional	1.00			1.00			1.00		
Manager	1.11	0.96, 1.27	0.15	1.15	0.98, 1.36	0.09	1.01	0.72, 1.41	0.97
Clerical worker	1.23	1.00, 1.51	0.05	1.28	1.10, 1.49	0.002	1.09	0.74, 1.60	0.67
Sales worker	1.00	0.85, 1.18	0.97	1.05	0.91, 1.22	0.5	1.04	0.76, 1.42	0.82
Service worker	1.06	0.88, 1.27	0.54	1.19	1.05, 1.34	0.009	1.31	0.79, 1.61	0.49
Skilled worker	1.05	0.87, 1.27	0.58	1.06	0.92, 1.22	0.4	0.82	0.56, 1.18	0.28
Semiskilled worker	0.97	0.78, 1.20	0.75	1.21	1.02, 1.22	0.03	1.16	0.77, 1.76	0.48
Unskilled worker	1.50	1.00, 2.25	0.05	1.46	1.04, 2.05	0.03	1.24	0.67, 2.31	0.48
Work hours per week									
11 to 39	1.00			1.00			1.00		
40	1.13	1.01, 1.28	0.04	1.12	0.99, 1.27	0.7	1.07	0.82, 1.40	0.63
41 to 50	1.17	1.03, 1.33	0.01	1.21	1.03, 1.43	0.02	0.79	0.60, 1.03	0.08
51 or more	1.29	1.10, 1.52	0.002	1.31	1.09, 1.58	0.005	0.98	0.69, 1.38	0.90

this chapter only as they constituted a very small percent of the population. While not ideal, these categories are generally accepted as broad indicators of racial inequality and its effects on the health of these populations.

African Americans: A Well Documented Pattern

Racial and occupational segregation and the resultant health disparities among workers [61] may persist partly due to transformations in global economic labor trends and changes in immigration patterns during the last several decades. Findings from this research are consistent with the widely recognized ethnic health disparity patterns associated with hypertension and obesity.

For example, analysis of the CHIS data shows that compared with White Americans, African Americans had the highest rates of hypertension and obesity among all groups. As indicated in Table 2, after controlling for demographic variables, biological risk factors, socioeconomic status, and work-related variables, African Americans were 65% (OR = 1.65, CI = 1.34, 2.03) more likely to have hypertension, compared to Americans of European lineage. African Americans were 63% (OR = 1.63, CI = 1.34, 1.99) more likely to be obese, compared to Americans of European lineage. They were also 29% more likely to be diabetic. This finding is consistent with documented evidence that African Americans have the highest prevalence of hypertension, obesity, and diabetes [11].

African Americans were disproportionately among the lowest socioeconomic status groups in the CHIS data, with nearly 15% living below the Federal Poverty Level, second only to Latinos (26%). Most African Americans are also concentrated in clerical work and blue-collar or service work, which are also risk factors for hypertension and obesity (Table 1). Some researchers argue that living on a low income in itself creates uncertainty, insecurity, and feelings of a lack of control over one's life—a potent psychosocial stressor (see chapter 3) [62]. These living conditions create stress that acts through psychological and biological pathways to impact one's cardiovascular system. Adverse social environments also lead to lipid abnormalities, high blood pressure, and clotting disturbances through the sympathetic nervous system and the hypothalamic pituitary-adrenal axis [62-65].

Asian Americans: The Model Minority Myth?

Asian Americans are predominantly young in terms of population age structure, compared to White Americans, although not as young as the Latino American group in the CHIS data. The major contributing factor to the Asian American age structure is immigration. Although the total population size is much smaller than that of Latino Americans in the United States, Asian American population growth has been rapid in the last decade, with the greatest concentrations in California, New York, and Hawaii.

Historically, Asian Americans have been considered "the model minority," a homogeneous group, or the "healthiest ones among all." However, in part, because of these myths, Asian American health issues historically have been overlooked. Asian Americans have been considered passive, compliant, and without problems or needs [66]. Moreover, a stereotype has prevailed that Asian American immigrants to the United States tend to be highly educated and from middle or upper classes, and so are presumably healthier. A number of researchers have contended strongly that the model of healthy and middle-class Asian Americans and Pacific Islanders is a myth. This myth has been "unwittingly" sustained because of lack of adequate data on Asian Americans from lower socioeconomic status groups or from recent Asian immigrant groups for whom English is a second language [67]. The importance of collecting disaggregate data on different Asian ethnic groups needs to be emphasized [68].

The CHIS study data demonstrate that Asian Americans are a heterogeneous group in terms of socioeconomic status. Although more than half (56%) of them had college or higher education, the proportion of Asian Americans with less than a high school education (8%) is still higher than that of White Americans (5%), and Asian Americans were twice as likely to live in poverty. In addition, Asian Americans did not appear to be the healthiest group, according to this study. The likelihood that Asian Americans reported having hypertension or diabetes was not significantly lower than that of White Americans. Moreover, compared with all other groups, Asian Americans were more likely to have a sedentary lifestyle, which is a risk factor for hypertension and obesity. However, Asian Americans were 68% less likely to be obese compared to all other groups, the only area showing Asian Americans to be healthier.

However, it is important to recognize that this study also suffers from the limitation of aggregating all Asian American and Pacific Islander groups. This study is not able to depict the health disparities among different Asian ethnic groups [68].

Latino Americans: A Paradox?

Strong inverse relationships between socioeconomic status and cardiovascular diseases in African Americans and White Americans have been well recognized previously [17-20]. Surprisingly, Latino Americans have been shown to have lower rates of chronic illnesses, such as cancer and heart disease, compared with Americans of European heritage and other ethnic groups, even though they are disproportionately among the lowest socioeconomic status groups. Scientists have had a difficult time explaining this fact and call it the "Hispanic Epidemiological Paradox." This issue has given rise to heated debates since the end of the 1980s [23, 25, 69] and the findings of this study contribute to this discourse.

As Table 1 indicates, Latino American workers in California had the youngest age structure among all groups, with 56% aged 18 to 35, compared with White Americans (34%), African Americans (42%), and Asian Americans (42%). Latino Americans were more likely than any other race/ethnic group to work in service occupations (16%), such as restaurant workers, caretakers, and house cleaners; or semiskilled or unskilled occupations, such as truck drivers, gardeners, construction laborers, material moving workers, or agricultural workers. Almost half (44%) had less than a high school education, dramatically higher than African Americans (6%), Asian Americans (8%), and White Americans of (5%), possibly related to the high proportion of immigrants in California's population. By far the group with the highest proportion living in poverty, more than a quarter (26%) of Latino Americans had a household income below the Federal Poverty Line.

Latinos in California were 77% more likely to have diabetes (OR = 1.77, CI = 1.39, 2.26), compared to White Americans. The disproportionately higher prevalence of diabetes in the Latino American group revealed by this study is consistent with evidence found in many existing studies. Recent research indicates that the high prevalence of diabetes in the Latino American population may be attributed to genetic susceptibility or changing lifestyle patterns among Latino American immigrants, including a high-sugar, high-fat diet and a low level of physical activity [70, 71].

Despite a higher rate of diabetes, Latinos were 15% less likely to have hypertension, compared to White Americans (Table 2). The low prevalence of hypertension among the Latino American working age population in California, despite concentration in occupational sectors known to be at risk (e.g., unskilled workers), may be partly related to the asymptomatic nature of hypertension and lack of access to health care. There also may be significant under-reporting of illnesses among workers who have low-paid and low-skilled jobs or who are undocumented immigrants [72]. The high proportion of younger workers may account for a delay in prevalence of hypertension. More research is needed because other risk factors or protective factors for hypertension among the Latino American groups are unclear.

THE GROWING EPIDEMICS

CHIS data showed that some 15% of California workers reported having hypertension, about 4% reported having diabetes, and 18% were obese. These data represent a population of approximately 2,400,000 with hypertension, 2,900,000 with obesity, and 570,000 with diabetes in California in 2001. These figures are, however, undoubtedly an underestimation of the reality due to the self-reported nature of these health conditions [73, 74].

Ethnic groups in the United States with a Latino-American heritage have experienced the most rapid population growth in a number of states, including California, Texas, and Florida. The total Latino American population in the country had a 50% increase during the decade between 1990 and 2000, with immigration playing a key role. It is projected that Hispanics will become the majority in California by 2040 [75]. Even though Latinos report a lower prevalence of hypertension and obesity, given their concentration in low-paid, low-skilled occupations, occupational health issues for Latino American workers can no longer be overlooked, nor in the decades to come.

Studies show that diabetes impacts employment, absenteeism, and work productivity [55, 76] and that obesity is strongly associated with absenteeism and other health risks [47]. Moreover, obesity also may act as a co-risk factor for the development of a number of work-related diseases, such as occupational asthma and cardiovascular disease. It is theorized that obesity may modify the worker's response to occupational stress, immune response to chemical exposures, and risk of disease from occupational neurotoxins [47].

Work-induced risk factors, such as long work hours and sedentary work, are contributing to the epidemic of obesity, one which will be far greater than the epidemic of the present, while the changing ethnic fabric of the population in the coming decades will no doubt exacerbate significantly the epidemic of diabetes. The anticipated and alarming growth in the epidemics of obesity and diabetes, influenced by both changing patterns of work and ethnicity, will act like a tsunami, contributing to both hypertension and cardiovascular diseases which will, in turn, have tremendous impacts at both the societal and individual levels. Given the poor efforts toward preventing and treating the present epidemics of obesity and diabetes, there is little reason to think that status quo measures will be more successful in addressing epidemics of a far greater scale. Prevention is, and will continue to be, critical.

REDUCING WORK-RELATED HEALTH DISPARITIES

What should be done to reduce work-related health disparities among workers in the United States? Ethnicity-based research argues the importance of collecting adequate data on Asian Americans, recent and undocumented Latino immigrants, and to disaggregate data on different ethnic groups [68]. Industry-specific research calls attention to the need to reduce or eliminate the most hazardous substances from workplaces [77]. Studies on socioeconomic status and cardiovascular disease emphasize the need to increase opportunities for stable employment with increased wages through various mechanisms such as living-wage ordinances, higher minimum wages, and improved access to health insurance coverage [64]. Research on long work hours stresses the urgency to develop regulations regarding limiting working hours for adults in the United States [4]. In addition, research on the relationship between work and obesity highlights the need to create more opportunities for physical activity at work sites and to recognize the detrimental nature of sedentary work. It is necessary to address work, health, and obesity without using approaches that are prejudicial, discriminatory, stigmatizing, or punitive. Reducing obesity and increasing physical activity will in turn contribute significantly to preventing diabetes and hypertension [47].

In response to current and anticipated demographic trends in the United States and California in particular, the findings in this chapter support the need to develop empirical studies with more complex research designs and with multidisciplinary perspectives that explore not only demographic, socioeconomic, and biological risk factors, but also risk factors at work. The risk factors at work should include both environmental exposures related to hazardous substances, as well as psychosocial risk factors that are related to work organization. By going beyond the boundaries of either the ethnicity-based or industry-based approaches, we can uncover new ways of thinking about health disparities in order to better address the health issues of workers from different racial and ethnic backgrounds at risk.

The workforce in the United States has become more ethnically diverse and this fact is more striking in California than in any other state in the country. The trend is anticipated to continue over the next decade [78]. As these demographic changes continue to unfold in many parts of the United States, especially California, the importance of addressing race/ethnic health disparities will become magnified. Hypertension, obesity, and diabetes are the three most prevalent health conditions, with workers of racial and ethnic minority backgrounds experiencing an excess burden. Reducing these health disparities for all Americans ranks among our nation's foremost health challenges [79]. To advance our understanding of these health disparities, we need new data and new approaches to exploring risk factors and protective factors. This research agenda must become a priority in many related disciplines, especially occupational health.

REFERENCES

1. Ashford, N. A., The Economic and Social Context of Special Populations, *Occupational Medicine,* 14:3, pp. 485-493, 1999.
2. NORA, National Occupational Health Research Agenda: The Special Populations at Risk, 1999, cited, available from: http://www2a.cdc.gov/nora/NaddinfoSpecPops.html
3. NRC, The Changing Nature of Work: Implications for Occupational Analysis, National Research Council (U.S.). Committee on Techniques for the Enhancement of Human Performance, 0309065259, x, 364 p., 1999.
4. Yang, H., P. L. Schnall, M. Jauregui, T. C. Su, and D. Baker, Work Hours and Self-Reported Hypertension among Working People in California, *Hypertension,* 48:4, pp. 744-750, 2006.
5. Mokdad, A. H., E. S. Ford, B. A. Bowman, et al., Prevalence of Obesity, Diabetes, and Obesity-Related Health Risk Factors, 2001, *Journal of the American Medical Association,* 289:1, pp. 76-79, 2003.
6. Gregg, E. W., Y. J. Cheng, B. L. Cadwell, et al., Secular Trends in Cardiovascular Disease Risk Factors According to Body Mass Index in US Adults, *Journal of the American Medical Association,* 293:15, pp. 1868-1874, 2005.
7. Ogden, C. L., M. D. Carroll, L. R. Curtin, M. A. McDowell, C. J. Tabak, and K. M. Flegal, Prevalence of Overweight and Obesity in the United States, 1999-2004, *Journal of the American Medical Association,* 295:13, pp. 1549-1555, 2006.
8. Mokdad, A. H., B. A. Bowman, E. S. Ford, F. Vinicor, J. S. Marks, and J. P. Koplan, The Continuing Epidemics of Obesity and Diabetes in the United States, *Journal of the American Medical Association,* 286:10, pp. 1195-1200, 2001.
9. Burt, V. L., P. Whelton, E. J. Roccella, et al., Prevalence of Hypertension in the US Adult Population: Results from the Third National Health and Nutrition Examination Survey, 1988-1991, *Hypertension,* 25:3, pp. 305-313, 1995.
10. CDC, *High Blood Pressure Fact Sheet, 2006,* cited 2007, available from: http://www.cdc.gov/dhdsp/library/fs_bloodpressure.htm
11. CDC, National Diabetes Fact Sheet: General Information and National Estimates on Diabetes in the United States, 2005, cited 2007, available from: http://www.cdc.gov/diabetes/pubs/pdf/ndfs_2005.pdf.
12. Rabin, K. R., Y. Kamari, I. Avni, E. Grossman, and Y. Sharabi, Adiponectin: Linking the Metabolic Syndrome to Its Cardiovascular Consequences, *Expert Review of Cardiovascular Therapy,* 3:3, pp. 465-471, 2005.
13. Cooper, R. and C. Rotimi, Hypertension in Blacks, *American Journal of Hypertension,* 10:7(Pt 1), pp. 804-812, 1997.

14. Daniel, H. I. and C. N. Rotimi, Genetic Epidemiology of Hypertension: An Update on the African Diaspora, *Ethnicity and Disease,* 13:2(Suppl 2), pp. S53-66, 2003.
15. Flegal, K. M., C. L. Ogden, and M. D. Carroll, Prevalence and Trends in Overweight in Mexican-American Adults and Children, *Nutrition Review,* 62:7(Pt 2), pp. S144-148, 2004.
16. Frumkin, H., E. D. Walker, and G. Friedman-Jimenez, Minority Workers and Communities, *Occupational Medicine,* 14:3, pp. 495-517, 1999.
17. Harrell, J. S. and S. V. Gore, Cardiovascular Risk Factors and Socioeconomic Status in African American and Caucasian Women, *Research in Nursing & Health,* 21:4, pp. 285-295, 1998.
18. Kaplan, G. A. and J. E. Keil, Socioeconomic Factors and Cardiovascular Disease: A Review of the Literature, *Circulation,* 88:4(Pt 1), pp. 1973-1998, 1993.
19. Pickering, T., Cardiovascular Pathways: Socioeconomic Status and Stress Effects on Hypertension and Cardiovascular Function, in *Socioeconomic Status and Health in Industrial Nations: Social, Psychological, and Biological Pathways,* Adler, N. E. and M. Marmot (eds.), Annals of the New York Academy of Sciences, New York, pp. 262-277, 1999.
20. Winkleby, M. A., C. Cubbin, D. K. Ahn, and H. C. Kraemer, Pathways by Which SES and Ethnicity Influence Cardiovascular Disease Risk Factors, *Annals of the New York Academy of Sciences,* 896, pp. 191-209, 1999.
21. Srinivasan, S. and T. Guillermo, Toward Improved Health: Disaggregating Asian American and Native Hawaiian/Pacific Islander Data, *American Journal of Public Health,* 90:11, pp. 1731-1734, 2000.
22. Yu, E. S. and W. T. Liu, US National Health Data on Asian Americans and Pacific Islanders: A Research Agenda for the 1990s, *American Journal of Public Health,* 82:12, pp. 1645-1652, 1992.
23. Markides, K. S. and J. Coreil, The Health of Hispanics in the Southwestern United States: An Epidemiologic Paradox, *Public Health Report,* 101:3, pp. 253-265, 1986.
24. Magana, A. and N. M. Clark, Examining a Paradox: Does Religiosity Contribute to Positive Birth Outcomes in Mexican American Populations?, *Health Education Quarterly,* 22:1, pp. 96-109, 1995.
25. Palloni, A. and J. D. Morenoff, Interpreting the Paradoxical in the Hispanic Paradox: Demographic and Epidemiologic Approaches, *Annals of the New York Academy of Sciences,* 954, pp. 140-174, 2001.
26. Cooper, R., J. Cutler, P. Desvigne-Nickens, et al., Trends and Disparities in Coronary Heart Disease, Stroke, and Other Cardiovascular Diseases in the United States: Findings of the National Conference on Cardiovascular Disease Prevention, *Circulation,* 102:25, pp. 3137-3147, 2000.
27. Lenfant, C., Conference on Socioeconomic Status and Cardiovascular Health and Disease, *Circulation,* 94:9, pp. 2041-2044, 1996.
28. CHIS, California Health Interview Survey. Survey Methodology and Sample Design, 2003, cited 2004 Nov, available from: http://www.chis.ucla.edu/methods_design.html
29. Ponce, N. A., S. A. Lavarreda, W. Yen, E. R. Brown, C. DiSogra, and D. E. Satter, The California Health Interview Survey 2001: Translation of a Major Survey for California's Multiethnic Population, *Public Health Report,* 119:4, pp. 388-395, 2004.
30. ILO, Key Indicators of the Labour Market, 2002, cited; retrieved, 2005 March, 15, available from: www.ilo.org
31. Caruso, C., E. M. Hitchcock, R. B. Dick, J. M. Russo, and J. M. Schmit, *Overtime and Extended Work Shifts: Recent Findings on Illnesses, Injuries and Health Behaviors,*

National Institute for Occupational Safety and Health (NIOSH), Cincinnati, OH, pp. 1-49, 2004.

32. van der Hulst, M., Long Work Hours and Health, *Scandinavian Journal of Work Environment and Health,* 29:3, pp. 171-188, 2003.

33. Landsbergis, P., Long Work Hours, Hypertension, and Cardiovascular Disease, *Cadernos de Saúde Pública,* 20:6, pp. 1746-1748, 2004.

34. Dembe, A. E., J. B. Erickson, R. G. Delbos, and S. M. Banks, The Impact of Overtime and Long Work Hours on Occupational Injuries and Illnesses: New Evidence from the United States, *Occupational and Environmental Medicine,* 62:9, pp. 588-597, 2005.

35. Dong, X., Long Workhours, Work Scheduling and Work-Related Injuries among Construction Workers in the United States, *Scandinavian Journal of Work Environment and Health,* 31:5, pp. 329-335, 2005.

36. Hoshuyama, T., Overwork and Its Health Effects—Current Status and Future Approach Regarding Karoshi, *Sangyo Eiseigaku Zasshi,* 45:5, pp. 187-193, 2003.

37. Buell, P. and L. Breslow, Mortality from Coronary Heart Disease in California Men Who Work Long Hours, *Journal of Chronic Disease,* 11, pp. 615-626, 1960.

38. Sokejima, S. and S. Kagamimori, Working Hours as a Risk Factor for Acute Myocardial Infarction in Japan: Case-Control Study, *British Medical Journal,* 317:7161, pp. 775-780, 1998.

39. Liu, Y. and H. Tanaka, Overtime Work, Insufficient Sleep, and Risk of Non-Fatal Acute Myocardial Infarction in Japanese Men, *Occupational and Environmental Medicine,* 59:7, pp. 447-451, 2002.

40. Uehata, T., Long Working Hours and Occupational Stress-Related Cardiovascular Attacks among Middle-Aged Workers in Japan, *Journal of Human Ergology (Tokyo),* 20:2, pp. 147-153, 1991.

41. Kawakami, N., S. Araki, N. Takatsuka, H. Shimizu, and H. Ishibashi, Overtime, Psychosocial Working Conditions, and Occurrence of Non-Insulin Dependent Diabetes Mellitus in Japanese Men, *Journal of Epidemiology and Community Health,* 53:6, pp. 359-363, 1999.

42. Nakanishi, N., K. Nishina, H. Yoshida, et al., Hours of Work and the Risk of Developing Impaired Fasting Glucose or Type 2 Diabetes Mellitus in Japanese Male Office Workers, *Occupational and Environmental Medicine,* 58:9, pp. 569-574, 2001.

43. Nakanishi, N., H. Yoshida, K. Nagano, H. Kawashimo, K. Nakamura, and K. Tatara, Long Working Hours and Risk for Hypertension in Japanese Male White Collar Workers, *Journal of Epidemiology and Community Health,* 55:5, pp. 316-322, 2001.

44. Nakanishi, N., K. Nakamura, S. Ichikawa, K. Suzuki, and K. Tatara, Lifestyle and the Development of Hypertension: A 3-Year Follow-Up Study of Middle-Aged Japanese Male Office Workers, *Occupational Medicine (London),* 49:2, pp. 109-114, 1999.

45. Hayashi, T., Y. Kobayashi, K. Yamaoka, and E. Yano, Effect of Overtime Work on 24-Hour Ambulatory Blood Pressure, *Journal of Occupational and Environmental Medicine,* 38:10, pp. 1007-1011, 1996.

46. Iwasaki, K., T. Sasaki, T. Oka, and N. Hisanaga, Effect of Working Hours on Biological Functions Related to Cardiovascular System among Salesmen in a Machinery Manufacturing Company, *Industrial Health,* 36:4, pp. 361-367, 1998.

47. Schulte, P. A., G. R. Wagner, A. Ostry, et al., Work, Obesity, and Occupational Safety and Health, *American Journal of Public Health,* 97:3, pp. 428-436, 2007.

48. Gangwisch, J. E., S. B. Heymsfield, B. Boden-Albala, et al., Short Sleep Duration as a Risk Factor for Hypertension: Analyses of the First National Health and Nutrition Examination Survey, *Hypertension,* 47:5, pp. 833-839, 2006.

49. Singh, M., C. L. Drake, T. Roehrs, D. W. Hudgel, and T. Roth, The Association between Obesity and Short Sleep Duration: A Population-Based Study, *Journal of Clinical Sleep Medicine*, 1:4, pp. 357-363, 2005.
50. Gottlieb, D. J., S. Redline, F. J. Nieto, et al., Association of Usual Sleep Duration with Hypertension: The Sleep Heart Health Study, *Sleep*, 29:8, pp. 1009-1014, 2006.
51. Moreno, C. R., F. M. Louzada, L. R. Teixeira, F. Borges, and G. Lorenzi-Filho, Short Sleep Is Associated with Obesity among Truck Drivers, *Chronobiology International*, 23:6, pp. 1295-1303, 2006.
52. Kohatsu, N. D., R. Tsai, T. Young, et al., Sleep Duration and Body Mass Index in a Rural Population, *Archives of Internal Medicine*, 166:16, pp. 1701-1705, 2006.
53. Lee, S., G. A. Colditz, L. F. Berkman, and I. Kawachi, Prospective Study of Job Insecurity and Coronary Heart Disease in US Women, *Annals of Epidemiology*, 14:1, pp. 24-30, 2004.
54. Kroenke, C. H., D. Spiegelman, J. Manson, E. S. Schernhammer, G. A. Colditz, and I. Kawachi, Work Characteristics and Incidence of Type 2 Diabetes in Women, *American Journal of Epidemiology*, 165:2, pp. 175-183, 2007.
55. Stewart, W. F., J. A. Ricci, E. Chee, A. G. Hirsch, and N. A. Brandenburg, Lost Productive Time and Costs Due to Diabetes and Diabetic Neuropathic Pain in the US Workforce, *Journal of Occupational and Environmental Medicine*, 49:6, pp. 672-679, 2007.
56. ADA, T. A. D. A., *Diabetes Symptoms, 2007*, cited 2007, available from: http://www.diabetes.org/diabetes-symptoms.jsp
57. Karasek, R. A., T. G. Theorell, J. Schwartz, C. Pieper, and L. Alfredsson, Job, Psychological Factors and Coronary Heart Disease. Swedish Prospective Findings and US Prevalence Findings Using a New Occupational Inference Method, *Advances in Cardiology*, 29, pp. 62-67, 1982.
58. Schnall, P. L., J. E. Schwartz, P. A. Landsbergis, K. Warren, and T. G. Pickering, A Longitudinal Study of Job Strain and Ambulatory Blood Pressure: Results from a Three-Year Follow-Up, *Psychosomatic Medicine*, 60:6, pp. 697-706, 1998.
59. Landsbergis, P. A., P. L. Schnall, T. G. Pickering, K. Warren, and J. E. Schwartz, Life-Course Exposure to Job Strain and Ambulatory Blood Pressure in Men, *American Journal of Epidemiology*, 157:11, pp. 998-1006, 2003.
60. National Research Council, *The Changing Nature of Work: Implications for Occupational Analysis*, Committee on Techniques for the Enhancement of Human Performance: Occupational Analysis, Commission on Behavioral and Social Sciences and Education, National Academy Press, Washington, DC, 1999.
61. Frumkin, H. and G. Pransky, Special Populations in Occupational Health, *Occupational Medicine*, 14:3, pp. 479-484, 1999.
62. *Eliminating Racial & Ethnic Health Disparities, 2007*, cited 2007. Available from: http://www.cdc.gov/omh/AboutUs/disparities.htm
63. Raphael, D., Inequality Is Bad for Our Hearts: Why Low Income and Social Exclusion Are Major Causes of Heart Disease in Canada, 2001, cited, available from: http://depts.washington.edu/eqhlth/paperA15.html
64. Raphael, D. and S. Farrell, Income Inequality and Cardiovascular Disease in North-America: Shifting the Paradigm, *Harvard Health Policy Review 2002*, cited Volume 3 Number 2, available from: http://hcs.harvard.edu/~epihc/currentissue/fall2002/raphael-farrell-ref.php
65. Schnall, P., K. Belkic, P. A. Landsbergis, and D. Baker, Why the Workplace and Cardiovascular Disease?, *Occupational Medicine: State-of-the-Art Reviews*, 15:1, pp. 1-5, 2000.

66. NHLBI, *Addressing Cardiovascular Health in Asian Americans and Pacific Islanders,* NIH Publication No 00-3647, National Heart, Lung, and Blood Institute (NHLBI), National Institutes of Health, (ed.), 2000.
67. Yu, E. S., An Overview of the U.S. Health Data for Asian Americans and Pacific Islanders: Sources, Limitations, and Potential Solutions, *Asian American and Pacific Island Journal of Health,* 4:1-3, pp. 68-71, 1996.
68. Chen, M. S., Jr., Cardiovascular Health among Asian Americans/Pacific Islanders: An Examination of Health Status and Intervention Approaches, *American Journal of Health Promotion,* 7:3, pp. 199-207, 1993.
69. Patel, K. V., K. Eschbach, L. A. Ray, and K. S. Markides, Evaluation of Mortality Data for Older Mexican Americans: Implications for the Hispanic Paradox, *American Journal of Epidemiology,* 159:7, pp. 707-715, 2004.
70. Hallman, D. M., E. Boerwinkle, V. H. Gonzalez, B. E. Klein, R. Klein, and C. L. Hanis, A Genome-Wide Linkage Scan for Diabetic Retinopathy Susceptibility Genes in Mexican Americans with Type 2 Diabetes from Starr County, Texas, *Diabetes,* 56:4, pp. 1167-1173, 2007.
71. Hallman, D. M., J. C. Huber, Jr., V. H. Gonzalez, B. E. Klein, R. Klein, and C. L. Hanis, Familial Aggregation of Severity of Diabetic Retinopathy in Mexican Americans from Starr County, Texas, *Diabetes Care,* 28:5, pp. 1163-1168, 2005.
72. Brown, M. P., A. Domezain, and N. Villoria-Siegert, Voices from the Margins: Immigrant Workers' Perceptions of Health and Safety in the Workplace, 2002, available from: www.iosh.ucla.edu
73. Bergmann, M. M., E. J. Jacobs, K. Hoffmann, and H. Boeing, Agreement of Self-Reported Medical History: Comparison of an in-Person Interview with a Self-Administered Questionnaire, *European Journal of Epidemiology,* 19:5, pp. 411-416, 2004.
74. Klungel, O. H., A. de Boer, A. H. Paes, J. C. Seidell, and A. Bakker, Cardiovascular Diseases and Risk Factors in a Population-Based Study in the Netherlands: Agreement between Questionnaire Information and Medical Records, *Netherlands Journal of Medicine,* 55:4, pp. 177-183, 1999.
75. Rand, Rand California's Population and Demographic Statistics: Total Population Estimates in California, 2003, cited 2004, available from: http://ca.rand.org/stats/popdemo/popest.html
76. Tunceli, K., C. J. Bradley, D. Nerenz, L. K. Williams, M. Pladevall, and J. Elston Lafata, The Impact of Diabetes on Employment and Work Productivity, *Diabetes Care,* 28:11, pp. 2662-2667, 2005.
77. Murray, L. R., Sick and Tired of Being Sick and Tired: Scientific Evidence, Methods, and Research Implications for Racial and Ethnic Disparities in Occupational Health, *American Journal of Public Health,* 93:2, pp. 221-226, 2003.
78. *U.S. Interim Projections by Age, Sex, Race, and Hispanic Origin,* U.S. Census Bureau, Population Division, Population Projections Branch, 2004.
79. OMHD, *Eliminating Racial & Ethnic Health Disparities, 2007,* cited 2007, available from: http://www.cdc.gov/omh/AboutUs/disparities.htm

CHAPTER 9

Work, Psychosocial Stressors, and the Bottom Line

Maritza Jauregui and Peter L. Schnall

The bottom line: it reflects a company's profitability or lack thereof, the profit that a particular company has made after all expenses and taxes have been paid. In an economic environment increasingly filled with global business competitors employing relatively cheap labor and inexpensive materials, many companies, including those in the United States, have had to think of creative ways to cut expenses in order to keep their bottom lines from shrinking. In this type of high pressure environment, where products often have limited pricing power, the primary focus is on improving productivity, and employee health remains a secondary concern, something to be dealt with as the need arises, not something in which to invest one's hard-earned capital.

From a purely economic standpoint, we believe that treating employee health in this manner is a mistake. While workplace injury rates appear[1] to have declined substantially since the Bureau of Labor Statistics first began reporting such data in the 1970s, with 4 years of consecutive declines between 2003 and 2006 [1], the physical environment is not the only contributor to employee ill health. According to the National Institute of Health, 60-80% of workplace accidents are stress-related. Preceding chapters have illustrated how a wide range of workplace organization and job characteristics can function as psychosocial stressors that have serious impacts on employee health and illness. Some of these stressors, such as heavy workload demands and conflict, appear to play significant roles in the development of burnout, anxiety, and depression (see chapter 7) while others, such as job strain, shift work, and long work hours, have been implicated in physical injuries and the development of cardiovascular disease (see chapter 6). In trying to reduce costs, companies frequently make changes in the ways in which work is organized and in individual

---

[1] Workplace injury and illnesses are affected by underestimates due to underreporting by employees and to regulatory changes in recordkeeping since 1992.

job requirements. Many of these changes can end up hurting rather than bolstering their bottom line by adding to health-related costs.

Downsizings and layoffs are other cost-cutting measures. Research into downsizing conducted by the American Management Association (AMA) for CIGNA found that 70% of the companies that had experienced downsizings and layoffs reported a substantial increase in disability claims, even with fewer employees [2]. According to Robert Morgan, President of Spherion Corporation's human capital consulting group, more than 50% of the people who left merged organizations did so because of merger-related stress. Dr. Mitchell Marks, an M&A consultant and organizational psychologist, said that companies "underestimate how much human pain is required to get to the financial gain, if they get the gain at all." In fact, 75% of the 37,000 deals recorded by Thomson Financial Securities will fail to achieve the intended financial goals [3].

If a relationship exists between work organization and health, then injuries and illnesses are not just the concern of the individual employee but are also the responsibility of the companies that create the deleterious working conditions. Moreover, there is a point for each company at which the enhanced productivity, if any, that results from organizational changes will be offset by the increased cost that results from damage to the workforce—unless, of course, the costs are externalized by replacing sick and injured workers with healthy ones.

DIRECT COSTS

Both the direct costs of treating work-related illnesses and injuries and the indirect costs or resultant deficits in the amount of work or ways in which the work is done are borne to some extent by the employer. Although employers rarely pay directly for medical, hospital, and pharmaceutical expenses, employers do pay the health insurance premiums, disability, and workers' compensation benefits.

According to the Institute for Health and Productivity Studies, the top physical health conditions financially affecting large U.S. employers through direct costs were chronic maintenance of angina pectoris, essential hypertension, diabetes mellitus, mechanical low back pain, acute myocardial infarction, chronic obstructive pulmonary disease, back disorders other than low back, traumatic spine and spinal cord, sinusitis, and diseases of the ear, nose, throat, or mastoid processes [4]. Six of these 10 conditions have been associated with psychosocial stressors in past studies (see chapters 6 and 7). The top mental health conditions were: bipolar disorders; depression; neurotic, personality, and non-psychotic disorders; alcoholism; anxiety disorders; acute phase schizophrenia; and psychoses. Of these conditions, anxiety disorders, depression, and alcoholism have been shown to have some roots in workplace stressors.

Health Care Premiums

One hundred and fifty-five million non-elderly Americans rely on employers as their main source of health insurance [5]. Sixty-one percent of employers provided coverage for more than 60% of all Americans in 2006 [6]. Ninety-eight percent of all workers participating in employer-sponsored plans had prescription drug benefits in 2006 [7]. According to a 2007 survey of 170 of the United States' largest Fortune 1000 companies with operations in multiple locations nationwide, health care premium costs for U.S. employers were projected to rise by 7%, or two-thirds higher than the consumer price index for the year in which the survey was conducted [8]. Respondents reported spending more than $15 billion annually in premium costs for insured health and dental plans and premium equivalents in the form of estimated benefit and administrative costs for self-insured plans. These were the costs for employers who subsidize only 78% of this year's premium costs, thus leaving their employees to cover the remaining 22% in premiums in addition to deductibles, co-payments, and co-insurance.

According to Kaiser, health care costs have grown at an average annual rate of 9.8% since 1970 or, on average, 2.5 percentage points faster than the U.S. gross domestic product (GDP), faster than overall inflation (3.5%), and wage gains (3.8%) [7]. This figure was corroborated by Towers Perrin's finding that the cost of individual health insurance premiums has increased by more than 60% in just the past 5 years [8]. Kaiser found that premiums for family coverage have increased by 87% since 2000, with current average annual premiums for employer-sponsored coverage at $4,242 for single coverage and $11,480 for family coverage [7].

Health care costs encompass goods and services such as hospital stays and prescription drugs, dental services, and equipment purchases. More than half of the total costs are attributed to hospital care and physicians' services. Any increase in chronic illnesses, such as the ones clearly associated with exposures to workplace stressors, would serve to increase these costs.

Whereas premiums have increased between 8% and 14% every year since 2000, inflation and changes in employees' earnings were in the 3 to 4% range for the same period [7]. This means that workers have to spend more of their income every year on their portion of health care coverage and expenses. The amount of these costs covered by the employer versus the employee varies depending upon the industry and the employer's ability to pay. Sometimes, employers cut costs by requiring the employee to pay a greater percentage of the premiums; at other times they must shoulder greater co-pays at each office visit. Yet other times, the employer may reduce wages or limit wages in order to set off the rising costs associated with health care benefits. According to the U.S. Census Bureau, the percentage of businesses offering health benefits has steadily fallen since 2000 [6]. In addition, health benefits vary considerably by firm size. Nearly all companies with 50 or more employees offer coverage, with firms with more than 200 employees particularly stable over the years, states the Kaiser report [7]. Only 48% of the smallest companies (three to nine workers) offer health benefits (down from 57% in 2000), compared to 73% of firms with 10 to 24 workers, 87% of firms with 25 to 49 workers, and more than 90% of firms with 50 or more workers [7].

One surprising finding in the Towers Perrin study was that there was a wide variation in per capita costs even among companies of similar sizes offering similar benefits. One in five respondent companies reported increases in costs of 11% or greater [8]. Those that reported smaller increases or no increases all had several characteristics in common, the most common being an emphasis on finding more solutions that address the underlying causes of health care cost increases, i.e., preventable illnesses and injuries. Given that many stressors are organizational in nature, it would be an easy place to start making changes in order to see a reduction in costs.

Disability and Workers' Compensation

Disability claims are often associated with blue-collar work and workplace accidents, but 90% of workplace disabilities are the result of illness, not accidents [9]. Psychosocial factors contribute to workers' compensation and disability claims when they play a role in producing health outcomes, usually illnesses, which are recognized as compensable. The research described in some of the other chapters relating job strain and other psychosocial factors to repetitive motion injuries and back and neck injuries is an example of work-related health outcomes which carry a significant cost to the workers' compensation system. On the other hand, a number of health conditions, such as burnout, hypertension, and cardiovascular disease (CVD) which appear to be the result of exposure to workplace psychosocial stressors, are not recognized as yet as work-related disorders. The exclusion of these illnesses from workers' compensation coverage suggests two important and interrelated issues. First, despite a substantial body of scientific literature linking these conditions to causes in the workplace, they are considered primarily to be caused by individual-level risk factors, e.g., inability to cope with stress, poor diet, and exercise and other lifestyle choices. Second, the costs of including these "ordinary diseases of everyday life" must be seen as overly burdensome to the system. However, not including them simply offsets the costs onto health care, partly resulting in escalating health insurance premiums paid by employers anyway. This argument has yet to impact disability and the workers' compensation system.

Disability represents dollars paid in lieu of wages to employees who cannot work because of physical or mental impairments. Direct disability costs include temporary disability, permanent partial, and permanent total disability, disability pension, the disability component of Social Security, and miscellaneous accident insurance. Some economists also include workers' compensation—both medical and indemnity. When an employer purchases insurance to cover the costs of disability benefits, the premiums paid plus the internal expenses of administering the program constitute the direct cost of disability benefits. For self-insured employers, the cost is the actual payout for salary continuance or disability benefits plus the present value of future benefits for these claims. The employer's administrative cost is also usually included [10].

Workers' compensation insurance is mandated by law in all 52 states in the United States. Currently, workers' compensation insurance for employers is compulsory in all states except New Jersey and Texas. Five states, Wyoming, West

Virginia, Washington, Ohio, and North Dakota, require employers to use the state fund as the exclusive insurer. Most states make no numerical exceptions for minimum number of employees per firm in order to require workers' compensation insurance. Six have exceptions for those who employ fewer than three employees, two states have exceptions for fewer than four employees, and four states have exceptions for five or fewer employees. Almost all states provide full medical benefits as part of workers' compensation. Although this insurance is mandatory in most states, benefits vary by state. Benefits for total temporary disability and permanent total disability can vary from 66%-^{2}/₃% of the worker's wages before disability to 80% of the worker's spendable earnings, while those for permanent partial disability range from 55% of the worker's wages before disability to 75% of the worker's spendable earnings [11].

The same way that benefits vary by state, the division of premium contributions between employer and employee also varies. According to the Kaiser report, premiums vary from 9% employee cost and 91% employer cost in Hawaii, to 25% employee cost and 75% employer cost in Alabama. The average cost for employers in all states is 82%. Family premiums also vary in division of cost, from 33% employee/67% employer in South Dakota, to 15% employee/85% employer in Michigan. The average contribution for all employers in all states for family premiums is 76% [7].

Because these contributions are mandated by law and because several states require use of the state fund as the primary insurer, many states have sought to reform their workers' compensation programs in order to cut back on costs to both the states and the employers. One example of this is the state of California, which has one of the most expensive workers' compensation systems in the country. Passed by the state's legislature in 1913, California's workers' compensation law was a no fault-system designed to shield employers from liability regardless of fault and provide workers with appropriate benefits for all work-induced injuries and illnesses. The system costs California employers more than any other state and provides the third lowest benefits to workers. In 1993, compensation costs in California were $9 billion/year. In 2002, the costs had risen to $32 billion [12].

In an attempt to reform the system, the state of California passed legislation in 2002, 2003, and 2004. The legislation enacted in 2002 sought to address the fact that the system had not seen a benefits increase since 1996. The legislation enacted in 2003 and 2004 sought to change some of the provisions passed in 2002. Overall, it is thought that these reforms have decreased overall costs by 45%, but this interpretation is based on several assumptions, including that there has been no change in the types of industries in the state; that if there had been no reforms that the claims costs would have remained more or less the same between 2003 when the first set of changes took effect and 2006 when a study was conducted to assess the impact of the reforms; and that the reported rates are accurate [12]. Findings from a study of the financial impact of these reforms have shown that most of these assumptions were met and that it is reasonable to assume that the 45% cut in costs is also correct, with the caveat that it is too soon to understand the long-term effects.

A 45% cut in costs to the system and subsequent reduction in premium costs for the employer seems like a very good thing on the surface. Unfortunately, some say that these changes will cut costs in the short term and increase them in the long term. The primary way in which costs were cut was by precluding medical care that was deemed unreasonable, unnecessary, or deleterious. This meant primarily cutting out physical therapy and chiropractic services and reducing the total number of occupational therapy sessions to 24, regardless of the severity and type of injury. A second source of savings is in a reduction in total payouts for injuries. In some cases, this reduction is quite significant. For instance, someone who has had an injury that requires spinal vertebral discs to be fused would have received $100,000. Now the same person would receive $10,000 in benefits. This reduction in benefits is even extreme compared to most other states. For example, a loss of a foot in other states would merit an average benefit of $81,000. After the reforms in California, the same injury would merit a benefit of $28,820.

Regardless of the repercussions to the injured individuals or the moral implications, these types of reforms to cut costs may not make sense financially in the long term. The reason they make sense on the surface is because they cut expenses immediately, thus allowing employers to increase their bottom lines via fewer direct expenses. The reason this may not be the best option is that direct costs are only a percentage of the costs that employers pay when an employee becomes injured or ill and reduced short-term services for workers' compensation may result in more long-term illnesses.

INDIRECT COSTS

Indirect costs are more difficult to calculate than direct costs, yet they account for more than half of the expenses associated with employee ill health [13]. The difficulty in calculating these costs lies in the choice of perspective used for the calculations and the fact that there are many layers to the costs involved. Indirect costs will also vary by occupation, industry, illness, race, and gender [14].

In general, indirect costs are the added costs to employers from increased workplace absenteeism/sick leave; short-term and long-term disability management; diminished productivity at work in the form of presenteeism; increased employee turnover; and the cost of law suits related to stress and mental health issues. The National Institute for Occupational Safety and Health estimated these associated costs at more than $200 billion annually for U.S. industry in 1999 if one only took into account absenteeism, tardiness, and employee turnover [15]. Using Kaiser's finding that health-related costs have increased on average 9.8%/per year, and taking into account a total rate of inflation of 25.36% from June 1999 to June 2007 [6], this figure is closer to $407.5 billion today.

As mentioned above, individual indirect costs are difficult to calculate. From the perspective of the individual, indirect costs would include costs to the worker associated with any impairment or loss in the ability to work as manifested through unpaid sick leave and decrement in income while on disability. It would also take into account the loss of an individual's ability to engage in leisure activities because of morbidity or cost of the loss of financial contributions to the worker's dependents due to early mortality. In general, this accounting method values human life in terms of a person's income or value of leisure time. This is a correct formula for calculating indirect cost, but in reality, it has more to do with the cost to the employee than the cost to the employer.

An alternative perspective is a public health perspective. Public health practitioners take a societal perspective to indirect costs, which is based on the idea that the value of an individual's work and thus the cost associated with their inability to work can be measured by the individual's potential to generate income. This perspective is based upon the neo-classical economic model which assumes that a person's earnings reflect a person's productivity and thus their contribution to society. It is the perspective most commonly used by economists when calculating health-related indirect costs.

The greatest drawback of the public health perspective is that it undervalues workers who earn at the lowest levels. In addition, some have argued that this perspective does not truly reflect the needs of the employer because an employer would be more interested in the cost of lost production and idle assets due to morbidity and the costs of re-hiring and retaining replacement workers in the case of mortality than in the present value of future earnings foregone [16]. For this reason, this section on indirect costs will report on findings from studies that have used the more common "lost-wages" approach to calculating indirect health-related expenses and thus more closely reflect the costs to the business sector and society as a whole, as well as findings from studies that have used newer models for accounting for indirect costs that are meant to more closely reflect the costs to individual employers.

Mortality

Indeed, there are many layers of costs related to work-induced injury or illness. Indirect costs depend not just upon the accounting method used, but also upon the level of severity of the illness or injury. The most severe case, of course, would be the case of worker death. Indirect costs associated with worker mortality would include the cost of replacing the employee, which will be further examined under the heading of turnover, and the value of lost future income.

Simply replacing the employee is not the employer's only concern. The death of an employee has other repercussions, including an increase in work burden, and thus increased psychosocial stressors on the remaining employees on top of any mental health effects that the death may have had on individual co-workers, thus affecting their levels of productivity and their own chances of suffering from ill health. According to Pollard, increased work burden has been shown to significantly increase psychological distress and systolic blood pressure [17].

Disability

The total indirect cost of disability is calculated as the sum of hidden costs and management costs. Although employers intuitively acknowledge the hidden costs of disability, usually they are unable to measure these costs even in organizations with sophisticated databases. The primary component of hidden disability costs is usually lost productivity, which can be calculated in terms of individual salary plus benefits for the time the employee is not fully replaced. The assumption is that an employee will produce a value amount equivalent to, if not more, than the amount that individual is being paid by his or her employer. This factor will be further discussed in the next section on productivity.

Disability management costs include programs designed to prevent the occurrence of disabilities or minimize their impact if they do occur. The costs of these programs include overhead costs associated with establishing and administering the programs, as well as case management expenses, return-to-work programs, wellness programs, employee assistance plans (EAP), medical clinics specializing in minimizing disability, and safety programs [18].

Specific Illnesses/Morbidity

Earlier in this chapter, we mentioned the illnesses found to have the greatest impact on business expenses in terms of direct costs. It may come as no surprise that these same illnesses have been identified as causing the most in terms of indirect costs to the employer [4]. Approximately half of these identified illnesses have been associated with workplace stressors. Table 1 is a chart of the indirect costs to the employer associated with some of these illnesses. The data are based on findings from Goetzel et al. [4]. Indirect costs to employers per employee are calculated by adding the total costs from presenteeism (decreased work performance), absenteeism, and short-term disability management.

The calculation uses the 2001 average hourly compensation rate of $23.15 as a basis for calculating costs for absenteeism and presenteeism. The third column of the table adjusts for the updated hourly compensation rate for 2007 ($25.91) according to the Bureau of Labor Statistics. Although the increased hourly compensation rate somewhat adjusts for inflation rates, assuming that hourly compensation

Table 1. Indirect Costs for Employers of Work-Related Illnesses
($ per Person/per Year)

Medical condition	Indirect cost 2001 ($)	Indirect cost adjusted compensation rate ($)	Indirect cost adjusted total inflation rate ($)
Depression	293.85	328.88	343.95
Heart disease	102.62	114.85	120.12
Hypertension	300.88	336.75	352.18
Diabetes	182.16	203.88	213.22
Migraines/ chronic headaches	196.70	220.15	230.24

rates are keeping up with inflation, it does not adjust for the inflated cost of idle assets; thus, it is best to also adjust for the total inflation rate, which in this case would be 17.05% from June 2001 to June 2007 [6].

PRODUCTIVITY

Productivity measures are being used more often in business to calculate costs other than direct and indirect costs related to illness. These are often "hidden costs" which have been strongly associated with exposure to psychosocial stressors at work, including turnover, absenteeism, and "presenteeism" or decreased work performance. Unlike illness or injury costs, these costs evolve as employees seek to cope with difficulties that may arise in their personal lives (e.g., caring for a sick parent or children), as well as from exposure to a stressful work environment. Locating the causes of these productivity issues needs to extend beyond the individual's private life to consider causes in the work environment.

Turnover

Increased turnover rates have been associated with several psychosocial stressors in the workplace including lack of work-life balance [19], effort-reward imbalance [20], and job strain [21]. It has been estimated that up to 40% of turnover can be attributed to stressors at work [22]. The 2000 Integra Realty Resources study found that 19% of respondents had quit a job in the past because of stress [23].

Replacing an employee can be a very expensive proposition. Once the employee decides to leave or is fired, there are the costs of separation pay in the case of termination, cost of the exit interviewer's time, and administrative, accounting, and legal costs. Vacancy costs include overtime pay for remaining employees, the cost of temporary workers, minus the amount saved in wages and benefits from having one less employee. During the vacancy period, there are hiring costs, which include advertising for the position or use of a hiring agency, the cost of screening applicants, the cost of interviews, testing costs, administrative, accounting and legal costs, and the possible costs related to travel and moving expenses and the cost of medical exams. After a new employee is hired, there are still formal training costs, other staff time for on-the-job training, and salary during formal and informal training. These are just the direct costs of replacing an employee. On another level, there are indirect costs such as the cost of lost productivity during transition, lost sales, lost intellectual capital, lost or damaged relationships with customers, the cost of rebuilding relationships inside and outside of the company, integration costs for the new employee, impacts on co-workers due to increased stressors resulting in increased absenteeism and lost productivity, cost impacts on suppliers due to interruption of efficiencies, cost of inefficiencies on the part of the departing employee, and the cost of inefficiency due to learning curves on the part of the new employee.

It is estimated that turnover costs average 120-200% of the salary of the position affected [24]. A research study by Nextera Enterprises Inc. suggested that industries with high turnover rates, such as retail, have 38% lower earnings and stock prices

due to replacement costs alone [25] and another study of 1,750 American manufacturing plants found that workers at plants with a turnover rate of less than 3%
had nearly 170% of the productivity of those at plants with turnover rates of
more than 20% [26].

Absenteeism/Sickness Absence

The nature and number of employees' unscheduled absences has changed significantly over the last several years. According to the 2006 CCH Unscheduled
Absence Survey, absenteeism is up at its highest reported rate, yet personal illness
as a cause of absenteeism has dropped from 45% of total unscheduled absences
in 1995 to 35% in 2006 and workplace stress has increased from causing 6% to
12% of unscheduled absences in the same time period [27]. It is important to
note that the other non-health-related reasons given for absenteeism—family issues,
time for personal needs, and an "entitlement mentality"—all can be interpreted as
indicators of psychosocial workplace stressors, such as lack of work-life balance
and effort-reward imbalance.

In general, the following demographic characteristics have been associated with
increased absenteeism: being female, full-time, high tenure, low wage [28], working
in the health and social services industries or working for a company with more
than 500 employees [29], and belonging to a union [30]. The following work factors
have been associated with sickness absence in past studies: long hours worked;
work overload and high pressure; lack of control over work; lack of participation
in decision-making; poor social support; and unclear management and work role.
One recent study by Andrea et al. [31] found that job characteristics such as lower
levels of decision latitude (i.e., job control) and the presence of one long-term
disease were the strongest predictors of sickness absences exceeding a 1-month
duration. A meta-analysis conducted by Darr reviewed 175 studies that examined
the relationship between stress at work and absenteeism [32]. They concluded
that an indirect causal relationship exists whereby stressors cause illness which
then results in increased absenteeism. They also found a direct relationship by
which absenteeism resulted as an adaptive coping response to the effects of stress by
limiting exposure at times when the individual was most vulnerable to ill health.
Regardless of whether absenteeism is used as a stress moderator or whether it is an
indirect cause of stress in the workplace, it still affects the bottom line.

According to the U.S. Bureau of Labor Statistics, companies lose approximately
2.8 million workdays each year because of unscheduled absences in the workplace
[15]. In 2002, the average cost of this absenteeism was estimated at $789.00/worker/
year nationally or, for large employers, more than $3.6 million/year/per company
[15]. A more recent study conducted by CCH Incorporated found that the
absenteeism rate has been increasing steadily since 2000, and along with it, the
average per-employee direct payroll cost [27]. Overall, they found that unscheduled
absences have increased by a total of 24% within this 5-year period. Many of
the costs associated with absenteeism stem from the need to hire temporary staff,
pay overtime to permanent staff or overstaffing to prevent loss of productivity during

unscheduled absences. Those companies that do not do this pay in other ways when the increased burden of work affects the rest of their workforce.

Decreased Work Performance (Presenteeism)

There is a problematic assumption that an employee who is not absent is being productive. Therefore, an employee who is present longer at work should be producing more. However, even when employees are physically present at their jobs, they may experience decreased and below-normal work quality—a concept known as "presenteeism." A major concern to employers, this phenomenon is often referred to as LPT or LWPT (lost (work) productive time), and is characterized by 1) time not on task, 2) decreased quality of work, 3) decreased quantity of work, and 4) unsatisfactory employee interpersonal factors. Some data suggest that presenteeism is a larger productivity drain than either absenteeism or short-term disability. In 1999, the Employee Health Coalition of Tampa, Florida, found that lost productivity from presenteeism was actually 7.5 times greater than productivity loss from absenteeism [33].

Overall, presenteeism is costly to the employer and the workforce. It has been estimated that presenteeism costs U.S. companies $250 billion/year or approximately $2,000 per worker/year [34]. Presenteeism has been identified in studies of specific illnesses in the workplace, including migraines and depression [35], as well as studies of work-life balance [36].

A study conducted by Stewart et al. [37] found that productive time lost due to common pain conditions such as headaches, back pain, and arthritis costs U.S. employers more than $61 billion each year and that most of that lost time is caused by impaired performance at work rather than workplace absence. Unfortunately, the costs of presenteeism are compounded because employees who work when ill generally cost more in the long run from increased utilization of general and mental health services and short-term disability.

An economic analysis of several health and insurance databases by Goetzel et al. found that presenteeism was most likely to be associated with the following conditions in order of economic impact to employers: arthritis, hypertension, depression/sadness/mental illness, allergies, migraine/headaches, cancer, asthma, heart disease, and respiratory infections [4]. The average annual loss per company per employee per condition was $156.66. Below is a chart reflecting costs to the employer due to some of these specific illnesses. All data in Table 2 are based on findings from Goetzel et al. [4], and are calculated based on indirect costs to employers per employee due to total costs from presenteeism.

The calculation uses the 2001 average hourly compensation rate of $23.15 as a basis for calculating costs for presenteeism. The third column of the table adjusts for the updated hourly compensation rate for 2007 ($25.91) according to the Bureau of Labor Statistics. Although the increased hourly compensation rate somewhat adjusts for inflation rates, assuming that hourly compensation rates are keeping up with inflation, it does not adjust for the inflated cost of idle assets, thus, it is best to also adjust for the total inflation rate, which in this case would be 17.05% from June 2001 to June 2007 [6].

Table 2. Indirect Costs to Employers per Employee Due to
Total Costs from Presenteeism

Medical condition	Presenteeism cost 2001 per person/per year	Presenteeism adjusted compensation rate	Presenteeism adjusted total inflation rate
Depression	246.00	275.33	287.94
Heart disease	70.53	78.94	82.55
Hypertension	246.73	276.15	288.80
Diabetes	158.75	177.68	185.82
Migraines/ chronic headaches	189.23	211.79	221.49

Presenteeism often occurs when workers come to work even when they are not feeling well. Employers often blame individual workers for decreased productivity at work, yet the reasons for working when ill vary. Some working people feel they have a commitment to the job including to co-workers and the company. Others cannot afford to take sick days or to go on disability, many have no entitlement to paid sick days, and others are afraid to lose their jobs (employment insecurity) by not being ever-present on the job. Sometimes it is for a combination of these reasons. Oftentimes, presenteeism is a response to job stressors, overwork, and company policies. According to the CCH, 2006 Unscheduled Absence Survey disciplinary action remained the single-most used absence control program, with 91% of surveyed organizations reporting its use [27]. Employers want their employees on the job and using as few sick days as possible, but relying on disciplinary action to control absenteeism actually can be more costly because it can produce presenteeism.

CONCLUSION

Employers are often under pressure from analysts, board members, creditors, and shareholders who demand to see positive short-term performance indicators such as revenue growth, positive financial ratios, and earnings. When the economic market becomes more competitive, ethical behavior and long-term goals appear to become of less importance than short-term gains. Business leadership (management) is just as fearful of employment insecurity as the people they employ. The inability to produce an increase in shareholder value is a sure way to make that employment insecurity a reality. In addition, top management and policy-makers are often tempted by lucrative bonuses that make short-term objectives much more appealing than long-term goals. These pressures can force decision-makers to push their managers and employees to meet objectives that can be both unreasonable and unsustainable. In order to meet these objectives, managers often adopt policies and create corporate cultures that encourage unhealthy working environments.

The direct and indirect costs to companies discussed in this chapter can be estimated in the hundreds of billions of dollars and are the consequences of the way work is organized. These costs reflect social decisions on the part of ownership and management as to how to maximize productivity and a lack of awareness of the harm resulting from these decisions. In short, unhealthy work environments are ripe with stressors that will cause illness and eventually take their toll on workers and on the bottom line. Simply because stress is not a standard accounting line item on a financial spreadsheet does not mean that it is insignificant in its financial toll on organizations. This chapter has presented a small amount of the evidence showing that stressors can have both direct and indirect costs to businesses.

REFERENCES

1. *OSHA News Release: Statement by U.S. Secretary of Labor Elaine L. Chao on 2006 Workplace Injury and Illness Rates,* October 16 2007, cited 2008 04/24/08], OSHA News Release, available from: http://www.dol.gov/opa/media/press/osha/osha20071599.htm
2. Auman, J. and B. Draheim, The Downside to Downsizing, in *Benefits Canada,* pp. 31-33, May 1997.
3. Lublin, J. S., Mergers Often Trigger Anxiety, Lower Morale, *The Wall Street Journal,* January 16, 2001.
4. Goetzel, R. Z., S. R. Long, R. J. Ozminkowski, K. Hawkins, S. Wang, and W. Lynch, Health, Absence, Disability, and Presenteeism Cost Estimates of Certain Physical and Mental Health Conditions Affecting U.S. Employers, *Journal of Occupational and Environmental Medicine,* 46:4, pp. 398-412, 2004.
5. Claxton, G., J. Gabel, I. Gil, et al., Health Benefits in 2006: Premium Increases Moderate, Enrollment in Consumer-Directed Health Plans Remains Modest, *Health Affairs Web Exclusive,* pp. w476-w485, 2006.
6. U.S. Census Bureau, Revised CPS ASEC Health Insurance Data, March 23, 2007. http://www.census.gov/hhes/www/hlthins/usernote/schedule.html
7. Kaiser Family Foundation (KFF) and Health Research and Educational Trust (HRET), *Employer Health Benefits 2006 Annual Survey,* Author, Washington, DC, September 2006.
8. Towers Perrin, 2007 Healthcare Cost Survey, March 2007, cited March 2007, available from:
http://www.towersperrin.com/tp/getwebcachedoc?webc=HRS/USA/2007/200703/07HCSSfinal.pdf
9. Woodward, N. H., Supplemental Ltd Plans Can Reduce Executive Discrimination—Focus on Technology—Long-Term Disability, *HR Magazine,* December 1998.
10. Knowles, S. and P. D. Owen, Educational and Health in an Effective-Labour Empirical Growth Model, *Economic Record,* 73, pp. 314-328, 1997.
11. Clayton, A., Workers Compensation: A Background for Social Security Professionals, *Social Security Bulletin,* 65:4, 2003/2004.
12. State of California Commission on Health and Safety and Workers' Compensation, *2006 Annual Report,* December 2006.
13. Goetzel, R. Z., The Financial Impact of Health Promotion and Disease Prevention Programs—Why Is It So Hard to Prove Value?, *American Journal of Health Promotion,* 15:5, pp. 277-280, 2001.

14. Waehrer, G., J. P. Leigh, D. Cassady, and T. R. Miller, Costs of Occupational Injury and Illness across States, *Journal of Occupational & Environmental Medicine,* 46:10, pp. 1084-1095, 2004.
15. NIOSH, Costs of Absenteeism, cited 2002, available from: http://hr.cch.com/default.asp?subframe=/press/releases/101602a.asp
16. Berger, M. L., J. F. Murray, J. Xu, and M. Pauly, Alternative Valuations of Work Loss and Productivity, *Journal of Occupational & Environmental Medicine,* 43:1, pp. 18-24, 2001.
17. Pollard, T., Changes in Mental Well-Being, Blood Pressure and Total Cholesterol Levels During Workplace Reorganization: The Impact of Uncertainty, *Work & Stress,* 15:1, pp. 14-28, 2001.
18. Chelius, J., D. Galvin, and P. Owens, Disability: It's More Expensive Than You Think, *Business and Health,* 11:4, pp. 78-84, 1992.
19. Hobson, C. J., L. Delunas, and D. Kesic, Compelling Evidence of the Need for Corporate Work/Life Balance Initiatives: Results from a National Survey of Stressful Life Events, *Journal of Employment Counseling,* 38, pp. 38-44, 2001.
20. Hasselhorn, H., P. Tackenberg, and R. Peter, Effort-Reward Imbalance among Nurses in Stable Countries and in Countries in Transition, *International Journal of Occupational and Environmental Health,* 10:4, pp. 401-408, 2004.
21. de Croon, E., J. Sluiter, R. Blonk, et al., Stressful Work, Psychological Job Strain, and Turnover: A 2-Year Prospective Study of Truck Drivers, *Journal of Applied Psychology,* 89:3, pp. 442-454, 2004.
22. Hoel, H., K. Sparks, and C. Cooper, *The Cost of Violence/Stress at Work and the Benefits of a Violence/Stress-Free Working Environment,* International Labour Organisation (ILO), Geneva, Switzerland, 2001.
23. Flash, What Is the Cost of Employee Turnover?, *Compensation & Benefits Review,* September/October 1997: Article # 8582, 1998.
24. Phillips, J., The Pricetag on Turnover, *Personnel Journal,* 69:12, p. 58, 1999.
25. Sibson Consulting, *Employee Turnover Depresses Earnings, Stock Prices by 38%, Nextera Research Study Shows,* PR Newswire, Princeton, NJ, 2000.
26. Jusko, J., Paying the Price (Cost of High Employee Turnover to Manufacturing Production), *Industry Week,* 2000.
27. CCH Incorporated, 2006 CCH Unscheduled Absence Survey, cited June 1, 2007, available from: http://hr.cch.com/topic-spotlight/hrm/101206a.asp
28. Drago, R. and M. Wooden, The Determinants of Labor Absence: Economic Factors and Workgroup Norms across Countries, *Industrial and Labor Relations Review,* 45:4, p. 776, 1992.
29. Akyeampong, E. and J. Usalcas, Work Absence Rates 1980-1997, *Statistics Canada,* Cat. No. 71-535-MPB, No. 9.
30. Vistnes, J., Gender Differences in Days Lost from Work Due to Illness, *Industrial and Labor Relations Review,* 50:2, pp. 304-323, 1997.
31. Andrea, H., I. J. Kant, A. J. H. M. Beurskens, J. E. M. Metsemakers, and C. P. van Schayck, Associations between Fatigue Attributions and Fatigue, Health, and Psychosocial Work Characteristics: A Study among Employees Visiting a Physician with Fatigue, *Occupational and Environmental Medicine,* 60:(Suppl 1), pp. 99-104, 2003.
32. Darr, W., *Examining the Relationship between Stress and Absenteeism: A Research Synthesis,* Concordia University, Canada, p. 191, 2005.
33. Loeppke, R., P. A. Hymel, J. H. Lofland, et al., Health-Related Workplace Productivity Measurement: General and Migraine-Specific Recommendations from the Acoem

Expert Panel, *Journal of Occupational & Environmental Medicine,* 45:4, pp. 349-359, 2003.

34. *BNA Human Resources Bulletin,* December 2002.

35. Druss, B., M. Schlesinger, and H. M. Allen, Depressive Symptoms, Satisfaction with Health Care, and 2-Year Work Outcomes in an Employed Population, *American Journal of Psychiatry,* 158:5, pp. 731-734, 2001.

36. Higgins, C., L. Duxbury, and D. Coghill, Voices of Canada: Seeking Work-Life Balance, Report for Canada's Department of Human Resources and Skills Development (HRSD), in *The 2001 National Study on Balancing Work, Family and Lifestyle,* 2003.

37. Stewart, W., J. Ricci, E. Chee, S. Hahn, and D. Moganstein, Cost of Lost Productive Work Time among US Workers with Depression, *Journal of the American Medical Association,* 289:23, pp. 3135-3144, 2003.

PART III

Interventions

OVERVIEW

The final section of this book describes some of the more innovative stratagems taking place in American society and elsewhere related to the protection of workers' health. Revealed repeatedly in this section are successful approaches to changing and improving work organization in order to diminish or eliminate threats to workers' health. They employ two common elements: they draw on the body of scientific knowledge and rely on principles of collectivity. Underlying these elements is the notion of "balance of power" between workers and managers. It is clear that maintaining an understanding of what is demonstrated in the scientific literature, or at least liaising with people who are abreast of the body of knowledge, is important in achieving positive change. With these powerful tools in hand, numerous successful work organization change interventions have been achieved, using varied approaches. Innovative stratagems tailor the approach used to the nature of the workforce, the workplace, the type of work performed, and the type of labor-management relations and agreements that may exist.

Successful change initiatives described in this section have drawn on the strength and power that exist in collective bargaining agreements, labor-management partnerships, and from participatory action research. What is perhaps the most important message emerging from part III of this book is that strong collective voice is the singularly most important element found among all of the various interventions described. To date, few work organization change initiatives have succeeded in the absence of strong collective voice. Strong laws and regulations are also essential and much needed, but also need to be respected and enforced. During the last 25 years, the United States has witnessed a diminished lack of commitment to existing laws and regulations. Shown throughout this section, laws and regulations alone are not enough to protect workers' health; other mechanisms are needed to ensure the implementation of statutory laws and regulations.

A recent article by Nichols et al. [1] found that for the protection of workers' health, workplaces where trade unions have input into health and safety committees and where there are union representatives are to be preferred to those where there is no such trade union input or no representation. Some Western European countries introduced regulatory measures for regional or territorial safety representatives—a mechanism whereby trade union resources in the health and safety field can be extended to vulnerable workplaces.

The protection of workers' health has not been a priority on management agendas in the United States similar to most other countries. One major reason for this is the lack of adequate and strong statutory regulation in the United States. Over the last 20 years, statutory regulation has shifted to be dominated by "voluntary" initiatives, often presented as "safety culture" themes. Such themes risk being mere euphemisms when voluntary initiatives are backed up by little or no enforcement and little threat of penalty for wrong-doers. Without statutory regulations, enforcement, financial incentives, and strong collective voice, workers' health remains conspicuously absent from management agendas.

Weak statutory regulation and diminished collective voice are two obvious reasons for the lack of widespread initiatives. Deborah Gordon, Maritza Jauregui, and Peter Schnall provide in chapter 10 unique evidence and analysis of some heretofore un-described reasons for the lack of attention paid to the impacts of work organization on workers' health. A lack of dialogue and a lack of common understanding about the meaning and context of work stress among various key stakeholders—including business, unions, government, and researchers—appear to be holding back advancement in this area. Through interviews with key informants, Deborah Gordon describes how various stakeholders may appear to speak the same language while in reality they are not and they lack a common understanding of terms, experiences, approaches, and perceptions about the adverse effects of work organization today. Improved communication is, therefore, an essential area for future work among all of the key stakeholder groups, bearing in mind the social, political, and economic disincentives for management to make changes based on any such common understanding.

Regardless of stakeholder differences, a wide variety of interventions and prevention programs have been developed and used to reduce job stressors and the health problems they cause. These interventions can be carried out at the level of the job, at the level of the organization, at the level of the individual, or at a state or national level through laws and regulations. In chapter 11, Paul Landsbergis reviews the various levels of work organization interventions and the different stages of prevention, exploring collective work alternatives in contrast to Fordism and lean production in automobile manufacturing. Among his conclusions, he finds that effective interventions tend to be those involving "systems approaches," which focus on both primary prevention, that is, changing the causes of work stress such as work schedules and workload, and include secondary and tertiary levels of prevention, with programs to help employees suffering symptoms of stress or who have become ill due to job stressors. Landsbergis' review of the literature reveals that effective interventions also include meaningful participation of employees, increasing employees' job control, and ensuring top management support.

Participatory Action Research (PAR), a multidisciplinary research methodology for the epidemiological study of health issues in worker populations, is presented by Ellen Rosskam in chapter 12. The chapter discusses how PAR, by incorporating the knowledge and participation of workers themselves in the research process, is leading to concrete, measurable improvements in worker health and working conditions. By using the example of her recent work with airport check-in workers, Rosskam concludes that it is precisely through intervention-based research and the adequate evaluation of that research that public health and occupational health make advances.

Chapter 13 by Ray Antonio, June Fisher, and Ellen Rosskam, highlights the way in which the problems in the work environment of the San Francisco Municipal Railway (MUNI) workers impact the health of San Francisco transport workers. Union-management-researcher collaboration on a study of hypertension and work stress among San Francisco bus drivers led to a unique intervention program aimed at improving the difficult working conditions that bus drivers face. The outcomes demonstrate how research findings can be combined with union organizing efforts to achieve sustainable improvements and policy-level changes. The research and interventions described in this chapter focused on the work environment, not on individual behaviors. Trade union/researcher participatory action research aimed at structural, not individual level, change is also presented by Mike Casey and Ellen Rosskam in chapter 14. They show how union organizing and collaborating with labor-supportive researchers led to significant changes aimed at reducing injuries among hotel room cleaners in San Francisco. The chapter outlines the effects of downsizing, cost-cutting, and the resulting intensification of workloads on the health of hotel workers—particularly exacerbated post-9/11—and the organizing efforts of union members in San Francisco around these issues. By carrying out a housekeeping workload study, the local union was able to help workers success-fully negotiate a new contract that made important advances toward alleviating the impacts of workload on housekeepers.

Lilia Garcia presents in chapter 15 the accomplishments of the Maintenance Cooperation Trust Fund (MCTF). Established under the auspices of the Taft Hartley Act, MCTF represents non-union janitors in their quest to recover back wages or in other legal claims (e.g., OSHA violations) against unscrupulous employers and to establish a "level playing field" for the janitorial industry. Employers of unionized workers in the janitorial industry pay into the MCTF and the fund is governed by both employers and the union (in this case the Service Employees International Union local), representing another form of labor-employer collaboration.

Sociopolitical and structural obstacles inhibit occupational physicians from more direct access to the workplace. In chapter 16, Dean Baker, Marnie Dobson, and Peter Schnall explore the role of occupational and environmental medicine (OEM) as a location of intervention. The substance of occupational medicine is constrained by the limits of the workers' compensation system of reimbursable work-related illnesses as well as by the costs to the employer. In the United States, OEM doctors working for companies or contracted as consultants lack the power or authority to be able to conduct surveillance programs or to recommend workplace interventions, yet models exist in other countries where OEM doctors do have such authority, backed by national policies. The authors conclude that a paradigm shift is called for, which must be accompanied by government regulation requiring employers to create healthy work environments, and that implementing a national health care system or national insurance program is the key obstacle to overcome in order to develop a public health approach to the workplace based on prevention.

Stephen Smith's innovative essay in chapter 17 offers an essential series of interventions for those workers on the "front line" of the fast-growing service sector of the economy. Many service workers perform "emotional labor," putting on a "front" or a "smiling face" in order to serve customers or the general public. Smith suggests ways to mitigate the possible negative human costs for emotional laborers by recommending a "Commission of Inquiry" to better understand the conditions of emotional labor, better training of emotional laborers, and calls for us as members of society to participate in improving the conditions for the workers from whose services we often benefit.

In response to the changes in the conditions of work brought about by globalization and economic liberalization, Ellen Rosskam proposes in chapter 18 an expanded concept for the way in which "occupational health and safety" is understood and defined. A "rights-based" approach for redefining concepts underlying the field of occupational health is proposed as a departure from medical, engineering, and technocratic approaches to occupational health. The proposed approach is based on principles of universalism and basic rights due to all citizens. A work security index is presented as a benchmarking system for evaluating how well local, state, or national level governments perform in protecting workers' health.

REFERENCE

1. Nichols, T., D. Walters, and A. Tasiran, Trade Unions, Institutional Mediation and Industrial Safety: Evidence from the UK. *Journal of Industrial Relations,* 49:2, pp. 211-225, 2007.

CHAPTER 10

Stakeholder Perspectives on Work and Stress: Seeking Common Ground

*Deborah R. Gordon, Maritza Jauregui,
and Peter L. Schnall*

Most would agree that work, health, and illness cause serious concern for many people in the United States today: from a crisis in the workers' compensation system to one around health insurance and work; from the problems resulting from an aging workforce to a crisis over the excessive cost of health care in general; from the downsizing and outsourcing of industries to the upsizing of job demands, work load, and pace of work; and from the crumbling of hard-earned protections of worker health and safety to the increasing identification of sweat-shop conditions both abroad and in the United States. In fact, work, ill health, and their costs frequently figure center stage—explicitly or implicitly—in many important societal battles over the relative responsibilities of government, business, and individuals for the health and sickness of the citizens of the United States. And it is common knowledge today that a pressured work pace and excessive workload are stressful, that too much stress at work is bad for your health, and that it is increasing. Yet, any consensus about this common knowledge quickly dissolves into a series of disconnects when addressing the hotly contested topic of work-induced stress.

• Yes, on the one hand, discussion of work stress is ubiquitous and a worldwide concern [1-3]; in 2003, three million hits were made on the words on the internet [4]. From one-third to one-fourth of sampled workers in the United States report that they are "very" or "always" stressed at work [5]; a similar situation is found in Europe [6], Australia [3], and Brazil [1]. Some analysts seek to explain the "work stress epidemic" and its powerful hold on public and scientific imaginations [7-9], including very public litigation cases.

  Yet the very experience of work stress by employees, particularly its deleterious impact on mental and physical well-being, is often minimized and even denied by employers [3, 9].

173

• One reads that job stress is one of the most costly of all disabilities to employees, to the state, and one would assume to employers [2, 3, 10], in that the median absence for disability due to stress is four-fold longer than the median for disability from other causes [11] and that health care costs for cases with high stress are 50% higher than other illnesses [1].

Yet these costs are rarely calculated or named in the cost-accounting and calculations of productivity used by business; little research on the impact of work stress on the organization has been conducted [6], and full and precise figures of cost are not at hand [1].

• From the perspective of business and management, work stress is often considered fundamental to high productivity. As affirmed by one business administrator interviewed for this chapter, "Stress is positive, it motivates, increases productivity, gets the most out of you."

Yet most of the literature in occupational health documents the many negative health and well-being consequences of this stress for employees [1-3].

Can they be talking about the same "work stress?" Can they be counting the same costs? In many cases, the answer is "No."

Adversarial relations are almost inherent in a capitalist economic system, as ready-made labels such as "labor" and "management" indicate, making the quest for a common ground and shared language about the nature and extent of work stress a serious and political challenge; much is at stake in the naming. One potential mediator in this picture has been science, carrying its own authority by virtue of its rigorous commitment to objectivity and therefore presumed neutrality. But as the debate about climate change and other topics illustrates daily, politics and economics have everything to do with what scientific knowledge gets produced, heard, interpreted, implemented, translated, ignored, or quashed.

Such could well be the case with the substantial and convincing international body of scientific knowledge that documents the impact of stress on worker health engendered by the way work is organized—from cardiovascular disease [12] to musculoskeletal disorders [13-15] to depression and metabolic disorders [6, 16]. This particular model of job stress—variously referred to as workplace stressors, work-related stress, psychosocial stressors in the workplace, job-strain, effort-reward imbalance, organization of work and occupational health and safety [17]— locates the primary sources of stress, "the stressors," in the work environment, specifically in particular ways in which work is organized.

The models and questionnaires used to measure and interpret this stress aim primarily at describing *the workplace characteristics, not the employee's emotions.* Several particular job characteristics have been identified as hazardous with long-term exposure. One is the job-strain model [18], in which strain results from a combination of high psychological demands coupled with low control over carrying out the work tasks. The second, the effort-reward imbalance model [19], locates the primary source of stress in a perceived imbalance between the effort one puts out and the rewards one receives. In other words, a sensed lack of reciprocity experienced over time has been shown to arouse stress and have health consequences for the people involved. The terms organization of work or work organization were initially used to refer to these characteristics of high-demand/low-control, high-effort/low-reward. They gained additional meaning in the 1990s and beyond with the increasing changes in the organization of work, such as lean production and contingent work [17].

In sharp contrast to European countries (such as Sweden, Finland, and Denmark) and Japan, where this knowledge is more readily produced and has been translated into European Union workplace policies, guidelines, and legislation [2, 6], in the United States this same body of knowledge has had little diffusion and impact on policy, medical practice, occupational health, and even the labor movement. This is so despite explicit recognition in government-sponsored National Institute for Occupational Safety and Health (NIOSH) publications and research agendas of the impacts of work-induced stress on health and the importance of work organization in determining health outcomes [17, 20]. Instead, in the United States, most interventions to reduce job stress, such as stress management programs, have focused primarily on treating the individual worker, aiming at differential individual vulnerabilities rather than on the systemic characteristics of the workplace [5]. More importantly, concerns for the health consequences of the ways people work are being trumped by employment insecurity (job loss, in particular) and the loss of health benefits.

Why has this information had such minimal impact in the United States? Why do these disconnects persist? What are the political, economic, and cultural dynamics of the limited circulation and impact of this approach to work stressors? And what can be done about it?

It was these questions and the fundamental contrast between the robust and important body of knowledge and its relative silence in the United States that were the impetuses for epidemiologists Drs. Peter Schnall, Dean Baker, Paul Landsbergis, and Julia Fawcett—all university-affiliated researchers and leaders in occupational health—to propose convening a state Forum in California in 2004 at which the multiple players (stakeholders) in the field could come together. As director of the Center for Social Epidemiology, Schnall had already established a website on work and stress (www.workhealth.org) as well as the California Work and Health Study Group (CWHSG) that met bi-annually in Northern and Southern California to present and discuss issues related to work, stress, and health. After a few years of meetings of the California Study Group and international meetings (such as the International Conference on Occupational Health) with European, Japanese, and other colleagues working on similar questions, the contrast between the growing body of knowledge and its application in Europe and Japan, and its lack of diffusion in the United States became the object of reflection and concern, leading to the proposal for a state Forum. High priority was given to involve influential representatives from both the major camps—business/management and labor—and to expand the network to include new people and constituencies.

The challenge of seeking a common language began immediately in planning the Forum. What to call the Forum? How to propose it? Whom to invite? How to conduct it in a way that would make the various constituencies feel it worth their while to participate? They were all questions actively and repeatedly discussed among the planning committee formed for the Forum.

One strategic approach taken to help answer these questions was to carry out exploratory, anthropological research in the form of interviews with opinion leaders of various constituencies, both state-wide in California and nationally. The research questions were guided by four aims: 1) to gain an empirical description of the interviewees' awareness and understanding of this body of data about psychosocial stressors and their health implications, including familiarity, understandings and associations with some of the technical terms used; 2) to identify current priorities and perspectives of different stakeholders; 3) to identify potential speakers and participants for the Forum; and 4) to provide feedback to the Forum planning committee on language (e.g., what to call the Forum), content, and process based on stakeholders' current priorities and suggestions. In this way, the research itself constituted an intervention, by expanding the network, by spreading the word about the Forum, by interviewing and exploring potential candidates for speakers at the Forum, as well as by exploring the extent of familiarity and understanding of concepts and health problems amid a range of informants.

In this chapter, we present and analyze our findings from this research project and the Forum itself as follows: 1) the technical terms in this epidemiological research used to specify stress caused primarily by the social environment of work—job strain, effort-reward imbalance, psychosocial stressors, and work organization—are minimally known, poorly understood by many of the stakeholder groups, and often lumped together with more diffuse and psychological notions of stress used in everyday and professional contexts; work stress was nearly always considered something a worker experiences and declares; 2) the term "stress"—and more specifically "work stress" or "job stress"—is powerfully multi-vocal and steeped with conflicting political, economic, moral, and ideological implications that vary significantly according to power relations as reflected in class, gender, age, industry, and perspective, thus making the politics of speaking about and recognizing work stress a highly contested issue; and 3) many political, economic, and cultural obstacles limit the impact of this social view of workplace stressors. Foremost among the cultural is the hegemony of an individualist approach to health and illness that places responsibility for health on the individual, that preserves the autonomy of the free-market, that calculates on the basis of short-term rather than long-term costs, and that makes even conceptualizing linkages between the social environment and stress extremely difficult.

AN INTERVIEW STUDY OF OPINION LEADERS

The interview study with opinion leaders from a range of constituencies or stakeholder groups involved in work and health took place in 2003 and 2004 and was designed and directed by medical anthropologist Gordon and epidemiologist/occupational health physician Schnall. As leaders, most of the informants were not rank-and-file employees, but were asked to speak about those whom they represented. The interview questions—many open or semi-structured— were first pilot-tested with colleagues in public and occupational health in California, and then at a national conference on workers' compensation held in Southern California in May 2003. The latter brought together a broad spectrum of national leaders, including some from NIOSH. Whenever possible, these pilot interviews were conducted with at least two team members present, both for evaluation and standardization of the interviews. The interviews were also used to solicit suggestions of content and people to invite to the Forum. Some of the initial interviews in particular, were partial but useful in contributing another "voice" and material for understanding a perspective.

Purposive, opportunistic, and then snow-ball sampling led to more than 40 conversations/interviews with representatives of different target groups, which were conducted either face-to-face or by telephone.[1] As ethnographer of a study of psychosocial work stressors among hospital workers [21, 22] (the GROW study), Gordon also drew on a few interviews conducted with relevant personnel in that study.[2] The interviews lasted from 15 to 60 minutes and, when possible, were taped and later transcribed. Table 1 shows the breakdown of the informants in the different groups. All but one person agreed to be interviewed, though logistical difficulties prevented a few interviews from ever being realized. Five closed questions were added to the questionnaire after a couple of months and posed, whenever possible, to the last 27 subjects. The explicit purpose of these exploratory data, however, was to further understanding and communication, rather than to statistically document the situation.

STAKEHOLDER PERSPECTIVES

The worlds of work and health constitute a complex, diversified field characterized by distinct but overlapping and interacting networks and languages. These are not groups, per se, but are often identified as such based on shared interests and perspectives. The term "stakeholder" captures a fundamental question around which groups differ or join: what is at stake for people in a particular situation strongly determines what they see and don't see, what their priorities are, and how they approach the situation. This factor is the basis of what philosophers and social scientists call "positionality" [23].[3] Therefore, an important question considered for

---

[1] The majority of interviews were conducted by Dr. Gordon. A number of interviews in Southern California were conducted by Dr. K. Patel-Coleman and Dr. M. Jauregui.

[2] We acknowledge Dr. Paul Blanc, the Principal Investigator of the Grow Study, which was funded by NIAMSKD, RO1 AR47798, for permitting use of some interviews included and analyzed.

[3] "Positionality" refers to the idea that no one can ever be outside of a position and that each position offers a particular "take" on a situation. This means not an end to objectivity, only that we must take this positionality into consideration in order to reach real objectivity.

Table 1. Stakeholder "Groups" and "Sub-Groups"
(Study Sample N = 41)

Academia	Business	Labor
N = 6	N = 8	N = 8
*epidemiology	*owner and VP of Health	*regional labor union
*public health	services of large industry	representatives
*health policy	*lobbyist for small	*director of the Federation o
*business	independent businesses	Labor
*occupational medicine	*consultants for workers'	*heads of labor
	compensation of large	*labor educator
Government	corporations	*union coordinator of health
N = 4	*occupational consultant	and safety
*national,	for Fortune 500 companies	*coordinator of health and
*state,	*medical director for large	safety at large industry
*local, and	industry	*coordinator of workplace
*international		health and planning
Legislative	**Health Care Providers**	**Workers' Compensation**
N = 2	**and Public Health**	N = 5
*lobbyists to California	N = 4	*Commission Directors;
legislature	*HMO, public hospital	medical director of a state
	HR administrator	fund; insurers
Community Groups	**Media**	**Foundations**
N = 1	N = 2	N = 1
*Asian Immigrant	*Newspaper Journalists	*Small, international,
Women's Association		labor-oriented

each stakeholder group was, What is or was at stake for them in recognizing or not the connections between work organization and health outcomes?

Here we describe the perspectives of three of the important stakeholder groups we identified: 1) academics/government/work stress researchers; 2) business, management or supportive of business; and 3) labor or supportive of labor. The descriptions are based on interviews with opinion leaders from each group or sub-group as well as recourse to written material used by the informants or written by or about them. The goal here is both to track the extent of mutual language and understanding around work stressors as well as to understand some of the logic or rationale of these stakeholders, the different worlds they inhabit, their priorities, and what is or would be at stake for them if this work environment model of stress had more impact.

1) Academic Perspectives

We are grouping together the academics, government representatives—NIOSH or Cal-OSHA—and other researchers under the shorthand label academics as they share a similar commitment to science and research, and in this case, share the basic tenets of the work stress models under consideration. Nonetheless, they are heterogeneous in their areas of specialty, as indicated earlier in Table 1, as their ideology, as well as their priorities, commitments, and responsibilities differ, particularly between the academics and government people. Academics represent a stakeholder group with particular investment in the production of knowledge about work stress that follows the strictures of scientific validity and is thus recognized as valid and credible among international scientific colleagues. As employees themselves, academics are also invested in producing research publications in order to fulfill their professional obligations and receive recognition and economic advancement within their fields and institutions. However, many academic stakeholders in the area of work organization also share a fundamental political commitment to improving the work environment and health of working people either directly through workplace intervention research or indirectly through promoting changes to social policy. Some, like the group organizing the original California Forum, try to bridge divisions by collaborating with non-academic stakeholder groups such as business and labor unions.

Languaging Stress

As a whole, and almost by definition, the informants (n = 9) were nearly all familiar with the scientific terms proposed—work stress, work organization, job strain, effort-reward imbalance, psychosocial stressors—although they differed in their commitment to using the terms, in some of their interpretations, and expected implications. Whether or not someone uses the term stress or work stress, however, depends not only on their own interpretation of the concept, but how they expect it to be interpreted, and the types of social, political, economic, psychological, and moral implications they expect it to have. This is best captured by Dr. Z, a government administrator and supporter of the work organization and stress model, when he said:

> I don't use the term [stress] because it's considered pejorative, psychological, and mental. Speaking about stress is complaining you're not tough enough. You should knuckle down and do the job. Work stress is often understood as a problem with the individual.

Another leading epidemiologist who has done work in this area said he stopped using the term stress because of all of its ambiguity. The fundamental survival issue, he has concluded, is around control—that people, both at work and in the rest of their lives, need to experience a sense of control over their immediate environment.

Priorities in Work and Health

What were considered to be the most burning issues in 2004 for these academic stakeholders? Several were noted: the changing nature of the work relationships and work organization in today's labor market and their implications in particular, for the increase in employment insecurity; the crisis of the family and child care that is being created by long working and commuting hours, multiple jobs, and the implications for them over the long run. The most pressing health problems mentioned were ergonomics and musculoskeletal injuries of all kinds; blood pressure and cardiovascular disease were more distant concerns.

The general consensus among those having this stakeholder perspective is that work stress is "a very big problem," "of epidemic proportions," according to some. The general assumption is that a great deal of work-induced stress is not being diagnosed; some may in fact show up as elevated blood pressure only at the workplace and not in the doctor's office. This lack of diagnosis may, in fact, explain a great deal of occult hypertension (see chapter 6).

2) Business Perspectives

What we are calling business perspectives is also a heterogeneous field marked by fundamental diversity related to enterprise size—small (10 or fewer employees), medium, and large. This is particularly true for the "small guys" who must compete with the "big guys." With small businesses, usually the owner manages what there is of a health and safety program; with larger employers and corporate businesses, one or more designated and trained persons usually carry the responsibility for health and safety issues. Dominant health problems differ among the manufacturing and services businesses, yet among the small businesses across the board, accidents are the major problem.

Another important distinction affecting perspectives within a stakeholder group is the extent to which someone takes in "the big picture." Among business informants, this could be personnel in organizational development or health and safety consultants to the companies, such as Dr. Y, who notes the large difference between his own (educator of health and safety managers) and his clients' (the managers themselves) first responses to a presentation on the concept of the health implications of organization of work:

> I guess it was a little too abstract for them . . . I think this [work organization] is a very interesting area . . . it's a huge unknown in the area of occupational safety and health, how all of that impacts. It's almost like we're making sure this earth is fine, but we've left the galaxy totally unexplored. But that's just me. [As a consultant], I'm allowed to think that way because I'm allowed to look at the bigger picture. A lot of our client or member companies—they have a day-to-day job to do, which is to deal with hazards in the workplace, as they are known and recognized today. And that's a full plate. They don't need to be further challenged. (educator/consultant to occupational health and safety managers)

Languaging Stress

On the whole, few business informants recognized technical terms, such as job strain, effort-reward imbalance, or psychosocial stressors, or the specific meanings of the term work organization, e.g., low control, high demand, meant by academics and government people. Most considered "work organization" to be similar to "working conditions" and the way one's work is organized. But not everyone, as the small business lobbyist indicated:

> Yes, the way work is organized affects the health and safety of working people . . . this is my perception of what you mean by work organization. But in terms of how many hours you work a day, how many breaks, whether you perform repetitive tasks or in terms of physical labor. . . . I would think that would affect your health, your well-being, your whole attitude toward your job. Yet I'm unsure if they (small businesses) have the financial flexibility to make their employees' work more interesting. . . . Breaks . . . is an interesting question. I'm not sure if we've ever done a survey on that. One would hope the employers would provide [breaks]. But as no survey has been done, I have no answer to that.

As the ability or not to take timely breaks has been shown to impact worker health, ignorance about this fundamental issue is noteworthy.

Work Stress

Most consider work stress to be mental stress, not physical stress, i.e., having to lift too much. Several informants immediately underscored the positive side of stress or distinguished between good work stress and bad work stress. "The good stress," one risk manager posited, "it's what needles you, stretches you, and gets you and others to do the best. I don't want a workplace that's all vanilla." A workers' compensation manager for management seconded the notion: "We have to have stress or we'll be dead. If you want to make the company so safe, so non-demanding, the company won't survive. . . . I worry about a company's success if they would need to support a non-stressful model." Not surprisingly, this informant does not consider work stress to be a major issue in the workplace, as work stress for her means reimbursable by workers' compensation.

From this perspective, then, the survival of the company *depends* on work stress and demanding work. And in this context, management's work is to select appropriate employees from the beginning, culling out the wrong people for the jobs. Bad work stress was attributed to a bad fit between the work environment and the individual who is unable to complete the amount of work before him or her. Even so, management must still identify the breaking point: "You need to find out where the breakpoint of productivity is: how to assess that? Because people do break down. Organizational development people who do surveys to get the pulse need to help with that" (Risk Manager).

Nearly everyone did associate work stress with elevated blood pressure or heart attacks. Referring to the small business owners, the lobbyist said:

> I think they would laugh and say, "No shit, Sherlock, or something like that!!"
> Yeah. I mean, if you're stressed out, trying to run a business, and you got a heart problem, it doesn't take a rocket scientist to figure that out . . . it's a matter of

being able to find a way to cope with it . . . you need to sleep more, eat less, have a better diet, work a little less, do your job differently, that kind of stuff. Easier said than done. I think the more successful someone is, the easier it is to have the luxury of organizing your life a little better . . . very definitely—the more profit you have, the more flexibility. I know there are studies . . . showing how income affects safety.

We hear, then, that the negative impact of stress on cardiovascular problems is taken for granted, is a concern to owners as well, but not easily avoided. But some respondents were careful to distinguish between the *association* between work and cardiovascular disease and cardiovascular disease being "work-related." "It's decided on a case by case basis. We look at most people's personal health habits. There is always stress. Bad work stress can exacerbate a problem. But we found it rare that it causes these conditions." Today it is not uncommon to find defibulators on the walls and blood pressure machines in large companies, indicators of the pervasive epidemic of hypertension in our society.

Priorities in Work and Health

The costs of health insurance and workers' compensation insurance were cited most often as the most or nearly the most burning issues for business people, both for the large businesses but especially for the small ones:

> What figures in a small guy's mind is workers' compensation. For the . . . small businesses, trying to afford health insurance is their main worry: only half the members are able to provide health insurance; those who don't—it's because they can't afford it. And as hiring and retention of qualified employees is a real problem, one of the reasons they all want to offer health insurance is to compete with the larger guy down the street. (Small business lobbyist)

Most, in fact, think that stress at work is a big problem:

> Yes, for small business owners, due to low profit margins, few people performing the job. They probably work 60-70 hours/week. That to me spells . . . stressful. And they like to do that because they like to run their own show. [And what about the employees in this situation?] I have trouble speaking for employees because they can go elsewhere. I think it's more on the owner. The employee might have the same stress as in a large business.

The darker side of work stress for the employers and managers, themselves, however, is sometimes addressed. Environmental Health and Safety (EHS) managers of Fortune 500 companies, for example, were presented a talk entitled, "Stress is the Cocaine of Corporate America," which they reportedly found extremely interesting and sobering. It spoke of the need for these EHS managers to be good role models for the employees, to start taking care of themselves and recognize their own "addiction" to stress, and to understand the serious health consequences of stress over the years, particularly as a precursor to middle-aged heart attacks and blood pressure problems. These business executives themselves, needed help in setting limits, one of the interventions organizations commonly offered to deal with work stress. One can imagine they view work stress of employees through this prism.

In sum, stress is taken for granted, is a charge for many corporate employees, almost an addiction, from which they may need to wean themselves. It is accepted and considered good and fundamental for productivity. Yet it is also seen as a problem, both for management and employees. Little distinction was made between the stress of white-collar workers and blue-collar or service-sector workers.

What is at stake in the recognition of stress for business stakeholders? First at stake is more money for health care and workers' compensation insurance, as the fear is that speaking about a new hazard will "open a flood of unjustified compensation claims." As it is, we are told that small businesses often need compliance assistance programs, and many are already unable to meet the current standards of health and safety. Many companies are still very concerned about their workers' compensation claims and injury/illness logs, the current standards. They are the immediate wolves at the door, they are the indicators against which the health and safety and risk managers are judged, and they feel they are very stretched with these hazards as it is. The idea of considering work organization and its implications for health opens up a new and vague area of potential hazards presented in terms that remain at an abstract level, that feel far-fetched and like pie-in-the-sky types of problems—e.g., worrying about an employee's sense of control on the job or the long-term impact of job stress when they are worried about the immediate, in-your-face issues of injury, illness, and absences and the huge insurance rates they must pay.

Also at stake is industry productivity, as discussed, and the issue of control at work and how much control employees should have, as well as the relevance of stress and its health implications for their own way of life and their own health vulnerability.

How is work stress being addressed? In some places, such as small businesses in the construction industry, "It's called the local tavern after work." One noted a United Auto Workers' plant that actually allowed visits to the pub during lunch hour. Smaller companies rarely provide any organized health activities. Employee Assistance Programs (EAPs) are a second source of dealing with work stress on an individual basis. Most large companies have stress programs for those individuals who are considered unable to manage the stress due to their own personal limits, where they teach employees skills for setting limits to their work and offer them support.

The indicators of work and health status that a company uses appear to be based, in many cases, on the traditional injury and illness rates that have ruled occupational health for many years and that address the traditional recognized physical, chemical, ergonomic, and environmental toxins, not the psychosocial ones. These are consequential vs. leading indicators. Both small and large businesses also appear to rely on frequent surveys and polls taken of their own clientele as indicators of where things stand. These are the data that are developed and appear to be listened to most when making decisions regarding health and work; research results in journals seem to play a small role and are not always considered good science—"if you want to know, I think many of those studies [that link blood pressure and heart attacks to work] are poppycock." Academia (perhaps excluding Business Management) appears not to be considered an important resource by many. Organizational development people do frequent surveys "to get the pulse" of their organization.

In order to reach business people, the consensus was that health and productivity must be considered together: "Health without productivity will be resented. We're trying to survive. We have dips. You don't understand the real world. Bring productivity and health costs together in a meaningful way. People want better bank for the money." (Workers' compensation administrator in a Fortune 500 company)

However, as an epilogue: it appears that the bottom line—the impact of health expenses—has been hit so hard it has triggered a new orientation to the problem. As employers are responsible for assuring not only a safe workplace, but paying the health insurance of their employees *and* their families' health, not just occupational illness and injuries but non-occupational health as well has begun to take center stage under their surveillance. A new frontier is opening which integrates health prevention at the workplace and health promotion beyond it.

Among the business stakeholders, there is consensus that workers are being asked to produce more with fewer personnel and less time. They all know they are being asked for more of themselves as well. But businesses have not studied the short- or long-term impact of this leaner workforce and continue to measure injury and illness logs while lacking indicators of the costs of injury and stress to productivity. Stress is a common term, has colloquial use, is understood in so many different ways, is something that most business people have experienced and about which they often speak in terms of their own approach.

3) Labor Perspectives

Like the informants grouped in the business perspective, the labor or labor-supportive informants, hereafter referred to as labor, presented a heterogeneous picture: from leaders of state labor federations to state leaders of international unions, to an occupational health manager working for a large automobile union, to a labor educator, to a leader of a professional association of health care workers. Most informants were affiliated with the labor union movement and therefore represent a distinct political position compared to the larger category of labor which might also represent non-unionized working people. We focus on union representatives and affiliates because historically labor unions represent the voice of working people and are an important collective strategy and legal mechanism (i.e., collective bargaining) for improving working conditions.

Languaging Stress

On the whole, the terms used by these stakeholders differed from those of the work stressor researchers, in part, a function of their connotations. "Stress," several pointed out, "is considered a negative among non-service workers, a type of complaining, as if someone is not up to the job." A couple pondered the possibility that it was different in the service occupations which involve more women and more people-to-people work and where the term stress seems to be more frequently used and less negatively interpreted.

When academic researchers try to reach people in labor, they encounter something of a catch-22 in communication. On the one hand: in order to avoid confusion with the abundant uses of the term stress and to distinguish themselves from the dominant psychological and popular interpretations of work stress, work stressor scientists select and use language carefully. Yet, on the other hand, their use of this technical language is often perceived as "jargony," exclusive, and alienating, unnecessarily complicated, impersonal, distancing, and abstract to many non-experts.

Other than the university-affiliated labor educator and a union health and safety manager, few informants knew or used the terms job strain, effort-reward imbalance, and psychosocial stressors. Some terms, such as job strain, were associated with a similar meaning in colloquial use, such as physical strain: "I assume it means lifting, physical strain" (Union leader). The meaning of effort-reward imbalance was easier to figure out, in terms of pay and what you get in rewards; psychosocial stressors: "Sounds like a management term to blame workers for problems" (Union leader).

The term work organization tended to have weak communicative value to leaders, who found it abstract, alienating, another sign of academia being cut off from the real world. The term working conditions was considered better. Issues of job control were referred to as responsibility without authority. The overall comments by a leader of the Council of Unions about these terms were instructive and influential: "These terms are very alienating. They're vague, they're abstract, there are no causes mentioned." Instead of the term work organization, originally in the title of the Forum, which he also found to be "very vague and abstract," he suggested we speak about "your job, your health."

Many labor stakeholders think stress is a big problem at work. However, "people do not want to talk about it, and will not do so unless they are very close to each other. Stress is a dirty word to the union; it means you can't take it." A couple pointed out the gendered nature of talking about stress: "It's gender- and industry-related. To speak of stress is not macho. You find it particularly among men, especially in factory workers. It appears to be more acceptable in the health care industry where people work with people" (Labor educator). Another, a state union leader, thought about the question: "Now it may be that people who work with people or maybe women, I don't know that yet, but there seems to be both their gender and type of work-related issue that the use of the term stress in the health care industry is quite frequent." According to a health care leader, work stress was traditionally considered in terms of job satisfaction; the novelty now is to consider it in terms of its health implications. One gets the sense that much of what is referred to as work stress is taken for granted, nothing new, nothing to comment on, by workers and some union people alike.

On the other hand, many expressed concerns for the increased pace, workload, and work pressure. Labor stakeholders spoke of understaffing, downsizing, working conditions, patient/nurse ratios, and the increase in employment insecurity. This means that on the ground, they were concerned with the same types of problems as the work stressor researchers, albeit referred to with different, more specific terms. Most agree that there has been downsizing and more pressure, but that there has been no study of the effect of it on employees.

One union manager for an automobile company was concerned with the increase of physical stress placed on workers, that they are required to work faster and harder for longer periods of time, and that the unrelenting quantity becomes stressful for the workers. "There is only one speed now," he pointed out, "and that is *very fast.*" He described the sharp increase in productivity and attention required by the workers. Whereas in the past they would be required to attend about 40 out of 60 seconds, it is now 50 out of 52 seconds. The pace means that downtime has been nearly eliminated, leaving the body and mind little, if any, time to recover.

Priorities in Work and Health

Given the declining power of labor unions over the last 50 years, labor's struggles have increasingly focused on retaining jobs, deflecting wage losses, and preserving health benefits, while occupational health and safety issues have taken a back seat as a priority. The economic context for the labor movement may partly account for what appears to be a "disconnect" between the academic stakeholders' scientific knowledge about work stress and many labor union informants' reticence to prioritize the issue of stress because it is seen as an individual issue, and blamed on the weakness of individual workers.

At the top of the most pressing problems for labor named by these stakeholders were securing health insurance and wages and problems of staffing and increasing temporary work. In fact, one can imagine a great deal is traded in exchange for health insurance. The most pressing health problems are ergonomic (musculo-skeletal); they are the most visible, most directly related to work, costly, and negatively affected by stress. Work stress is understood as intangible, hard to measure, and difficult to regulate.

"WORK STRESS" ACROSS STAKEHOLDERS: SUMMARY AND ANALYSIS

Stress at work appears to be the metaphoric elephant in the room in today's work settings. Most know or feel it, are quite aware of it, but do not call it directly or by the same name. And importantly, few link it with health. A multitude of reasons contribute to these two related phenomena—that it is known but not named or called by the same term and that it is not being linked to health and safety implications.

First, stress is taken for granted, it is adapted to, which is the very nature of the stress response—it naturally allows people to stretch themselves. But it is not meant to be chronic and daily. Nearly all informants from all groups, in fact, agreed with the statement that "one could be stressed without being aware of it." Second, it is increasingly considered to be normal, a characteristic of work that is caused by an economic squeeze, that is being carried out quite deliberately and often together with layoffs, such that many people are made to feel they are lucky simply to have a job, no matter what the working conditions, and afraid to speak about stress out of fear of losing their jobs. This factor makes staffing and health insurance over-riding priorities for unions. Third, the aforementioned circumstances contribute to a sense that the problem is so big and expensive that little can be done to solve it. It was described as hopelessness on the part of labor (employees, unions, and managers) about actually doing anything to ameliorate the situation and was echoed by business-oriented health and safety managers who rolled their eyes in response to the work organization material. Labor and business all feel pressure to lower the costs of workers' compensation for known and recognized injuries and illnesses. Fourth, a bad experience of stress claims in the 1980s further soured business and management people against recognizing it. Yet the stress cited of these stress claims—by definition "episodic" and not "chronic"—is *not* the same stress— chronic, long term—whose health consequences these researchers are concerned about. Fifth, speaking about job stress is often considered morally derogatory for many union people mostly men and workers in manufacturing—a sign of weakness. This evaluation was also shared by many in the business community who considered speaking of job stress as a sign of individual weakness and failure. Sixth, staffing and understaffing issues are among the most common ways of referring to work stress. In some cases, such as understaffing in hospitals, the two words—stress and staffing—are spoken together. The terms "the way work is organized" or "work organization," on the other hand, appear to communicate little of the specific meanings they hold for the researchers. Finally, the experience of stress is ubiquitous, experienced by people at all levels of the hierarchy.

Three recurring constellations of meanings or echoes were most associated with the terms work stress, work-related stress, or job stress:

1. Individual, mental, and equated with feeling stressed and or speaking about it; many—labor men and leaders, as well as business informants—considered it complaining, anti-macho, and more pejoratively, morally weak and or "psych cases"—inseparable from individual characteristics and individual life. For many, the association of stress with subjective evaluation puts it into the category of the immeasurable, which is a major problem for business which feels that stress is exploited for any number of emotional reasons, job-related or not.

2. Working conditions such as understaffing, patient ratio, high pace: "Yes, it's [stress] a pretty huge problem in health care due to understaffing." "Yes, it's a very big problem in health care: 'I can't handle the stress,' you'll hear that often." (A union person)

3. Positive charge that contributes to productivity, that gets things done, that is good, and that we all feel and sometimes thrive on.

In short, stress is a very complicated, powerful, multi-vocal term, which has many different resonances among the different stakeholder groups, but with little explication of the different meanings.

CONCLUSION

Mediators and Translators

To find a common ground among diverse stakeholders first requires knowledge of each others' respective grounds, worlds, perspectives, and languages. It means listening, seeing, knowing. The lack of common ground contributes to the fact that the links between work stress and cardiovascular problems, for example, have not yet penetrated the fields of general or cardiac medicine or even labor.

a) Academics: Further interaction among stakeholders could focus on particularly strategic groups for mediation and translation. Based on this research and the knowledge imparted at the Forum, academics who are committed to putting knowledge into action and to using research to foster communication have a good orientation for achieving this end. Greater effectiveness will require using different modes of communication with different groups. The numbers and tables that speak so clearly and interestingly to many of the epidemiologists, for example, lacked context and meaning for many non-epidemiologists who sought trends, contexts, narratives, stories, ways of interpreting the data. It will require translating the very precise, technical language that is developed and used to further understanding and to refine theories into terms that are more comprehensible and that can reach varied audiences.

b) Mediators in occupational health and safety: Another set of professionals, already situated between academia, government, business, and health and safety [material] are consultants to occupational health and safety managers. In this study, we saw how one of these consultants, "allowed to take in the large picture," could grasp the whole world that was opened by the work organization and health research in a way that those working close to the ground could not.

Similarly, groups that bridge the academia/labor fields are also particularly valuable in translating among groups and putting the theories into practice. Exercises such as risk mapping of stress, carried out by labor educators with workers, such as those at the Labor Occupational Health Program at the University of California, Berkeley, identify problem spots in the work process and environment. While some translation between academia and workers does take place, productive links are missing between academics and labor leaders and labor in general. The sparse use and familiarity with stress models and theories by labor stakeholders is striking, given that stress researchers share many of labor's orientations and values.

Beyond the Individual to the Social

The eminent English anthropologist, Marilyn Strathern, writes, "You can tell a culture by what it can and cannot bring together" [24]. Culture as "what you cannot bring together" is well illustrated by the NIOSH leader and his explanation as to why he avoids using the term stress: "Health is strongly tied to individuals. Stress is considered psychological, mental, a problem with the individual. *It is extremely difficult to think of stress as located in a social phenomenon such as work organization*" (italics added). Indeed, that has been the case.

Finding common ground means addressing shared cultural orientations that are pervasive, appear natural, but which need to be questioned. We live in a society that puts more and more emphasis on the individual, on individual risk, on individual responsibility for that risk, and on individual accountability for dealing with that risk. It is a ubiquitous world view that has its grip on most of us. Because of this characteristic, we have increasing difficulty conceiving of social phenomenon. The uphill battle the work stressor school faces in the United States is clearly related to its postulating essentially a social etiology of work stress, locating the problem in the way work is organized. We lack language that clearly addresses the social *qua* social and which does not convert the social into the psychological or the individual.

As long as individualism remains such a dominant frame, as long as freedom is understood as freedom *from* restrictions and regulation and not freedom *from* insecurity or unhealthy work, as long as health is located in the individual, as long as stress is considered a mental problem of the individual, it will be very difficult for this approach to worker health to make dramatic in-roads. The careful work its authors do to distinguish this paradigm from others is quickly lost in the consumption and the translation. Similarly, reports of worker stress studies that are lassoed into the cause to show how much stress there is in different parts of the world further confuse the matter—what is meant by stress? Is it only what is self-reported? Indeed, judging from data indicating an epidemic of occult hypertension in the United States, self-reports of stress are unreliable and lead to gross under-diagnosis of hypertension in society [12].

The different schools of work stress research and the social determinants of health need to join forces to resist, as Willis writes, "the neo-liberal economic climate that defines work stress as essentially a personal lack of individual adaptation, rather than a symptom and result of unhealthy work environments" [4]. Clear ideological barriers impede recognizing social causes of work stress, which obviously lead to questioning the social order.

One thing is very clear from the above study and analysis: a major obstacle to recognizing connections between types of work organization and health outcomes is fear of the responsibility for cost and change. The threat that identifying new work-related illnesses will translate into expanded grounds for workers' compensation claims and more costs for employers is a major deterrent to recognizing more workplace etiologies. Further, the dual role of employer and insurer that many companies play gives companies great power and interest in determining what will be recognized as illness or not, particularly work-related. Thus, *diagnosis of illness* must be separated from the *responsibility for it*. For as long as recognizing stress caused by the way work is organized is associated with *responsibility* for it, the real work-related impacts of work on health, particularly around the huge and expensive issue of heart problems, will be resisted by business. While legislatively responsible for controlling the impact of work on the health of their workers, the fact that business perceives itself as laden with responsibility for workers' health naturally makes them particularly close and puts them in the position of policeman. It is yet another stark consequence of not having separate, free, and universal health care. As long as health insurance in the United States remains tied to employment, businesses and organizations will continue to play the role of policeman over workers' health and make every effort to diminish and defer the impacts of work-induced stress on health.

The vital need for control and influence, a sense of fairness, a sense of competence, and a sense of appropriate reward are not just important values to strive for or keys to work satisfaction. What this line of stress research underlines is that these experiences are fundamental for health [25, 26] and their absence or defilement entails the absence of vital life necessities. *Control and fairness at work need to be understood as public health matters.* In this era of health promotion and prevention, policing and punishing overweight individuals because of their elevated risk to health should not proceed without due attention to the known social sources of ill health in the workplace and the appropriate oversight for their contribution to ill health. Much like clean air, a sense of control over one's work tasks and of fairness in one's work contract appear to be vital human necessities whose absence damages not only the spirit but also the body and health.

The stress response, as so many researchers have pointed out, offers humans and animals extra resources to face an emergency. It is meant to respond to a state of exception. But the exception is now becoming the norm as the increasing pace, intensity, and quantity of work is so demanding that it requires, on a daily basis, the extra energy of the stress response. Indeed humans are continuously adaptive and very often do come up with what is needed to respond to a situation. But such adaptation comes at a price, and when the price is paid with health, the price can indeed be very high. One successful means of continuing to exploit the extra energy workers' bodies produce through the stress response is to preserve ignorance of its actual long-term impact, specifically its costs to the worker, his or her family, the organization, the government. Such ignorance is maintained through strategically under-studying the costs, ignoring scientific results that indicate otherwise, keeping the impact of intensified production disconnected from health outcomes, keeping adverse health outcomes displaced and disconnected from their real causes, and in the case of stress, remaining focused on the immediate present and the individual, as opposed to the long-term and the collective. In today's language, what is not measured remains essentially invisible. Such is undoubtedly part of the story of the limited impact of international research that links specific working conditions with chronic stress and its expensive, dreaded, and very costly long-term health consequences.

REFERENCES

1. Rossi, A. M., P. L. Perrewé, S. L. Sauter, and S. M. Jex, Foreword, in *Stress and Quality of Working Life: Current Perspectives in Occupational Health,* Rossi, A. M., P. L. Perrewé, and S. L. Sauter (eds.), IAP, Greenwich, CT, pp. ix-xi, 2005.
2. Dollard, M., N. Skinner, M. R. Tuckey, and T. Bailey, National Surveillance of Psycho-Social Risk Factors in the Workplace: An International Overview, *Work and Stress,* 21:1, pp. 1-29, 2007.
3. Peterson, C. L. (ed.), *Work Stress: Studies of the Context, Content, and Outcomes of Stress,* Baywood, Amityville, NY, 2003.
4. Willis, E., Foreword, in *Work Stress: Studies of the Context, Content and Outcomes of Stress,* Peterson, C. L. (ed.), Baywood, Amityville, NY, pp. vii, 2003.
5. Sauter, S. L. and L. R. Murphy, Approaches to Job Stress in the United States, in *Stress and Quality of Working Life: Current Perspectives in Occupational Health,* Rossi, A. M., P. L. Perrewé, and S. L. Sauter (eds.), IAP, Greenwich, CT, pp. 183-197, 2005.
6. Levi, L., The European Commission's Guidance on Work-Related Stress and Related Initiatives: From Words to Action, in *Stress and Quality of Working Life: Current Perspectives in Occupational Health,* Rossi, A. M., P. L. Perrewé, and S. L. Sauter (eds.), IAP, Greenwich, CT, pp. 167-182, 2005.
7. Wainwright, D. and M. Calnan, *Work Stress: The Making of a Modern Epidemic,* Open University Press, Buckingham, UK, 2002.
8. Peterson, C., *Work Stress: A Sociological Perspective,* Baywood, Amityville, NY, 1999.
9. Dollard, M., Introduction. Costs, Theoretical Approaches, Research Designs, in *Occupational Stress in the Services Professions,* Dollard, M., A. Winefield, and H. Winefield (eds.), Taylor and Francis, London, UK, pp. 1-43, 2003.
10. Cooper, C., P. Dewe, and M. O'Driscoll, *Organizational Stress: A Review and Critique of Theory, Research, and Applications,* Sage, Thousand Oaks, CA, 2001.
11. Webster, T. and B. Bergman, Occupational Stress: Counts and Rates, *Compensation and Working Conditions,* 4:3, pp. 38-41, 1999.
12. Schnall, P. L., K. Belkic', P. Landsbergis, and D. Baker, The Workplace and Cardio-vascular Disease, *Occupational Medicine,* 15:1, pp. 1-322, 2000.
13. Krause, N., D. R. Ragland, J. M. Fisher, and S. L. Syne, Psychosocial Job Factors, Physical Workload, and Incidence of Work-Related Spinal Injury: A 5-Year Prospective Study of Urban Transit Operators, *Spine,* 23:2507, p. 16, 1998.
14. Johnson, J. V., Occupational Stress, in *Preventing Occupational Disease and Injury,* Weeks, J. L., B. S. Levy, and G. R. Wagner (eds.), American Public Health Association, Washington, DC, pp. 464-473, 2004.
15. Rosskam, E., *Excess Baggage: Leveling the Load and Changing the Workplace,* Baywood, Amityville, NY, 2007.
16. Rugulies, R., U. Bultmann, B. Aust, and H. Burr, Psychosocial Work Environment and Incidence of Severe Depressive Symptoms: Prospective Findings from a 5-Year Follow-Up of the Danish Work Environment Cohort Study, *American Journal of Epidemiology,* 163:10, pp. 877-887, 2006.
17. Sauter, S. L., W. S. Brightwell, M. J. Colligan, et al., *The Changing Organization of Work and Safety and Health of Working People: Knowledge Gaps and Research Directions,* NIOSH, CDC, Cincinnati, OH, 2002.
18. Karasek, R. and T. Theorell, *Healthy Work: Stress, Productivity, and the Reconstruction of Working Life,* Basic Books, New York, 1990.

19. Siegrist, J., Adverse Health Effects of High-Effort/Low-Reward Conditions, *Journal of Occupational Health Psychology*, 1, pp. 27-43, 1996.
20. Howard, J., Navigating Uncharted Territory in Occupational Safety and Health Research: 21st Century Challenges, in *Conference of the Association of Industrial Hygiene*, Dallas, TX, 2003.
21. Gordon, D. R., G. M. Ames, I. H. Yen, M. Gillen, B. Aust, R. Rugulies, J. W. Frank, and P. D. Blanc, Integrating Qualitative Research into Occupational Health: A Case Study among Hospital Workers, *Journal of Occupational Environment Medicine*, 4:4, pp. 399-409, 2004.
22. Rugulies, R., J. Braff, and J. W. Frank, et al., The Psychosocial Work Environment and Musculoskeletal Disorders: Design of a Comprehensive Interviewer-Administered Questionnaire, *American Journal of Industrial Medicine*, 45, pp. 428-439, 2003.
23. Haraway, D., Situated Knowledges: The Science Question in Feminism and the Privilege of Partial Perspective, in *Simians, Cyborgs, and Women*, Haraway, D., Routledge, New York, pp. 183-201, 1991.
24. Strathern, M., *Reproducing the Future: Anthropology, Kinship, and the New Reproductive Technologies*, Manchester University Press, Manchester, UK, p. 2, 1992.
25. Kivimaki, M., M. Elovainio, J. Vahtera, and J. E. Ferrie, Organizational Justice and Health of Employees: Prospective Cohort Study, *Occupational and Environmental Medicine*, 60, pp. 27-34, 2003.
26. Ferrie, J. E., J. Head, M. Shipley, J. Vahtera, M. G. Marmot, and M. Kivimaki, Injustice at Work and Health: Causation, Correlation, or Cause for Action?, *Occupational and Environmental Medicine*, 64:6, p. 428, 2007.

CHAPTER 11

Interventions to Reduce Job Stress and Improve Work Organization and Worker Health

Paul A. Landsbergis

Interventions or programs to improve the organization of work and reduce the impact of stressful jobs on our health can be conducted in a wide variety of ways. Changes can be made at the individual level, at the level of the job, at the level of the organization, or from outside the organization through laws and regulations. The U.S. National Institute for Occupational Safety and Health (NIOSH) developed a summary of levels of interventions and categories of prevention (Table 1) [1]. The author's additions to NIOSH's original version of this table are in italics.

Within each level, interventions can be considered primary, secondary, or tertiary prevention. *Primary prevention* refers to efforts to protect the health of people who have not yet become sick. *Secondary prevention* involves early detection and prompt and effective efforts to correct the beginning stages of illness (for example, reversing high blood pressure, buildup of plaque in the arteries, or chronic insomnia, before a heart attack occurs). *Tertiary prevention* consists of measures to reduce or eliminate long-term impairments and disabilities and minimize suffering after illness has occurred (for example, rehabilitation and return-to-work after a heart attack) [2].

Historically, *legislative/policy* interventions have been more common in Europe [3] and Japan [4] than the United States [5], with exceptions, such as U.S. state laws banning mandatory overtime or providing minimum staffing levels for nurses, or the new California paid family leave law [6]. In the United States, ergonomics regulations have also addressed issues of work organization, although such efforts have been very general and have met with considerable resistance [5]. The only existing state regulation, the California Standard on Repetitive Motion Injuries, requires that "the employer shall consider engineering controls . . . and administrative controls, such as job rotation, work pacing or work breaks." The OSHA Ergonomics Program Standard, rescinded in 2001, describes administrative controls for musculoskeletal disorder risk including "employee rotation, rest breaks,

Table 1. Levels of Work Organization Interventions
and Stages of Prevention

Levels of intervention	Primary	Secondary	Tertiary	Typical intervention methods
Legislative/ Policy	Work hour limits, *ban mandatory overtime, staffing requirements*	Workers compensation	Social Security Disability	*Legislation, regulation*
Employer/ Organization	Work-family programs; *Workplace health & safety programs; New systems of work organization; Work-site surveillance*	Health promotion programs; *Work-site surveillance*	Company provided long-term disability; Return to work programs	*Collective bargaining; Worker ownership; Employer-initiated programs/policies, including contingent work, downsizing, new systems of work organization*
Job/Task Characteristics	Job/task redesign; Job rotation; *Integrated workplace health-health promotion programs*	Provision of light duty jobs		*Labor-management committees, initiatives; Action research; Employer-initiated job redesign*
Individual/ Job interface	Health promotion programs	Stress management programs		*Employer-initiated programs; Labor-management initiatives*
		Employee assistance programs Disease management programs		

Note: Additions to NIOSH's basic model by the author included in italics.

alternative tasks, job task enlargement, redesign of work methods and adjustment of work pace" [5].

National Work Environment laws enacted in Scandinavia in the 1970s gave workers far greater influence in the workplace. In 1991, a series of amendments to the 1977 Swedish law specified that:

• Employees are to be given opportunities to participate in the arrangement of their own work situation.

- Technology, the organization of work, and job contents are to be designed so that the employee is not exposed to physical and mental loads that may lead to ill-health or accidents.
- Pay systems (such as piece work) and work schedules that involve an appreciable risk of ill health or accidents are not to be used.
- Strictly controlled work is to be avoided or restricted.
- Work should afford opportunities for variety, social contacts, cooperation, and a connection between individual tasks.
- Working conditions should provide opportunities for personal and occupational development as well as for self-determination [7, p. 22].

In addition to national laws, European-wide initiatives have included: a European Union directive on June 12, 1989 to "alleviate monotonous work at predetermined pace to reduce health effects"; a European Commission Guidance document on work-related stress in 2000; and an agreement on work-related stress by major employer and union federations in Europe on October 8, 2004, which states that,

> [A]ll employers have a legal obligation to protect the occupational safety and health of workers. This duty also applies to problems of work-related stress in so far as they entail a risk to health and safety.
> Anti-stress measures could include:
> clarifying the company's objectives . . . ensuring adequate management support for individuals and teams, matching responsibility and control over work, improving work organization . . . training managers and workers [on job stress] . . . provision of information to and consultation with workers and/or their representatives [8].

Employer/organizational level interventions tend to target human resource policies (for example, work-family or health promotion programs) and organizational climate (for example, efforts to make the workplace climate more supportive). Occupational health and safety and work-site surveillance programs to monitor both employee health and features of work organization are appropriate at this level. However, employers have also put into place more controversial "interventions" in order to improve productivity, quality, and profitability. They include new systems of work organization, such as "lean production" or "total quality management" (TQM) [9], and downsizing [10], which can hurt workers' health.

Interventions at the *job/task* level focus on job redesign, job enrichment, or increased job control or participation in decision making and can result from methods such as action research or labor management committees or initiatives.

WORK SITE SURVEILLANCE

In 1998, experts in Japan, Europe, and the United States called for a program of surveillance at workplaces and monitoring at national and regional levels in order to identify the extent of work-stress related health problems and to provide baselines against which to evaluate intervention efforts. They recommended that workplaces measure both workplace stressors and health problems known to result from such stressors [11].

In the United States, occupational and environmental medicine clinics can play a key role in such surveillance efforts. In addition to clinical care, such clinics conduct research, and provide patient education, industrial hygiene and ergonomics services, and social work and support groups [12]. Thus, a team approach is recommended in which epidemiologists work together with clinicians, health educators, ergonomists, psychologists, and other health professionals to identify high-risk workplaces and jobs, facilitate the provision of clinical care, and design and implement workplace interventions.

The surveillance team needs to discover whether the current occupation(s) is high risk; whether workers are exposed to any workplace physical, chemical, work schedule or psychosocial risk factors for disease; and whether any such have been increasing over time [13]. Questionnaires, such as the Job Content Questionnaire [14], the Effort-Reward Imbalance Questionnaire [15], and the Occupational Stress Index [16], can help measure job characteristics and job stressors. Workplace screenings should be conducted for biomedical risk factors, such as high blood pressure [17]. Such surveillance can help to identify clusters of work-related hypertension and help target work sites for primary and secondary prevention programs. Another key part of surveillance is taking an occupational history of workers to see how long they have been facing workplace risk factors for disease, and what types of risk factors [18].

Such surveillance would be an important part of the newly developing field of occupational cardiology, which would link cardiologists, health promotion experts, and occupational health specialists. In addition to efforts described above, they would develop return-to-work guidelines for cardiac patients, including workplace modifications, and expand the use of ambulatory (portable) monitors to measure blood pressure or heart rate [19].

ACTION RESEARCH

Action Research (AR) involves a partnership between outside experts and members of an organization aimed at meeting both research and intervention goals. Employees are involved in an empowering process of defining problems, developing intervention tactics, introducing changes that benefit employees, and measuring the effects of the changes [20, 21]. AR emphasizes employee influence, input, and control for organizational change. It is consistent with the emphasis in work stress research on increasing employees' levels of control at work to improve employee health.

AR efforts to reduce job stressors and improve worker health have been common in Scandinavia [22-24]. For example, an intervention among Swedish civil servants included worker committees which developed and carried out action plans to reduce work stressors. Stimulation from work and autonomy over work significantly increased in the intervention group but remained the same in the control group. There was also a trend toward increased supervisor support in the intervention group.

and a decline in the control group. Finally, a reduction in heart disease risk (a significant improvement in lipid profiles) occurred in the intervention group, but not in the control group, suggesting that the intervention was "heart healthy" [25].

An intervention on an inner city bus line in Stockholm was begun to reduce traffic congestion and improve passenger service. During planning, interest developed on the part of the municipal workers union and researchers to study stress and the health of the drivers. The intervention included a number of components designed to diminish time-pressure and promote traffic flow, for example, changed lanes and routes, signal priority, redesigned bus stops and an information system. This led to a significant decline in "job hassles per hour" and in systolic blood pressure (–10.7 mm Hg) in the intervention group [26].

COLLECTIVELY BARGAINED APPROACHES

More typical in the United States have been employer or researcher-initiated job redesign programs (some using action research principles), or collectively bargained initiatives (including programs established through labor-management committees). Collective bargaining is the traditional strategy used by employees to improve working conditions [23, 27, 28]. Contracts can moderate job demands, increase employee job control and job skills, and help provide a more supportive atmosphere, through provisions on job security, work standards, work assignments, performance evaluations, technological change, harassment, discrimination, staffing, comparable worth, skills training, and career development. By providing employees with a voice in improving working conditions and protection from arbitrary decisions through seniority provisions, a grievance procedure, or labor-management committees, collective bargaining agreements can help reduce job stress [23, 27, 28].

Examples include a reduction in the number of rooms to be cleaned per day bargained by hotel room cleaners in San Francisco [29] (see chapter 14), or efforts by nurses' unions to bargain for bans on mandatory overtime and minimum staffing levels for hospital nurses. Collective bargaining has also modified stressful lean production to some extent—through creating more moderate work demands (through more staff, and control over line speed and job standards), by increasing job control (for example, by electing team leaders, ability to transfer, joint committees), ergonomics programs, and less arbitrary access to training [9].

Unions have also bargained for child and elder care, family and medical leave, alternative work schedules, and working part-time with benefits [30-32]. However, collective bargaining has rarely been evaluated for its effect on improving workplace health or reducing job stress.

JOB REDESIGN

A number of studies have evaluated labor-management programs that attempted to improve the design of jobs. They included programs to reduce "burnout" symptoms among state child protection agency employees through a labor-management committee and new technology [33] to increase participation in decision-making through labor-management committees at an automobile manufacturer [34], and to reduce work-related musculoskeletal disorders (such as carpal tunnel syndrome and tendonitis) through job redesign at a meatpacking plant [35].

A recent intervention program at a Canadian hospital included a team that was developed according to the principles of German "health circles" [36], which have shown their effectiveness in the prevention of stress at work in Europe [37]. The principles of these health circles are: a) operating in small groups; b) including group members at different levels of the organization; c) regularly scheduled work meetings; d) preferably 8-10 meetings; e) meetings led by an external moderator; and f) individual knowledge of team members used as input for finding solutions to problems at work. The ultimate objective of health circles is to recognize and eliminate problems at their source [38]. The team included two researchers, one research assistant, three head nurses, and three registered staff nurses (one from each targeted care unit), one nurses' aide and one reception one representative from human resources and one from nursing, as well as two local union representatives (nurses and nurses aides' unions). A 1-year follow-up has shown positive health benefits from this intervention [39].

The New York City Worksite Blood Study was not an intervention study; however, blood pressure and job characteristics were measured at baseline and 3-year follow-up in eight workplaces. Among 195 men, who went from a situation of job strain at baseline to no job strain 3 years later, levels of blood pressure at work significantly dropped (−5.3 mm Hg systolic, −3.2 mm Hg diastolic) [40], suggesting that an intervention study designed to reduce job strain would achieve similar benefits.

NEW SYSTEMS OF WORK ORGANIZATION

New systems of work organization, such as "lean production" and "total quality management," have been introduced by employers throughout the industrialized world to improve productivity, product quality, and profitability [9]. Lean production, developed at Toyota, Nissan, and other Japanese manufacturers, was based on "quality circles," "just-in-time," and team working [41]. However, few studies have examined the impact of such new systems on occupational injuries or illnesses or on job characteristics such as job strain, which has been linked to high blood pressure and heart disease. Existing studies provide little evidence to support the claim that lean production "empowers" automobile workers. In fact, auto industry studies suggest that lean production creates an intensified work pace and increases job demands. Increases in workers' decision-making authority and skill levels are small or temporary, and their authority and skills typically remain low. In physically demanding jobs, the intensification of labor appears to lead to increases in musculoskeletal disorders [9]. NIOSH is concerned that

> . . . various worker participation or involvement strategies may often be more ceremonial than substantive, having little meaningful influence on worker empowerment—or perhaps even eroding workers' means to influence job conditions through more traditional labor-management mechanisms such as collective bargaining [42, pp. 15-16].

"Taylorism," the traditional assembly-line approach to job design and mass production, which was introduced at the beginning of the twentieth century, was based on the idea that management planned work while workers carried out work. This approach contributed to workers' stress-related illnesses, "burnout," alienation [9, 43], and high rates of absenteeism in a tight labor market [41]. Various "interventions" were developed to try and reform this system, including human resources and personnel management beginning in the 1930s and Socio-Technical Systems (STS) design, first developed in England in the 1940s and 1950s. The Scandinavian version of STS, "field experiments with autonomous work groups and related forms of work organization emerged . . . in the early 1960s . . . beginning with the Industrial Democracy Program in Norway," a collaboration between labor federations, employer federations, and researchers [43, p. 9; 44, p. 529]. Supervisors were "replaced by 'contact people' elected by and responsible to the groups" [44, p. 527].

The Japanese lean production approach primarily measured success through measures of interest to management, such as productivity and product quality. However, the Scandinavian experiments were also judged by their benefits to work organization and workers' health. Scandinavian research during the 1960s and 1970s demonstrated the stressful and illness-producing effects of the assembly-line approach, of machine-paced work, monotonous and repetitive work, lack of contact with co-workers, piece-rate payment systems, and authoritarian control of the worker [43], as well as demonstrating the benefits of the STS approach: "The new work organization has meant a richer job content, increased dignity for workers, increased solidarity among workers, increased trade union activity and strength, as well as a more effective use of productive resources in the company" [44, p. 527].

Results of these work experiments as well as the political strength of the labor movements in Norway and Sweden led to interventions on a national level—the Work Environment Acts, which gave workers greater influence over the work environment [43] and which spurred further efforts to humanize work. Evaluations of thousands of work life programs in Sweden and Norway provide evidence of increased job control, increased employee health and satisfaction, and increased productivity [3]. Improved job content not only benefited workers' health on the job, but their life outside the job. Swedish national surveys showed that workers whose jobs became more "passive" over 6 years reported less participation in political and leisure activities. In contrast, workers in jobs that became more "active" participated more in these activities [45, p. 53].

A recent Swedish field study showed that systolic blood pressure, heart rate, adrenalin, and fatigue increased significantly from the start to the end of a day shift on a traditional auto assembly line, but not at a more flexible work organization with small autonomous groups having greater opportunities to influence the pace and content of their work. And, unwinding after work (shown by a drop in adrenalin levels) occurred in workers in the more flexible work organization, but not after work on a traditional auto assembly line—especially for women workers [46].

Work humanization experiments in Scandinavia were conducted in a wide variety of workplaces, but the most well known were at Volvo [47] and Saab [48]. The auto assembly plant in Uddevalla, Sweden, which opened in 1989, was the culmination of years of experimentation at Volvo [49]. Instead of an assembly line, parallel teams built complete cars, with cycle times of 1.5-7 hours in contrast to the 60 second standards of typical assembly lines, and with greatly improved ergonomics [50]. However, in the midst of a recession in 1993, and a period of excess capacity, Volvo closed the Uddevalla plant. The causes of the closure, including organizational politics, have been debated. However, there is evidence that the productivity of the plant was competitive [49-51] with either the traditional or the lean production versions of assembly line work. The plant closing prevented the adequate evaluation of this experiment. We can only imagine that if the cost of injuries and chronic illnesses, absenteeism, and turnover caused by assembly line work were added to the equation, the STS experiment at Uddevalla might have been superior on purely economic measures; it was clearly healthier for workers than assembly line work.

WORKPLACE DEMOCRACY/WORKER OWNERSHIP

These Scandinavian efforts are examples of (limited) attempts to achieve greater workplace democracy. In a few cases, progressive employers have carried out such reforms. For example, employees in the successful Brazilian company Semco [52] have the right to approve every item of expenditure, veto new product ideas, and freely question everything in the company. More systematic efforts to achieve workplace democracy have occurred through producer cooperatives and other forms of worker ownership.

A worker cooperative is a corporation owned and controlled by the people who work in the company. The largest system of cooperatives is Mondragon, in the Basque region of Spain, but there are also many worker cooperatives in India, Italy, England, and other countries, including an estimated 500 in the United States [53]. Mondragon Corporacion Cooperativa has 120 different companies, 42,000 worker-owners, 43 schools, one college, more than $4.8 billion of business annually in manufacturing, services, retail and wholesale distribution, and is expanding. The workers elect management, and each enterprise has a committee that considers issues of health, safety, environment, and the social responsibilities of the enterprise [54]. Some critics claim, however, that tensions exist between business demands in the global economy and maintaining the principles of cooperation and employee control at Mondragon [55].

"Employee Stock Option Plans" (ESOPs) are cousins of worker cooperatives. In an ESOP, workers are offered, or required, to buy ownership stock in the company they work in. However, ownership rarely comes with decision-making powers that control the business, which is an important element of the worker cooperative model. Decision-making power in an ESOP remains with the majority stock owners, which may not be the worker-owners [53].

Employee ownership is sometimes seen as a last option for failing businesses. For example, following the factory closings, bankruptcies, and economic collapse in Argentina in 1999-2000, more than 150 abandoned or bankrupt factories or businesses have been taken over by their former employees, now as worker-owners. According to anecdotal reports, they are now producing on an industrial scale under worker control, with humanely paced assembly lines, support for family members, and morale-boosting conditions such as adequate staffing [56, 57]. Few cooperatives and worker-owned businesses have been evaluated for their impact on worker health and safety. However, to the extent that such experiments lead to increases in levels of workers' control, other things being equal, such improvements in work organization would likely result in improved physical and mental health for workers.

OTHER EMPLOYER-INITIATED INTERVENTIONS

In other cases, in order to enhance productivity or profitability, employers have carried out less sophisticated "interventions," that is, simply reducing the size of their workforce or "downsizing." A growing body of research provides evidence showing that downsizing can hurt the health of workers. For example, among those who *remained* on the job, downsizing has been associated with increases in fatal occupational injuries in the United States [58], musculoskeletal injuries and pain in Finland [59], sickness absence and rates of death from heart disease over 7.5 years among Finnish municipal workers [10], and minor psychiatric disorders and increases in blood pressure among male government employees in Great Britain [60].

HEALTH PROMOTION/STRESS MANAGEMENT

Another approach to dealing with workplace stressors has been to provide employees with personal strategies for coping with stress through stress management programs or programs to help them change unhealthy behaviors (for example, smoking, lack of exercise, poor diets) which can develop from or be maintained by stressful jobs. However, cardiac risk factor counseling may not be very effective if isolated from addressing the working conditions which may be at the root cause of, or significantly contributing to, cardiac risk factors, particularly among workers with a heavy burden of job stressors: "Despite devotion of substantial time and the use of state-of-the-art methods . . . our efforts applied systematically among pro-fessional drivers were, at best, only minimally effective, unless there was a con-comitant amelioration in stressful working conditions" [61].

In the United States, most efforts to reduce the health impact of work stressors have focused solely on personal stress management [62]. While stress management programs can have positive benefits, most have limited follow-up periods (only 23% > 6 months). Thus, it is not known whether or how long the benefits last. Benefits are also seen in control groups, and about one-third of participants fail to learn techniques, indicating that such approaches are not appropriate for everyone [62]. If employees return to an unchanged work environment and to high levels of job stressors, the benefits that may have been gained from a stress management program are likely to be eroded [63], if not entirely un-done.

Few health promotion programs have "focused on the physical, psychosocial, or policy work environment" [64, p. 1137]. Many "programs have emphasized risk-factor reduction strategies . . . , but have not integrated disease prevention and safety programs with organizational policies to enhance the physical and social quality of the workplace" [64, p. 1137]. Another limitation is the tendency for less participation by higher-risk, that is, poorer or less educated employees [65]. In other words, traditional health promotion programs in the United States have maintained a focus on the individual, and not on the root causes of disease risk in the workplace, such as work organization and management practices, which create stress and promote unhealthy behaviors. Traditional health promotion programs have also not been accepted or accessible to blue-collar or lower income workers. However, new programs have been developed that attempt to integrate health promotion with occupational health, and attempt to meet the needs of blue-collar or lower-income workers.

INTEGRATED HEALTH PROMOTION-OCCUPATIONAL HEALTH PROGRAMS

The previously mentioned action research intervention among Swedish civil servants included a personal "health promotion" component, involving relaxation training and an education program on job stress [25]. However, there was no comprehensive health promotion program. A number of researchers have recommended integrating workplace health promotion and occupational health, to develop "complementary behavioral and environmental interventions" [66, 67], or, as NIOSH recommends, the "combination of workplace and worker-directed measures" [68]. Several good examples of them now exist. For example, the WellWorks Project, a randomized controlled trial conducted in 24 worksites in Massachusetts, found a significant association between participation in nutrition and environmental exposure-related activities. These findings suggest that "participation in programs to reduce exposures to occupational hazards might contribute to blue-collar workers' participation in health promotion activities . . . when workers were aware of change their employer had made to reduce exposures to occupational hazards, they were more likely to participate in both smoking control and nutrition activities" [69, p. 191].

Barriers to participation in the WellWorks Project, such as blue-collar workers' time constraints and job responsibilities, were addressed, for example, through negotiation of time-off for participation in health promotion activities [70].

A program provided to Dutch manufacturing employees included individual-level exercise, health education and social skills training programs, as well as organizational-level support for lifestyle improvement (for example, an exercise facility, smoking policy, and healthier cafeteria food) *and* provided workers with greater influence over production decisions, greater task variety, job rotation, and training, leading to reduced cardiovascular disease risk, greater job control and reduced job demands, improved ergonomics and reduced absenteeism [71].

An action research approach can also be used to carry out integrated health promotion-occupational health programs. For example, following the publication of research showing that bus drivers in Denmark had high rates of heart disease [72], the Copenhagen Healthy Bus project was implemented. More than 200 interventions to improve the health, well-being, and work environment of 3,500 Copenhagen bus drivers were carried out between 1999-2004, with labor, management, and researcher cooperation. The interventions focused on: *lifestyle* (smoking cessation, healthy diet courses, and fresh fruit available in garages); *job characteristics/work organization* (more flexible schedules, meeting drivers' wishes on rotation and schedules, and better communication between management and drivers); *education and training* (personnel management and communication for managers, handling threats and violence, and "knowing your bus"); and the *physical work environment* (more resources for bus preventive maintenance and joint labor-management meetings) [73].

While such an integrated approach is not yet common in the United States, some positive developments exist. A new form of a "health risk appraisal" has been developed which goes beyond asking workers about their health behaviors (such as smoking, exercise, and diet) and reviews policies on the extent to which companies provide support for exercise programs, smoking-cessation programs, or healthy food in their cafeterias, *and* policies on organizational level "interventions" such as flexible work schedules and collective bargaining [74].

EVALUATIONS OF WORK REDESIGN AND ORGANIZATIONAL INTERVENTIONS

A new comprehensive review concludes that "systems approaches" (emphasizing primary prevention, integrating primary with secondary and tertiary prevention, including meaningful participation of employees), are the most effective in dealing with the organizational and individual impacts of job stress [75]. An earlier reviewer similarly argued, "Work redesign to enrich jobs (such as by increasing employees' job control) is therefore a powerful stress-reduction intervention which has potentially important business benefits" [76].

These reviews are consistent with research on job redesign and work organization changes that lead to lower injury rates, which include: empowerment of the workforce, job autonomy, and delegation of control; good relations between management and workers; low stress and low grievance rates; and encouragement of the long-term commitment of the workforce [77, 78].

At least one NIOSH researcher has concluded that key ingredients of successful interventions include risk analysis, a combination of workplace and worker-directed measures, a participative approach, and top management support [68]. Semmer similarly argued that "interventions are likely to be the most promising if they involve a participative approach, are based on a sound analysis of pressing problems, from which necessary steps are inferred in a systematic way, combine work-directed and person-directed interventions, and encourage management support" [79].

However, not all reviewers have been this positive. For example, in their 1998 review of the literature, Parkes and Sparkes concluded " . . . the studies do not present a convincing picture of the value of organizational interventions designed to reduce work stress . . . and tend to be difficult to interpret, causally ambiguous, inconsistent, based on small samples, and/or statistically non-significant." They specified that "socio-technical" interventions, reducing stress by changing objective aspects of the work situation (such as work schedules or workload) were particularly successful. However, "psychosocial" interventions and enhancing job satisfaction and performance by modifying employees' perceptions of the work environment (by increasing, for example, levels of perceived autonomy, social support, communications, and role clarity) were slightly less consistent, although still encouraging [80].

CONCLUSION

A wide variety of interventions and prevention programs have been developed and used in order to reduce job stressors and the health problems they cause. These interventions can be carried out at the level of the job, throughout the organization, at a more personal level, or at a state or national level through laws and regulations. It is important that the effects of interventions be carefully observed, measured, and documented [81].

Work organization and job stressors are also shaped by the competition employers face in the global economy. Thus, solutions to the problem will also need to be international in scope. The European-wide regulations and labor-management agreements that deal with job stress are one example of solutions achieved through national regulations while addressing organizational levels, and which are international in scope by encompassing all of the countries of the European Union.

While more research on the effectiveness of different types of interventions would always be useful, the existing research allows us to draw various conclusions. For one, effective interventions tend to be those involving "systems approaches," which focus on *both* primary prevention, that is, changing the causes of work stress, such as work schedules and workload, *and* include secondary and tertiary levels of prevention, with programs to help employees suffering symptoms of stress or who have become ill due to job stressors. Additionally, the existing research allows us to conclude that effective interventions also involve meaningful participation of employees, increasing employees' job control, and ensuring top management support.

We should continue to be persistent and creative in developing, carrying out, and evaluating workplace changes designed to improve workers' health. Listening to employees about their concerns, their pain, and the solutions they recommend is a key principle of this effort. The following chapters provide some excellent and more detailed examples of interventions carried out to reduce stress and create healthier work—and workers.

FOR FURTHER READING

For those planning intervention programs in your workplace, you can find further details on successful programs in:

LaMontagne, A., T. Keegel, A. Louie, A. Ostry, and P. Landsbergis, A Systematic Review of the Job Stress Intervention Evaluation Literature: 1990-2005, *International Journal of Occupational and Environmental Health*, 13, pp. 268-280,

2007. Open access at www.ijoeh.com. Appendix with details of reviewed studies is available in pdf format at www.ijoeh.com

Semmer, N., Job Stress Interventions and the Organization of Work, *Scandinavian Journal of Work, Environment and Health*, 32:6(Special Issue), pp. 515-527, 2006.

Semmer, N., Job Stress Interventions and Organization of Work, in Quick, J. and L. Tetrick (eds.), *Handbook of Occupational Health Psychology*, American Psychological Association, Washington, DC, pp. 325-353, 2003.

REFERENCES

1. Murphy, L. and S. Sauter, Work Organization Interventions: State of Knowledge and Future Directions, *Soz-Praventivmed*, 49, pp. 79-86, 2004.
2. Last, J., *A Dictionary of Epidemiology*, Oxford University Press, New York, 1995.
3. Levi, L., Legislation to Protect Worker CV Health in Europe, *Occupational Medicine: State-of-the-Art Reviews*, 15:1, pp. 269-273, 2000.
4. Shimomitsu, T. and Y. Odagiri, Working Life in Japan, *Occupational Medicine: State of the Art Reviews*, 15:1, pp. 280-281, 2000.
5. Warren, N., U.S. Regulations for Work Organization, *Occupational Medicine: State-of-the-Art Reviews*, 15:1, pp. 275-280, 2000.
6. Milkman, R. and E. Appelbaum, Paid Family Leave in California: New Research Findings, in *The State of California Labor 2004*, University of California Press, Berkeley, 2004.
7. Levi, L., Work Stress and Health: Research Approaches and Health Promotion Strategies, in *Behavioral Medicine: An Integrated Biobehavioral Approach to Health and Illness*, Araki, S. (ed.), Elsevier, New York, 1992.
8. European Trade Union Confederation, Union of Industrial and Employers Confederations of Europe, European Association of Craft Small and Medium-Sized Enterprises, and European Centre of Enterprises with Public Participation and of Enterprises of General Economic Interest, *Framework Agreement on Work-Related Stress*, cited 2004, available from: http://www.etuc.org/a/529
9. Landsbergis, P. A., J. Cahill, and P. Schnall, The Impact of Lean Production and Related New Systems of Work Organization on Worker Health, *Journal of Occupational Health Psychology*, 4:2, pp. 108-130, 1999.
10. Vahtera, J., M. Kivimaki, J. Pentti, et al., Organisational Downsizing, Sickness Absence, and Mortality: 10-Town Prospective Cohort Study, *British Medical Journal*, 328:7439, p. 555, 2004.
11. The Tokyo Declaration, *Journal of the Tokyo Medical University*, 56:6, pp. 760-767, 1998.
12. Herbert, R., B. Plattus, L. Kellogg, et al., The Union Health Center: A Working Model of Clinical Care Linked to Preventive Occupational Health Services, *American Journal of Industrial Medicine*, 31, pp. 263-273, 1997.
13. Belkic, K., P. Schnall, and M. Ugljesic, Cardiovascular Evaluation of the Worker and Workplace: A Practical Guide for Clinicians, *Occupational Medicine: State of the Art Reviews*, 15:1, pp. 213-222, 2000.
14. Karasek, R. A., G. Gordon, C. Pietrokovsky, et al., *Job Content Instrument: Questionnaire and User's Guide*, University of Southern California/University of Massachusetts, Lowell, Los Angeles/Lowell, MA, 1985.

15. Siegrist, J. and R. Peter, *Measuring Effort-Reward Imbalance at Work: Guidelines*, University of Dusseldorf, Dusseldorf, 1996.

16. Belkic, K., C. Savic, T. Theorell, and S. Cizinsky, *Work Stressors and Cardiovascular Risk: Assessment for Clinical Practice. Part I, National Institute for Psychosocial Factors and Health. Section for Stress Research*, Karolinska Institute, WHO Psychosocial Center, Stockholm, 1995.

17. Schnall, P. and K. Belkic, Point Estimates of Blood Pressure at the Worksite, *Occupational Medicine: State-of-the-Art Reviews*, 15:1, pp. 203-208, 2000.

18. Schnall, P., K. Belkic, P. Landsbergis, et al., Hypertension at the Workplace-Often an Occult Disease: The Relevance and Potential in Japan for Work Site Surveillance?, *Japanese Journal of Stress Science*, 15:3, pp. 152-174, 2000.

19. Belkic, K., P. Schnall, P. Landsbergis, and D. Baker, The Workplace and CV Health: Conclusions and Thoughts for a Future Agenda, *Occupational Medicine: State of the Art Reviews*, 15:1, pp. 307-322, 2000.

20. Susman, G. and R. Evered, An Assessment of the Scientific Merits of Action Research, *Administrative Science Quarterly*, 23, pp. 582-603, 1978.

21. Israel, B., S. Schurman, and J. House, Action Research on Occupational Stress: Involving Workers as Researchers, *International Journal of Health Services*, 19:1, pp. 135-155, 1989.

22. International Labor Office, *Conditions of Work Digest: Preventing Stress at Work*, International Labor Office, Geneva, Switzerland, 1992.

23. Landsbergis, P. A., S. J. Schurman, B. A. Israel, et al., Job Stress and Heart Disease: Evidence and Strategies for Prevention, *New Solutions*, 3:4, pp. 42-58, 1993.

24. Mikkelsen, A., P. O. Saksvik, and P. Landsbergis, The Impact of a Participatory Organizational Intervention on Job Stress in Community Health Care Institutions, *Work & Stress*, 14:2, pp. 156-170, 2000.

25. Orth-Gomer, K., I. Eriksson, V. Moser, T. Theorell, and P. Fredlund, Lipid Lowering through Work Stress Reduction, *International Journal of Behavioral Medicine*, 1:3, pp. 204-214, 1994.

26. Rydstedt, L. W., G. Johansson, and G. W. Evans, The Human Side of the Road: Improving the Working Conditions of Urban Bus Drivers, *Journal of Occupational Health Psychology*, 3, pp. 161-171, 1998.

27. Landsbergis, P. A. and J. Cahill, Labor Union Programs to Reduce or Prevent Occupational Stress in the United States, *International Journal of Health Services*, 24, pp. 105-129, 1994.

28. Landsbergis, P., Collective Bargaining to Reduce CVD Risk Factors in the Work Environment, *Occupational Medicine: State-of-the-Art Reviews*, 15:1, pp. 287-292, 2000.

29. Lee, P. and N. Krause, The Impact of a Worker Health Study on Working Conditions, *Journal of Public Health Policy*, 23, pp. 268-285, 2002.

30. AFL-CIO Working Women's Department, *Bargaining Fact Sheet: Control Over Work Hours and Alternative Work Schedules*, AFL-CIO Working Women's Department, Washington, DC, 2001.

31. Grundy, L., L. Bell, and N. Firestein, *Labor's Role in Addressing the Child Care Crisis*, Foundation for Child Development, New York, 1999.

32. Dones, N. and N. Firestein, Labor's Participation in Work Family Issues: Successes and Obstacles, in *Learning from the Past—Looking to the Future*, Beem, C. and J. Heymann (eds.), The Work, Family and Democracy Project, Racine, WI, 2002.

33. Cahill, J. and L. H. Feldman, Computers in Child Welfare: Planning for a More Serviceable Work Environment, *Child Welfare*, 72, pp. 3-12, 1993.

34. Israel, B. A., S. J. Schurman, and J. S. House, Action Research on Occupational Stress: Involving Workers as Researchers, *International Journal of Health Services,* 19, pp. 135-155, 1989.

35. Smith, M. and D. Zehel, A Stress Reduction Intervention Programme for Meat Processors Emphasizing Job Design and Work Organization, *Conditions of Work Digest,* 11:2, pp. 204-213, 1992.

36. Beermann, B., K. Kuhn, and M. Kompier, Germany: Reduction of Stress by Health Circles, in *Preventing Stress, Improving Productivity European Case Studies in the Workplace,* Kompier, M. and C. Cooper (eds.), Routledge, New York, pp. 222-241, 1999.

37. European Agency for Safety and Health at Work, *How to Tackle Psychosocial Issues and Reduce Work-Related Stress. Systems and Programmes,* 127, Office for Official Publications of the European Communities, Luxembourg, 2002.

38. Bourbonnais, R., C. Brisson, A. Vinet, M. Vezina, and A. Lower, Development and Implementation of a Participative Intervention to Improve the Psychosocial Work Environment and Mental Health in an Acute Care Hospital, *Occupational and Environmental Medicine,* 63, pp. 326-334, 2006.

39. Bourbonnais, R., C. Brisson, A. Vinet, M. Vezina, and A. Lower, Effectiveness of a Participatory Intervention on Psychosocial Work Factors to Prevent Mental Health Problems in a Hospital Setting, *Occupational and Environmental Medicine,* 63, pp. 335-342, 2006.

40. Schnall, P. L., P. A. Landsbergis, J. Schwartz, K. Warren, and T. G. Pickering, A Longitudinal Study of Job Strain and Ambulatory Blood Pressure: Results from a Three-Year Follow-Up, *Psychosomatic Medicine,* 60, pp. 697-706, 1998.

41. Ramsay, H., From Kalmar to Koromo, in *International Workshop on Worker Participation: What Can We Learn from the Swedish Experience?* Cressey, P. (ed.), European Foundation for the Improvement of Living and Working Conditions, Dublin, Ireland, pp. 133-145, 1992.

42. National Institute for Occupational Safety and Health, *The Changing Organization of Work and the Safety and Health of Working People,* NIOSH, Cincinnati, OH, 2002.

43. Gardell, B. and B. Gustavsen, Work Environment Research and Social Change: Current Developments in Scandinavia, *Journal of Occupational Behavior,* 1, pp. 3-17, 1980.

44. Gardell, B., Worker Participation and Autonomy: A Multilevel Approach to Democracy at the Workplace, *International Journal of Health Services,* 12, pp. 527-558, 1982.

45. Karasek, R. and T. Theorell, *Healthy Work: Stress, Productivity, and the Reconstruction of Working Life,* Basic Books, New York, 1990.

46. Melin, B., U. Lundberg, J. Soderlund, and M. Granqvist, Psychophysiological Stress Reactions of Male and Female Assembly Workers: A Comparison between Two Different Forms of Work Organization, *Journal of Organizational Behavior,* 20, pp. 47-61, 1999.

47. Ellegard, K., T. Engstrom, and L. Nilsson, *Reforming Industrial Work—Principles and Realities in the Planning of Volvo's Car Assembly Plant in Uddevalla,* Swedish Work Environment Fund, Stockholm, 1991.

48. Swedish Work Environment Fund, *Man and Technology in Interaction: The Saab Body Shop in Trollhattan, Sweden,* Swedish Work Environment Fund, Stockholm, 1989.

49. Sandberg, A. E., *Human Resource, Management, and Personnel: Enriching Production: Perspectives on Volvo's Uddevalla Plant as an Alternative to Lean Production,* Avebury, Aldershot, 1995.

50. Berggren, C., *Volvo Uddevalla: A Dead Horse or a Car Dealer's Dream?,* Royal Institute of Technology, Department of Work Science, Stockholm, Sweden, 1993.

51. Berggren, C., Nummi Vs Uddevalla, *Sloan Management Review,* 35:2, pp. 37-45, 1994.

52. Semler, R., *The Seven Day Weekend,* Portfolio, New York, 2003.
53. Padgham, J., Worker Cooperatives, *Bulletin of the University of Wisconsin Center for Cooperatives,* 5, 2002.
54. The Oklahoma City Catholic Worker, *Mondragon: A Better Way to Go to Work?,* cited 2008, available from: http://www.justpeace.org/mondragon.htm
55. Wikipedia, *Mondragón Cooperative Corporation,* cited 2008, available from: http://en.wikipedia.org/wiki/mondrag%c3%b3n_cooperative_corporation
56. Ballve, M., The Silent Revolution, *Orion Magazine,* July/August 2006.
57. Magnani, E., *El Cambio Silencioso,* Prometeo, Buenos Aires, 2003.
58. Richardson, D. and D. Loomis, Trends in Fatal Occupational Injuries and Industrial Restructuring in North Carolina in the 1980s, *American Journal of Public Health,* 87, pp. 1041-1043, 1997.
59. Vahtera, J., M. Kivimaki, and J. Pentti, Effect of Organizational Downsizing on Health Employees, *Lancet,* 350, pp. 1124-1128, 1997.
60. Ferrie, J. E., M. J. Shipley, M. Marmot, S. Stansfeld, and G. D. Smith, The Health Effects of Major Organisational Change and Job Insecurity, *Social Science and Medicine,* 46, pp. 243-254, 1998.
61. Fisher, J. and K. Belkic, A Public Health Approach in Clinical Practice, in *The Workplace and Cardiovascular Disease Occupational Medicine: State of the Art Reviews,* Schnall, P., K. Belkic, P. A. Landsbergis, and D. Baker (eds.), Hanley and Belfus, Philadelphia, PA, pp. 245-256, 2000.
62. Murphy, L. R., Stress Management in Work Settings: A Critical Review of the Health Effects, *American Journal of Health Promotion,* 11, pp. 112-135, 1996.
63. Nowack, K., Screening and Management of the Workplace in Relation to Cardiovascular Disease Risk, *Occupational Medicine: State-of-the-Art Reviews,* 15:1, pp. 231-233, 2000.
64. Stokols, D., K. R. Pelletier, and J. E. Fielding, Integration of Medical Care and Worksite Health Promotion, *Journal of the American Medical Association,* 273:14, pp. 1136-1142, 1995.
65. Lewis, R. J., W. H. Huebner, and C. M. Yarborough, Characteristics of Participants and Nonparticipants in Worksite Health Promotion, *American Journal of Health Promotion,* 11, pp. 99-106, 1996.
66. Heaney, C. A. and R. Z. Goetzel, A Review of Health-Related Outcomes of Multi-Component Worksite Health Promotion Programs, *American Journal of Health Promotion,* 11, pp. 290-308, 1997.
67. Dejoy, D. M. and D. J. Southern, An Integrative Perspective on Work Site Health Promotion, *Journal of Occupational Medicine,* 35:12, pp. 1221-1230, 1993.
68. Murphy, L. and S. Sauter, Work Organization Interventions: Status of Research and Practice, in *The Way We Work and Its Impact on Our Health,* Center for Social Epidemiology, Los Angeles, pp. 121-125, 2004.
69. Sorensen, G., A. Stoddard, J. K. Ockene, M. K. Hunt, and R. Youngstrom, Worker Participation in an Integrated Health Promotion/Health Protection Program: Results from the Wellworks Project, *Health Education Quarterly,* 23, pp. 191-203, 1996.
70. Sorensen, G., J. S. Himmelstein, M. K. Hunt, et al., A Model for Worksite Cancer Prevention: Integration of Health Protection and Health Promotion in the Wellworks Project, *American Journal of Health Promotion,* 10:1, pp. 55-62, 1995.
71. Maes, S., C. Verhoeven, F. Kittel, and H. Scholten, Effects of a Dutch Work-Site Wellness-Health Program: The Brabantia Project, *American Journal of Public Health,* 88:7, pp. 1037-1041, 1998.

72. Tuchsen, F. and L. A. Endahl, Increasing Inequality in Ischaemic Heart Disease Morbidity among Employed Men in Denmark 1981-1993: The Need for a New Preventive Policy, *International Journal of Epidemiology*, 28, pp. 640-644, 1999.

73. Poulsen, K., S. Jensen, E. Bach, and J. Schostak, Using Action Research to Improve Health and the Work Environment for 3500 Municipal Bus Drivers, *Educational Action Research*, 15:1, pp. 75-106, 2007.

74. Golaszewski, T. and B. Fisher, Heart Check: The Development and Evolution of an Organizational Heart Health Assessment, *American Journal of Health Promotion*, 17:2, pp. 132-153, 2002.

75. LaMontagne, A., T. Keegel, A. Louie, A. Ostry, and P. Landsbergis, A Systematic Review of the Job Stress Intervention Evaluation Literature: 1990-2005, *International Journal of Occupational and Environmental Health*, 13, pp. 268-280, 2007.

76. Parker, S. K., P. R. Jackson, C. A. Sprigg, and A. C. Whybrow, *Organisational Interventions to Reduce the Impact of Poor Work Design*, The University of Sheffield/Health & Safety Executive, Sheffield, UK, pp. 1-30, 1998.

77. Shannon, H., J. Mayr, and T. Haines, Overview of the Relationship between Organizational and Workplace Factors and Injury Rates, *Safety Science*, 26:3, pp. 291-217, 1997.

78. Hale, A. and J. Hovden, Management and Culture: The Third Age of Safety. A Review of Approaches to Organizational Aspects of Safety, Health and Environment, in *Occupational Injury: Risk, Prevention and Intervention*, Feyer, A. M. and A. Williamson (eds.), Taylor & Francis, London, UK, 1998.

79. Semmer, N., Job Stress Interventions and the Organization of Work, *Scandinavian Journal of Work, Environment and Health*, 32:6(Special Issue), pp. 515-527, 2006.

80. Parkes, K. R. and T. J. Sparkes, *Organizational Interventions to Reduce Work Stress. Are They Effective? A Review of the Literature*, HSE Books, Sudbury, 1998.

81. Semmer, N., Commentary II. Health Related Interventions in Organizations: Stages, Levels, Criteria and Methodology, *Soz-Praventivmed*, 49:89-91, 2004.

CHAPTER 12

Using Participatory Action Research Methodology to Improve Worker Health

Ellen Rosskam

A variety of catalysts can lead to changes in work organization. Informally collecting information, talking with workers, observing work processes, examining workers' compensation or absenteeism records, or simply getting an impression by listening to what people say in the workplace can indicate that a problem may exist which is causing health issues. Formal research is a useful tool that often helps trade unions, management, and policymakers to guide work organization change. Research can be used to provide the empirical foundation needed to lead to policy-level changes or to create change at the level of the organization. The collaboration between workers, management, and researchers often is helpful to identify or describe worker health issues. Participatory Action Research (PAR) is presented in this chapter demonstrating a methodology appropriate for the epidemiological study of health issues in worker populations. The chapter will explore why PAR is useful for and consistent with an examination of jobs or workplaces as entire systems, as opposed to viewing worker health outcomes as the outcome of individual behaviors or as the result of single work tasks or exposures. A variety of examples are provided where PAR has been used for the study of work-related health issues leading to concrete, measurable improvements in worker health and working conditions.

RESEARCH IN THE PAR CONTEXT

Research oriented toward action and/or change can apply in several contexts including: 1) the professional expert model, in which the researcher makes a study and recommends a course of action to decision-makers in the organization studied; 2) action research controlled by the researcher, in which the researcher aims to be a principal change agent as well as controlling the research process; or 3) participatory action research, in which the researcher seeks to involve some members of the organization studied as active participants in all stages of the research/action process [1].

Investigations in the PAR context incorporate a systematic effort to generate knowledge about specific conditions that can influence changes in a given situation (e.g., in a community or a workplace). The term "action" in PAR indicates that the research is meant to contribute to change efforts or accompany action by the participants, such as workers and their representative trade unions, or change for employers through an interactive research-learning process. PAR in the workplace is a process of systematic inquiry in which those who are experiencing a work-related problem participate with trained researchers in deciding the focus of knowledge generation, in collecting and analyzing information, and in taking action to improve the conditions or resolve the problem entirely [2].

Researchers in the PAR vein reject the separation of theory from practice and view science as best advanced when theory and practice, research and action, are linked together. PAR breaks the mold of conventional research in its process of reflection and action, carried out *with* people rather than *on* them, using a "bottom-up" approach, where local knowledge and priorities form the basis for the research and planning process.

Participatory action researchers put into question domination and dominating research structures and relationships, including how actual organizational structures, processes, and practices shape and influence the ways in which those holding decision-making power relate to those not holding decision-making power. This questioning is particularly relevant and important to work-related research given the complex nature of worker-management relationships; indeed it is the very process of human inquiry that provides the impetus toward action. At its core, PAR on work-related health issues promotes worker participation in decision-making in the workplace, which implies an inherent redistribution of power between workers and management. In workplace PAR, this can also be conceived of as sharing and providing information and access to resource mobilization to help others as well as oneself [3].

The Theoretical Roots of PAR: A Multidisciplinary Methodology

PAR has its academic roots in sociology, social psychology, psychology, organizational studies, and education. The converging of these various disciplines has made PAR relevant for use by the Tavistock Institute of Human Relations in London and the Work Research Institute in Oslo, both of which have carried out extensive work studying, applying, and promoting PAR. In Norway, PAR has been used for decades because the methodology allows for the generation of situation-specific knowledge within a broad-based context. Interest in participatory research emerged in Norway as an outgrowth of a national enactment of an innovative work environment law in 1977 based on workers actively participating in studying and changing their own workplaces and focusing on improving and democratizing working conditions. This led to the need for more participatory and action-based research and techniques to be developed.

The domain of PAR methodology includes the principles of participation, reflection, and empowerment of groups seeking to improve their social or work situation. PAR pioneers such as Kurt Lewin have focused on learning about social systems by trying to change them. Lewin, for example, used PAR and experience with group discussion methods and group dynamics in studies aimed at solving social and organizational problems, rather than using research to resolve purely theoretical issues. Key to Lewin's approach was linking research to empowerment and principles of democracy. Recognizing the importance of social context in order to understand an individual or a group problem—workplace or organizational, Lewin pushed forward the use of theory to improve real situations and problems [4]. *"[C]ausal inferences about the behavior of human beings are more likely to be valid and enactable when the human beings in question participate in building and testing them"* [5]. To achieve that which is *enactable*, PAR involves participants in the research process, enabling them to give and get valid information, make choices freely, including the choice to participate in the research or not, and generate their own commitment to the results of the research.

While Lewin is credited with the development of PAR methods, much of the theoretical base on which PAR is built is inspired by the later work of Brazilian educator Paulo Freire. The central premise of Freire's work is that education is not neutral; workers bring their life experiences and expectations into learning environments, and leave with the consequences of the interaction. Freire's work in education made an important contribution to the process of knowing and learning through an on-going process of action and reflection, inspiring many researchers to develop PAR methodology [6].

One of the key aspects of PAR that distinguishes it from other research methods, such as the professional expert model, lies not in the methods but in the attitudes and beliefs of the researchers, specifically how they view the locus of control in the research process. Participatory researchers view society and social change from a perspective that recognizes that change sometimes occurs through conflict between groups, and that society often benefits some at the cost of others, particularly those who are socially and economically marginalized. This contrasts with an equilibrium perspective toward such groups.

Another key distinction between PAR and the "professional expert model" in particular, is that research conducted within the professional expert model is aimed at government-imposed standards. While this assumption remains unspoken, it is a critical determining factor in how such research is conceived, designed, and conducted. Rarely does research aimed at government-imposed standards include participation of the workers who such standards are meant to impact, or direct intervention, monitoring, evaluation, and enforcement of such standards. In the present era of anti-regulation, PAR becomes quite important because of its inherent participation and intervention-based orientation as well as its in-built focus on change from *within* a workplace, union, company, or organization. Indeed, in an *anti-regulation* era, strengthening workers' knowledge, and participation, self-monitoring and enforcement of standards *within* workplaces take on a dimension of far greater importance than in periods of strong, committed government monitoring and enforcement of standards. In the United States, the last two decades have been dominated by "voluntary initiatives" and "self-regulation by management," with few results to be lauded to date. Concomitant with and further degrading conditions in this era of anti-governmental regulation, results generated by professional expert-based research are often ignored, leading to less and less protection for working people. Under such conditions where interventions are not strongly promoted and governed by local, state, or federal governments, more PAR is needed to strengthen collective efforts around workers' health and community-based efforts, and to create opportunities for interventions at the level of the organization.

Applying PAR as a methodology requires ensuring that those participating in the research feel that the researchers have genuine respect for them and their experiences, that their opinions are valued, and that they are perceived as partners in the process. Research tool choice should depend on what is being studied as well as why a subject is being studied. PAR can be used to extend the principles of education for empowerment, which espouse learning that is participatory, based on real-life experiences. The primary purpose of PAR has thus often been to encourage the poor and oppressed, and those who work with them, to generate and control their own knowledge. As a research methodology, PAR assumes that knowledge generates power and that people's knowledge is central to social change.

While the role of any researcher is to be a learner, in PAR, the researcher's role is to be a co-learner and a co-producer, learning alongside the stakeholder groups, relinquishing the role as the sole "expert" [4]. Developing an organizational learning process requires the initiative to be located within the organization itself. The needs of the organization inform the research questions and come from within the organization. The participatory researcher's task is to contribute to the discovery and development of the conditions necessary for a process to be self-sustaining. Extending this thinking to organizational change indicates that a change process may be established as a result of the co-learning that has taken place during the research process. The participatory researcher need not be the problem-solver and in fact, probably should not be seen as having a technocratic role. The chance of success in a participatory research change process is high because the change agents are both multiplied and motivated.

Researchers using the PAR methodology need to remain flexible given that there are other key stakeholder groups who will be defining and determining forces in how the research process is implemented. Each situation will be different, depending on its context, the participant group, the subject being studied, and the empowering actions desired at the end. It is important that the research is aimed at a change process such that the information generated by the research is transmitted to and remains with the participants of the study when completed. To do this successfully, researchers need to develop alliances with existing groups who should have ownership over a change process, such as trade unions and managers supportive of and participating in a workplace improvement effort through research. Where unions do not exist or where they lack strength, notwithstanding, PAR can be conducted together with other types of organized groups, such as community groups, grassroots organizations, non-governmental organizations, or simply together with willing management. For PAR to be effective, it is desirable for a change component to be planned—or at least envisioned—from the research design stage, and it is necessary to engage in the process with people who have the power to institute those desired changes.

PAR methodology has been used in community development and health-related research, such as with community health workers and nurses, in industrial and other types of organizations. PAR also has led to a major expansion of the scope of scientific research in the field of agriculture, where it has been widely applied [1]. In these settings, researchers using PAR have focused primarily on oppressed groups in order to empower and generate collective action, where new knowledge based on research led to local level and industrial actions aimed at improvements for workers.

PAR has also been used as a methodology to address community and organization issues, including management and labor issues in various countries [1]. PAR has been used extensively in organizational development in industry, and by management applying human resource theories, particularly those with a systems perspective focusing on the fit, or lack of fit, between work and family, for example, or between the organization and implementation of work and people's psychosocial needs. PAR has evolved into a research perspective with many variations today. When participatory systems work well, they produce results because they apply a wide range of information and ideas to problems in an organizational context.

Typically, in addressing problems stemming from the workplace, PAR researchers view research as serving the broader purpose of empowering workers to take an active part in making their workplace and/or community safer, rather than simply encouraging worker compliance with health-oriented or safety rules. The extension of worker involvement in production is for workers to participate in the research process when examining work processes, particularly processes flawed in design, as demonstrated by occupational injuries and illnesses. Involving workers in the research process can promote organizational learning and can catalyze organizational change from within, without any stimulation by outside researchers.

PAR for Workplace-Based Research

The application of PAR methodology in occupational health research, therefore, starts from a belief that adults are self-motivated and rich with information that has immediate application to their lives and work. In research where workers' health is in question due to work processes, some degree of change in the organization is likely to be necessary to prevent further work-related injury and illness.

Few problems can be resolved in modern industrial organizations through the use of any single academic discipline; the complex nature of work calls for integrating ideas and methods from a variety of disciplines. The increasingly complex nature of the workplace gives rise to greater need to understand the causes and methods of prevention of work-related accidents, injuries, and illnesses, and the transmission of this information to workers, managers, and others is a critical dimension of preventing these negative outcomes. Important advantages of PAR methods include the qualitative information obtained about workers involved in the study, the potential to obtain a precise picture of work-related risks and the root causes, and the semi-quantitative data on adverse health outcomes. Use of the research as a means of catalyzing a process of consciousness-raising and organization among workers is a further advantage, enabling positive actions for workplace improvements. Learning which draws on real-life experiences, incorporates dialogue between and among educators and workers, and engages in a critical analysis of the organizational and system-wide causes of problems could be aimed at worker action and empowerment. Participatory research is based on the same philosophy [7]. As a research methodology, PAR assumes that knowledge generates power and that people's knowledge is central to social change. PAR puts workers and their priorities first.

PAR methodology incorporates the recognition that the research process can be a tool to encourage workers to question and challenge the very systems that may keep them passive and not able to participate in decision-making, which in turn adversely affects their well-being. Dialogue and participation in the research process are means for workers to gain a critical understanding of the causes of workplace problems and their role in accepting or challenging these forces. Where workers are consulted and participate in projects likely to affect them, positive outcomes and changes are more likely to be sustainable in part because participants can critically analyze the barriers to change in systems of work organization.

PAR in the workplace, like education, is most effective when it includes a holistic view of the context of behaviors, including an analysis of obstacles to safe or healthful work practices, without becoming narrowed to specific individual behaviors or competencies. Employing a holistic and systems view is concordant with the reality that improvement in working conditions takes place in a wider organizational context of worker and management relations.

The need for a holistic view of occupational disease is a compelling reason for occupational physicians to view workers as members of an occupational health team [8]. Mergler [9] pointed out that the participation of workers in occupational health research can take two forms: 1) where workers contribute their knowledge of working conditions and health problems to provide a better understanding of the conditions and their impact; and/or 2) where workers participate in all stages of the design and implementation of the project.

Notwithstanding, success for change to improve workers' health and to make changes in the organization of work depend largely on collectivity. Where workplaces are unionized and backed by a strong trade union, the chance for success is greater than where collective voice is lacking. But even collective voice alone may not suffice. Using research to implement work organization and policy changes generally requires the existence of collective bargaining agreements, which provide workers with the strong bargaining chip they need to implement change.

The Challenge of Existing Methods in Occupational Health Research

While research using action-oriented methodologies in work-related health studies does exist, the epidemiology and occupational health literature remain dominated by studies applying purely quantitative methods. Within what is considered the "scientific paradigm," research methodologies that will lead to generalizing research findings to large groups and using research methods that are meant to remove "biases" by randomizing the selection of participants in studies and the recipients of interventions are the methods attributed the "gold stamp" of credibility as scientific methodology. Yet the over-reliance on quantitative cross-sectional or cohort designs and the use of validated measures without incorporating the perspectives of workers inadvertently results in research findings that all too often seem remote from the everyday working conditions of specific workplaces.

In conducting PAR-based occupational health research, both qualitative and quantitative techniques can be applied. Quantitative techniques may include survey-based data collection and systematic analysis by structured questionnaire with closed and open-ended questions. Qualitative techniques may include structured individual interviews with open-ended questions, participant observation on the job, focus group interviews, and discussions, videotaping, and examination of work processes, workstation analysis, document and archival review, and a broad or well-defined literature review. Engaging in discussion with workers and management at various stages of the research process is an important means of increasing confidence in the research findings by both groups and can strengthen the process and outcomes aimed at eventual change.

While PAR is a validated scientific methodology, because it involves stakeholders in the research process and aims to contribute to a change process many in the scientific community do not consider that it is a methodology with an equal stamp of credibility. The scientific literature based on purely quantitative cross-sectional or cohort studies lacks participation by workers and a focus on strategies for change. It is a major reason that such studies seldom contribute directly to improving workers' health and working conditions, nor do they provide employers with the benefits that come with attention and commitment to worker health and well-being (such as reduced absenteeism, increased and improved productivity, improved workplace morale, reduced insurance costs, and a more healthy society overall). Since too few researchers include a link between research and action in occupational health research, conducting research together with workers, trade unions, and managers using a PAR methodology would be a marked improvement.

The U.S. National Institute for Occupational Safety and Health (NIOSH) has made ensuring the link between research and practice a key focus in its present program of work. The participation of stakeholder groups in the research process helps to ensure the relevancy of issues addressed and questions asked to investigate those issues. The interpretation of findings also can be conducted with input from the stakeholder groups that could complement the researchers' analysis.

CASE EXAMPLES OF OCCUPATIONAL HEALTH
STUDIES USING PAR

The chapters by Antonio, Fisher, and Rosskam (chapter 13) and by Casey and Rosskam (chapter 14) in part III of this book describe PAR studies that led to improvements in the health, well-being, and working conditions of hotel room cleaners and urban bus drivers in San Francisco. Comparisons by Laurell et al. [10] of workplace-based study results based on PAR methodology made with results from an individual questionnaire have affirmed PAR-generated results as more revealing than individual questionnaire-generated results.

Hugentobler et al. [11] used PAR methods to implement a longitudinal multi-methodological research and intervention project investigating occupational stress, psychosocial factors, and health outcomes; their findings were combined with intervention to improve worker health. Israel, Schurman, and Hugentobler [12] used PAR methodology to better understand and try to reduce the negative effects of work-related stress. Ritchie [13] described the workplace as a useful venue for research, where social and environmental factors in a work environment can be relatively easily explored, a defined community where one can legitimately explore and help to develop improvement-oriented and empowerment-based strategies for action. Schurman [14] used a PAR approach to study stress in an automobile factory, involving the factory workers in the investigation. The process was designed to improve the system's performance through work organization redesign and to contribute to the body of scientific knowledge at the same time.

Occupational Health Research with Direct Policy
Impact: PAR with Airport Check-in Workers [15]

Rosskam applied PAR methodology in a study of airport check-in workers. The process and findings led to direct improvements at various airports and contributed to policy changes in multiple countries [16]. In a pioneering study, PAR was used to examine the occupational health of airport check-in workers and the management practices that contribute to and create the existing conditions of work in that occupation.

The investigation began with the simple observation of problems related to work organization and work design. After it was established that the International Transport Workers' Federation (the ITF is the international trade union representing civil aviation workers) considered the working conditions of airport check-in workers to be a priority for research and policy-related action, the necessary research partners were mobilized by the principal investigator, in collaboration with the ITF.

Partners in the research included the Canadian Centre for Occupational Health and Safety, employers at all of the airports studied, and unions at local, national, and international levels in the two countries studied. Management and labor were involved from the design stage and involved throughout the research process. Meetings with management and union representatives at individual airports took place at different stages of the process. Focus group workshops were held at numerous international meetings organized by the international union. The study was conducted in two countries—Canada and Switzerland. The national unions in both countries were involved in the process through information exchange and exchange of ideas. Ultimately, the single most important counterpart in the study was the head of the Civil Aviation Section at the International Transport Workers' Federation, who was involved in the entire research process, and who made himself available to the principal investigator to guide, answer questions, provide input, review documents, and assist in analyzing the research findings. His commitment enabled the principal investigator to participate in various meetings of international working groups to meet with union representatives of check-in workers in order to obtain their direct input to the research design and its process, and to create a knowledge base on which the union would later build a campaign. Three different airports of varying sizes served as the study sites, ranging from a small regional airport to large international airports. The investigation looked at three different types of baggage check-in mechanization, from manual to fully mechanized systems.

A variety of research tools were used in the study. They included a questionnaire that presented a body map where check-in workers could indicate exactly where on their body they experienced pain, if indeed they had pain; examination of national workers' compensation records; work analysis; interviews with workers and supervisors; focus group discussions at trade union working group meetings and conferences, and discussions with management and unions at all of the airports studied.

Airport check-in work is predominantly, but not exclusively, a female occupation. There is a significant gap in the knowledge base of most jobs as they are performed, particularly jobs performed by women. The job of airport check-in workers is characterized as one that is high in demand but low in worker decision-making latitude. It is low-status, low-wage work. During the last 20 years, the occupation has been de-professionalized and lowered in status due to liberalization and globalization. Airport check-in work causes a high degree of both acute and chronic physical strain as well as significant psychological distress in workers performing the job.

Examining airport check-in work requires a systems point of view in order to understand the various factors that may contribute to work-related injury or ill health in workers. PAR was extremely useful for the study of work organization factors among airport check-in workers because it allowed the research team to involve different individuals and groups in the research process. Through those various research partners and the trusted interactions, the research team was able to make discoveries that otherwise would not have been possible during a research process.

The scope of the investigation was large, looking at the contribution of management practices to physical strain and psychological distress in check-in workers, the contribution of the physical design and operation of the baggage check-in system to musculoskeletal disorders (MSDs), and the impacts of the specific characteristics that typify jobs predominantly performed by women, such as lack of autonomy, lack of voice in decision-making, low-wage and low-status work, and lack of employment security. The study also examined the impacts of violence and the effects on workers from interacting with the public. In many service-sector jobs, including airport check-in work, the emotional labor associated with dealing with the public can contribute to psychological distress and MSDs in workers. Interaction with the public also can be a source of satisfaction and motivation on the job for many workers.

The study found that MSDs are widespread among check-in workers working at fully mechanized check-in systems and at semi-mechanized systems. MSDs in check-in workers result in disability, lost work time, and reduced job performance. The results of the investigation revealed that more than half of the workers surveyed live with severe chronic shoulder and/or lower back pain. Nearly 80% live with pain in multiple places of their body at once. More than 70% of respondents said that they often lose sleep due to neck pain in particular. Two-thirds said their performance on the job was diminished due to back and shoulder pain. A silent "occupational culture of pain" emerged as the norm most check-in workers lived with, at all of the study sites, but the prevalence and severity of the problems were not reflected in employers' injury reports. While management reports revealed low official levels of absenteeism due to work-related ill health, it became apparent that workers seldom reported their chronic MSDs to management. Workers appeared to live with body pain day in and day out as the norm. The reasons that workers seldom reported their occupational injuries and took time off from work appeared to be a phenomenon related to the fact that work-related MSDs are not recognized, compensable occupational diseases in either of the two study countries. Thus, for workers to simply find a physician who could diagnose their health problems correctly, link them to their work, and help to ensure proper treatment and compensation when needed is very difficult. The organization of work was found to contribute to MSDs at all three study sites. The study found that management externalized the costs of work-related injuries and illnesses with the costs being borne by the workers and their families.

While fully mechanized systems of baggage check-in are meant to obviate the need for workers to lift and carry baggage, in reality check-in workers often lifted, hauled, dragged and carried thousands of kilograms of baggage every day, twisting and turning in awkward positions, even when the system was fully mechanized. This investigation discovered that fully mechanized baggage check-in systems do not prevent MSDs and other types of problems that they were thought to obviate.

Psychological distress and violence emerged as major factors linked to organizational factors and management practices, with negative effects on worker health and productivity. Substantial violence toward check-in workers emerged as a significant finding, where 1 in 20 reported having been physically assaulted on the job by passengers. The majority of check-in workers who participated in the study reported having been verbally abused by passengers. More than half perceived a substantial risk of violence on their job, which is associated with chronic, low-level stress and tension on a daily basis, contributing to and aggravating MSDs.

Violence and MSDs on the job were found to be gender neutral, meaning that male and female check-in workers suffered from both. The trend to un-employ senior level workers in the industry was one of the major causes identified as causing psychological distress among both younger and senior-level check-in workers. De-professionalization of the job, the irregularity of work shifts, the high-demand/low-control nature of check-in work, the lack of protective mechanisms against violence, and the absence of worker participation in any level of organizational decision-making or work design all were found to contribute to high levels of psychological distress, aggravating MSDs as well. Poor communication was found to be a problem at all three study sites, indicated by the significant difference between what workers reported and what employer injury reports revealed.

The study demonstrated the importance of looking at check-in work as an entire system of interacting factors. The results showed conclusively that the degree of mechanization of the baggage check-in system is not the only factor contributing to work-related health problems. Work-induced health effects also resulted from stress and violence, as well as from a lack of worker control over decision-making. Therefore, examining the degree of mechanization of baggage check-in systems alone as the means of preventing work-related health problems would be insufficient as a research approach. Applying a single-factor cause-and-effect research approach would result in overlooking the variety of other factors which were found to contribute to MSDs and other work-related health problems reported by check-in workers.

Numerous simple solutions were proposed by the investigators, based on the findings generated by this study. Floor mats, for example, could be introduced to provide support and relief for check-in workers who stand for prolonged periods. Adjustable furniture would help to relieve MSDs among check-in workers. Roller balls could be used to move baggage where a fully mechanized system cannot be introduced due to costs. High counters would help to protect workers against violent passengers. Introducing a universal baggage weight limit of 20 kilograms per passenger was proposed as a policy recommendation as well as expanding the occupational niche of check-in workers so that their skills could be used for more than simply checking-in passengers. Check-in workers are well placed and skilled at identifying potentially unruly or disruptive passengers. Their job could be expanded to apply those skills within a hierarchy of security measures to prevent potentially disruptive passengers from getting on airplanes, where they might place passengers and crew in danger. Check-in workers have skills that could be used to increase protection for ground staff, cabin crew, and passengers on board aircrafts.

PAR is an effective methodology to use to describe problems, to apply a systems view, to uncover factors contributing both to physical stress and psychosocial distress, and then to use the findings to improve work organization. Since the completion of the study of airport check-in workers, numerous positive changes have taken place. The changes have demonstrated improvements that can be generated by a PAR-based study. Some of the changes have been direct outcomes of this PAR, others have been related to it, and some have been indirectly linked.

Following dissemination of the study findings and discussion with the Canadian Auto Workers' Union (the CAW represents airport check-in workers across Canada), the local union together with management at one of the study site airports re-designed entirely all of the check-in work stations at that airport. A fully mechanized check-in system was installed to eliminate the need for workers to lift and carry bags being checked-in by passengers. The new system greatly helps to relieve the physical stressors on workers' bodies. The union also is following up on other issues related to the entire work "system."

A public seminar to present the results of the study was held in Switzerland. Participants included representatives of management from the study site airport in Switzerland, check-in workers, union representatives—including at least one collective bargaining agent, 15 labor inspectors, representatives from the national workers' compensation body, the regional Institute for Occupational Health, and the press. The seminar catalyzed action. The labor inspector responsible for the airport studied in Switzerland met with representatives of management and the union the week following the seminar. A process of negotiation began using the results of the investigation to improve check-in workers' working conditions, employment security, and income security. These outcomes took place after the research results were made public, however, it was the participation of the local and international unions and management throughout the research process that facilitated the ensuing pressure to introduce change.

Check-in work stations at the study site in Switzerland were designed for sitting work only, which has been linked to MSDs in this worker population. Using the study findings and recommendations made in a report for the study participants, an increase in task variety has been introduced to relieve the Swiss airport check-in workers from performing check-in work exclusively. According to airport management in April 2005, check-in workers now perform different functions in the airport, including spending more time on gate duties, and workers are rotated more frequently. The introduction of greater and more frequent task variety reduces the time spent performing check-in work only and has a number of beneficial outcomes. They include reduced body load from static posture, reduced exposure to awkward postures and lifting and carrying bags, diminished risk of exposure to violent passengers, reduced monotony on the job, and increased flexibility and freedom during the work day. According to airport management at that particular study site, some days are so busy that check-in workers do not even have time to go to the toilet. The introduction of this increase in task variety and flexibility in how work is organized and performed now enables workers to take a break when one is needed.

These changes will not necessarily eliminate all of the adverse outcomes discovered and described among check-in workers, but they are positive steps and hopefully will lead to further organizational changes in management practices. Change usually takes time and, more often than not, is incremental and step-wise. Often the very act of working toward and implementing one change leads to further changes over time. The empowerment aspect is worth noting here. By engaging and involving airport management, local, national, and the international trade unions in the research process, providing and discussing results and recommendations with them, the various stakeholders have been able to use the research in their own way among themselves to make positive changes appropriate to their own work and organizational context.

In addition to the outcomes mentioned above, which are directly related to the research process, there have been a number of developments in other countries and contexts. In 2004, a major airport in Scotland introduced an airport-wide regulation limiting all checked baggage to 20 kilograms. In April 2005, the International Air Transport Association (IATA), which represents the majority of airlines around the world, passed an important resolution that limits all checked baggage to a maximum of 32 kilograms for all classes of travel. All airlines adopting the resolution will require passengers to send by cargo any and all baggage exceeding 32 kilograms. Passengers who travel economy class will still be able to pay excess baggage fees for total baggage weight above the 20 kilogram limit, but only up to 32 kilograms. Business and first-class passengers will still be able to pay for excess baggage weight above their 30 kilogram total limit but also only up to the new 32 kilograms limit. Above 32 kilograms, baggage for passengers in any class will not be accepted for check-in. The resolution passed because of the extremely high level of disabling back injuries among airport baggage handlers, a predominantly male population, and associated high workers' compensation costs. The adoption of the resolution by airlines around the world will clearly have positive spin-off effects for airport check-in workers, reducing the amount of weight they end up lifting and carrying each day. It is another positive step and a public recognition of the risks to one occupational group—baggage handlers. Even if it was not intended for check-in workers, the spin-off effects benefit check-in workers as well.

The study prepared the groundwork needed for collective bargaining agents to take steps toward solving the problems identified among check-in workers. To get the information into the hands of collective bargaining agents around the world, in 2005 the International Transport Workers' Federation published a report of the study [17] and disseminated it to all of the collective bargaining agents of the ITF's global trade union affiliates. The ITF today represents 800,000 workers in 200 countries. The report provides empirical evidence for collective bargaining where such evidence did not exist before. The report is available both by direct mail and on the ITF web site. The Canadian Labour Congress and the CAW disseminated the ITF's report of the study to their affiliates and members at airports across Canada.

From the design stage of the study, both trade union and employer partners indicated their intent to make use of the results of this study. The ITF is extending their international media campaign against Air Rage to include ground staff as well as cabin crew. Using the study results, the extended campaign would aim to improve work conditions for ground staff in airports, re-professionalize the status of check-in workers, and prevent violence against check-in workers. The study results have been presented and discussed in international trade union health and safety conferences. Findings from the study have been presented at seminars at a variety of universities, in scientific conferences, at policy-making conferences, to business and management classes, and in public seminars for employers and the general public. The study was discussed at the Tripartite Meeting on the Civil Aviation Industry at the International Labour Office (ILO) in January 2002. Conclusions from that meeting called for the ILO to continue research and follow-up work from this study of check-in workers.

Articles about the study have appeared in trade union magazines, ILO publications, scientific journals, and in various newspapers, including full-page, front page newspaper articles. The ILO published a feature article on the study in its magazine *World of Work* [18]. (The ILO's magazine has an estimated worldwide readership of 30,000-50,000 and is published in English, French, Spanish, and German. Adapted versions of the feature story also were published in Russian,

224 / UNHEALTHY WORK

Chinese, Norwegian, Japanese, Danish, and Hindi.) The Canadian Auto Workers' union published a section on airport check-in workers, with findings from the study and photographs of workers from the three study sites, in their manual *Ergonomics in the Work Environment: A Manual for Workers*. The manual has been distributed widely by the CAW.

In 2003, the ILO's Socio-Economic Security Programme published a report of the study, which it made available to the ILO's major tripartite constituent groups around the world, including employers' organizations, workers' organizations, and governments. The ILO also made the report available to a broad range of academics world-wide, particularly social scientists in both developing and industrialized countries, and to a variety of non-governmental organizations. The Canadian Centre for Occupational Health and Safety distributed the ILO's report of the study among its tripartite constituents in Canada.

A short video was made using film footage from the three study sites for use at workshops, meetings, and international conferences. The video shows check-in workers performing their jobs at the three study sites, highlighting the risks of MSDs. The video has been provided to the ITF to distribute among its global affiliates.

Researchers in Malta and Ireland have conducted studies on airport check-in workers since this study was completed. In 2007, a male check-in agent in Italy, disabled from degenerative work-related injuries to his musculoskeletal system, was using the findings of the study to bolster his workers' compensation case.

The study generated new knowledge that people can use and which has been published in the scientific literature. This alone can be motivating for a researcher and occupational health practitioner. Yet most important is that this PAR study of airport check-in workers has been used to create positive change which has actually improved people's lives and which has contributed to an organizational learning process for the employers, workers, and unions involved.

PAR Compared with Other Research Methodologies

The professional expert model could be appropriate for examining the factors thought to contribute to a given health outcome. Case studies are not developed as a means of measuring a variety of causal factors. PAR, however, lends itself as a useful method by which multiple factors and outcomes can be examined. The direct involvement of study participants is a key means of learning about factors thought to contribute to or cause outcomes. The descriptive aspects of a case study model may be useful for detailing a worker population and depicting working conditions. A detailed work analysis is indispensable for understanding how jobs are performed. While observation and questioning can be applied in case study development, the researcher maintains a more distant attitude than that used in a PAR methodology. The difference in researcher attitude between PAR and the professional expert model is significant in determining how a study process unfolds. Where participants feel themselves viewed as the object of scientific research rather than part of a process designed to benefit them, engendering a sense of trust and involvement becomes more difficult.

For a worker health study, where a change process is part of the study design, direct involvement with the participants is essential. Direct involvement with participants is of particular importance to identify problems associated with the job, as the problems are best known by the person performing the job, such as through focus group discussions where workers are encouraged to be part of the PAR methodology as a key means of obtaining rich, qualitative information, and for obtaining support for participation in the study. Focus group discussions in multiple meetings were extremely helpful in defining the major issues for the study of airport check-in workers. Similarly, keeping management updated on the study progress and working directly with managers to obtain information maintains open lines of communication and helps to ensure transparency. Focus group discussions also can be useful for generating hypotheses.

In both the professional expert model and a case study methodology, there is no demarcation between theory and practice. In both of these methods, it is the researcher who defines the problem to be studied. There is no feedback mechanism built into these methodologies, no requirement that knowledge gained be shared directly with the study participants. The professional expert model contributes to the body of knowledge shared by only a limited group of "experts." These methods do not include an action component meant to contribute to change on the part of the workers participating in the study, nor are they designed to create a learning process for the participants. In contrast, PAR is designed to create a learning process among participants and to ensure the dissemination and application of knowledge and experience gained.

Limitations of PAR

One of the difficulties in PAR is to ensure that all groups understand the process and feel validated and valued in their contributions to the research design, process, and any outcomes. PAR researchers must be attentive to not speaking only in

Using PAR to Study the Causes of Stress and Fatigue in Civil Aviation Workers

The study of airport check-in workers led the international union to include the recognition, protection, and re-professionalization of check-in workers in its international campaigns. In 2006, at the request of its global affiliates (representing 800,000 civil aviation workers in 200 countries), the ITF spearheaded a global research project attempting to identify the causes of what seemed to be a pandemic of stress and fatigue among all civil aviation workers that they represent—including cabin crew, air traffic service workers, and ground staff workers (ground staff workers include check-in workers, mechanics, baggage handlers, security workers, caterers, cleaners, ticket sales/call center workers, and ramp workers). The study, using PAR as the methodology, collects time series data from 2000-2007, understanding that 9/11, 2001 was the trigger for the continuous degradation of civil aviation workers' conditions of work. The study is unique in its marrying measures of job strain, effort-reward imbalance, emotional labor, temporal factors, and burnout with measures of social and economic insecurity. Working closely with an international research team, the international union and its global affiliates meet with and maintain on-going dialogue with the researchers to define the conceptual framework, study design, time frame, financing of the study, development of three separate questionnaires for the three occupational groups, translation of each questionnaire into multiple languages, launching the questionnaires globally, collecting the data, entering the data, managing the database, and all of the many other aspects which are involved in a large global research project. Three questionnaires (each translated into eight languages) were sent to union representatives of the ITF's affiliates in 200 countries. The international union, based on its members' needs from around the world, is already working on a campaign strategy during the research process, planning the widest possible dissemination of the study findings to its global members, and particularly to its collective bargaining agents in 200 countries.

In October 2007, the principal investigator participated at the international union's international occupational safety and health working group meeting. At the meeting, the researcher was allowed wide scope and time to work directly with union affiliates representing ground staff and cabin crew in particular, to define the key issues and wording of the various questionnaires in development. Thereafter, dialogue continued for several months with various affiliates, the international union, and its advisors on precise wording and issues for the various questionnaires. Such open and unlimited access to technically knowledgeable people on the union side combined with their firm commitment to the study facilitates what is a tremendous and intensive process for a global study, where consensus-building is crucial at each step of the process. The study will be completed in 2009. A report of the findings and policy recommendations will be available from the International Transport Workers' Federation's Civil Aviation Section. Using the results of the investigation, the ITF will work with its global affiliates to build and implement campaigns to improve the conditions of work and health of civil aviation workers. The ITF will also use the findings in its work with regulatory bodies and airline management.

academic terms with the various groups, to not presume the same understanding of research terminology and of interpreting data, but without appearing condescending or technocratic. This entails a delicate balance on the part of PAR researchers, who should see themselves as learners and facilitators at the same time as being scientists. Listening to and learning from workers and managers about workplace issues is valuable and enriching, albeit time-consuming. PAR researchers have the additional responsibility to help the various participants learn from the process, which also can be time-consuming.

An additional difficulty in applying a PAR approach is arriving at consensus with workers and employers by establishing a relationship with each group and bringing them into the process. It can be both a difficult and a lengthy process for the researcher. The processes are more time-consuming than research based on the professional expert model, for example, where input from various groups is not involved and where consensus-building is not required at any stage. The consultative process in PAR methodology is likely, therefore, to be more costly in terms of researchers' time and in analysis of qualitative data.

As with any research methodology, there exists the potential for bias to be introduced. It can occur in defining the issues to be addressed or if various stakeholders want more emphasis on certain issues of greater importance or concern to them, which may also be areas of political concern. Stronger emphasis on particular issues by any one participating group could skew results. In working with management and unions, researchers must exercise caution to not fall into political traps based on the agendas of any one group. While the research team must gain the confidence of all groups involved, if they are perceived to lean more toward one group's interest than another's, they may lose the confidence of the other group. Maintaining what can be a delicate balance is necessary, as well as being perceived as neutral with all groups, while ensuring that all concerns are addressed.

There is also a risk of researcher bias through personal involvement with the participant community, as well as in any change process that may develop. The researcher can influence how the change process unfolds, how the research findings are interpreted and applied within and beyond the participating groups. Care must be exercised to maintain distance from the process, allowing the stakeholder groups to define how a change process is envisioned and formulated. In the end, it is the workers and managers who will have to live with the effects of any changes they implement, or any changes they do not implement, since non-implementation of changes, after awareness has been raised, can also have consequences.

A debate exists about the validity and reliability of data, in particular when they are qualitative and obtained through participatory appraisal. Data generated by PAR are open to various interpretations that can include the researcher and participant community designing the study together or researchers designing the study and then collecting the data with the help of the participating group. Perhaps this is the best means of ensuring that research contributes to an organizational change process given the complex nature of today's organizations.

CONCLUSION

PAR is important to research and to policy work. Some epidemiologists would challenge PAR as being "not objective." Many epidemiologists do not involve themselves in PAR because intervention studies are often more difficult to carry out than purely quantitative research, often take more time, and may cost more. Analyzing an existing data set can be easier than talking to groups of people, working to build consensus, and aiming for real change to improve workers' health. Notwithstanding, it is precisely through intervention-based research and the adequate evaluation of intervention-based research that public health and occupational health make advances. In order for research in occupational health to not remain in an "ivory tower," epidemiologists and other researchers should be aware of the importance of PAR, perhaps today more than ever before. Researchers, employers, trade unions, and policy-makers stand only to gain from encouraging and supporting joint research conducted together with working people.

REFERENCES

1. Whyte, W. F., *Social Theory for Action: How Individuals and Organizations Learn to Change*, Sage, Newbury Park, CA, p. 272, 1991.
2. Deshler, D., and M. Ewert, *Participatory Action Research: Traditions and Major Assumptions,* 1995, available from: http://tdg.res.uoguelph...pdrc/articles/article.1
3. De Koning, K., and M. Martin (ed.), *Participatory Research in Health: Issues and Experiences*, Zed Books, London, UK, 1996.
4. Elden, M., Political Efficacy at Work: The Connection between More Autonomous Forms of Workplace Organization and More Participatory Politics, *American Political Science Review*, 75:1, pp. 43-58, 1981.
5. Dash, D. P. (ed.), *Problems of Action Research—As I See It*, Lincoln School of Management, United Kingdom, 1998.
6. Freire, P., *Pedagogy of the Oppressed*, Continuum Press, New York, 1970.
7. Elden, M., Sharing the Research Work: Participative Research and It's Role Demands, in *Human Inquiry: A Sourcebook of New Paradigm Research*, Reason, P. and J. Rowan (eds.), John Wiley & Sons, Chichester, UK, pp. 253-266, 1981.
8. Wallerstein, N. and M. Weinger, Health and Safety Education for Worker Empowerment, *American Journal of Industrial Medicine*, 22, pp. 619-635, 1992.
9. Mergler, D., Worker Participation in Occupational Health Research: Theory and Practice, *International Journal of Health Services*, 17:1, pp. 151-167, 1987.
10. Laurell, A., M. Noriega, S. Martinez, and J. Villegas, Participatory Research on Workers' Health, *Social Science and Medicine*, 34:6, pp. 603-613, 1992.
11. Hugentobler, M., B. A. Israel, and S. J. Schurman, An Action Research Approach to Workplace Health: Integrating Methods, *Health Education Quarterly*, 19:1, pp. 55-76, 1992.
12. Israel, B. A., S. J. Schurman, and M. K. Hugentobler, Conducting Action Research: Relationships between Organization Members and Researchers, *Journal of Applied Behavioral Science*, 28, pp. 74-101, 1992.
13. Ritchie, J., Participatory Research in the Workplace, in *Participatory Research in Health: Issues and Experiences*, De Koning, J. and M. Martin (eds.), Zed Books, London, UK, pp. 205-215, 1996.
14. Schurman, S. J., Making The "New American Workplace" Safe and Healthy: A Joint Labor-Management-Researcher Approach, *American Journal of Industrial Medicine*, 29, pp. 373-377, 1996.
15. Rosskam, E., *Excess Baggage: Leveling the Load and Changing the Workplace*, Baywood, Amityville, NY, 2007.
16. Rosskam, E., *Working at the Check-In: Consequences for Worker Health and Management Practices*, University of Lausanne, Lausanne, 2003.
17. Rosskam, E., A. Drewczynski, and R. Bertolini, *Service on the Ground: Occupational Health of Airport Check-In Workers*, International Transport Workers' Federation, London, UK, 2003.
18. International Labour Office, *World of Work*, International Labour Office, Geneva, Switzerland, 2002.

CHAPTER 13

The MUNI Health and Safety Project: A 26-Year Union-Management Research Collaboration*

Ray Antonio, June Fisher,
and Ellen Rosskam

Participatory research findings and recommendations alone are not necessarily the answer to the problems being addressed in research. They do, however, lead to the development of guides, tools, factual arguments, and an agenda for change. Health and safety is about more than just the issues and problems on the job. Health and safety must be an issue at the collective bargaining table, and must be seen as a political and economic issue. It is an issue of standards and regulations to protect workers. It is an organizing tool that can constitute part of the foundation of any trade union, and will, undoubtedly, provide an on-going challenge. Health and safety is both a logical and excellent tool to use in empowering workers to address the problems they face everyday [1].

As a physician, June Fisher came to a fundamental understanding about the critical role of collaboration with workers in research projects devoted to studying and reducing health hazards in the work environment. She knew intuitively what work psychologists and sociologists—especially in the international arena—had demonstrated for some decades. In essence, it is the truth that empowering workers to make decisions at the workplace, and giving them the training and tools to make changes, is a critical factor for improving the work environment and reducing injuries and illnesses [2, pp. 29-35].

Hypertension and heart disease are quite prevalent among bus drivers and transit operators compared to workers in other occupations [3]. Constant vigilance and continuously managing conflicting demands characterizes driving for transit

*The authors would like to acknowledge and thank Len Syme, David Ragland, Birgit Greiner, and Nik Krause for their important contributions to the study.

operators in urban mass transit systems. Ensuring public safety is paramount, requiring drivers to pay close attention to increasingly congested traffic conditions while adhering to tight schedules and attending to passenger needs and satisfaction. Bus drivers, their unions, management, and clinical researchers have long been concerned about the link between the stressful aspects of the work environment and the high prevalence of hypertension and heart disease among transit workers. This chapter highlights the joint efforts of Ray Antonio, bus driver and union president, and Dr. June Fisher, Associate Clinical Professor of Medicine and clinician, to describe the ways in which problems in the work environment of San Francisco Municipal Railway (MUNI) workers impact the health of San Francisco transport workers.

The first part of this chapter is written from the perspective of Ray Antonio, a transit worker and retired President of Transport Workers' Union (TWU) Local 250A. He describes his experiences as a union representative and a bus driver in terms of the stressors to which workers are exposed in the San Francisco MUNI.

In the second part of this chapter, Dr. June Fisher, an Associate Clinical Professor of Medicine at the University of California, San Francisco (UCSF), describes the on-going research that investigates the link between stressful working conditions experienced by bus drivers and the prevalence of hypertension and cardiovascular disease among workers in this occupation.

Despite the existence of a federal mandate requiring biennial medical examinations for commercial drivers, the impact of the work environment on the health of drivers had been largely ignored prior to this study. In the late 1970s, Antonio and others in TWU Local 250A were able to negotiate into their contract with the San Francisco MUNI a more effective medical examination for drivers than those that had been routinely provided by the San Francisco MUNI. The examinations were required to fulfill the federal mandate. These more effective exams were performed at San Francisco General Hospital, under the direction of Fisher. A review of the first 1,000 expanded medical exams revealed that this cohort had a high rate of elevated blood pressure. With colleagues at UCSF and Berkeley, Dr. Fisher created a research project to utilize these more effective exams as the basis for ongoing surveillance and multidisciplinary studies to measure stress in the San Francisco MUNI environment, and its effects on various health outcomes, in particular hypertension. Based on this collaboration, various interventions have been implemented to improve the quality of the work environment and help prevent the development of hypertension. The results have been at times mixed or unexpected.

I. LIFE AS A BUS DRIVER: RAY ANTONIO

I began my career with the San Francisco MUNI. The Transport Workers' Union Local 250A represents bus drivers in San Francisco, and I was first hired as a bus driver in January of 1974. Later that year I became a full-time union representative, first as a grievance handler, grievance officer, then as a recording secretary, executive vice president, and finally as financial secretary/treasurer. In 1993, I decided that in order for me to be more successful in my career as a union representative, I needed to return to the work of driving a bus, to better understand the changes that had occurred since I first started working as a bus driver in 1974. I needed to return to driving a bus to better understand the impacts of those changes on drivers. Consequently, I took a one-term sabbatical from my job as a full-time union representative and went back to driving a bus. I drove that bus for 3 years. When the election came up, I decided to run for union president. I won that election, and served in the position of union president for two terms, until 2002.

Other than the New York subway system, San Francisco MUNI is the most heavily used transit system in the country. It employs more than 2,500 drivers, who prefer to be called "transit operators." They operate light-rail vehicles, diesel buses, electric buses, articulated buses, historical streetcars from different parts of the world dating back to the 1930s, and of course, the famous San Francisco cable cars. These vehicles are operated 24 hours a day, 7-days a week. In this chapter, I will describe what it takes to be a bus driver, what it is like to be hired as a bus driver, and once hired what bus drivers do at work. I will describe some of the problems that transit operators face everyday. I will also summarize the work that we have carried out under the Stress and Hypertension Study, which is the first hypertension study of bus drivers in the United States.

Being Hired as a Transit Operator

MUNI publicizes job announcements inviting people to apply for the job of transit worker. These announcements outline the specific requirements of the job so that applicants know what is expected. Drivers work under general supervision and are required to operate a variety of transit vehicles. The job announcement explains that the essential functions include transporting passengers along specific routes in a safe, timely, and courteous manner. It specifies that the transit operator makes designated stops as required, makes announcements of stops, transfer points, and points of interest, and that s/he must accept fares, issue transfers, and provide directional information. Operators are required to provide the highest level of professionalism in transit, offering safe and good service. They are responsible for the preparation of reports in the event of accidents or any incidents involving the riding public. The job announcement also specifies that the nature of work requires employees to work Saturdays, Sundays, holidays, and on any shift. Work hours and days off can change several times throughout the year. Employees are required to use both hands and feet for repetitive movement in the operation of a motor vehicle, work around moving machinery and equipment, are required to work in hot, cold, humid, and rainy weather, and may be exposed to dust, fumes, oils, lubricants, gases, and vapors.

In order to be hired, there are numerous requirements and regulations mandated by both the company and different levels of government, all of which must be respected. For example, MUNI, which hires bus drivers in San Francisco on behalf of the city and county of San Francisco, requires that drivers have had a regular Class C driver's license for at least 5 years and that they have maintained a good driving record. The latter is defined as having had no more than 2 moving violations in the last 3 years, no accidents in the last 3 years, and the license must not have been suspended or revoked in the last 3 years. The applicant is required to have had no convictions involving accidents, use of alcohol or drugs, reckless driving, or convictions for the sale, use, or possession of drugs. Requirements also include the ability to obtain a Class B commercial driver's license with passenger endorsement and no air break restriction. These requirements make it very difficult to qualify. Applicants have to pass a variety of tests and examinations, as well as meet specific driving requirements. Applicants also are required to qualify for a school pupil activity bus certificate, which is an additional state requirement to be issued by the Department of Motor Vehicles. Once these criteria are met, the applicant must pass both written and oral examinations, followed by MUNI's 35-day training period, which must be completed in full.

In addition to the company's minimum qualifications, there are certain medical requirements mandated by the state and federal governments. The State of California requires prospective bus driver candidates to pass initial medical exams and then to repeat the exams every 2 years throughout their driving career. Drivers cannot have a clinical diagnosis of uncontrolled high blood pressure when being considered for employment. They must not have a medical history of arthritic, orthopedic, muscular, or vascular disease, epilepsy or any cause of loss of consciousness, mental, nervous, organic, or psychiatric disorder. And they must not have a clinical diagnosis of diabetes requiring insulin. Recently, the federal government also imposed drug testing regulations requiring employees to be randomly tested if there is reasonable suspicion of illicit drug use post-accident, and requiring random testing during return to duty and during follow-ups post accident. These are just a few examples of the existing requirements by both the state and the federal Department of Transportation (DOT).

The Demanding Work of Bus Driving

Once hired as a bus driver, transit operators are required to work under varying conditions, with very demanding schedules. The job is very difficult work, at times dangerous. The late Dr. Bertil Gardell characterized the profession as one of the most highly stressful occupations in the world. He concluded in his research that transit operators are a high-risk group for deleterious health outcomes. He also found that the problems of driving buses and transit vehicles are similar in most urban areas, and that health outcomes are also very similar, regardless of country or nationality.

Some may perceive the job of transit operator to be fairly simple and routine, assuming that transit operators do nothing more than drive a bus from one bus stop to the next, open and close the doors, and let people on and off. The reality, however, is quite different from this simplistic image. Transit operators are constantly faced with both "internal stressors" as well as "external stressors," making their job very difficult every minute of the day, every day.

When drivers report for work, they do so while most other people are still asleep. They do this to ensure that the bus is out there, waiting at the bus stop to get people to work on time. Drivers can start work as early as four o'clock in the morning. The first thing they do is report to the station, or what is called a "division," where they pick up their "outfit." The outfit consists of the schedule for the day, the transfers, and any special instructions that are given to that group, for that day. The schedule that they pick up is their assignment for the day and the transit operator cannot deviate from that assignment. Operating in a timely manner, according to schedule, is a rule.

The schedule indicates the amount of time it should take the operator to travel from point A to point B. The schedule consists of three elements: the running time, the actual time that it takes to get from point A to point B, and some recovery time to assist the transit operator in recovering some of the time lost in case there are delays during the trip. There is also supposed to be what transit operators call the "layover time," which is the time remaining prior to the next scheduled departure time. There are two trips: an inbound trip and an outbound trip. Each trip is meant to have these three elements of scheduling.

When drivers are at work, they complain mostly about the pressures of trying to maintain a tight schedule and, of course, due to the tight schedule, drivers do not get the breaks that are built into the schedule. Breaks are often infrequent or nonexistent. During a shift, an operator can make up to 20 trips, each trip consisting of an inbound and outbound trip. Insufficient time needed to make the trip safely is a common and key complaint of drivers.

Split Shifts

Shift work requires drivers to contend with continually rotating patterns of early and late spells. Split shifts, a combination of a morning and afternoon/evening shift with a long break in between, are common [3].

Typically, urban transit operators may work split shifts, requiring them to work 12-15 hours a day. The split often requires 2 hours of unpaid time between assignments. For example, a driver may come to work at 6 a.m., which I have done when working a split shift, and finish work at 6 p.m. the same day. The cost of living is very high in San Francisco. This means that many people have to live outside the city, obliging them to commute to work. Some drivers, therefore, have to leave their homes by 5 a.m. in order to get to work at 6 a.m. If they work a split shift, there are 2 hours of unpaid time during the day that are supposed to be the worker's own time. Thus, a workday with a split shift may run from 6 a.m. to 6 p.m., with a 2-hour break from 11 a.m. to 1 p.m. With a 12- to 15-hour workday ending at 6 p.m., followed by a commute that may take up to 2 hours one way due to traffic conditions, drivers end up being away from home for 15 hours in a 24-hour period. Bus drivers suffer from the negative effects of odd shift hours and long working hours because transit operates 24 hours a day. For bus drivers, there is no such thing as day-work only.

Lack of Supervisor Support

In addition to the stress of long working hours, commuting, and shift work, bus drivers often suffer from a lack of support from their line supervisors. Line supervisors are meant to assist drivers in making transit line work more efficient. Rather than working in a proactive, professional manner, however, line supervisors often behave like policemen, looking for drivers' rule violations, which the supervisors then write up and give to management to discipline the driver. Drivers often are unjustly written up, including for extremely minor infractions. For example, running two minutes ahead of schedule is a rule violation in the company. If the street supervisor is at the corner and sees that a driver is running 2 minutes ahead of schedule, the supervisor could simply stop the bus and say, "Operator, what time do you have?" as a means of keeping the bus there until the correct departure time. This would help the driver and the public. Instead, however, more often than not, the supervisor will simply write up the driver as having committed a violation of rules, send the "report" to management, and let management decide what they want to do with the driver.

Driving a bus can be a dead-end job. There are virtually no opportunities for growth or advancement, and few supervisory positions. The few incentives that exist are only available to drivers with a high level of seniority, which entitles a driver to choose better hours, better days off, better work assignments, and better pay. Drivers not having a high level of seniority are not entitled to these choices. Interaction with management also can be problematic. In transit, people working in management typically do not have good management training. They apply punitive disciplinary practices because they view the passenger as the customer, and they consider that the customer is always right. The driver is, thus, considered wrong under almost any circumstance. Poor management training leads to poor managerial practices, which results in transit being seen as an arena for adversarial labor-management relations.

Managing the Public

Dealing with the traveling public is a challenge for transit operators. A wide variety of situations and difficulties arise every single day, some of which are potentially violent and threatening for the drivers. For example, there are passengers who do not want to pay the fare, or who argue about transfers and who abuse or cheat the system. Another problem is that in San Francisco, many passengers seem to think that public buses are rolling garbage cans. Such passengers leave food, drinks, and all kinds of garbage on seats and on the floor. These behaviors are perpetuated by the general public, including by working people who ride the buses every day to and from work. It is very common that people riding the bus to and from work bring their newspapers on the bus, read their papers on the bus, and upon leaving the bus simply leave their newspaper on the seat. From hour to hour, the garbage on the bus can accumulate significantly thanks to inconsiderate passengers. But the problem does not stop there. New passengers getting on the bus sometimes get irritated with the garbage and incidents can result, which can be difficult for the driver to manage. As well, the bus drivers have to think about this as an additional stressor in their workday, and have to clean up the bus from time to time, which is not meant to be part of their job requirements.

There are also problems with overcrowding and overloading the bus, often resulting from a missing bus. In the industry, this phenomenon is called the "missing leader" because for every bus on the line, there is the "leader," which is supposed to be the bus in front of an individual bus, followed by the "follower," which is the bus directly behind. Missing leaders or missing buses result from breakdowns, accidents, a driver who did not get to work on time, or a driver who was ill and therefore could not get the bus out. In the event of a missing bus, passengers waiting for a long time for the missing bus can get quite angry when the following bus shows up. Passengers express their anger to the driver, saying things such as, "Where have you been? Can't you guys do the right thing? Don't you guys work around here?" The driver on the receiving end of such passenger anger was in no way responsible for the missing bus, yet s/he is the one who ends up having to face any consequential passenger abuse, harassments, and threats.

Once a bus is overloaded due to a missing bus, other types of problems arise inside the bus. These situations generally result from overcrowding, compounded by passengers' heightened nerves due to their bus arriving late. Under these conditions, drivers may become the target of physical harassment, threats, and physical assault by unruly passengers. In addition, drivers have to face and deal with problems created by children and teenagers on the buses, who sometimes harass elderly passengers, creating problems for the other passengers as well. Even though some transit systems may have a police force, when drivers do end up needing help, there is often a lack of police security on the bus. In San Francisco, MUNI relies on the police department for transit security. It is not possible, however, to have a policeman on each and every bus. Therefore, when a situation does arrive where a driver needs help, there are difficulties in obtaining an immediate response to urgent problems. These various situations of difficulty can be extremely stress-inducing for drivers, and can contribute to adverse health outcomes in transit operators.

Traffic and Vehicle Stressors

Traffic problems are stressors that are beyond the control of the transport system and beyond the control of drivers. There is nothing that drivers can do about traffic. Nevertheless, the bus-riding public expects the bus to compete with and to be as fast as the automobile. The bus-riding public expects the bus and its driver to be there to accommodate them just like in a taxicab. There are also roadway problems, such as potholes and roadwork. The *Bus Only* lanes, or diamond lanes for carpools and buses, can be blocked with other traffic getting in the way. This induces stress in drivers and is a situation over which they have no control.

Poorly designed and poorly maintained equipment are other types of stressors that San Francisco transit operators have to face in their day-to-day work. Operators are constantly moving around physically, twisting and turning in awkward postures as they try to access controls situated in difficult-to-reach places. These frequent awkward movements affect drivers' backs, shoulders, knees, and legs.

Bus drivers often have limited or no access to restroom facilities or eating facilities. Yet when a bus has to stop and the public sees a driver getting out of the bus to go into a public place, rest area, or coming back with a bag or a sandwich, the public could write a complaint to the company and the driver might face disciplinary measures.

Bus drivers constantly fight the tilt of the road. Roadways are built with a tilt so that the rain can run off the road into the sewer system. Because buses usually have to travel in the far right lane, drivers are always fighting the tilt of the road, necessitating a movement of constantly pulling back to the left, in order to stay upright. The pull against the steering wheel creates a strain on the musculoskeletal system and can lead to chronic back problems for drivers.

Drivers face problems with other vehicles on the roadway, and their job has become even more difficult since bicycles became allowed in the middle of the roadway. When delivery trucks are double-parked, bus drivers have to take the risk of going around them, which increases the risk of an accident. Express trucks, taxicabs, bicycles, and other drivers are all competing for the city streets, sometimes leading to what is known as "road rage." Aside from the aforementioned factors on the bus line, the weather, political climate, the poor public image that the media gives to bus drivers, and overall economic conditions all contribute as well to the stress that bus drivers experience, consequently impacting their health and well-being.

Recommendations from the Field

Transit operators come into the system with a clean bill of health, with a clean criminal record, with a good driving record, and they are clean and sober. Once they begin to work, however, the nature of the job and the difficult working conditions induce serious health problems among transit operators. And those health problems result in significant impacts on individual productivity, motivation, mood, worker turnover, absenteeism, workers' compensation claims, accidents, health care costs, insurance costs, overtime costs, family life and family relationships, as well as on the overall functioning of the public bus transport system as a whole.

Identifying problems and working toward solutions, interventions, and policy-level changes are on-going processes for the union. While a number of changes already have been introduced in San Francisco, two critical areas still need to be addressed and resolved. First, bus drivers are not protected by legislative standards regulating working hours, overtime, or break times, unlike many other workers. The Department of Motor Vehicle Code allows employers to require bus drivers to work 12 hours within a 15-hour consecutive time period. Second, because there are no acceptable standards for realistic running times for buses, drivers are subjected to tight scheduling on a permanent basis. The demand for personal service by handicapped passengers and the elderly, and the need to maintain order in crowded buses creates a direct conflict with the need to keep to a tight schedule, particularly in dense traffic. Driving a bus for 12 hours a day is highly stressful. Drivers need some recovery time as well as some guaranteed rest time to help them maintain their health and well-being, while making those stressful and difficult trips all day long, in and out of the city.

II. THE SAN FRANCISCO MUNI STRESS AND HYPERTENSION STUDY: JUNE FISHER

In the 1970s, Ray Antonio observed that there seemed to be a great number of heart attacks among transit operators and felt that something needed to be done about it. Ray, and the many transit workers who have participated in our research, have been much-appreciated mentors, helping us to understand the system in which they work. In order to address the perceived high rate of heart attacks among bus drivers, the union first negotiated with management on the issue of medical examinations, which, prior to our study, were being performed by different private practitioners in many different settings. The quality of the exams, was, therefore, quite variable. The union negotiated for the exams to be centralized at San Francisco General Hospital. I was recruited to come in at that point and we agreed that we would use these mandated exams for the purpose of health surveillance. Ours is the only project of this nature in the United States and has been an on-going joint labor-management project for the last 28 years. There are between four and five million such medical exams being performed in the United States each year. Such a quantity of data represents a tremendous potential for evidence-based policy action. Unfortunately, however, this database is not being as fully utilized for research purposes as it could be.

Given the paramount importance attributed to public safety, bus drivers must maintain constant vigilance on the job. While safety is something everybody thinks about to some degree, the bus driver has to think about it all the time at a conscious level, even if s/he may not talk about it. Exercising constant vigilance bears a physiological effect on the body of the driver. It is not a question of being alert or being awake—bus drivers' safety vigilance has to be moment to moment. If you ride a bus with the driver as we have done many times, their constant vigilance is quite apparent. As researchers, we have been studying the link between the stressful aspects of bus driving and the high incidence of hypertension that has been shown among bus drivers worldwide.

This section of the chapter will provide a brief history of the federally mandated medical examinations and the beginnings of the ongoing San Francisco MUNI stress and hypertension study. Then it will highlight the studies that have supported the association between bus driver work stress and hypertension, as well as describe some of the conflicting findings that have been found while undertaking research on stress and bus driving in San Francisco. Finally, the chapter will describe the Ambassador Program, a unique intervention in San Francisco aimed at improving the difficult working conditions that bus drivers face, conditions which Ray Antonio described earlier in this chapter. The Ambassador Program is an outcome of our long-standing labor-research collaboration, whereby research findings are combined with the union's organizing efforts to achieve sustainable improvements and policy-level changes.

Public Safety and the Biennial Commercial Drivers' License Medical Exams

Public safety is the reason for the required biennial commercial drivers' license medical examinations, which are mandated by the federal Department of Transportation. Similar systems exist in many other countries for granting Class C commercial driving licenses. The existence of the required biennial medical examinations creates a "healthy worker effect," meaning that people who work typically are healthier than people who do not work. The required medical examination eliminates individuals who may have some health problems. Thus, as a group, newly hired bus drivers tend to be healthy individuals, similar to police, firefighters, and certain other groups. The medical examinations, however, ignore the impact of work on operator health and safety and the DOT regulations do not address the issue of the development of hypertension among bus drivers. While there are several million exams being conducted each year, they are not being used for ongoing surveillance of bus driver health effects resulting from the work environment.

In the case of bus drivers, the "healthy worker effect" and the required biennial medical examinations are issues of major importance in considering the impacts of work on bus drivers' health. Bus drivers start their bus driving careers in better health than most any other group of workers, in most occupations. Yet after approximately 5 years on the job, bus drivers start to show important and worrying signs of diminished health, in particular hypertension and the development of cardiovascular disease. These negative health outcomes and the time frame in which they start to be revealed point to the effects of chronic job strain, leading to depression and burnout, which occur after 5 to 6 years on a job with a high degree of job strain. In a nutshell, the evidence indicates that many bus drivers go from a state of extremely good health to a state of chronically poor health within 5 years on the job, due to excessive chronic job strain. Driving a bus may generate a worker's income but it sacrifices the worker's health in a relatively short time.

The San Francisco MUNI Stress and Hypertension Study

Back in 1976, Ray Antonio and the Transport Workers' Union (TWU) negotiated with MUNI to centralize the required medical exams. From that point onward, the team at the San Francisco General Hospital clinic reviewed thousands of exams and confirmed to both the union and management that the number of cases of high blood pressure appeared to be above average. In collaboration with TWU Local 250A, its members, and the San Francisco MUNI, researchers at the University of California, San Francisco and Berkeley began an on-going research program to investigate whether stressors on the job might be a cause of the observed high blood pressure and other deleterious health outcomes.

This agreement was the start of a new educational process for all of us. The union and management had to learn the whys and wherefores of good and valid medical research. We learned that the study of populations rather than an individual is called "epidemiology," that it is a discipline based on probability and requires complicated data-gathering and statistical analysis. . . . The most painful lessons were related to the costs of good research and the lack of funding available for occupationally related health research. The research staff also went through a learning process. They learned the operations of MUNI and how a transit system works, the daily routine of an operator, and the operator's perception of their work [1].

When we began our research work with the union, there were only 2 preexisting studies on cardiovascular disease and bus driving. The well-known studies by Morris, Heady, and Raffle [4, 5] conducted on a population of 31,000 male bus drivers in the United Kingdom found a 2.7 per 1,000 per year incidence rate of coronary heart disease, compared to a 1.9 incidence for bus conductors in the same study. The authors attributed this finding to the difference in physical activity, in that the conductors were climbing the stairs of the double-decker buses while the drivers were sedentary. The other study located was an abstract found in the Russian literature about a small group of hypertensive bus drivers [6]. Since then, there have been more than 60 studies worldwide confirming the high prevalence of hypertension and cardiovascular disease among bus drivers [3]. Ragland et al. [7] showed that bus drivers experienced higher rates of hypertension compared to controls drawn randomly from various occupations. A 1991 Swedish study found an 18% incidence of coronary heart disease for bus and tram drivers compared to a 6% risk for controls [8]. In a more recent study by Wang and Lin [9], Taiwanese male bus drivers were compared to skilled workers from the same company and were shown to have a significantly higher rate of hypertension (56% vs. 31%).

Numerous studies have found that bus drivers have higher rates of musculoskeletal disorders, general health problems, family problems, and health risky behaviors than the general population [10-12]. Examining the rates of hospital admissions, a study in Denmark found the admission rates highest for transit operators than for any other occupation, with transit operators being admitted to hospital for cardiovascular disease more often than for any other reason. As a result, legislators in Denmark allocated funding to conduct systematic interventions. Denmark is one of the few places in the world where this is being done [13].

Hypertension, Bus Drivers, and Stressful Work

The high incidence of cardiovascular disease that we observed among bus drivers was alarming. One of the goals of our research project was to collaborate with the union and management in an attempt to understand the nature of the link between bus driving and the elevated risk of heart disease. During "ride-alongs" with bus drivers, many of the members of the research team observed that the job characteristics in bus drivers' work environment appear to be quite stressful. The occupational stressors include: maintaining an intense pace in order to meet time schedules, foregoing breaks to make up time missed due to traffic conditions or due to extra time needed to help passengers, working 12-hour split shifts without being paid for a mandatory 2-hour break in between shifts, ergonomic risks from exposure to static seated posture for hours at a time and repetitive movements, exposure to the toxic fumes emitted by urban traffic, and managing hostile encounters with supervisors, managers, and the riding public.

In addition to physical exposures on the job, psychosocial stressors appear to play an important role in elevating bus drivers' blood pressure. Job strain, or the combination of a high level of demand on the job while having little control over the work environment, has been associated with an increased prevalence and incidence of coronary heart disease, even when controlling for typical risk factors such as age, race, cholesterol, and smoking [14-16], and with high blood pressure [17]. In one of our studies of bus drivers, while a higher than average incidence of hypertension was confirmed, we found no association between self-reported job strain, defined as high job demands and low decision latitude, and prevalence of hypertension [18]. However, more recent research by Greiner, Krause, and Ragland [19] has shown that it may be important to include objective assessments of stressors as well as individual level self-reports in order to predict hypertension.

> The most objective indices of job barriers and time pressure, obtained by observational interview, significantly predicted hypertension after controlling for age, gender and seniority. However, the more subjective indices based on each individual's self-report of frequency and intensity of stressors, were positively but not significantly associated with hypertension [19, p. 1089].

There are two possible additional reasons for the discrepancy between the two studies. First, within a single occupation, there may not be enough objective variance in generic job demands and decision-making latitude on the job to find associations with health outcomes [20]. Secondly, job demands, decision-making latitude, and job strain usually are measured by Karasek's Job Content Questionnaire (JCQ). The JCQ includes generic questions that can be used across occupations. In studies within a single occupation, however, occupation-specific questions (such as bus drivers' time constraints) may well have greater variation, and may be, therefore, better predictors of health outcomes.

To explore whether there is an association between the high prevalence of hypertension and the work environment of the transit operator, various risk factors for hypertension, such as race, low socio-economic status, length of time on the job, and coping mechanisms, must be taken into account. Older African American drivers have a higher hypertension prevalence rate than White drivers, indicating the effect of race on hypertension. Except for the 40-49 year age group, MUNI drivers have a higher prevalence rate than all other comparison groups.

When comparing hypertensive bus drivers with non-hypertensive bus drivers, hypertensives have a higher separation rate than non-hypertensives, which ends up costing several million dollars to the system. Drivers have also been shown to gain weight and increase their cigarette smoking and use of alcohol during non-working hours. Increases in eating, drinking, and smoking are "maladaptive coping mechanisms," behaviors that are, in a sense, used as a means of unwinding. Some bus drivers report drinking a six-pack of beer on a regular basis. Drivers are not at home very often because of their shifts, and depending on their shifts may seldom see their children during waking hours. These workers pay a high price for the work they perform, but their families also pay a high price for the worker's job as a bus driver.

Interventions and Psychosocial Stress: Academia, Labor, and Management

The MUNI health and safety project, through the Working Committee—a labor, management, researcher committee set up to facilitate the research project—became a mechanism for thinking about interventions in the *work environment,* rather than focusing solely on individual behaviors. The work of the project has resulted in a number of positive outcomes including Resolution 49,[1] changes to union contract language, and development of a national model for other transit unions.

Despite extensive literature demonstrating the impact of *work* on cardiovascular disease and fatigue in commercial drivers, the recent initiatives of the DOT regarding hypertension and fatigue focus solely on *individual* behavior. While there may be individual health behaviors that contribute to the prevalence of hypertension, such as obesity, smoking, and alcohol consumption, these are also "maladaptive coping mechanisms" resulting from the pressures of the job. A close investigation of the *objective* occupational stressors has shown a strong positive association with hypertension.

Today, internationally, there is a large network of people who have been working together conducting research on the effects of long work shifts, overtime, and fatigue. Figure 1 shows the logo used in the International Transport Workers' Federation annual "Fatigue Kills" campaign. The annual "Fatigue Kills" campaign led to millions of transit workers around the world demonstrating for improvements in their working conditions. Unfortunately, the transit unions in the United States did not participate in this campaign, fearing that supporting it would affect overtime pay, which is the basis for transit operators being able to earn a living wage. There is a genuine dilemma facing transit workers in the United States: on the one hand, research demonstrates that hypertension and cardiovascular disease can result from long working hours [3, 21], yet economically transit operators in the United States are compelled to continue working overtime in order to survive. An example based on how MUNI drivers get paid may serve to elucidate why this dilemma in the United States exists.

The salary for a MUNI driver is based on the average of the top two transit systems in the United States. Based on this system, the wages of MUNI drivers

---

[1] Resolution 49 talks about the creation of a national health center for bus drivers, and was passed at the Transport Workers' National Convention in 2000. To date, however, funding has not been allocated to create the center.

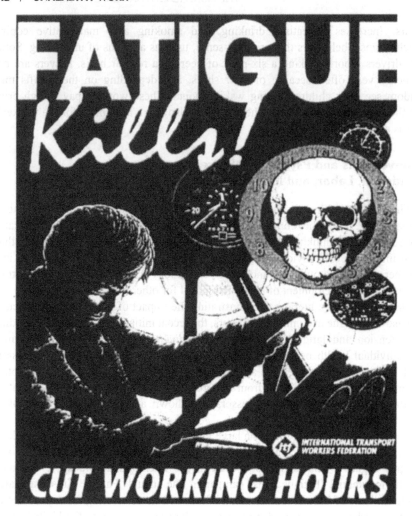

Figure 1. "Fatigue Kills" slide.

cannot exceed that average, and it effectively ties MUNI drivers' wages to the economic performance of the other two systems that are used as the benchmark. This means that if the other transit systems do not perform well, then MUNI drivers' wages go down. Even with collective negotiations, MUNI drivers' wages are, for the most part, fixed. The wage of a MUNI driver is insufficient to make ends meet in a family; a two-income household is needed for survival. The basis for drivers' wages explains why they need to work a great deal of overtime. The "Fatigue Kills" campaign aims to limit work hours to 8 hours per day, but this would make it impossible for drivers and their families to survive financially. Thus, while TWU supports the "Fatigue Kills" campaign, the limit it aims to implement is unlikely to be accepted by drivers since they would be deprived of the possibility of earning extra money, which they need to survive. If the "Fatigue Kills" campaign is implemented in the United States, it would eliminate overtime and split shifts, having a direct negative effect on workers' pay. One obvious alternative would be to ensure that drivers' wages are sufficient without overtime pay.

The Ambassador Program

A much-hailed joint labor-management initiative is the Ambassador/Friends of the MUNI Program, bringing hope to both MUNI operators and passengers. The overall purpose of the program is to improve service, working conditions, and relationships between operators and their riders. The program was brought about by the joint efforts and agreement of the Transport Workers' Union Local, the San Francisco Municipal Railway, together with representatives of the transport riders, and with the input of physicians and other researchers with expertise and concern about the health and well-being of the urban transport operators. The Ambassador Program is a pilot project. Initially the program will focus on 12 lines. When the program was first designed, it was envisioned that it would be rolled out throughout the system over time. However, it is highly unlikely due to both costs and difficulties experienced during the pilot phase of the program.

Issues at the heart of the program include:

- Increasing the number of transit operators to full strength.
- Revising schedules to be more realistic and to guarantee drivers' recovery time.
- Improving equipment so that working vehicles are provided.
- Upgrading and training for operators, to provide *transportation service rather than merely moving a vehicle from one place to the other.* Experienced operators would be offered the opportunity to become "line-trainers," and from this venerated position, provide guidance and share their skills with their colleagues.
- Involving and educating riders about how the system works and what kind of service riders can expect. The Ambassador Program will give operators the tools, the materials, and the training they need to reach out to the riders.

The program started on the 22-Filmore bus line. Everyone involved identified problem areas such as scheduling, passenger load, safety, and stress. In order to address these problems and to create a better working environment, it was agreed to add three more buses on the 22-Filmore line.

Unfortunately, trying to solve one problem ended up creating unforeseen new problems in other areas. For example, in order to add more vehicles to the 22-Filmore line, buses were cut from other lines, since surplus vehicles and drivers do not exist in the fleet. Thus, while attempting to correct problems on the 22-Filmore line, new problems ended up being created on the lines where buses were cut. This action resulted in problems in scheduling, passenger load, safety, and caused additional stress for the drivers on the lines that became newly short on vehicles. This was not a sustainable solution and not an acceptable intervention simply to make the Ambassador Program appear successful.

Additional steps have been taken to improve services on the 22-Filmore line, and by all accounts, operators are pleased. The next step is to discuss training needs and ideas with 22-Filmore line operators. The program has a coordinator who meets with operators, union leaders, and MUNI staff to put together all of the elements of the program. The support, ideas, and participation of transit operators are needed for the program to continue to succeed.[2] Working with fixed budgets and limited vehicles means finding solutions to problems is not simple or necessarily straightforward, even with cooperation from both union and management.

Recommendations for Change

It is time for an action-oriented agenda for change. The following recommendations should be implemented to begin to address the impact of occupational stressors on the high incidence of hypertension among urban transit workers:

- Promote worker and researcher collaboration on a broader basis.
- Influence DOT to mandate that data from the biennial medical exams be used as surveillance for health outcomes.
- Promote a paradigm shift on the part of the DOT from focusing solely on personal and lifestyle behavior to examining the impact of work on health outcomes.
- Ensure the provision of guaranteed and adequate rest breaks.
- Reduce working hours without decreasing income.
- Create a center for transportation worker health and safety. (This center was envisioned with the passage of Resolution 49. In the United States, a National Transportation Institute (NTA) exists, which conducts research but without the involvement of drivers or unions. The NTA does not address occupational health and safety or work standards.)
- Promote a "Transit First" policy. (San Francisco has a law that calls for a "Transit First" policy, which is meant to promote the use of public transportation. The policy gives buses and trains priority on the streets. The policy exists on paper, but has not yet been implemented because of the money required to do so. In addition to the issue of funding, implementing the "Transit First" policy would most likely unleash a major conflict between people who use their cars and the public transit system. If "Transit First" were to be implemented, it would effectively prohibit cars and trucks on certain streets. The commercial delivery sector, in particular, is strongly

[2] Article from *The MUNI Ambassador* (May 1998), published by the MUNI Improvement Fund, a joint project of the San Francisco Railway, The Transport Workers Union, and the City of San Francisco. For more information, call (415) 440-6823.

against losing the right for delivery trucks to have access to all streets since this would negatively impact the ability to make deliveries.

In response to demands made by the TWU Local 250A, efforts are being made to have operators drive on the same line as much as possible.[3] Doing so allows an operator to become familiar with his/her environment, including the passengers and all the specifics of the route. Knowing what to expect improves the level of the transit operator's control and is a key part of healthy-work practice.

CONCLUSION

Our project, a collaboration between TWU Local 250A represented by Ray Antonio in collaboration with Dr. June Fisher, and San Francisco General and researchers at the University of California, Berkeley is an important case example of how labor and researchers can work together to raise awareness of the deleterious health effects of stressful work environments. MUNI drivers begin their work life with a clean bill of health, however, the San Francisco MUNI Stress and Hypertension Study provided important results demonstrating that long-term exposure to elements of the bus driving work environment contribute to drivers' high rates of hypertension. Labor, management, and researchers came together and formed a committee to begin to address these concerns and were focused on making changes to the "objective" characteristics of bus driving rather than just focusing on the individual level behaviors of bus drivers.

While various interventions have been proposed and implemented, including Resolution 49, the International Transport Workers' Federation annual "Fatigue Kills" campaign, and the Ambassador Program, each of these programs had significant limitations including not being sufficiently funded to be effective. Much remains to be done to address the problems facing urban bus drivers. *Urban transit operators represent the eyes and the ears of the city.*[4] If the troubles of urban transit operators reflect the troubles of everyone in a city, then by extension the health of the city transit driver is inextricably linked to the health of the city. Efforts to improve their health are, therefore, in the interest of us all.

---

[3] This practice is part of the Ambassador Program, which includes the idea of having the same driver on the same line, in order to establish better relations with the traveling public. The philosophy behind this is that having a regular driver on any given line would enable the driver to develop a relationship with the regular traveling public on his/her line, which would also improve safety for the driver. This practice cannot be implemented, however, because of seniority provisions. Four times a year, MUNI drivers have a "sign-up" whereby drivers can select the work assignment they want based on line, hours, and days. These selections are based on seniority, which means that drivers with the most seniority get the best choices. Drivers with less seniority end up with what is left over, i.e., the worst lines, hours, days—the worst work assignments. Having the same driver on the same line all the time would conflict with the seniority provisions.

[4] This was a quote by Ray Antonio in 1978 when TWU started the project.

REFERENCES

1. Antonio, R., Worker-Researcher Collaboration with San Francisco Bus Drivers, *New Solutions: A Journal of Occupational and Environmental Health Policy,* 15:1, p. 40, 2005.
2. Deutsch, S., The Contributions and Challenge of Participatory Action Research, *New Solutions,* 15:1, pp. 29-35, 2005.
3. Tse, J. L. M., R. Flin, and K. Mearns, Bus Driver Well-Being Review: 50 Years of Research, *Transportation Research,* 9, pp. 89-114, 2006.
4. Morris, J. N., J. A. Heady, P. A. B. Raffle, C. G. Roberts, and J. W. Parks, Coronary Heart Disease and Physical Activity of Work, *The Lancet,* 1953a:2, pp. 1053-1057, 1953.
5. Morris, J. N., J. A. Heady, P. A. B. Raffle, C. G. Roberts, and J. W. Parks, Coronary Heart Disease and Physical Activity of Work, *The Lancet,* 1953b:2, pp. 1111-1120, 1953.
6. Long, L. and J. L. Perry, Economic and Occupational Causes of Transit Operator Absenteeism: A Review of Research, *Transport Reviews,* 1985:5, pp. 247-267, 1975.
7. Ragland, D., M. A. Winkelby, J. Schwalbe, et al., Prevalence of Hypertension in Bus Drivers, *International Journal of Epidemiology,* 16, pp. 208-214, 1987.
8. Rosengren, A., K. Anderson, and L. Wilhelmsen, Risk of Coronary Heart Disease in Middle-Aged Male Bus and Tram Drivers Compared to Men in Other Occupations: A Prospective Study, *International Journal of Epidemiology,* 20, pp. 82-87, 1991.
9. Wang, P. D. and R. S. Lin, Coronary Heart Disease Risk Factors in Urban Bus Drivers, *Public Health,* 46, pp. 149-155, 2001.
10. Greiner, B. A., N. Krause, D. R. Ragland, and J. Fisher, Objective Stress Factors, Accidents and Absenteeism in Transit Operators: A Theoretical Framework and Empirical Evidence, *Journal of Occupational Health Psychology,* 3, pp. 130-146, 1998.
11. Krause, N., D. R. Ragland, B. A. Greiner, S. L. Syme, and J. Fisher, Psychosocial Job Factors Associated with Back and Neck Pain in Public Transit Operators, *Scandinavian Journal of Work Environment and Health,* 23:3, pp. 179-186, 1997.
12. Grosswald, B., I Raised My Kids on the Bus: Transit Shift Workers' Coping Strategies for Parenting, *Journal of Sociology and Social Welfare,* 29:3, pp. 29-49, 2002.
13. Tuchsen, F. and L. A. Endahl, Increasing Inequality in Ischaemic Heart Disease Morbidity among Employed Men in Denmark 1981-1993: The Need for a New Preventive Policy, *International Journal of Epidemiology,* 28, pp. 640-644, 1999.
14. Karasek, R. A., T. Theorell, J. E. Schwartz, P. L. Schnall, C. F. Pieper, and J. L. Michela, Job Characteristics in Relation to the Prevalence of Myocardial Infarction in the US Health Examination Survey (HES) and the Health and Nutrition Examination Survey (HANES), *American Journal of Public Health,* 78:8, pp. 910-918, 1988.
15. Karasek, R., D. Baker, F. Marxer, A. Ahlbom, and T. Theorell, Job Decision Latitude, Job Demands, and Cardiovascular Disease: A Prospective Study of Swedish Men, *American Journal of Public Health,* 71:7, pp. 694-705, 1981.
16. Karasek, R. A., K. P. Triantis, and S. S. Chaudry, Coworker and Supervisor Support as Moderators of Associations between Task Characteristics and Mental Strain, *Journal of Occupational Behavior,* 3, pp. 181-200, 1982.
17. Schnall, P. L., C. Pieper, J. E. Schwartz, et al., The Relationship between "Job Strain," Workplace Diastolic Blood Pressure, and Left Ventricular Mass Index. Results of a Case-Control Study [published Erratum appears in JAMA 1992 Mar 4;267(9):1209], *Journal of the American Medical Association,* 263:14, pp. 1929-1935, 1990.

18. Albright, C. L., M. A. Winkleby, D. R. Ragland, J. Fisher, and S. L. Syme, Job Strain and Prevalence of Hypertension in a Biracial Population of Urban Bus Drivers, *American Journal of Public Health,* 82:7, pp. 984-989, 1992.
19. Greiner, B., N. Krause, D. Ragland, and J. Fisher, Occupational Stressors and Hypertension: A Multi-Method Study Using Observer-Based Job Analysis and Self-Reports in Urban Transit Operators, *Social Science and Medicine,* 59, pp. 1081-1094, 2004.
20. Schnall, P. L., P. Landsbergis, J. E. Schwarts, and T. G. Pickering, Job Strain and Hypertension, *American Journal of Public Health,* 82:2, pp. 320-321, 1994.
21. Yang, H., P. Schnall, M. Jauregui, T. Su, and D. Baker, Work Hours and Self-Reported Hypertension among Working People in California, *Hypertension,* 48:4, pp. 744-750, 2006.

CHAPTER 14

Organizing and Collaborating to Reduce Hotel Workers' Injuries

Mike Casey and Ellen Rosskam

Hotel workers have higher rates of occupational injury and illness compared to workers in the service sector at large, and hotel room cleaners appear to have worse overall health than that of the general U.S. population [1]. In 2002, hotel workers had 6.7 occupational injuries and illnesses per 100 full-time workers, compared to 4.6 in the service sector as a whole. Hotel workers also had higher rates for occupational injuries and illness resulting in lost workdays (1.8 vs. 1.3 per 100 full-time workers) [1]. During the last 25 years, changes in the hotel industry have affected the nature of work for hotel workers in San Francisco and have affected the kind of organizing efforts employed by Local 2 of UNITE HERE. This chapter outlines the effects of downsizing, cost cutting, and the resulting intensification of workloads on the health of hotel workers, as well as the organizing efforts of union members in San Francisco. In conducting a housekeeping workload study, collaboration with researchers at the University of California, San Francisco, helped workers success-fully negotiate a contract in 1999/2000 that made important advances toward allevi-ating the impacts of workload on housekeepers.

The detrimental effects of 9/11 on the hotel industry meant a lowering of occu-pancy rates and diminishing revenues for hotels in the first year to 18 months following that tragic day. This led to layoffs and fewer staff, resulting in increased workloads for the remaining housekeepers, for kitchen staff, and other classifi-cations. Future contract negotiations to try to change working conditions to alleviate the rates of injury among members in housekeeping and in the kitchens will require the continued help of both researchers and the public.

CHANGING DYNAMICS IN THE HOTEL INDUSTRY

Taken together, cooks, food servers, room cleaners, and related jobs comprise more than half of the hospitality workforce. Nationwide, hospitality accounts for 13% of all employment in cleaning and building services and 6% of all jobs in

249

food and beverage services. These two groups of occupations (cleaning and building services and food and beverage) employ 11.7 million workers in the United States, or nearly one in every 10 jobs, and a much larger share of those jobs at the bottom of the pay scale.

The quality of non-managerial jobs in hospitality has deteriorated on several dimensions in recent decades. During the 1960s and 1970s, work hours declined by nearly 25%. Due to the prevalence of part-time work, the average workweek has remained about 30 hours per week for the last two decades, while compensation remains quite low. Real hourly wages increased more slowly in the 1970s and declined in the 1980s (Figure 1) [2]. Average weekly earnings have remained stagnant for a generation [2]. When annual productivity growth fell significantly from the 1960s to the 1970s, hourly wage growth also fell significantly each year. Since the 1980s, however, employers have managed to restore productivity growth to post-World War II levels, yet workers have seen few, if any, of the benefits. Strikingly, productivity grew 12 times faster than wages between 1990 and 1995 [2]. The recent disjuncture between wage and productivity gains has contributed to soaring profitability in the industry. Pre-tax profits have doubled to $17 billion over the last several years. More than ever before, management is focused on short-term financial gain.

Besides a real decline in wages, the quality of employment in the hospitality industry also has declined substantially over the last two to three decades. Many of the jobs in these occupations offer low wages and benefits, unreliable work schedules, and limited career advancement opportunities. Employment is still segregated by race and gender. A large proportion of non-managerial workers are people of color, especially immigrants in back-of-the-house jobs that often do not require much communication with guests [2].

In the 1970s and 1980s, hotels in San Francisco were still largely family-owned and -operated. The industry, however, consolidated in the 1990s, with a handful of corporations owning most of the hotels, including Marriott, Hyatt, Hilton, Starwood, and Intercontinental. Increasingly, corporate operators are replacing local hoteliers.

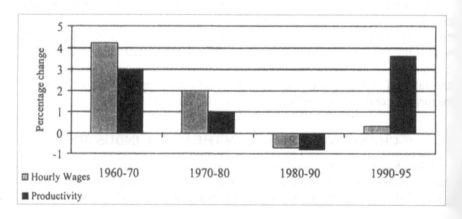

Figure 1. Wage and productivity growth, 1960-1995.
Source: Bureau of Labor Statistics.

These operators hire human resources managers who take control away from local management and exercise increasing influence over the work environment, contract negotiations, and labor costs from corporate offices far away from the hotels.

As a result of the increasing influence of remote corporate management and consolidation of the industry, there has been a disastrous downsizing in staff over the course of the 1980s and 1990s in particular. So much so that downsizing, outsourcing, subcontracting, and lean staffing are trademarks of the industry everywhere today in the United States. Big hotels, such as the Fairmont in San Francisco, which 15 years ago had as many as 700 workers, today operates with fewer than 450 workers. The St. Francis hotel in San Francisco had some 700 workers. Today it only boasts 550 to 600 workers. Ironically, while the hotel industry is reducing staffing levels, they are also increasing the level and quality of amenities. The result of this downsizing has been an increase in workload causing increases in work-related injuries. By 1999, when Local 2's contract came up for renewal, union members, particularly those in the area of housekeeping, had had enough.

The sad truth is employees of modern corporations have little reason to feel satisfied, much less fulfilled. Companies do not have the time or the interest to listen to them, and lack the resources or the inclination to train them for advancement. These companies make a series of demands, for which they compensate employees with salaries that are often considered inadequate. Moreover, companies tend to be implacable in dismissing workers when they start to age or go through a temporary drop in performance, and send people into retirement earlier than they want, leaving them with the feeling they could have contributed much more had someone just asked [3].

Local 2 won a very good contract in 1999/2000. Between 2000 and 2003, however, the impact of 9/11 took its toll, severely affecting the travel and hotel industries. Initially, post-9/11, the hotel industry suffered significant and drastic cuts in room occupancies. The industry responded by reducing room rates. The increase in hotel bookings by internet also has led to a dramatic reduction in room rates while also increasing occupancy rates, so employers have again instituted a whole new round of cost-cutting measures. Fifteen years ago it was recognized that a hotel functioning at 64% occupancy would allow the management to break even, with any income above 64% being pure profit. Today, 47% occupancy will allow a hotel to break even [4]. This lowering of the profit-making bar has occurred due to downsizing the workforce and augmenting the intensity and pace of work, which has decreased labor costs to such a point that even rising health care costs have not thwarted the profit margin.

Room cleaners organized a full year ahead of the 1999/2000 contract negotiations in order to demand reductions in workload. While hotel room cleaners in San Francisco had one of the better contracts in the industry, workers still were required to clean 15 rooms a day. This translates into making between 15 and 20 beds a day—most of which are king-sized beds, cleaning and scrubbing at least 15 bathtubs and toilets, and vacuuming and dusting 15 rooms. Cleaners have checklists they must go through methodically with as many as 120 items to be completed in a room in a 25-minute period. As a result of this heavy workload combined with constant time pressure, room cleaners were no longer willing to accept the conditions of work imposed by management. In the hotel industry, this translates into serious problems for management.

UNION RESPONSE TO HOUSEKEEPING
WORKLOAD STUDY

Local 2 of UNITE HERE in San Francisco, represents hotel workers, private clubs, stadium workers, and convention workers, and has approximately 9,000 members in San Francisco. There are an additional 3,000 members employed in San Mateo County properties. The Local is a result of several mergers back in the mid-1970s of bartenders, cooks, waiters, room cleaners, and bell persons combining into one consolidated union. Local 2's union members are from many backgrounds. Like most hotel unions in the country, Local 2 has international representation, with workers coming from China, Southeast Asia, the Philippines, Central and South America, Mexico, Africa, and Eastern Europe. Women workers make up more than half of Local 2's membership, and represent 99% of hotel room cleaners, with immigrants making up 90% of hotel room cleaners.

The Restaurant and Hotel Workers' Union, San Francisco, represents approximately 89% of hotel workers in full-service hotels in San Francisco, providing significant representation density. Good contracts result from that membership density. Yet the nature of the hotel industry in San Francisco and nationwide has been changing significantly over the last couple of decades, accompanied by the steady intensification of work and sizable increases in room attendants' workload. These changes have put in jeopardy the health and safety of union members in this industry.

In San Francisco, Local 2 developed a strategy for preserving or expanding the organized share of the workforce and therefore the bargaining power and political clout of non-managerial workers. On the one hand, Local 2 established a unique partnership with a dozen major full-service hotels to upgrade the quality of customer service and employment in the industry between 1994 and 2004. On the other hand, Local 2 also achieved a model ordinance that requires employers who receive economic development subsidies from the city to remain neutral in organizing drives. In effect, this dual strategy compensates employers under contract for the union premium and aggressively organizes non-union employers to even the playing field [1].

While progress was being made in the late 1990s toward better contracts, awareness was growing that hotel workers were burdened by worsening health.

For many years, these workers . . . had complained of high rates of injuries and musculoskeletal disorders. The union was aware that many had undergone surgery and several had become permanently disabled [1, p. 1].

By the 1990s it was well known that various work related psychosocial stressors, such as mismatches between high demands and low control (job strain) and high efforts and low rewards (effort-reward imbalance) had been shown to increase the likelihood of cardiovascular disease and musculoskeletal disorders [5-15]. However, most of the research demonstrating these links has been conducted with factory workers and civil servants. Little was known, therefore, about the impact of job stress in the rapidly growing numbers of low-wage and precarious service-sector jobs.

> Believing that these injuries could be job-related, the union leadership con-tacted the University of California at Berkeley's Labor Occupational Health Program (LOHP) to assess its interest in helping to conduct original research that would look at work load, health and employee/employer relationships. The union envisioned a study that would involve participatory action research (PAR) with hotel room cleaners themselves in the role of study collaborators [1, p. 1].

Based on this gap in knowledge and Local 2's awareness of a growing number of health problems among hotel housekeepers, in 1998, Local 2 initiated an investi-gation into the association between job stress and physical and psychological health outcomes in hotel room cleaners [16]. Working directly with the union local, LOHP served as an intermediary in carrying out the original research with university-based researchers at the University of California, Berkeley, School of Public Health. In addition to donating considerable amounts of their own time, the union allocated staff and dedicated substantial funding to the project. The union supplemented an initial grant of $30,000 from the Rockefeller Foundation with most of the additional $100,000 needed to see the project through to completion.

LOHP was responsible for direction of the project, coordination between the union and School of Public Health researchers, and facilitation and training of room cleaner groups involved in the project. LOHP identified as potential collab-orators public health researchers who were knowledgeable about and comfortable with the use of PAR. Niklas Krause, a physician and epidemiologist in occupa-tional and environmental medicine at the University of California, San Francisco, with extensive experience in collaborating with both unions and management, was the project's lead public health researcher. Pam Tau Lee, LOHP's Labor Services Program Coordinator, served as the project's co-director, and brought with her professional background personal experience as a room cleaner [1]. Consistent with the objectives of participatory action research, workers and researchers col-laborated in designing and carrying out all aspects of the study.

Designed to examine recent changes in housekeeping and the differences in their impact on room cleaners, the study involved conducting a survey of room cleaners at four full-service union-represented hotels in San Francisco. The survey was completed by 258 out of 373 day shift room cleaners (participation rate of 69%).

Focus Groups and Questionnaire

Focus groups with room cleaners were used as a key means of gathering information, establishing credibility, identifying risk factors, and prioritizing areas to be included in a questionnaire instrument. The questionnaire was developed in close collaboration with room cleaners, who provided extensive input at all stages of the questionnaire design, as well as with data input and analysis.

> The team agreed to an approach that would combine the knowledge of the workers and the best available science. A core group of 25 room cleaners was identified, whose racial/ethnic composition reflected that of the workforce: all but two (one each African American and white) were Latina, Filipina, and Chinese. All core group members were women, and they were chosen on the basis of the high regard in which they were held by peers and their tendency to seek out union representatives on job-related concerns. An effort also was made to include women with varying lengths of seniority . . . [1, p. 6].

Core group members attended six focus group sessions, held every 2 weeks for 3 hours after work. LOHP facilitated group discussions to look at workload, physical strain, relationship with management, and worker disability. The information that emerged from the discussions provided the study team with specific issues that formed the basis of more in-depth collaborative research [1]. To inform the focus group discussions while maintaining an emphasis on local capacity-building and empowerment, training on ergonomics and control measures was integrated into the focus group sessions. Adult education and interactive activities were used, including illness and injury reports, body mapping for workplace pain, brainstorming, and risk mapping. Participants drew maps of their workplaces on which they identified the physical, chemical, ergonomic, and other stressors to which they are routinely exposed. The risk maps were then used as a basis for discussion within the groups. The team used a mock hotel room as a prop during the group discussions. The mock hotel room was set up with two beds, a bathtub, a sink, furniture, and equipment. After participants were given a short introduction to ergonomic risk factors, "volunteers" went through the motions of cleaning a room, while the rest of the participants identified risk factors for injury. The process enabled the study team to discover that factors such as the weight and awkwardness of linen carts and vacuum cleaners, and ineffective cleaning products that required repeated scrubbing, were sources of ergonomic and other forms of stress [1].

Through this collaboration between university researchers, LOHP, room cleaners, and the union, a foundation for the sharing of power was created, and bridges built between the union and the academic researchers. One union spokesperson summed up in the following way the importance of the role of LOHP, the "third party" institution:

> We needed a third party to keep us [the union] in line. We had to be disciplined and learn how to participate but not taint the process. A third party helped us to sort through our concerns and helped us present these in a way the

researchers could understand. We didn't know anything about the world of the academics and we wouldn't have been able to figure out what to do without the help of people who understood us and understood the researchers as well [1, p. 5].

WHAT THE STUDY REVEALED

The findings from the collaborative research project were cause for serious concern. Ninety percent of room cleaners described their jobs as "physically demanding," and nearly 90% reported their jobs as becoming "more demanding" over the last few years. Eighty-three percent reported that the job required them to work very fast due to constant time pressure, and nearly 40% reported experiencing high levels of demand on the job with a low level of worker control over the organization and implementation of their work (i.e., job strain), a classic predictor of work-induced stress that can lead to long-term health problems. It has become common practice in the hotel industry to combine intensified workloads with irregular, often unpredictable, work hours, effectively shifting the burden of variation in hotel occupancy to workers. Many workers are essentially "on-call," meaning they are sent home when business is slow and held over for additional work hours when the occupancy rate is high, whether planned or unexpected.

A room cleaner typically arrives at work at 7:30 in the morning to receive her room assignments and keys. This means that many workers must rise at extremely early hours (such as 5:00 a.m.) in order to get to work on time, often traveling by public transport from areas far outside of San Francisco. The cleaner's tasks include loading the cart with linens, walking through the assigned area to determine which rooms are still occupied or have "do not disturb" signs, removing dirty linen from bathrooms, soaking the tub, bowl, and sink with cleanser, emptying the trash, stripping the bed, emptying the trash, checking under the bed, closet, and drawers, then cleaning and stocking the bathroom. The room cleaner then makes the beds, dusts the furniture, checks amenities, light bulbs, and other items in the room, organizes the closet, vacuums the carpet, and closes the windows and shades [2, p. 12].

A room cleaner in San Francisco does this an average of 14 times a day, including suites and special rooms.

Trash in the room was revealed to be a significant workload problem. Room cleaners today often end up removing far more garbage than in past decades due to the bags of brochures, papers, and trinkets that convention and meeting participants collect. Convention catalogs and brochures left in a room can weigh 10 pounds or more. Guests bring in take-out food, often leaving paper containers, cans, and bags on tables or in trash cans. More garbage means more trips to pick up trash and heavier trash cans, but all within the same allocated time frame, no matter what the extra trash load may be [1]. Workers have to pace themselves and solve problems throughout the day to make their room quota in a safe and healthy manner. Done well, housekeeping requires experience and skill, if not an actual educational credential. Cleaning most rooms involves facing a range of unexpected problems that must be solved quickly, often with little or no support.

Work intensity is related to a variety of factors, such as the number of special rooms, guests, amenities, and the like. Although these factors vary by market segment, their impact depends on policies and practices set within each hotel. Within the business travel segment, for example, the number of check-outs tends to be lower when guests arrive for conventions, conferences, or other extended stays. Because a checkout room takes more time to clean, one room may get dropped from the quota for every seven or eight checkouts. However, supervisors often respond by spreading out the number of checkouts across room cleaners to minimize the number of rooms dropped from the quota. That, in turn, increases the travel from room to room, the frequency of trips between floors, and the potential for logistical problems in stocking the carts, the linen closets, or both.

Three trends in the industry have contributed to an increase in the workload for room cleaners in recent years even at unionized hotels where the room quota has been established through collective bargaining. Employers have: 1) upgraded facilities to include two double beds per room (generally in non-luxury hotels) or more luxurious beds which can be much more difficult to make up; 2) increased amenities (coffee pots, mini-bars, fax machines, and the like); and 3) reduced support staff (especially inspectresses and housemen).

Luxury business hotel rooms often have one king-size bed, which are a major source of job stress and injury for room cleaners in those hotels. The linens are heavier, making the beds is more difficult, and the carts must be stocked more often. Room cleaners often use their hips and knees to help them move beds around within a limited space. Workers have not been involved in laying out the rooms, selecting the furniture or their own equipment, or other activities that could have prevented such problems. Bed linen also emerged as a major problem in the study because many hotels now use three sheets per bed and more pillows than in the past. A king-sized bed can require up to six or eight pillows, requiring more travel to and from the linen closet, again, with no additional time allowed to workers despite these significant changes in hotel room design.

Housekeeping workloads continue to increase as a result of the number of checkouts in a hotel. Doing a "checkout room" is more work than a "stay-over" room. Rushed rooms or rooms that are designated "VIP" also increase the workload pressure. Management often will say that everyone who stays in the hotel is a VIP, but in reality, some hotel customers are actual VIPs, while the rest of the clients may be told they are VIPs for marketing purposes. As a trade union local, HERE Local 2 has fought management over the issue of VIPs because true VIP rooms usually are extra work compared with other guest rooms. Management would insist that all rooms carried VIP status based on the notion that all guests were "very important." This led to a struggle to distinguish the difference in workload between a "typical" guest room and a room that might be extraordinarily dirty. Dirty rooms take longer to clean, particularly rooms where a rock band or high school tour group has stayed, for example.

Another issue over which the union struggles with management is the time spent traveling between floors. Hotel housekeeping workers use a large cleaning cart that they move between floors. In order to move between floors, they have to use the service elevators, which are used at the same time by room service attendants, bellmen, and other hotel classifications. Service elevators are the slowest elevators in the hotel. Time spent waiting on the landing for the elevators counts against the amount of time allocated to fulfill workload requirements. This factor alone has resulted in an underestimate of workload by management because it is not taken into account. Missed breaks are rampant among hotel housekeeping workers as they try to make up for this unaccounted time and fulfill workload requirements.

WIDESPREAD PAIN AND SUFFERING

Musculoskeletal Disorders

The collaborative research project of San Francisco hotel housekeeping workers discovered that the vitality and energy levels of room cleaners were lower than the U.S. average. Workers also reported higher levels of fatigue. In self-reports about the status of their own health, nearly 40% of workers in the study categorized their health as fair or poor.

Even in San Francisco, where workers have an independent voice in the workplace through their union, almost every room cleaner reported work-related pain. Nearly 75% of workers reported work-related pains severe enough to oblige them to see a doctor. As shown in Figure 2, one in four had to take time off from work due to pain, 24% of the room cleaners said they experienced severe pain in their lower back on a regular basis, and 84% of workers reported using some kind of pain medication. Self-rated general health among room cleaners was significantly lower than among the general U.S. population. Of the three-quarters of room cleaners who reported work-related pain or discomfort, in 73% of all cases it was

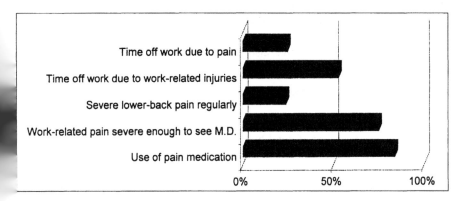

Figure 2. Reported pain, injuries, and time off work in San Francisco hotel room cleaners [19].

severe enough to visit a doctor and in 53% of all cases it was severe enough to take time off from work [17]. Only half of the affected workers reported their injuries to supervisors and even fewer filed for workers' compensation. Many managers believe that the widespread *perception* of heavier work loads stems mainly from aging. The high annual turnover rate among new employees and the high rates of musculoskeletal disorders among both younger and older employees, however, indicate that aging is not the primary cause of this widespread perception among workers [18].

Workers with greater job demands had a higher likelihood of suffering from back and neck pain, even after accounting for individual characteristics, cumulative work demands, care-taking responsibilities at home, and psychosocial job factors.

The increased burden of work for hotel room cleaners has resulted in a considerable level of job-related stress and injury. To highlight the widespread nature of these problems and the fact that they are not location-specific, more than three-quarters of room cleaners in a similar study in Las Vegas reported having work-related pain, and more than half had been obliged to take time off from work due to their pain. The 1-month prevalence of severe bodily pain was slightly over 40% for neck pain, 60% for upper back pain, and more than 60% for low back pain [18].

The Wear and Tear of Stress and Job Strain

In addition to high rates of musculoskeletal disorders, hotel housekeeping workers in both San Francisco and Las Vegas were shown to live with high levels of work-related stress. The San Francisco hotel workers' study found effort-reward imbalance and job strain to be highly prevalent and associated with poor physical and psychological health [16]. Nearly 40% of room cleaners experienced high levels of job strain, which was found to be associated with lower back pain and psychological exhaustion [16]. The findings suggest that about one-third of all room cleaners experienced high levels of job stress, but the level of job stress varied significantly between hotels, suggesting that there is a potential for preventing job stress through job redesign [18]. In addition, 30% of San Francisco room cleaners in the study experienced an imbalance between their work efforts and the material and non-material rewards they receive, also an important indicator of job stress [19].

Underreporting and Workers' Compensation

Additional similarities in findings have been noted between the Las Vegas and San Francisco studies of hotel housekeepers. Among the San Francisco room cleaners, workers averaged about 16 sick days per year for a total of 1,600 per 100 workers, although workers' sick days were not always reported as work-related. In spite of the significant burden of pain and suffering, a mere 23% of the San Francisco workers filed for workers' compensation for their work-related injuries or illnesses [2]. Consistent with those findings, in Las Vegas only 27% of workers said they had filed a workers' compensation claim for their injuries or illnesses [18].

In our study, the self-reported rate of injuries filed with workers' compensation in the last 12 months is 26.9 per 100 full-time employees (FTE). This rate is four times higher than the national incidence rate of 6.6 per 100 FTE (Bureau of Labor Statistics, 2003a) and 6.3 per 100 FTE in Nevada (Bureau of Labor Statistics, 2003b), for the Hotel and Lodging industry. It is nearly six times higher than the national incidence rate of 4.6 per 100 FTE for all jobs in the service sector (Bureau of Labor Statistics, 2003a). The significantly higher incidence rate of self-reported injuries in our study suggests substantial under-reporting by either workers to employers or employers to OSHA [18, p. 333].

It is likely that injuries are under-reported even among unionized workers because of the temporary or precarious nature of the job. Subtle or more overt messages from management lead workers to blame themselves for their injuries or internalize their pain so they can continue to work and earn an income, operating in what could be called an "occupational culture of pain." In such an environment, everyone you work with is suffering in similar pain, but no one talks that much about it, preferring instead to get on with the job, unless the worker becomes incapacitated due to pain or injury [20, 21].

Workers appear to prefer dealing with work-related pain on their own rather than risk loss of income, out-of-pocket medical expenses, or hostile or punitive responses from management. Underreporting of injuries, inadequate or delayed care, and failure to recognize and address hazardous working conditions can lead to the work-related health condition worsening and becoming chronic [22, p. 487].

Under-reporting of work-induced injuries shifts the cost away from the employers' liability insurance and often can lead to an increase in the overall cost of the employee's health insurance, which in turn can lead to increased pressure from employers during contract negotiations for union members to share the increased cost of health insurance. Health care costs continue to be a contentious issue for unionized workers during contract negotiations and is a major barrier for low-wage workers to be included in employer-based health plans.

Consequences of the "Lean" Machine

The hotel industry has adopted lean staffing arrangements even as the normal workload for room cleaners has increased. Hotels have reduced the number of inspectresses and housemen who would assist room cleaners with problem tasks or fill-in under certain conditions. Housemen perform certain problem tasks related to building maintenance. An increased burden of work for room cleaners results from an insufficient number of inspectresses and housemen, adding to room cleaners' "time squeeze," and increasing psychological stress and physical strain. In the San Francisco study, about half of the room cleaners reported that the reduction of inspectresses was a major problem for them [2].

RESEARCH AS PART OF UNION ORGANIZING
AND USING RESEARCH FOR CHANGE

The San Francisco hotel housekeepers' study marked the first time that Local 2 had ever conducted this type of systematic, participatory action investigation. The results gave credible, empirical weight to the union's demands and to seeking recognition for the problems addressed in collective bargaining negotiations. The research partnership provided survey results that were used in negotiations with management. Using the results of the investigation, workers organized across craft lines to help achieve the objectives of a stronger bargaining unit.

> Both academic partners and room cleaners themselves played a critical role at the bargaining table. At the union's request, the lead UC researcher presented the study findings at a joint contract negotiation session between union and management. A 45-minute presentation was made to the entire negotiating committee of over 100 people, including the union leadership along with many rank-and-file negotiators, the 23 hotel general managers, their lawyers, and human resources personnel. Well over 200 room cleaners came to hear the presentation and signify their support [1, p. 14].

The active involvement of the room cleaners themselves proved to be of critical importance at the bargaining table. During labor-management negotiations, six female room cleaners spoke on a panel.

> When the panel began, each woman told her life story, including the kinds of jobs she had held in her native country and here in the U.S., the injuries she had incurred as a room cleaner, and the results of these injuries, including severe pain, operations on wrists and shoulders, daily medications, and the wearing of braces. The women also talked about the physical and psychological demands of the job, and explained the hardship their injuries caused for them and their families (e.g., in leaving them with no energy for playing with their children or helping them with homework). Each of the speakers added that room cleaning involved by far the most difficult work she had ever done, and two cried openly during their testimony. In part because of their involvement in the research, the women could speak with great passion and clarity about their situation, the increase in workload they had experienced, and the proposals the union was making to protect their health [1, p. 15].

Housekeeping is the largest part of a hotel and a strong organizing force. Other departments are more separate; some traditionally have had conflict between them. Room cleaners, however, were able to organize across all craft lines and obtained solid support. Numerous actions were pursued, culminating on Labor Day weekend 1999, when approximately 1,500 people took to the streets of San Francisco to demonstrate, with 150 people conducting civil disobedience. That same weekend the press reported the data from the collaborative research. The media coverage proved to be a tremendous asset.

The 1999 actions, combined with the union's research findings, resulted in the most significant workload reduction ever achieved by the union local. The efforts resulted in reducing the workload from 15 rooms per day to 14 rooms per day. The union was able to convince management that still greater reductions for checkouts were needed. If a room cleaner had seven checkouts, one room could be dropped from their quota for the day. If a cleaner had 10 checkouts, they could drop two rooms from the quota. Additionally, room quotas have been decreased for traveling between floors to store or deliver cots and cribs. Workload restrictions on transporting bulk linen were also gained.

The study findings suggested opportunities to improve work organization, worker involvement, and career development in the hospitality industry. One strategy for improving the quality of housekeeping jobs is to re-design the staffing and work systems. The adoption of lean staffing arrangements has cut costs in the short term, but the technique is easy for rivals to duplicate, which only leads to a race to the bottom. The longer-term effect of heavier workloads for those who remain is likely to be a decline in customer service for the guests and an increase in health and safety costs (such as through documented absenteeism and worker compensation). A more durable source of advantage is the implementation of a new work system in which room cleaners take on many of the responsibilities once performed by inspectresses. But the transition to a new work system would require a revision of the current room quota underwritten by gains in customer service and health and safety. Indeed, lean staffing appears to have a significantly negative impact on room cleaners' perceptions of the quality of their job.

A consistent association has been established between lower injury rates and worker empowerment, among other factors such as active management in health and safety. Lower injury rates have been found where workers are expected by management to use their own initiative, rather than carry out tasks based on management instructions, where there is encouragement by management of a long-term commitment by workers, and where management-labor relations are good. In addition, companies which provide longer periods of safety training and continued safety training regularly and companies whose workers have longer seniority show lower injury rates and lower staff turnover [23].

Not surprisingly, and consistent with the evidence, hotel room cleaners' perceptions about the quality of their job are intricately linked to cleaners' relationships with supervisors. The San Francisco study revealed that good labor relations at a hotel were positively associated with room cleaners reporting that they receive respect and support from their supervisor.

> In cooperation with the union, management at the luxury hotel required the supervisors to attend a course on teamwork along with room cleaners. As a result, 91 percent of the room cleaners at the luxury hotel believe labor and management work together to solve problems, compared to 72 or 73 percent at the other three hotels [2, p. 18].

An important mechanism for improving the quality of housekeeping is to involve workers more in problem solving and decision-making away from their daily rounds. Hotel room cleaners, like all workers, know best the problems—and solutions—related to their job [24-30].

> Worker participation, effective use of worker voice, participatory ergonomics, or establishing changes in work conditions through participatory approaches involving both workers and managers, are demonstrated as central to reducing musculoskeletal disorders and improving overall workplace health and safety [21, p. 209].

Evidence suggests that positive management support results in fewer musculo-skeletal disorders, and even exerts a protective effect against musculoskeletal disorders by acting as a buffer against risk factors for physical strain and psychological stress [21].

> . . . organization policies may determine the possibility of worker participation in a broad range of company-level decisions. This possibility of participation can contribute to productivity and worker well-being (such as reduction in feelings of powerlessness). Union membership and membership in influential work groups must also affect the total picture of decision latitude available to the worker. These macro social factors may have direct effects on health and productivity as well as indirect effects through changes in the possibility of task control at the individual level. Factors similar to these have been found to contribute to psychological well-being [32, p. 141].

Local 2's room cleaner study placed a strong emphasis on building on the strengths of the room cleaner partners in the study, increasing their problem-solving abilities, and providing opportunities for them to articulate their concerns and issues, using their own voices [1].

Finally, an additional important strategy for improving the quality of work and employment in housekeeping is to improve training and promotion opportunities. With the transition to lean staffing arrangements, constructing job ladders with bridges between different departments could be a useful management approach, providing increased and more varied opportunities for workers in various hospitality categories, including room cleaners.

LOOKING FORWARD WITH GUSTO

While the new contracts mark important in-roads in improving hotel room cleaners' working conditions, the effects of the industry trend to downsize are being felt in the kitchens, where workers now face tremendous difficulties. Local 2 is organizing in the kitchens, while workers are conducting collaborative scientific studies, similar to those conducted with housekeeping workers. These actions helped prepare for recent contract negotiations in San Francisco. A number of alarming findings have been obtained through research conducted with kitchen workers. For example, the rate of injury among workers in the American workforce in general is 7.1 per 100 workers; however, in San Francisco's hotel kitchens, the injury rate is 53.6 injuries per 100 workers. Many of these injuries are unreported, because being a professional cook is a rather macho craft in many ways, for both men and women alike. If a cook cuts or burns him or herself, it is seen as simply *part of the job,* and thus very often goes unreported.

An additional problem in hotel kitchens is that increasingly there is more outsourcing of work. Widespread outsourcing has altered even the most customary features of hotel kitchen operations. Many of the items that appear on a menu will be outsourced. For example, hotel kitchens no longer make specialty soups; they purchase canned or pre-packaged soups instead. The widespread trend to outsource food preparation has resulted in an increased magnitude of injuries from the heavy lifting involved in moving prepackaged products from one area of the kitchen to the other.

CONCLUSION

The community and workforce development potential of the hospitality industry depends on the quality of work and employment in the sector. In addition to higher wages and benefits, local unions have championed innovations in work organization, worker involvement, and career advancement. National union centers have begun to commit resources to a comprehensive program for rebuilding union strength in dozens of markets around the country.

The 1999/2000 round of citywide bargaining in San Francisco improved the employment and advancement opportunities for low-income residents of the San Francisco Bay Area. The negotiated agreement raised the wages of room cleaners by 25%, from $12 to $15 per hour over 5 years. In the new contract set to expire in August 2009, room cleaners and other non-tipped workers will receive a $1 per hour increase effective August 2006, 2007, and 2008, which will bring room cleaners' wages to $18.09 per hour by the end of the contract. The 1999 agreement also contained provisions to improve room cleaners' health care, child care, elder care, and other benefits, and reduced the standard quota from 15 rooms to 14 per day. The agreement increased room cleaners' voice in work systems, staffing structures, and training and promotion opportunities. The agreement required class-A hotels participating in the San Francisco Hotel Partnership Project to form teams with the union to address the problems room cleaners encounter on the job, to increase workers' prospects for promotion into other occupations, and to improve the dispatch of workers to lucrative banquets and other special events. Local 2 has continued working with employers to establish an employment-linked training program to help low-income residents obtain better access to careers in hospitality, and at the same time improve the recruitment and retention of new employees.

In September 2006, the HERE Local 2 Negotiating Committee settled with the Multi-Employer Group (MEG) and other San Francisco hotels for a new collective bargaining agreement, to be effective until 2009. The agreement includes numerous gains for workers in multiple categories of the hospitality industry. For room cleaners, the tentative agreement includes further reductions in workload from the current maximum of 14 rooms per day to be cleaned. When six of those

14 are "checkouts," cleaners will have to clean only 13 rooms; when there are nine checkouts in a day, two rooms are to be dropped from the cleaning requirement. The hotels also agreed to some additional workload adjustments, which are of particular importance given the increase in injuries that room cleaners face due to the increased number of pillows and sheets, duvets, bigger beds, and more amenities.

The new agreement includes substantial improvements in drug benefits for workers and the coverage for dependents under the Vision Care plan. It also includes improvements to the pension plan and wage increases for workers in various categories. Most importantly, the union achieved agreement with the MEG allowing workers to organize without interference from management when new hotels are built or acquired in San Francisco or San Mateo counties, stronger protection of employment security, improved workload rights, and better immigration and hiring contract language.

The contract fight over workload and injuries has been a difficult fight, in particular over the issue of health care. The union has had to find a way around the workload issue, particularly in relation to hotel kitchen work. From Local 2's collaborative actions, we have learned that in order to achieve positive changes in the workplace, it is, first and foremost, workers who must take the lead. The workers have to organize, stand up, speak out, and take action. Of no less importance, credible, empirical evidence is needed that supports the claims that the union is making about workload, since management often discounts the union's claims as workers just "griping." Having community support, media and legal strategies, as well as empirical support from a university or an academic institution assists the workers in making successful workplace changes.

REFERENCES

1. Lee, P. T., N. Krause, and C. Goetchius, Participatory Action Research with Hotel Room Cleaners: From Collaborative Study to the Bargaining Table, in *Community Based Participatory Research for Health,* Minkler, M. and N. Wallerstein (eds.), Jossey-Bass, New York, pp. 390-404, 2002.
2. Parker, E. and N. Krause, Job Quality in the Hospitality Industry: Findings from the San Francisco Housekeeping Study, in *Report to the Rockefeller Foundation,* Center on Wisconsin Strategy, University of Wisconsin School of Public Health, University of California Madison, Berkeley, p. 23, 1999.
3. Semler, R., *Maverick: The Success Story Behind the World's Most Unusual Workplace,* Warner, New York, p. 107, 1993.
4. Bear Stearns, *Global Hotels,* 2, p. 12, September 2003.
5. Tuchsen, F. and L. A. Endahl, Increasing Inequality in Ischemic Heart Disease Morbidity among Employed Men in Denmark 1981-1993: The Need for a New Preventive Policy, *International Journal of Epidemiology,* 28, pp. 640-644, 1999.
6. Karasek, R. A., T. Theorell, J. E. Schwartz, P. L. Schnall, C. F. Pieper, and J. L. Michela, Job Characteristics in Relation to the Prevalence of Myocardial Infarction in the US Health Examination Survey (HES) and the Health and Nutrition Examination Survey (HANES), *American Journal of Public Health,* 78:8, pp. 910-918, 1988.

7. Karasek, R., D. Baker, F. Marxer, A. Ahlbom, and T. Theorell, Job Decision Latitude, Job Demands, and Cardiovascular Disease: A Prospective Study of Swedish Men, *American Journal of Public Health,* 71:7, pp. 694-705, 1981.

8. Karasek, R. A., K. P. Triantis, and S. S. Chaudry, Coworker and Supervisor Support as Moderators of Associations between Task Characteristics and Mental Strain, *Journal of Occupational Behavior,* 3, pp. 181-200, 1982.

9. Schnall, P. L., C. Pieper, J. E. Schwartz, et al., The Relationship between "Job Strain," Workplace Diastolic Blood Pressure, and Left Ventricular Mass Index. Results of a Case-Control Study [published Erratum appears in JAMA 1992 Mar 4;267(9):1209], *Journal of the American Medical Association,* 263:14, pp. 1929-1935, 1990.

10. Albright, C. L., M. A. Winkleby, D. R. Ragland, J. Fisher, and S. L. Syme, Job Strain and Prevalence of Hypertension in a Biracial Population of Urban Bus Drivers, *American Journal of Public Health,* 82:7, pp. 984-989, 1992.

11. Greiner, B., N. Krause, D. Ragland, and J. Fisher, Occupational Stressors and Hypertension: A Multi-Method Study Using Observer-Based Job Analysis and Self-Reports in Urban Transit Operators, *Social Science and Medicine,* 59, pp. 1081-1094, 2004.

12. Siegrist, J., Adverse Health Effects of High-Effort/Low-Reward Conditions, *Journal of Occupational Health Psychology,* 1, pp. 27-43, 1996.

13. Siegrist, J., Place, Social Exchange and Health: Proposed Sociological Framework, *Social Science and Medicine,* 51, pp. 1283-1293, 2000.

14. Siegrist, J., Effort-Reward Imbalance at Work and Health, in *Research in Occupational Stress and Well-Being,* Perrewé, P. L. and D. Ganster (eds.), JAI Elsevier, New York, pp. 261-291, 2002.

15. Siegrist, J. and M. G. Marmot, Health Inequalities and the Psychosocial Environment—Two Scientific Challenges, *Social Science & Medicine,* 58:8, pp. 1463-1473, 2004.

16. Rugulies, R. and N. Krause, *The Impact of Job Stress on Musculoskeletal Disorders, Psychological Exhaustion, and Subjective Health (SF-36) in Hotel Room Cleaners,* Congress of the International Society of Behavioral Medicine, Melbourne, Australia, 2000.

17. Lee, P. and N. Krause, The Impact of a Worker Health Study on Working Conditions, *Journal of Public Health Policy,* 23, pp. 268-285, 2002.

18. Krause, N., T. Scherzer, and R. Rugulies, Physical Workload, Work Intensification, and Prevalence of Pain in Low Wage Workers: Results from a Participatory Research Project with Hotel Room Cleaners in Las Vegas, *American Journal of Industrial Medicine,* 48, pp. 326-337, 2005.

19. Krause, N., P. T. Lee, R. Thompson, R. Rugulies, and R. L. Baker, Working Conditions and Health of San Francisco Hotel-Room Cleaners, in *Report to the Hotel Employees and Restaurant Employees International Union,* Berkeley, CA, 78 pp., 1999 (unpublished).

20. International Labour Office, *Economic Security for a Better World,* Geneva, Switzerland, 2004.

21. Rosskam, E., *Excess Baggage: Leveling the Load and Changing the Workplace,* Baywood, Amityville, NY, 2007.

22. Scherzer, T., R. Rugulies, and N. Krause, Work-Related Pain and Injury and Barriers to Workers' Compensation among Las Vegas Hotel Room Cleaners, *American Journal of Public Health,* 95:3, pp. 483-488, 2005.

23. Shannon, H., J. Mayr, and T. Haines, Overview of the Relationship between Organizational and Workplace Factors and Injury Rates, *Safety Science,* 26:3, pp. 201-217, 1997.

24. Smith, M., Psychosocial Aspects of Working with Video Display Terminals (VDTs) and Employee Physical and Mental Health, *Ergonomics,* 40:10, pp. 1002-1015, 1997.

25. National Institute for Occupational Safety and Health, *Participatory Ergonomic Interventions in Meatpacking Plants*, NIOSH, Department of Health and Human Services, 1994.
26. National Academy of Sciences, *Work-Related Musculoskeletal Disorders: A Review of the Evidence*, Washington, DC, 1998.
27. Bohr, P. C., B. A. Evanoff, and L. D. Wolf, Implementing Participatory Ergonomics Teams among Health Care Workers, *American Journal of Industrial Medicine*, 32, pp. 190-196, 1997.
28. Nagamachi, M., Participatory Ergonomics: A Unique Technology of Ergonomics Science, in *The Ergonomics of Manual Work: Manual Handling and Information Processing at Work*, Taylor and Francis, London, UK, pp. 41-48, 1993.
29. Jensen, P., Can Participatory Ergonomics Become the Way We Do Things in This Firm—The Scandinavian Approach to Participatory Ergonomics, *Ergonomics*, 40:10, pp. 1078-1087, 1997.
30. EU Advisory Committee on Safety Hygiene and Health at Work, May 2001.
31. Faucett, J. and D. Rempel, VDT-Related Musculoskeletal Symptoms: Interactions between Work Posture and Psychosocial Work Factors, *American Journal of Industrial Medicine*, 26, pp. 597-612, 1994.
32. Karasek, R. A., Control in the Workplace and Its Health-Related Aspects, in *Job Control and Work Health*, Sauter, S. L., J. J. Hurrell, and C. L. Cooper (eds.), Wiley, New York, pp. 129-159, 1989.

CHAPTER 15

The Maintenance Cooperation Trust Fund: Combating Worker Exploitation and Unfair Competition through Collective Action with Responsible Employers*

Lilia García

The Maintenance Cooperation Trust Fund (MCTF), established in 1999, is a janitorial watchdog organization created by the Service Employees International Union (SEIU) Local 1877, and its signatory contractors. The MCTF is a Taft-Hartley Trust Fund that addresses the issues of the growing predatory economy in the janitorial industry. A Taft-Hartley trust fund is financed by employers, governed by both the contributing employers and the respective union, and established with a specific purpose.[1] In the case of the MCTF, the purpose was to combat the growth of unfair competition in the janitorial industry. The MCTF's mandate is to investigate and expose the use of illegal and unfair business practices in the janitorial industry. Its mission is to abolish such practices from the industry.

[1] The Taft-Hartley Act, also known as the Labor Management Relations Act of 1947, later amended by the Labor Management Cooperation Act of 1978, provided for the establishment of labor management cooperation committees. The MCTF is an example of a labor management cooperation committee. The 1978 amendment created the possibility for signatory employers and the respective union to create a fund that would be jointly managed. Taft Hartley entities have specific criteria of what they can or cannot do depending on their mission. The MCTF, for example, cannot organize a labor union and does not carry out arbitrations. Breaking the trust document would allow employers to remove their funding for the Taft Hartley. Taft Hartley entities do not have members; they are legal organizations and cannot be compared with collective bargaining agreements.

*I dedicate this chapter to my mentor, Edward Tchakalian, who taught me all I know. Particular thanks are given to Ellen Rosskam for her significant contributions to this chapter.

Over the last four decades the janitorial industry has gone through a significant structural shift with the introduction of "low balling contracts." Up until the mid-1960s to early 1970s, the subcontracting of janitorial services was limited in nature. This practice protected the industry from unscrupulous contractors, as most businesses were medium- to large-sized operations that operated within the law. In the mid-1970s building owners decided to increase the subcontracting of janitorial services. Today, up to 77% of building owners subcontract janitorial services in order to cut costs. The consequence of this business decision and the motivation behind it has been a downward spiral for the industry. In an effort to cut costs, building owners lowered the bar and encouraged unlawful business practices by their contractors. Today the bidding process in the industry is a rat race to the bottom. Workers are left in exploitative conditions, responsible employers are left without a fair marketplace, and the general public loses billions of dollars in tax revenue each year while absorbing millions more due to uninsured worksite accidents. All this, so that a few already wealthy business people can increase their profits even more.

Every day the janitorial industry is again defined by responsible contractors being underbid by competitors who break the law in order to offer a lower bid to client companies (such as the building owners and retailers who solicit the janitorial services). Unscrupulous employers often do not pay workers the minimum wage, do not pay for overtime, do not comply with health and safety regulations, and do not purchase appropriate, if any, workers' compensation insurance. These unlawful business practices allow a contractor to offer a much lower cost for service—as much as a 60% lower cost in some of the more egregious cases. Given such realities, establishing the MCTF was a simple strategic business investment for those employers who follow the rules and who were not afraid to partner with the union in order to create a structure through which a plan of action could be implemented.

Addressing unfair competition is complex in an industry dominated by contractors whose cost of entry is relatively low. In general, the growth of unfair competition is due to the exploitation of workers, low balling contracts, and a lack of enforcement. With these fundamental problems in mind, the MCTF developed a four-pronged approach to address such unsavory realities in the industry. The approach focuses on:

1. Impacting Employment Law Investigation and Advocacy
2. Agency Reform
3. Legislative Reform
4. Education and Outreach

THE UNDERGROUND JANITORIAL INDUSTRY

In the 1960s, most workers in the janitorial industry were African Americans whose jobs were predominately unionized and who were paid up to $12.00 an hour with benefits. In the 1970s, however, there was a strong move on the part of client companies to cut costs by increasing the outsourcing of janitorial services. Most large high-rise buildings had been committed to union contracts, but as the industry moved to cut costs contracts were opened to non-union companies. This business decision encouraged the creation of small-sized companies that were not beholden by contract to union wages and benefits. Such contractors tend not to have a physical office space. Employees typically know only the first name of their supervisor, whom they tend to see only on paydays, if at all. "Fly-by-night" contractors develop operations that allow them to disappear without any trace. Such contractors want to be ready to run in case workers understand their rights and decide to exercise them. Concurrent with the shift to subcontracting also came a significant change in the demographics of the janitorial work force.

THE IMPACTS OF DEMOGRAPHIC CHANGE

By the early 1980s, the janitorial industry's workforce consisted of predominantly foreign-born Latino and Latina workers, who were predominantly monolingual in Spanish, with limited literacy in their native language. These same characteristics describe today's janitorial workforce in California. Many hold multiple jobs, have no health insurance, lack access to even basic health care, and do not have personal transportation. Many are unfamiliar with their workplace rights and the protective mechanisms available to them under the law.

Old patterns of immigration continue, persisting due to the universal search for a living wage in the face of economic hardship in many countries. Similar to other service industries, the labor pool in the janitorial industry tends to be immigrant-based and made up of people desperately in need of work. A worker's immigration status may be the most influential element affecting his or her employment relationship. The non-union sectors of the janitorial industry have come to be dominated by predatory employers who seek out a vulnerable work force to intimidate and exploit. These immigrant workers make a significant contribution to the American economy with their labor. These realities, combined with the plethora of non-established contractors dominant in the industry, result in an extremely hazardous work environment. Janitors often are left with their wages unpaid, left with an injured body with no affordable treatment available or provided, and left with chronically deteriorating health due to work exposures that they have not yet realized. Janitors are left to face the daily reality that they can be fired unjustly at any moment, knowing that no action will be taken against their employer who broke the law—yet again.

A Day in the Life of Refugio Morales

Let me introduce you to Refugio Morales. Refugio is an immigrant from the State of Puebla, in Mexico. He is married with two children and also supports his elderly mother. He left his home in search of employment. The State of Puebla continues to suffer from a prolonged period of economic deprivation. Refugio was unable to find a job that would allow him to support his family's needs, so he went to the United States in search of work. "In Puebla I worked like a dog and got nothing. At least here I get something we can live on, even if it's not what is just." Like many other Poblanos, Refugio found work cleaning large chain grocery stores. "A lot of my cousins and uncles work in the stores. They told me they could get me work." Refugio works long hours, from 11 p.m. to as late as 10 a.m. the next day, 7 days a week. "It depends on when the store receives freight; those days are always longer. We don't get days off. You don't show up, you lose your job." Refugio was paid with personal checks that often bounced. He was paid a flat rate of $550.00 every 15 days. He recalls organizing a work stoppage because the subcontractor he worked for did not pay the workers for seven weeks. "What could we do? It's not right, I understand this, but we didn't feel like there was much we could do, except take away our work. But really, we all just wanted to work and get paid." That subcontractor never did pay the workers. He eventually "disappeared" into the night, and could not be found.

When asked about health and safety, Refugio laughed when we asked if he had received any training or protective equipment or what would happen when a worker got hurt.

> We got hurt all the time, but what could you do? Why would I tell my supervisor—so he'd fire me? One time a co-worker did report that he had slipped while waxing the floor and the supervisor told him to take an aspirin and keep working. Another time, when Hipolito got pricked with a used needle that was sticking out of a trash can, his boss told him to wash with soap and water and keep working. For us, we have no protections. The only person to count on is you, so be careful and don't get hurt, because there is no one to take care of you. Luckily, I never got seriously hurt but you can't tell me these chemicals don't hurt us. They do. I've been doing this for 11 years, and I know I have a hard time breathing. I cough a lot more too. Most don't think the liquids are bad, but they are.

After he led the work stoppage in Ventura County, California, Refugio received a call from his mother in Puebla who scolded him for bringing trouble to his uncle, a subcontractor, as Refugio led others to organize and fight for their rights. Refugio's uncle had become one of the subcontractor's "problems" in southern California. Refugio's mother expressed such anger that he actually began to doubt what he was doing, wondering whether anything was ever going to change as a result of his organizing. One day he came by the MCTF office. He was profoundly sad and quiet. He swivelled around in an office chair, leaning back on the wall, with his baseball hat low over his face and he said to me, "One day you said we were like family." I nodded "yes."

> Then if we are family, I need to tell you that I can't do this anymore. Nothing ever works out, nothing has changed, and for what? I came here to earn money to support my family, not because I wanted to, but because there was no work that we could survive off in Puebla. And that is what I'm going to do. I don't need the headache of my mom being mad and worried. As it is, I haven't been able to send her what she needs because the check bounced again.

For a couple of hours, I tried my best to understand the motivation behind what he said because this was not the Refugio I had known for over two years. And then I understood. He was right. In his world, in his immediate reality the organizing was counterproductive to meeting his daily needs. My check never stopped coming, did it? Refugio helped me to personify what is often intellectualized. Luckily, the fight was a long legal one, and with time he became re-engaged, because his passion to stop the injustice was greater than his fear. Refugio taught me that courage meant taking action, in spite of and in the face of fear.

Employers who subcontract in the janitorial industry are all too familiar with the obstacles facing immigrant workers. Predatory subcontractors actually seek out immigrant workers precisely because such workers generally are both unfamiliar with and extremely hesitant to assert their rights. Such employers take advantage of the existence of a vulnerable workforce that is relatively easy to exploit, often acting in direct defiance of existing labor laws. The non-established employers, for example, typically operate in an informal manner, not using formal job applications and providing inadequate entry-level training. They often underreport or do not report at all the existence of their employees and the wages paid, and use intimidation tactics to ensure that workers remain silent. Within this grim new context of the janitorial industry, the MCTF's primary strategy includes educating janitors about their workplace rights, reinforcing that *all* workers are meant to have the same rights regardless of immigration status. Defusing this "bomb" helps not only the workers, but responsible employers as well since it removes the immigration factor from the competition.

EDUCATION AND OUTREACH

Traditionally, workers are considered the target group for education and outreach. In a service industry like the janitorial industry, however, it has been our experience that combating the predatory economy requires reaching out to decision-makers at all levels, including client companies, contractors, regulatory agencies, elected officials, and janitors. The MCTF generally focuses on client companies, regulatory agencies, and janitors. In addition to reaching out to these decision-makers through personal meetings, the MCTF also produces documentation that exposes the systemic abuses in the industry and makes recommendations for addressing the problems.

Nevertheless, the most critical and challenging contact to make is with the janitors themselves. Unlike many industries where workers work a regular shift from 8 a.m. to 5 p.m., janitors can be characterized as an "invisible" workforce, one which begins work at 5 p.m. and continues working through the night until 10 a.m. the next day, in some cases. By the time janitors enter the building where they work, most office workers have gone home for the day. The regulatory agencies that bear the responsibility to conduct education and outreach efforts on behalf of the state tend to miss this nighttime slot, thereby leaving the janitors without a government-initiated outreach effort.

Unlike the Los Angeles garment industry, where a concentration of workers can be found in specific geographical areas, janitors can be found everywhere that there are physical buildings. MCTF investigators, therefore, conduct worksite visits to make initial contact with janitors. It is the only means of contacting a janitor without some other connection, such as through a family member, friend, or contractor. The goal of these outreach efforts is to explain to the workers that they have rights, that their employers are obliged to provide certain conditions, that if their employers do not comply with the regulations then workers can take specific actions, and that the MCTF is committed to changing the way business is done in the industry by holding employers and decision-makers accountable.

Given that the individuals making up this particular workforce move around a lot, at times holding two or three jobs simultaneously, and considering that many do not have home telephone numbers, visiting workers in their homes is essential in order to build a relationship with them. MCTF representatives conduct in-depth interviews with workers in their homes. The interviews are critical for the building of trust between the workers and the MCTF investigators. Without this investment, it would be very difficult to get workers to talk to the MCTF investigators. This type of outreach is essential to successful enforcement and long-term change in the industry.

We do not offer janitors a legal service; we offer them a plan that can win if they partner with us and assert their own power. All janitors who have a claim must participate in an interactive leadership training series that makes clear how their hazardous work environment is connected to the industry structure, and how MCTF's strategy addresses these realities. From the outset, the janitors need to understand that in order to win we all have important roles to play, especially them. It is a challenging task because the legal system within which we operate has significant limitations that often are unjust. The underlying objectives of our trainings are to provide janitors with the tools to assert their rights, to become familiar with the laws their employers need to follow, to understand the industry structure, to understand how the legal system works, and to engage in substantive discussion on how together we can change the industry. Within this context, we expose to the janitors the potentially severe injustices that they may face. While a law may exist, without a reasonable agency representative and a strong advocate, there is a good chance that the employer will get away with violating janitorial workers' rights. In fact, even with all of the necessary legal and advocacy components in place, one can still lose. This is precisely why we impress upon janitors that the legal avenue is a strategy that has important limitations and that alone it will not achieve institutional change in the industry.

One of the ways we tackle the immense obstacle of fear present in janitorial workers is by working with the government. We get government representatives to sit down in a room together with janitors so that the workers can hear directly from a government representative that they do have rights and that the government agency is there to help them. As an example of the MCTF's efforts to increase janitors' knowledge base of the law, between 2001 and 2002 we collaborated with the Labor Occupational Safety and Health (LOSH) Program at the University of

California, Los Angeles (UCLA) to develop a training module specific to janitorial workers. Over a period of 14 months, more than 300 janitors participated in a training course where they heard from representatives of the California Occupational Safety and Health Administration (Cal/OSHA) and health and safety advocates. These specialists focused on helping the janitors to work more safely and to learn what to do if workers noticed something wrong on the job. While this initiative has been an excellent start, more work is needed, and the MCFT will continue to open the door for agencies to facilitate their outreach to janitors.

The State of California requires that the following notices be posted by janitorial employers:

* *Industrial Welfare Commission wage order 5-2001*
* *Industrial Welfare Commission minimum wage order*
* *Payday notice*
* *Cal/OSHA form 200*
* *Workers' compensation insurance* poster
* *Harassment or discrimination in employment is prohibited* poster
* *Notice to employees concerning disability benefits and unemployment insurance*

It is important that janitors file complaints with Cal/OSHA when necessary and appropriate. Before this can happen, however, workers need to be provided with information and have their skills and knowledge built to create the confidence needed to deal with official agencies. On their side, regulatory agencies need to ensure that they address janitorial workers in a language that the workers can understand. Workers are unlikely to file a complaint if they cannot understand the information on forms received in the mail. Correspondence should, therefore, be in the complainant's own language (Spanish) and there should be an increase in the numbers of bilingual inspectors in California's regulatory agencies. As well, the regulatory agencies would do well to conduct proactive outreach to janitorial workers, as a means of collecting information on an on-going basis, rather than working on a reactive basis. For this to work, information has to be disseminated through workplaces, organizations like the MCTF, SEIU, community groups, and employers.

INDUSTRY TRENDS AND THE COST TO CALIFORNIA—
THE GROWTH OF UNFAIR COMPETITION

Tax and Workers' Compensation Fraud

Aside from systematic wage violations, there are a number of significant and troubling trends in the predatory sector of the janitorial industry, including tax and insurance fraud. Many small contractors performing cleaning work hire janitors as "independent contractors" and not as employees, to avoid paying social security, workers' compensation, and fringe benefits. These contractors typically pay workers in cash, saving the contractor approximately 8% of their tax burden by not withholding state or federal deductions from employees' paychecks. An employer who does not pay taxes by not declaring workers, and who does not pay accurate and sufficient workers' compensation insurance, can easily have up to a 60% advantage over an employer who pays taxes and insurance.

The hiring of janitorial workers as "independent contractors" is an issue central to the ongoing exploitation of janitors. Based on legal definitions, janitors do not meet the criteria for classification as an "independent contractor." The nature of the work relationship that janitors have with contractors defines such workers as "employees," according to the Internal Revenue Service. The contractor has the right to direct and control how the worker performs the task for which s/he was hired, including when and where the work is performed, the tools or equipment used, where supplies and services are purchased, what work must be performed by a specific individual, and the sequence or order that must be followed in carrying out the prescribed work. These criteria are used to distinguish an "employee" from an "independent contractor." An "employee" must be declared as such by the employer, with all required deductions taken from the employee's wages and required contributions made by the employer. The overwhelming majority of janitorial workers do not qualify as "independent contractors" and are exploited by the continued use of this fraudulent tax status, which is to the advantage solely of the employer.

When wages are not reported by not declaring the employee, the employers' workers' compensation insurance premiums are significantly lower. This manipulation of the law constitutes insurance fraud. Contractors often purchase insufficient workers' compensation coverage or simply do not report workplace accidents, because reporting an accident may trigger the workers' compensation system for an injured employee, which in turn may increase the employer's insurance premium.

A related problem arising from the lack of outreach efforts in this workforce is that the workers themselves often do not report work-induced injuries. Workers' reluctance to report injuries usually is due to fear of getting fired, lack of knowledge about how to report, to whom, and what the procedures are, lack of knowledge of their rights, and lack of awareness about chemicals that they work with and any illnesses or injuries that may result. The MCTF's experience shows that with awareness-raising, education, and advocacy, even frightened, vulnerable workers will report work-related injuries or illnesses once they understand their rights and the state and federal mechanisms and procedures that exist to help them assert their rights.

The non-reporting of work-related injuries serves to perpetuate a host of problems. For example, data about risks in the janitorial industry are, therefore unreliable, as they are based on gross underestimations of the incidence of janitors work-related injuries and illnesses. The underestimation in turn affects both regulatory and research attention given to the industry, and distorts both state-wide and national cost estimates of insurance paid out to workers' compensation in the industry. This is one industry-based example demonstrating one way that national occupational injury and illness data become, and remain, gross underestimates, and unreliable.

The frauds perpetrated by contractors in the janitorial industry create a significant burden on the California taxpayer. In 2003, the California State Employment Development Department reported a mere 39 audits, the results of which revealed $7 million in un-assessed taxes. At a time when the State of California is facing a critical fiscal crisis, there is a serious need to look at the business sector, at the underground economy, and at those employers who are placing a direct and significant burden not only on responsible employers, but also on California taxpayers. It is the latter who pays, ultimately, the costs related to this type of illegal activity. The Department of Insurance reports that California absorbs approximately $3 billion annually in costs associated with uninsured work-related accidents. If an injury is severe enough, workers will go to an emergency room at a county-funded hospital, which results in the state compensating the most costly type of health care.

HEALTH AND SAFETY EXPOSURES

Most janitors do not receive any type of health and safety training, neither at the start of a job nor thereafter. Many do not receive personal protective equipment, such as gloves, masks, or goggles. Many mix chemicals on the job, heightening the potential for exposure to dangerous chemical mixtures. Few people ever think about health and safety exposures in the janitorial industry. Contractors often trivialize the issue by suggesting that the chemicals used in cleaning are not noxious. Cal/OSHA works very hard to address all kinds of problems throughout the state; however, the reality is that they are focused on industries such as construction, where there are more immediate and serious problems, including loss of limbs and, unfortunately, fatalities. Construction is also an industry where the workers' compensation system is more likely to get triggered in the event of an accident. Therefore, the fact that this costs employers and insurance companies' money means there is more public pressure and greater visibility of the problems, particularly when fatalities occur.

Chemical Exposures

Janitorial workers are at high risk of serious adverse health effects resulting from their occupational exposure to a variety of chemicals. Cleaning products often contain poisonous chemicals. Home cleaning products alert consumers to the dangers of eye and skin irritation, advising consumers to prevent the product from contacting eyes, skin, and clothing. Warning labels on consumer cleaning products are common, such as the following:

> *Danger: Corrosive. Causes eye and skin burns. Avoid contact with eyes, skin and clothing. Avoid breathing vapor. Use only with adequate ventilation.*

Indeed, commercial-grade cleaning products almost always have warnings on the labels, recommending that the user wear gloves, masks, and goggles in order to prevent exposure to the dangerous chemicals in these products. Such commercial-grade product warning labels may look like the following:

> *Causes severe burns to skin and eyes. Avoid breathing dusts or mist. Wear eye protection, chemical resistant gloves, clothing and footwear to prevent skin contact. Do not get product on skin. Wear protection such as goggles or side shield safety glasses, clothing, or rubber gloves to prevent prolonged skin contact when using product.*

Yet despite these warning labels, most of which are written in English, many workers talk to the MCTF about health problems they are experiencing, which are known to result from exposure to the chemicals they use at work. Workers describe having difficulty breathing, or having skin irritations on their hands and on their feet, after using the various chemicals at work on a daily basis. Many develop severe headaches, have blurred vision, and complain of seeing diamonds in their vision after a while. Sometimes janitorial staff may mix chemicals together from unlabelled bottles, which can result in a dangerous combination. Many contractors do not provide appropriate protective equipment, do not conduct monthly training programs, or communicate effectively to employees about how to deal with injuries, accidents, or health problems. Workers are largely uninformed about the hazards of the products they are using everyday, the known health effects, and the danger of mixing chemicals. Consequently, slow and chronically deteriorating health problems are common among janitorial workers. They include respiratory problems, including a high (and increasing) rate of asthma among janitorial workers [2], skin irritations, bleeding noses, headaches, back injuries, blurred vision, and pregnancy complications. Many of these problems are due to chemical exposures, compounded by extreme insecurity leading to chronic physical and emotional strain.

Janitorial workers suffer from exposure to carbon monoxide (CO), emitted by the machines used to buff floors, a task often performed in unventilated areas. This practice amounts to carbon monoxide exposure in confined space conditions. Evidence demonstrates an association between carbon monoxide exposure and female reproductive health damage, as well as CO being a risk factor for adverse pregnancy outcomes, including causing fetal death and spontaneous abortion [1].

Following media reports of janitors being rushed to the hospital after passing out from exposure to poisonous chemicals on the job, awareness of the risks of exposure to carbon monoxide increased. Yet the hazardous effects of CO exposure are not limited to janitors. Once the janitor completes his or her work and a building is closed until the next day, or until the Monday following a weekend, a dangerous and persistent level of chemical exposure can remain stagnant in the building's ambient air. Office workers, students, children, elderly people, or anyone else with business or activity in the building where such chemicals have been used in cleaning become at risk of suffering the potentially serious effects of carbon monoxide exposure. In December 2002, for example, 60 children and three adults fell ill at a day care center in Gulfport, Mississippi, from exposure to carbon monoxide fumes. Many required hospitalization. The fumes were emitted the previous night during janitorial cleaning with a propane floor buffer used with inadequate ventilation. The fumes remained in the building throughout the following day, a Monday, poisoning people in the building. The cleaning crews had buffed the floors at the day care Sunday night, the Associated Press reported; fire officials said the fumes created by the propane buffer remained in the building Monday morning and throughout much of the day while fire crews ventilated the facility [1].

Inadequate ventilation is a common problem in commercial real estate buildings as well. High-rise and other commercial buildings often do not have windows that can be opened from the inside (commonly known as "sealed buildings"), or are kept locked up for security reasons, making it impossible for janitors (or inhabitants) to open doors to the outside to increase ventilation. The first to suffer from exposure due to insufficient ventilation are the janitors. The retail sector is another area where insufficient ventilation tends to be an important problem. Windows are either nonexistent (such as in department stores and supermarkets) or sealed from the inside. And here too, for security reasons janitorial staff are not permitted to open doors. Consequently, for janitors who work with toxic chemicals or propane floor buffing machines, the chemical exposure over an 8-hour period, or more, can be extremely significant.

Consistent with this history of exposure to chemicals in enclosed or confined spaces is the finding that work-related asthma is particularly high among janitors and cleaners. One study estimated janitors and cleaners in California to have the highest rates, at 625/million workers (higher even than firefighters at 300/million workers), compared to the rate among all California workers (75/million workers) after adjusting for underreporting [2]. A recent literature review shows that research on the health effects of janitorial work exposures is relatively scarce and is usually limited to community studies of mortality. High rates of asbestosis, a fibrotic lung disease caused by exposure to inhaled asbestos fibers, have also been associated with janitorial or cleaning work [3]. In a San Francisco study of adults with gliomas (a common type of primary malignant brain tumor), janitors along with other blue-collar workers likely to have chemical exposures such as firefighters and textile workers, were found to have elevated odds ratios compared to controls [4].

Musculoskeletal Disorders, Stress, Strain, and Violence

In addition to working with chemicals in closed buildings lacking fresh air or proper ventilation, janitorial workers are at high risk of developing severe musculoskeletal disorders. Their work involves repetitive motions using machines, pushing and carrying heavy equipment and awkward, bulky materials. Workers routinely move furniture. They overreach with the arms and shoulders in order to clean above their heads and to clean places that are difficult to reach. They adopt deep knee bending and twisting postures repeatedly during a work shift in order to reach electrical outlets. Janitorial workers use repetitive motions throughout their entire work shifts, day after day. These awkward and repetitive movements put them at high risk of back, neck, and shoulder injuries.

Janitors work odd shifts, often working back-to-back multiple long shifts. Working at night, often in isolated places that are deserted after day shift workers go home, exposes janitorial workers—especially female janitors—to the risk of violence. Shift work is a cause of chronic fatigue and stress, made even worse when workers have no say in their choice of work shift.

Many janitors clean public toilets and sinks. Without proper protective equipment and training, workers are at risk of infection from stool-borne diseases, such as hepatitis, typhoid, and salmonella. Protective gloves are a necessity, but undocumented janitorial workers in particular do not always receive such equipment from their employers. Toilets are an enclosed space with poor ventilation relative to the strong chemical cleaning products used. This leaves workers at risk of inhaling fumes in excessive quantities. Without proper training, workers may not know the importance of proper hand washing to ensure that no fecal matter has contaminated their skin, which can then be ingested by eating or smoking with contaminated hands. Diseases picked up through exposure to fecal matter in toilets can easily be transmitted to entire families, compounding workers' difficulties if they fall ill.

Janitors also suffer from job strain. Janitorial work is relatively high in physical demand, with workers having little or no control over the organization of their work. Work which is high in demand but low in worker control has been shown to lead to cardiovascular disease and hypertension, as well as a range of adverse psychological effects, including depression and burnout [5-9]. Janitorial workers are isolated from decision-making processes at both the level of the contractor and the customer. The pace of their work is dictated to them, with time pressure a constant on the job. Workers are obliged to complete cleaning a fixed amount of space in a given amount of time, similar to hotel housekeeping workers. The floor space that janitorial workers are told to clean on a work shift often is too large for the time allocated. This puts workers under constant physical and emotional strain to complete the job, at a predetermined standard of quality, in an insufficient amount of time, resulting in job strain.

The work performed by janitors can be equated with production line work that is mundane, repetitive, boring, with little or no opportunity for growth, learning, skills, or career development, with low worker decision latitude, high in demand, carried out under constant time pressure. The scientific literature documents the combination of these factors as causing hypertension, leading to cardiovascular disease, long-term chronic health problems, and even death, particularly among workers living in extreme insecurity, who are unable to afford health care [10-13]. Working for wages that are below subsistence level, lacking health or pension benefits, lacking employment security, and lacking recognition for work accomplished leads to an obvious imbalance between the effort required to perform the job and the rewards gained for the work. An imbalance between efforts and rewards for work performed has been shown to contribute to high stress, leading to potentially serious health outcomes [14, 15].

An additional problem facing janitorial workers in particular is the non-compliance with health and safety regulations by contractors. This constitutes serious negligence on the part of contractors, given the wide variety of hazardous exposures that janitorial workers face on the job.

IMPACTS OF LOW-WAGE WORK

While janitors face a number of work organizational exposures that may cause them suffering and harm, the impact of low-wage work cannot be ignored. Janitors employed by predatory contractors are paid below subsistence level wages because contractors vie for workers who will accept the lowest wages. This labor market approach has far-reaching consequences for individuals and for society. The repercussions include wages that are disconnected from current costs of living, health care, education, and pension plans, and mean that janitors employed by predatory contractors have little chance of envisioning an old age free from poverty.

Janitors often have no choice but to work two or three jobs at the same time, simply to survive in poverty. Working multiple jobs means very long working hours (a risk factor for hypertension), as well as living with chronic sleep deprivation. Adding up the number of hours per day spent working at one or more jobs, time spent commuting (often on public transport which can consume many more hours than commuting by car), child care, food shopping, the preparation of meals, and carrying out necessary household chores, the tally quickly reveals little more than 4 to 5 hours per day left for sleep. Such a life pattern leaves no time for rest (not sleep) or relaxation, which are as important for health and well-being as sleep and food. Add to this the extreme difficulty of fulfilling family life responsibilities while working nights and weekends on a regular basis, and a picture of permanent "time squeeze" becomes more than evident. Time squeeze causes workers to live under permanent psychological stress and physical strain.

Chronic sleep deprivation due to shift work (night work in particular), frequent overtime work, from working multiple jobs, and from working 7 days a week, compounded by poor nourishment (due to insufficient wages to purchase quality food products, plus lack of time to prepare and eat proper meals) and a high level of chronic stress due to insecurity, bear a negative effect on the human immune system, attacking the overall state of an individual's health. Chronic tension, fatigue, and a consequently weakened immune system can leave janitorial workers more susceptible to adverse effects caused by work-related exposures, most notably chemical exposures and musculoskeletal disorders.

Chronically exhausted workers are also more susceptible to viral and bacterial illness. Wage workers in the United States, subject to conditions of precarious employment, generally receive no entitlement to paid sick leave. For a janitor, with wages that are below subsistence level, missing work due to illness can mean not making it through the month financially, and may mean not having food to eat. Low wage workers, such as janitors, cannot afford to miss even 1 day of work. Janitorial workers typically suffer from "presenteeism," whereby they must go to work no matter how ill or injured they may be, even when they should be recuperating at home. Working when ill means that an illness may get worse instead of better. Workers with high rates of "presenteeism" may end up missing more work (and wages) when they are ill, if continuing to work means their illness becomes more severe, necessitating more recovery time.

When occupational accidents occur, the contractors of janitors often are quick to find the workers at fault, often citing worker carelessness as the cause. Yet upon closer examination, janitors' occupational injuries, as in most other occupations, usually are only one factor within a larger context. Many employers argue that programs to protect workers' health are too costly and not cost beneficial. Yet there are multiple hidden costs that demonstrate precisely the opposite. If janitorial workers received a wage sufficient to live on working only one job, they would have more possibility to sleep and eat properly, and to reduce their stress levels by not living in a permanent state of extreme insecurity. (The costs of unhealthy work organization are discussed in chapter 9.) These "basics" are essential for any individual to be able to maintain their personal health and to maintain concentration on the job. Similarly, when workers are fully informed about their rights and about the mechanisms available to them to assert their rights if needed, they feel less vulnerable. Knowledge, information, and mechanisms to exercise one's rights reduce human insecurity. The income and employment insecurity that janitorial workers live with day in and day out cannot, and should not, be excluded from any discussion of work-related hazards in the janitorial industry.

Janitorial workers are largely Spanish-speaking only, often with limited literacy in Spanish. Many janitorial workers would like to learn English. Yet, if a worker has no single hour in a day available to learn English due to exploitation through chronic overwork, he or she will remain permanently outside "the system," simply by not knowing English. Getting access to and obtaining essential information and resources available to the public become extremely difficult for workers who are outside of "the system." Janitorial workers are forced to manage everything in their lives through informal support networks. Yet such networks are not always reliable, particularly when everyone else in the support network is equally vulnerable. Income insecurity, employment insecurity, collective voice representation insecurity, and poor working conditions collectively can wield negative impacts on the health of janitorial workers.

CONCLUSION

Through its four-pronged strategy, the MCTF works to address various fundamental factors that bear severe negative impacts on the livelihood, health, and well-being of janitorial workers in California. The MCTF seeks to redress the unacceptable treatment of janitors when they are not paid their wages, when they are intimidated into not exercising their rights, and when they are exposed to physical hazards on the job.

Notwithstanding all of our efforts, the MCTF recognizes that all of the elements of the organization's strategy fail to address the root cause of the exploitation of janitorial workers: the capitalistic hegemony. The dominant economic, political and structural forces mean that the janitorial industry will continue to prey on the most vulnerable link, simply to increase profit. Nonetheless, by operating within a practical framework, the MCTF attempts to make the capitalist system more accountable, to make government more effective, and to facilitate the empowerment of janitorial workers.

REFERENCES

1. Frazer, L. M. and M. L. Hage, *Reproductive Hazards of the Workplace,* Van Nostrand Reinhold, New York, 1997.
2. Reinisch, F., R. J. Harrison, S. Cussler, et al., Physician Reports of Work-Related Asthma in California, 1993-1996, *American Journal of Industrial Medicine,* 39:72, pp. 72-83, 2001.
3. Wagner, G. R., Asbestosis and Silicosis, *The Lancet,* 349(9061), pp. 1311-1315, 1997.
4. Krishnan, G., M. Felini, S. E. Carozza, R. Miike, T. Chew, and M. Wrensch, Occupation and Adult Gliomas in the San Francisco Bay Area, *Journal of Occupational and Environmental Medicine,* 45:6, pp. 639-647, 2003.
5. Karasek, R., D. Baker, F. Marxer, A. Ahlbom, and T. Theorell, Job Decision Latitude, Job Demands, and Cardiovascular Disease: A Prospective Study of Swedish Men, *American Journal of Public Health,* 71:7, pp. 694-705, 1981.
6. Karasek, R. and T. Theorell, *Healthy Work: Stress, Productivity, and the Reconstruction of Working Life,* Basic Books, New York, 1990.
7. Karasek, R., Job Demands, Job Decision Latitude and Mental Strain: Implications for Job Redesign, *Administrative Science Quarterly,* 24, pp. 285-308, 1979.
8. Belkic, K., P. L. Schnall, P. Landsbergis, and D. Baker, The Workplace and CV Health: Conclusions and Thoughts for a Future Agenda, *Occupational Medicine: State of the Art Reviews,* 15:1, pp. 307-322, 2000.
9. Landsbergis, P., P. L. Schnall, T. G. Pickering, K. Warren, and J. E. Schwartz, Life Course Exposure to Job Strain and Ambulatory Blood Pressure among Men, *American Journal of Epidemiology,* 157:11, pp. 998-1006, 2003.
10. Landsbergis, P. A., J. Cahill, and P. L. Schnall, The Impact of Lean Production and Related New Systems of Work Organization on Worker Health, *Journal of Occupational Health Psychology,* 4:2, pp. 108-130, 1999.
11. Landsbergis, P. A., P. L. Schnall, D. Deitz, R. Friedman, and T. Pickering, The Patterning of Psychological Attributes and Distress By "Job Strain" and Social Support in a Sample of Working Men, *Journal of Behavioral Medicine,* 15:4, pp. 379-405, 1992.
12. Landsbergis, P. A., P. L. Schnall, J. E. Schwartz, K. Warren, and T. G. Pickering, Job Strain, Hypertension and Cardiovascular Disease: A Review of the Empirical Evidence and Suggestions for Further Research, in *Job Stress 2000: Emerging Issues,* Sauter, S. and G. P. Keita (eds.), American Psychological Association, Washington, DC, 1993.
13. Landsbergis, P. A., S. J. Schurman, B. A. Israel, et al., Job Stress and Heart Disease: Evidence and Strategies for Prevention, *New Solutions,* 3:3, pp. 42-58, 1993.
14. Siegrist, J. and M. G. Marmot, Health Inequalities and the Psychosocial Environment—Two Scientific Challenges, *Social Science and Medicine,* 58:8, pp. 1463-1473, 2004.
15. Siegrist, J., Adverse Health Effects of High-Effort/Low-Reward Conditions, *Journal of Occupational Health Psychology,* 1, pp. 27-43, 1996.

CHAPTER 16

Occupational and Environmental Medicine in the Twenty-First Century

Dean Baker, Marnie Dobson, and
Peter L. Schnall

The role of occupational medicine physicians in the treatment of occupational illness and injury is a challenging aspect of efforts to mitigate the adverse effects of work on health and promote healthy work. In many respects, the practice of occupational medicine has become a "last resort" attempt to put the human body back together after the deleterious effects of work have reached a medically diagnosable stage. This treatment and rehabilitation focus represents a stark contrast from the earlier and perhaps idealized concept of occupational medicine as a specialty area of preventive medicine that would emphasize prevention and worker population health. Currently, occupational and environmental medicine (OEM) is one of the smallest specialty fields in the medical profession. The field has been slowly constricting around a diminishing workers' compensation system, with decreasing attention to workplace-based prevention programs. Today most OEM specialists practice purely within traditional clinical settings with little awareness of actual workplaces and the working conditions of their patients. While theoretically it may be possible for these practitioners to obtain a clinical history about working conditions, almost no OEM residency programs provide formal training in how to ask about work organization and work-related psychosocial stressors.

OEM specialists also face impediments to prevention-oriented practice. Employers rarely invite—and many do not even allow—OEM specialists to visit workplaces. Insurers do not provide reimbursement for OEM specialists to engage in prevention-oriented programs or visit workplaces to evaluate cases of work-related illnesses. Although workers' compensation systems in the United States have functioned relatively well for the treatment of *acute* workplace injuries, these systems do not function well for work-related chronic illnesses because employers can use many strategies to challenge whether *chronic* illnesses are work-related. In most states, the injured employees are responsible for paying their medical bills until the workers' compensation claim is resolved, so these challenges by the employers

284 / UNHEALTHY WORK

can delay payments, resulting in pressure on the injured employees to agree to smaller benefits in order to settle their claim. Furthermore, in many states workers' compensation insurers and employers have been successful in pressuring legislatures to pass laws that specifically prohibit workers' compensation for the health effects resulting from chronic work stressors. It is difficult for OEM specialists to spend much effort in preventing, diagnosing, or treating health effects associated with work organization and work-related psychosocial stressors when the specialists have little awareness of the issues, no formal training on assessment and prevention strategies, restricted access to workplaces, and financial and legal disincentives to get involved.

We explore the changing role of OEM in the workplace, describing current trends in occupational medicine practice and the reasons for the changing nature of OEM practice, including the context of rising health care costs, industry control over occupational medicine, the weakening of the workers' compensation system, and the decreasing economic viability of the practice of occupational medicine. Finally, we suggest some possible directions that might re-focus the field toward primary prevention and a greater role in encouraging healthier work environments.

HISTORICAL BACKGROUND OF OEM IN
THE UNITED STATES

The American Association of Industrial Physicians (AAIP) was formed after World War I in 1915 as the first professional association representing industrial physicians who had gained prestige due, in part, to their participation in the war effort. The association was later renamed the Industrial Medicine Association (IMA) and is now known as the American College of Occupational and Environmental Medicine (ACOEM). While most members of the AAIP, IMA, and subsequent ACOEM work less than full-time in occupational medicine, according to Joseph LaDou, M.D., the associations' leadership has consisted largely of full-time "company doctors" employed by major industrial corporations. These company doctors have been linked with conservative sensibilities in support of industry self-regulation, and advocating for industry interests in scientific findings influencing public health [1, 2]. Criticisms have also been made of individual occupational health physicians. In many industries, OEM doctors were hired by the company and found themselves with conflicted loyalties, on the one hand to the company that hired them, paid them, and had the power to fire them and on the other hand to their ethical and moral commitments to their patients.

The 1970s saw a burgeoning in occupational medicine as a medical specialty after Congress passed the Occupational Safety and Health Act (OSHA) in 1970 and created the National Institute for Occupational Safety and Health (NIOSH). Interest in occupational medicine as a career grew among medical students and primary care physicians. Occupational medicine programs and short courses were established and grew at many U.S. medical schools. In 1972, NIOSH reported an enormous shortage in the human resources needed to implement the OSHA Act, including an estimated shortage of 3,000 occupational physicians, 1,000 industrial hygienists and 10,000 occupational health nurses [2, 3]. In 1978, NIOSH estimated that an additional 20,000 physicians with short-term competency training should be added as part-time OEM doctors [2, 3]. Membership in the ACOEM grew to a high of 6,500 but has subsequently declined to about 5,000 [2, 3]. The development of these agencies coincided with what, in retrospect, came to be seen as a high-water mark for occupational health efforts by organized labor and public health professionals in the 1970s.

Since the 1970s, occupational medicine has faced a significant decline in the number of specialists being trained, in the viability of occupational medicine practices, and in the amount of reimbursement received from workers' compensation, despite the increasing size of the U.S. workforce over the last several decades. In other countries, such as in western and northern Europe and Scandinavia, occupational medicine doctors play a more important role within industry because of governmental regulations that give them greater authority to extend their care of patients into the workplace itself (e.g., where they may recommend their patient's return-to-work (RTW) be to limited work duties or suggest some other forms of job redesign).

CURRENT TRAINING OF OEM DOCTORS

According to the ACOEM, the mission of the field of occupational and environmental medicine is "devoted to prevention and management of occupational and environmental injury, illness and disability, and promotion of health and productivity of workers, their families, and communities."[1] However, most training focuses on clinical care, i.e., treatment and not prevention.

OEM doctors can be divided for the most part into two categories: 1) generalists who are often trained only through independent study or short courses and who are grounded in clinical practice, and 2) specialists who are usually trained through formal OEM residency programs and who are expected to have, in addition to clinical practice, competencies in "public health, prevention, epidemiology, toxicology, and research methods."[2] Training for specialists often involves practicum (hands-on) experience in the workplace where physicians learn about hazard recognition and control as well as the clinical specialty of occupational medicine.

OEM is a component core of the American Board of Preventive Medicine. After receiving their initial clinical training, OEM resident doctors then receive training that emphasizes preventative medicine and surveillance. This training includes the development, implementation, and evaluation of screening programs to identify risks for disease and to promote wellness. It also prepares physicians to design and conduct surveillance programs in the workplace and/or community in order to detect environmental contamination, to use biomarkers to identify exposure, and to apply

[1] ACOEM vision and mission statement http://www.acoem.org/Vision.aspx Accessed 9/14/2007].
[2] ACOEM, Preamble to Competencies www.acoem.org/oem.aspx

individual or community-based interventions when indicated to mitigate exposures or improve health outcomes. However, OEM physician participation in workplace surveillance and screening is very limited in practice.

There is a broad list of competencies guiding the OEM doctor,[3] from screening or secondary prevention to documentation of exposure and its early health effects, to assessment and diagnosis. OEM doctors manage workers' compensation cases as well as fitness for duty and return to work assessments. Typically, the following tasks are part of the function of an occupational medicine specialist's duties: 1) screening, such as organization-based screening programs for tuberculosis, musculoskeletal disorders, or chemical exposures; 2) assessment and diagnosis of workplace risk factors, individual risk factors, pre-clinical effects, and clinical effects; 3) treatment and management of existing work-related health conditions, determining whether a person suffers from a work-related condition, conduct treatment and long-term disability management; 4) fitness for duty and return to work; 5) prevention, workplace health promotion which typically has focused on reducing individual behavioral risk factors such as smoking cessation, exercise etc.; and 6) consultations for individuals and management.

Although prevention is a core component of OEM competencies, treatment of health problems recognized by workers' compensation as work-related, particularly those related to chemical or physical exposures in industrial workplaces, predominates. The competencies listed by the ACOEM, however, are broad, ranging from public health and surveillance, to dermatology and infectious diseases, to management and administration. Competencies in cardiology also are included, as described by the ACOEM:

> Individuals with underlying cardiac risk factors and disease may encounter special concerns in safety-sensitive jobs, while working around certain chemical agents, and in performing exertional labor. OEM physicians assist patients, employers, primary care physicians and cardiologists in the secondary and tertiary prevention of cardiac disease, as well as the accommodation of workers with cardiac concerns. The perspective of the OEM physician is particularly useful in placing workers in special assignments such as emergency response, hazardous waste, forklift, and respirator use. OEM physicians may also be the first providers to respond to a cardiac emergency such as a myocardial infarction in the workplace.[4]

The fact that competencies regarding cardiovascular disease (CVD) are limited to chemical exposures and physical work capacity may be due, in part, to the limited awareness within OEM, and the field of medicine more broadly, of the role of work organization and psychosocial stressors in the development of hypertension and CVD. Issues of RTW to environments that are cardionoxious (i.e., where workplace

---

[3] ACOEM competencies http:/.www.acoem.org/oem.aspx [Accessed 9/14/2007].

[4] ACOEM cardiology clinical competency http://www.acoem.org/oem.aspx [Accessed 9/14/2007].

psychosocial stressors such as job strain, are reported as being present) is not yet a part of the training of OEM physicians. Nor is there awareness of the fact that working people with previous myocardial infarctions (MI) are at greater risk of a repeat MI if they return to the same stressful work environment in which they had their first MI. Also as previously mentioned, OEM physicians are not trained to take a comprehensive work history to identify those aspects of the psychosocial work environment that play a role in the etiology of CVD and many health problems for which the worker is being seen by the OEM doctor. There remains a great need for the training of OEM physicians to better incorporate public health-based prevention-oriented competencies that reflect state-of-the-art knowledge of etiologic processes.

CONTEMPORARY OCCUPATIONAL MEDICINE PRACTICE

Historically, the practice of OEM has been closely tied to the workplace. In the past, companies directly employed doctors and other health professionals to ensure the well-being and productivity of their workforce. Companies like General Motors have had on-site clinics for decades, offering primary or urgent care to employees or referring them to their family doctor or other specialist. In the 1970s, hospitals and specialty clinics opened occupational medicine departments and added occupational medicine to their own hospitals to care for their employees. Small and medium-sized enterprises never have had workplace health programs, although larger companies appear to be returning to company health clinics [4]. Today the vast majority of occupational medicine residents tend to practice in traditional medical care organizations with a reciprocal decline in workplace-based practices.

Medical care organizations that employ OEM doctors are likely to use what could be called the "restaurant model" of services rather than the "partnership model." The "restaurant model" presents a list of services and allows the client (generally employer) to select what services they want to purchase. Below is an example of one such list of services as advertised on the internet by Partners Occupational Medical Services Ltd.[5]:

- Complete Alcohol/Drug Testing and Related Services
- 24 Hour Post-Accident Services
- Post-Offer/Pre-Placement Testing (ADA Compliant)
- Post-Offer/Pre-Placement Ergonomic Testing
- Medical Services
- Out of Area Case Management by our Doctors via telephone 24 hours a day.
- Foreign Travel Immunizations (including Yellow Fever)
- Direct Company access to our Physicians

[5] http://www.partnersoccupationalmedicalserviceds.com/how_can_we_help.htm

One may note that the above list of services includes no mention of conducting any workplace-based health surveillance or prevention. In a "restaurant model," employers may request only "hearing conservation" or "drug testing on employees," which, while potentially important services, may be inadequate to allow the OEM doctor to recommend other screening for important health conditions or risks within the industry. The role of the occupational health professional in a "restaurant model" is limited and controlled. In such situations, employers are not generally interested in a broad partnership with occupational health professionals and employees.

In order for organizational change to lead to the prevention of work-related health problems, the relationship between employers, workers, and OEM doctors must be founded upon cooperation. When employers select only specific, limited services from a list offered by the OEM practices, the OEM specialists cannot offer services based on medical judgment, screening, or surveillance, and the OEM specialists' role is curtailed.

There are examples of more collaborative partnerships between OEM doctors, employers, and unions (see chapters 13 and 14). As one example of a collaborative partnership, the San Francisco MUNI system worked with its union and occupational medicine doctors to identify the work-related causes of bus drivers' high rates of hypertension (see chapter 13).

CURRENT TRENDS AND LIMITATIONS IN OEM

Since the boom of OEM in the 1970s, the field has shown a marked decline. According to the ACOEM, the proportion of physicians working for corporations fell from 80% to 20% over 10 years. Workers' compensation insurance carriers delayed increases in reimbursements so payments for medical care and lost wages have not kept up with inflation while state insurance programs stopped or even reversed increases in fee schedules. Occupational medicine doctors have been forced to leave the specialty because practices were running into serious financial difficulties. Political and economic pressure from employers, insurers, and pro-business state legislators has limited workers' compensation benefits to workers. In California, as in other states, state legislatures have sought to "restrict or eliminate claims for stress or mental disorders" [3].

As U.S. employers are responsible for paying the health care costs of their employees, including the costs of occupational medicine, OEM doctors have had a long history of close cooperation with industry. Although labor supported the OSH Act and a pro-worker movement also evolved within occupational medicine, the ACOEM has been dominated over time by company doctors who have, at various times, advocated less for the interests of worker-patients than for the interests of the industries for which they work [1]. The question of whether company doctors are co-opted by the employers they work for is a complex issue and one not easily evidenced. Many labor struggles were initiated on just this premise in the past. For example, the views expressed by John L. Lewis, former President of the United Mine Workers' Union, summed up the role of "company doctors" as follows:

A company doctor does much more than treat the sick and injured. He acts as the company representative in compensation cases. He is the company agent in insurance claims. He determines the physical fitness of job applicants. The company selects a doctor of its own choosing. Although his salary is paid out of deductions from the miners' wages, the doctor works for the company, not the employees. A doctor thus selected testifies against workers in compensation cases where the company disputes the extent of an employee's injuries. He does the company's bidding in passing upon the physical fitness of job applicants [5, p. 20].

Since many OEM doctors in specialty groups are economically dependent on services requested by their employer clients, they may be more likely to base their practice on an employer's "bottom line" perspective. The OEM doctors can rationalize that the company's "bottom-line" is directly associated with the interests of employees, since a prosperous company will stay in business and continue to provide work for employees. Given the irregular past history of some "company doctors" there is concern about the independence of OEM doctors who work directly for employers or primarily serve employer clients. However, as evidenced by the ACOEM statement of ethics, it is clear that OEM doctors, for the most part, are guided by the principles of medicine and must act in the best interests of the patient.

At present, larger employers are outsourcing occupational health professional services, so there are fewer corporate or worksite based professional positions than ever before. Although doctor groups may be technically independent of employers, there is considerable competition between groups for contracts and it is highly probable that compliance with the employer's needs is paramount.

Occupational health professionals, because of the structure of their employment in specialty groups contracted to employers or within medical organizations, have little or no influence or authority over the work environment, and instead tend to focus primarily on symptoms and disability treatment or management. As a result, the institutional culture of occupational medicine has evolved to focus primarily on doctors working in a clinical environment to treat individuals with occupational diseases or disability at the behest of the company and seeking to manage occupational illness claims, and perhaps to ensure there are as few claims considered work-related as possible. As such, the public health paradigm has been de-emphasized in OEM practice, either because it is considered beyond an employer's interest in basic medical services and case management of workers' compensation claims, or because it is not very strongly present in most traditional medical organizations, where many occupational medical professionals are employed. This is a primary limitation of the current practice of occupational medicine that means doctors are unlikely to visit workplaces or develop relationships with others in the organization to encourage primary prevention because they are not paid or reimbursed to do so.

Given the reduction in ACOEM membership and participation in the field, the continuing decline in reimbursement for workers' compensation practice, and the growing irrelevance of a public health prevention paradigm, what are the future prospects for the field? Will it continue to represent primarily the interests of employers while dwindling in numbers and relevance? There are certainly alternative possibilities that could increase the relevance of the specialty and return it to its origins in the public health arena. The next two sections will evaluate possible future directions for the field as well as the possibilities for overcoming the very real structural obstacles that exist because of the dominance of industry in determining the nature and scope of occupational health and safety in the United States.

AN OUNCE OF PREVENTION: FUTURE POSSIBILITIES FOR OEM

There is a growing body of evidence (discussed in Part II of this book) that the way work is structured, in addition to chemical and physical exposures, affects a range of mental and physical health problems not yet fully recognized as being work-related. This evidence suggests that the organization of work itself can be detrimental to individuals through prolonged exposure to forms of psychosocial stress that are derived from the intensification of work demands, a continuing lack of control over the pace and variety of work performed, as well as longer work hours, less (or no) vacation time, irregular shifts, and increasingly precarious job security. Psychosocial hazards in the workplace come at a high cost to the health and well-being of workers, to the productivity of industry, and contribute greatly to the overall costs of ill health borne by society (see chapter 9). The available evidence of the long-term health impacts of psychosocial exposures at work borne by individuals, including hypertension and CVD [6], burnout and depression [7, 8], musculoskeletal disorders and injuries [9], should be sufficient for OEM doctors to consider the role of psychosocial stressors and to advocate for improving workplaces as OEM has done in other countries around the world. Even where OEM doctors have become advocates for the industries in which they work, the costs of psychosocial exposures to these industries in terms of labor force productivity should be incentive enough for OEM doctors to encourage their clients to consider primary prevention efforts.

Intervening at the level of work organization is, however, currently at odds with the treatment and rehabilitation focus of most OEM doctors. Notwithstanding, in order to prevent many of the health problems plaguing the U.S. workforce and decreasing the productivity of American companies, OEM as a field must champion such a paradigm shift. Given the challenges facing the OEM field, the OEM discipline must expand beyond its current focus on the treatment of workers' compensation illnesses and injuries by emphasizing primary prevention in the workplace— which indeed is one of the fundamental principles defined by the American Board of Preventive Medicine that certifies occupational medicine specialists. While this is hardly an effortless task, certainly one fraught with many obstacles, and perhaps outside the power and authority of the OEM field, there are new trends and concrete goals that could begin to inform discussions about future directions for the field.

The Return of Company Health Clinics

According to a health care specialist quoted in a 2006 *New York Times* article [4], soaring health care costs may be encouraging the return of the company clinic, offering employees faster more convenient service, lower out-of-pocket expenses, a reduction in hospital emergency room referrals and specialists, all for a savings of between "1.5 and 2 million dollars a year for a 1,000 employee company" [4]. Large corporations are becoming frustrated with rising health care costs; the company-run "wellness" clinic with a prevention focus may be the way of the future. While companies appear willing to incorporate a secondary prevention focus in the clinics, their purpose is twofold: 1) to improve the health of their employees, and 2) to contain rising health care costs. Given economic realities, companies will seek to defray the health care costs of their employees while maintaining a commitment to productivity even at the expense of the health of their employees.

While the possibility of companies directly employing OEM doctors again within worksite clinics is unlikely and potentially problematic on a large scale, it could be an appropriate location as a means of revitalizing OEM as a prevention-oriented health field. OEM doctors could provide leadership in the development of prevention-oriented clinics, even if only working there part-time. Worksite occupational health clinics could provide an excellent venue for health promotion activities particularly if reinforced by company policies supporting the goals of the intervention. However, if workplace psychosocial exposures are to be effectively addressed, it is essential that OEM doctors advocate moving beyond the traditional health promotion paradigm that is common in the United States.

The traditional focus in health promotion programs has been on the behavior of individual workers—on physical activity, nutrition, weight management, and tobacco control. Alternative models, particularly in Europe and growing in the United States, incorporate both programs focused on individual risk factors as well as on the work environment. The focus on the work environment highlights how personal health practices, physical environment, and the workplace social environment all combine to influence employee health.

OEM doctors located within an on-site company clinic are in a position to expand traditional health promotion by working along with other occupational health professionals to advocate for enhanced workplace surveillance programs to identify work-related psychosocial stressors and hypertension, for example. As part of a multidisciplinary company team, OEM doctors could be integral to dealing appropriately and effectively with work organization issues. As part of a public health strategy, a team approach is recommended in which OEM doctors work together with other occupational health professionals such as industrial hygienists, health educators, ergonomists, occupational health psychologists, and epidemiologists to identify high-risk workplaces and occupations and to help design and implement workplace interventions [10]. OEM doctors also can consult for workplace-based labor-management committees to help evaluate the impact of job redesign programs and to help convince employers of the long-term benefits of the programs for improving productivity and employee well-being. The OEM doctor has a potentially pivotal leadership role in creating a healthy work environment and the return to the company clinic may be a location where it could be realized.

Healthy Work Environment National Policies

In many European countries and Japan, an important step has been the implementation of "healthy work" policies at national and multi-national levels [11]. For example, the European Network for Workplace Health Promotion (ENWHP) is a network of occupational health and safety institutions and agencies in 31 member countries committed to developing organizational, individual, and national level practices which ensure a healthy work environment.

According to the ENWHP's vision on its website:

> Healthy work is the result of an interplay of various factors. The most important factors or workplace health determinants include:[6]
> - The values and policies of decision-makers within organizations (private-sector companies, public administrations, health care facilities, institutions in the area of education, etc.) and outside at the level of social security and policy-making
> - The specific form of the culture of participation within and outside organizations
> - Leadership and management practices
> - The production concept and principles for daily work organization
> - The provisions for job security
> - The quality of the working environment
> - Personal health practices & lifestyle habits

This represents an integrative approach to ensuring worker health which includes both individual level behavioral factors as well as the overall quality of the working environment. Many European governments, such as Sweden, Norway, Denmark, and the Netherlands, have instituted healthy work environments as official policy.

Advocating Workplace Surveillance

An alternative to the current individual treatment-based approach would involve an expanded paradigm of occupational medicine that envisions occupational medicine doctors as managers of a multidisciplinary team of occupational health workers focused on: 1) documenting the work environment characteristics and potential health effects in clinical practice; 2) developing partnerships and increased emphasis on workplace-based practice; and 3) implementing greater workplace screening and surveillance. Surveillance is the systematic on-going collection, collation, and analysis of data and the timely dissemination of information to those who need to know so that action can be taken. The final step in the surveillance process is the application of the collected data to prevention and control.

---

[6] The vision of the ENWHP, European Network for Workplace Health Promotion 2006 http://www.enwhp.org/index.php?id=16

Healthy work policies worldwide recommend establishing a system of workplace surveillance to identify high-risk work environments and concomitant noxious psychosocial risk factors associated with negative health outcomes. It has not yet been achieved on a broad scale in the United States. The 1998 Tokyo Declaration, developed by occupational health researchers, scholars, and professionals recommends: ". . . *surveillance* at individual workplaces and *monitoring* at national and regional levels, in order to identify the extent of work-related stress health problems and to provide baselines against which to evaluate efforts at amelioration." They recommend that workplaces assess both workplace stressors and health outcomes known to result from such exposures (e.g., repetitive work and WRMDs) on an annual basis.

Surveillance to begin assessing the risk factors for CVD located in the workplace is an example of how this reinvention of OEM might operate, particularly in workplaces with high demands and low control or discretion over one's tasks, i.e., job strain. To know where to intervene, the prevalence of both noxious exposures that could be risk factors for CVD and cases of CVD must be mapped—i.e., surveillance. Such a map will facilitate the identification and management of individual exposed workers with varying CVD severity, who may benefit from either workplace interventions (to prevent the onset of disease) or early clinical intervention prior to the onset of symptoms. Worksite screening would produce prevalence data on cardionoxious exposures (e.g., job strain) and on work-related CVD (including occult hypertension).

There are several urgent clinical problems facing OEM physicians that grow out of our understanding of the role of workplace psychosocial factors in health and illness. Among them is the issue of return-to-work (RTW) after a myocardial infarction and the widespread occurrence of occult hypertension, defined as the presence of high blood pressure during the workday combined with normal blood pressure in the doctor's office. Recent research suggests that 15% or more of working men and women have "hidden hypertension" prior to developing elevations detectable in the doctor's office. The recognition of this epidemic is one of the reasons for increasing urgency in conducting wide-scale surveillance of the workplace.

Workplace Interventions and Medical Authority

Interventions to improve work organization through job redesign, reducing psychosocial stressors related to the work environment, and creating more healthy work organization have been documented [12-14]. Efforts to regulate or to collectively bargain problems with work organization or reduce psychosocial stressors have had limited success in the United States [15, 16]. Adding to the difficulties, health professionals in the United States do not have the authority to prescribe workplace interventions as part of their treatment plans for injured workers. However, legislation in Scandinavia, the European Union, and Japan provide valuable models for the United States as a way of regulating work organization and job stressors as health hazards [17, 18]. In Japan, occupational medicine professionals may legally prescribe changes and employers have an obligation to consider their recommendations.

WORKING THROUGH THE OBSTACLES

The current difficult state of OEM is influenced by several social factors that determine the practice of occupational medicine. We recognize that there is an enormous gulf between the needs of large companies to control health care costs and maintain productivity and the needs of working people to enjoy a healthy working environment. One consequence is that the very paradigm of medical science as a public health enterprise, as well as the etiology of many illnesses, is a contested area. Part of the reason for the delay in incorporating recently gained knowledge about the role of psychosocial stressors in the practice of occupational medicine is that notions of work-related causality are strongly opposed by many groups due to their substantial economic threat. Just imagine what the consequences would be if CVD was recognized as a work-related disorder in all occupations as it is currently for firefighters and police in most states. Thus, the practice of OEM is constrained by large social forces attempting to limit notions of causality and focus causality at the individual level as opposed to the workplace.

A second large structural constraint is that the system in the United States of dealing with work-related health care costs places most of the burden on the workplaces. Given the ever-increasing share of the GDP being consumed by health care and the rising cost of health care as a component of product cost, U.S. companies are at a severe disadvantage compared with foreign competitors. For example, one major reason for the decline of the U.S. auto industry is the spiraling cost of health care to U.S. companies, a burden not shared by non-U.S. car manufacturers which have the advantage of health care costs being borne by society as part of a national health care system. In fact, the dysfunctional U.S. health care system is a major obstacle to the development of an OEM practice that extends to the workplace and practices primary prevention. As long as new discoveries of cause are tied to the workplace under the current system, employers will be inclined to oppose recognition because of the threat of economic disadvantage. Given these structural obstacles, we suggest some possible areas the field of OEM could focus on in order to overcome these obstacles and to begin to grow and achieve greater relevance within the public health movement.

New Training: Acknowledging Psychosocial Risks

It is recommended that as a field, occupational medicine needs to acknowledge the important role that work organization and psychosocial factors play in the development of chronic health problems, including psychological distress, musculo-skeletal disorders, and CVD, inter alia. In turn, this reconceptualization leads to the conclusion that OEM doctors will need improved knowledge and skills in the assessment and management of the role of work organization factors, individual risk factors, and potential health and behavior outcomes. Given the current practice of OEM in the United States, competencies still focus mainly around the treatment and management of workers' compensation cases. Health professionals are inadequately trained to assess work organization issues, particularly those resulting in psychosocial exposures. Improving occupational histories and documentation by using standardized psychosocial stressor instruments could be an important addition to OEM practice.

A successful paradigm shift toward the public health movement will require concerted efforts to recruit general practitioners into OEM training programs and an ideological focus on primary prevention, work organization, and the detrimental health effects of psychosocial work exposures. Management of surveillance programs, worksite redesign interventions, research methodologies, as well as training in the coordination of a multi-disciplinary team, including industrial hygienists, nurses, and occupational health psychologists will be essential to incorporate more fully into OEM training programs. In addition, there needs to be an increased emphasis on the prevention paradigm, including negotiating employment contracts for OEM doctors that provide incentives and rewards for additional non-clinic activities such as going out to workplaces and focusing on prevention.

Industry Allies or Outsiders:
A Case for Governmental Regulation

Since many OEM doctors in specialty groups are economically invested in a contract with an employer or directly employed by a company they may be more likely to base their practice on an employer's "bottom line" perspective, even if that means a lack of will to participate in primary prevention. Given the declining effectiveness of workers' compensation as a system of reimbursement for work-related illnesses and injuries, employers are benefiting from macro level structural changes to the U.S. occupational medicine reimbursement system without having to pressure OEM doctors to deny cases of occupational illness.

Some employers are motivated by the societal value of providing meaningful and healthy work. However, intrinsic to capitalist industry and the competition of a global marketplace, work must be structured based on the profit-interest of the company or the risk of being out-competed. There are employers who institute health and safety measures because of government regulation and/or because of "enlightened self-interest." Even in some small companies where there may be long-term personal relationships between an employer and a small number of employees, there may be greater incentives for an employer to balance growth and profitability in the interest of providing a healthy work environment to retain employees. However, for the vast majority of worksites in the United States, it is the viability and profitability of the company that really determines the structure of the work environment.

Relying on large or small companies to ignore their "bottom line" in favor of protecting the health and safety of their employees is neither likely nor recommended. Instead, occupational medicine professionals need to encourage employers to recognize the health and productivity benefits of having a healthy workplace.

It is an argument and a perspective focused on capital preservation where the well-trained employee is recognized as a valuable resource. Ultimately, the real challenge for occupational health professionals and others committed to "healthy work" is to show the cost effectiveness of organizational change that incorporates healthy work programs. It is, nonetheless, important to note that in the short term the cost of changing organizational practices may be less than attractive to the employer's "bottom line," but is highly cost effective in the long term.

In addition, some of the cost impacts of psychosocial work organizational factors are never borne by employers; many illnesses resulting from prolonged work-related psychosocial stress exposure, such as hypertension, are not manifested until employees are older and out of the workforce. The costs of such illnesses, which end up being medicalized and treated as an effect of aging, become an "externality" and therefore of little importance to companies. The ultimate costs become borne by the affected individuals, by taxpayers, and by society overall, hardly an incentive for employers to change their organizational practices.

How viable is the idea then to convince employers to form on-going partnerships with occupational health professionals, under the management of OEM doctors, to conduct surveillance for physical or chemical hazards, let alone psychosocial exposures? Given the evidence that most states are decreasing workers' compensation benefits and that many potential work-related illnesses are not being reimbursed, it is unlikely that surveillance aimed at discovering new work-related illnesses will be welcomed by employers or by the workers' compensation system.

OEM doctors working for companies or contracted as consultants or for services within specialty groups do not as yet have the power or authority to gain the cooperation of employer clients to conduct surveillance programs or to recommend workplace interventions. Yet other countries provide models in which OEM doctors do have such authority, backed by national policies. It is probable that the paradigm shift in OEM will only bring about effective change if it is accompanied by government regulation requiring employers to create healthy work environments.

We suggest that the model serves as a rallying point for the paradigm shift in OEM. For example, the ACOEM or other professional occupational health organizations should be advocating similar and more expanded roles for OEM doctors to be incorporated into U.S. industry. Doing so would require a familiarity with the weight of scientific evidence showing clear connections between the organization of work and health outcomes. A convincing argument to U.S. legislators would be evidence demonstrating that the ultimate cost of unhealthy work environments, in the long run, is borne by taxpayers and not industry. Prevention comes with a cost, but there are enormous savings to be made in allaying the costs of treating chronic diseases such as heart disease, hypertension, and depression (see Chapter 9).

Implementing a national health care system or national insurance program is the key obstacle to overcome in order to develop a public health approach to the workplace based on prevention and to implement a progressive OEM agenda. Without a national health care system or a national insurance program, many workplaces will continue to oppose interventions aimed at the workplace. Yet with such a system in place, economic obstacles will be considerably diminished making it possible for health care workers to work collegially and collaboratively with both employers and employees. Most importantly, establishing a national or governmental source of payment for health care cost—including payment for OEM services—would extract the OEM practitioner from their uncomfortable role of serving two masters.

REFERENCES

1. LaDou, J., D. Teitelbaum, D. Egilman, A. Frank, S. Kramer, and J. Huff, American College of Occupational and Environmental Medicine (ACOEM): A Professional Association with a Dubious History of Service to Industry, *Journal of Occupational and Environmental Medicine,* 13:4, pp. 404-426, 2007.
2. La Dou, J., The Rise and Fall of Occupational Medicine in the United States, *American Journal of Preventive Medicine,* 22:4, pp. 285-295, 2002.
3. LaDou, J., The Rise and Fall of Occupational Medicine, cited 9/14/2007, available from: http://www.sfms.org/AM/Template.cfm?Section=Home&TEMPLATE=/CM/HTML Display.cfm&SECTION=Article_Archives&CONTENTID=1523
4. Freudenheim, M., Company Clinics Cut Health Costs, *New York Times,* January 14, 2007.
5. Krajcinovic, I., *From Company Doctors to Managed Care,* Cornell University Press, New York, 1997.
6. Belkic, K., P. A. Landsbergis, P. Schnall, et al., Psychosocial Factors: Review of the Empirical Data among Men, in *The Workplace and Cardiovascular Disease Occupational Medicine: State of the Art Reviews,* Schnall, P., K. Belkic, P. A. Landsbergis, and D. Baker (eds.), Hanley and Belfus, Philadelphia, PA, pp. 24-46, 2000.
7. Ahola, K., T. Honkonen, M. Kivimaki, et al., Contribution of Burnout to the Association between Job Strain and Depression: The Health 2000 Study, *Journal of Occupational and Environmental Medicine,* 48:10, pp. 1023-1030, 2006
8. Van Der Doef, M. and S. Maes, The Job Demand-Control(-Support) Model and Psychological Well-Being: A Review of 20 Years of Empirical Research, *Work & Stress,* 13:2, pp. 87-114, 1999.
9. Krause, N., D. R. Ragland, J. M. Fisher, and S. L. Syne, Psychosocial Job Factors, Physical Workload, and Incidence of Work-Related Spinal Injury: A 5-Year Prospective Study of Urban Transit Operators, *Spine,* 23:2507, p. 16, 1998.
10. Herbert, R., B. Plattus, L. Kellogg, et al., The Union Health Center: A Working Model of Clinical Care Linked to Preventive Occupational Health Services, *American Journal of Industrial Medicine,* 31, pp. 263-273, 1997.
11. The Tokyo Declaration, *Journal of the Tokyo Medical University,* 56:6, pp. 760-767, 1998.
12. Murphy, L., J. Hurrell, S. Sauter, and G. E. Keita, *Job Stress Interventions,* American Psychological Association, Washington, DC, 1995.
3. International Labor Office, *Conditions of Work Digest: Preventing Stress at Work,* International Labor Office, Geneva, Switzerland, 1992.
4. Landsbergis, P. A., S. J. Schurman, B. A. Israel, et al., Job Stress and Heart Disease: Evidence and Strategies for Prevention, *New Solutions,* 3:4, pp. 42-58, 1993.
5. Warren, N., U.S. Regulations for Work Organization, *Occupational Medicine: State-of-the-Art Reviews,* 15:1, pp. 275-280, 2000.

16. Landsbergis, P., Collective Bargaining to Reduce CVD Risk Factors in the Work Environment, *Occupational Medicine: State-of-the-Art Reviews*, 15:1, pp. 287-292, 2000.
17. Levi, L., Legislation to Protect Worker CV Health in Europe, *Occupational Medicine: State of the Art Reviews*, 15:1, pp. 269-273, 2000.
18. Shimomitsu, T. and Y. Odagiri, Working Life in Japan, *Occupational Medicine: State of the Art Reviews*, 15:1, pp. 280-281, 2000.

CHAPTER 17

Emotional Labor and the Pursuit of Happiness

Stephen Lloyd Smith

REASON TO BE CHEERFUL

Alongside stories of starvation, disease, crime, violent conflict, and abuse, today's headlines make winking references to the reform of earthly feelings and the right to happiness; for essential to the idea that the world is appalling in some respects is the notion that in these same respects it could be made better. For example, a war might end in peace, care of the elderly could be improved, and violence toward nurses reduced. If we really had lost faith in decency and progress, bad news from New Orleans would not count as news at all. We'd shrug it off, thinking, "So what? Nothing could be done anyway." Paradoxically, then, bad news entails reasons to be cheerful. Nor do we live in a Heav'n or Hell of our own creation as the Devil suggests in Milton's *Paradise Lost.* Our mood depends on others and that is why New Orleans was truly hellish, both for fearful police officers and the mistrustful residents whom they were supposed to be protecting.

Indeed, millions of "front-line" workers are employed especially to ease the passage of our day: in an emergency, at departure points, while traveling and on arrival; or seeking hospitality and entertainment. Most (not all) make our world better, but only if those workers are looked after too. The reader will have been a client of innumerable front-line encounters under different conditions, perhaps a sympathetic police officer, a care-worn nurse, an over-enthusiastic waiter, an indifferent actor, a considerate dentist, a sanguine driving instructor, a prickly airport check-in worker; perhaps an affable priest or a burnt-out consul. How many of those encounters had been legislated for? What were the hours of work? Were the conditions of work proportionate to the demands of the job? What was being transacted? What was the pace? What set the duration of each encounter? Was it OK? Were you aided or harmed?

Western employment has shifted toward jobs which entail working on "people's nerves" and there are many architects of our emotions besides ourselves. Hochschild calls them *emotional laborers* [1]. They staff call-centers, reception desks, TV stations, educational establishments, border crossings, retreats, auctions, heritage centers, crematoria, sales floors, hospital wards, rest homes, airports, prisons, theaters, police stations, cruise liners, leisure centers, wedding registries, family courts, cinemas, hotels, bars, rock festivals, parliaments, clubs, political conferences, sales conventions, war cabinets, truth-and-reconciliation hearings, rehab centers, and so on. These are legitimate places where feelings have been *industrialized*, sometimes on a bigger scale than steel-making.

It is a massive workforce: *half* of U.S. female employees, a *quarter* of its male employees, Hochschild estimates. It includes police officers, nurses, flight attendants, teachers, bar-staff, performers, DJs, MCs, undertakers, counselors, debt-collectors, beauticians, nannies, tour-guides, therapists, counselors, estate agents, train guards, foster parents, social workers, and so on. Tom Paxton sang, "In ten years we're gonna' have a million lawyers." It has happened: more than a million who sway the feelings of clients, judges, and jurors.

The sheer number of emotional laborers, the fact that we are their clients and that their conditions of work affect their ability to affect us properly, mean that they matter very much. Their potential for good is great, but so is the potential for abuse (trigger-happy police officers, malicious jailers (and dangerous extortionists) and malicious doctors). So what about working conditions for "front-line" workers themselves—the sometimes exhausted, sometimes terrified, sometimes blasé guarantors of our well being? Emotional laborers are *paid to affect our feelings.* By comparison with other workers, emotional laborers can enter a relationship (with clients) that is more dynamic, demanding, and compelling than any worker's contact with materials (miners with coal) or constructs (architects and plans).

CO-PRESENCE

Emotional labor is done in the presence of other human beings: sales worker with customers, counselors with clients, nurses with patients, wardens with prisoners, performers with audiences, teachers with students, 911 call-handlers with frightened citizens, undertakers with the bereaved, and priests with parishioners.[1] Compared to *manual labor* and *mental labor,* the special feature of *emotional labor* is that its "object" is not mundane material (like coal) or mental abstractions (like plans). As Hochschild points out, the object is our feelings. Therefore we the client *constitute a large part of the emotional laborer's "conditions of work"* and, as well as making a difference to us, we make a difference to them. The circumstances of each encounter can also be affected, for better or worse, by third parties: unions, management, industrial associations, professions, governments, codes of practice,

---

[1] I don't just mean physical presence. Telephone counseling is also done in the presence of the other person . . . for example 911 call handling or suicide counseling. Where personal health and safety is at stake, the counselor needs to be attuned to the other person, not least to build an accurate picture of their clinical or security needs and what intervention is necessary. And that other person can surely tell whether or not they matter especially.

and conflicting aims. Moreover, moods are also infectious, so one encounter influences the next.

"HELL IS OTHER PEOPLE"

Front-line work can entail conditions which prejudice both parties—abusive prisons, over-stretched social work, airport chaos, pressure-selling, abandoned cities. Sartre exclaimed that "Hell is other people!" and front-line workers and clients are vulnerable to hellish behavior under hellish conditions, particularly if both parties are self-obsessed "hearts." The *heart* metaphor for feelings [2] does not lend itself to solving the situations described later and it is in the defense of their "precious" hearts, that emotional laborers may adopt a mask that creates empty service encounters. I'd also leave out the "Devil's" self-help theory that one is responsible for one's own happiness and misery. It is wrong to expect individuals to become happy single-handed because feelings are social and circumstantial.

However, instead of seeing others as indulgent, hellish, and depleting soul-stealers, intent on ripping-out your "heart"—*users* whose presence makes life worse—it is possible to build on an objective common interest between worker and client that is mutually nourishing (even in jails). Political constituencies may exist between prisoners' groups and governors, patient groups and nursing unions, student unions and teaching unions. Something like this happened in the expanding European and North American cities of the nineteenth century, when the rhetoric of *Civic Gospel* and "Brighter and More Beautiful" cities transformed an individual's life chances in the name of the "greatest happiness for the greatest number" of people [3]. The reform of front-line work promises to be easier and cheaper.

Why easier to accomplish? Compare emotion with clothing made by children. Child labor does not affect the warmth of the garment, yet it was disturbing enough to be quickly forbidden in Europe and America. It should be easier to gather support for the reform of emotional production, because if conditions are poor, they affect everybody's experience *immediately* and we are all clients of emotional labor across a wide range of service industries. It is "really-in-your-face." Elder abuse in nightmarish nursing homes matters because most have parents to worry about. A doorstep security worker who is over their legal hours might switch from "engagement" with dangerously uninhibited party-goers to "herding" them instead, therefore overlooking lethal danger signs. Likewise, fearful police matter to fearful residents because of the risk of mutual violence. All such cases qualify as *headline news* about which "something needs to be done now," whereas factory children are more easily hidden.

A COMMON INTEREST BETWEEN CLIENT AND PROVIDER

By taking the long view of reform—since about 1845—we see that straightforward government interventions, underscored by the labor movement, have transformed labor and living conditions for the better. So why not the emotions as well?

We are no longer "stalked by death" every day of our lives; water is safe to drink, trains don't crash, and employers can be busted for health and safety violations. When it comes to reforming emotional labor and improving well-being today, we can trust the same handful of uncomplicated nineteenth-century research methods and moral principles which won *massive* improvements to public health and bodily security in the advanced capitalist societies. These principles and methods included: 1) *utilitarianism*—"the greatest happiness of the greatest number"; 2) *simple correlations* such as between "wholesome water" and less infectious disease, shorter hours and longer lives, or between equality and happiness; and 3) *popular mobilization*. We still need the indignation, urgency, and hope typical of epidemiologists, health officials, clinicians, relief workers, and trade unionists.

The one extra cheerful consideration to add in reforming life on the front-line, is that as well as deserving careful treatment from emotional laborers, the "other guy" also owes something to front-line workers in return. Indeed both sides have an objective, common interest in good conditions of emotional labor because if the carer sustains damage they will be in no fit state to offer the help that clients need: trigger-happy cops, burned-out clinicians, disaffected teachers, call-handlers past caring. This plain and communicable idea, the fourth principle to add to the ones above, of a common interest between client and provider, will serve us very well. On past reckoning, there is 50 years of improvement to accomplish, using these four principles. It's starting to happen, but our next great social project is threatened by the same opposing principle which delayed previous reforms.

Universities are alive with discussion about the emotions[2] and there are scores of TV shows and "airport books" pursuing happiness, often with an emphasis not on mutual care, but on "self-help" and making your own "Heav'n." A British reality-TV show expressed the similar idea that women can redeem their lives by associating bad feelings with old clothes, throwing away their wardrobe and making the "new me" through new clothes, casting out demons in a kind of ritual *exorcism* enabled by the market.

This is an extension of the self-help/market principle which always mistrusted collective improvement. The social reformers were right that there would have to be public solutions to squalor and disease, rest breaks, statutory train-braking systems, municipal schools, police, and firefighters. Though the "economizers" fought back bitterly, as with cutting working hours, public sanitation, clean water, and railway safety, reform of emotional labor is certain once the mutuality principle is seized. Likewise, it is quite easy to see that the principles of self-help, personal redemption, and laissez-faire fail on the front-line because most such encounters are not one-way (my way) but *two-way* (you and I, you and we, them and us) and dependent on circumstances:

$$\frac{(\text{provider conditions} \leftrightarrow \text{client conditions})}{\text{time}}$$

---

[2] See for example *The Journal of Happiness Studies: The International Journal of Work Organization and Emotion.*

The special two-way (often multi-way) quality of emotional labor is recognized in everyday language. People can be "too much in-your-face," "too intense," or "over-the-top." We ask of them, "Are you for real?" "Are you fake?" "Are you off your head?" "Are you being *funny* with me or what?!" "Are you fed up?" "Are you a *shit*?" "You're the best!" Southern Africans acknowledge the wider principle of "becoming-people-through-other-people" over time, rather than being completely individual individuals. The philosopher Levinas calls for heteronomy instead of *autonomy*, meaning "put the Other first" . . . the obligation to the other arises from *face-to-face contact* [4]. Nor is it difficult to see that if the client is wild, then conditions are uncomfortable, possibly life threatening for the emotional laborer— that New Orleans officer perhaps—and that the conditions of labor in a police station should accommodate the highest degree of care and security for all.

Although the interdependence can be quite complex, everyday expressions identify each problem well enough. The genius of this immediate, real-time relationship between emotional laborer and client is that it contains a mighty potential for dialogue-based reform. If both sides "put the Other first," perhaps not there and then, but by paying higher taxes and getting better service, we can get wonderful "flip-overs" in the worst of situations:

- The patient and doctor "ease up on each other," recognizing that they are *both* mortal and fallible and that "shit happens." Patients teach their doctors how to be better patients themselves. Courage circulates instead of anxiety [5].
- The Finance Director makes a one-off cash injection to increase permanent nursing levels, which is more than offset by cuts in the casual nursing budget and improved patient care.
- The comedian gets a second chance by going off-stage and coming back on to start over. The audience "hangs on in there." The promoter abandons the tour, the performer rests, but the earnings are good the following season. Performers look after each other backstage, rather like police officers and suicide counselors do.
- Students count as ends in themselves and the tutor is happy to repay the help which s/he received during some crisis they overcame many years ago. The word gets out that this is a good university and a vicious circle is exchanged for a virtuous one.

The fixes are winking at us. How to figure them out? Best of all, the excellent funeral director, custody sergeant, nurse, or tutor propagate good practice in *each others'* fields. My police confederates have much to offer my nurse confederates and vice-versa. My favorite undertaker (*Gilman's* from Tooting, South London) could teach the awkward coroner so much about death, composure, and "being there." The student could teach the tutor "how to be real" (humility). Clients, police officers, nurses, bus drivers, undertakers, and coroners can all meet for a "system conference" on, say, "just cities after the deluge." People can stop "behaving like assholes."

Travelers in the United States know that competitive individualism need not wreck civility, and service encounters are typically good or even slightly over-the-top. The screw-you principle can work against "user" workers as well as against "user" clients because the cumulative price paid by "users" everywhere is perpetual mistrust by others (experienced by door-to-door sales workers, for example). We learn to recognize cheesy tactics, over-acted sincerity and their breathless speed, set at "hurry-on-to-the-next-call-to-make-the-percentages-work-for-me." The less we trust them, the more calls they have to make. Selfish dictators seed the whirlwind that blows them away.

But the cumulative lesson is that encounters do need regulating. So what kind of regulation? "Market discipline" spawns "customer focus," "mystery shoppers,"[3] "output measurement," "relationship marketing,"[4] "performance targets," and "payment-by-results." These can be used as sticks to beat workers so their customers get a surface-acted 0.2-second smile, or weird hospitality, which has no place in a popcorn queue. It is peculiar and wrong when the sales worker's scripted "hello" sounds like one which they should keep for special friends and family (see Hocshchild on "recurrent flight training"). It feels *yucky*. *Output* measurement overlooks *outcomes* in favor of what's measurable, which is often trivial and spoils good outcomes [6]. What's happening here is that for all the pretense, the customer is really a means to market share and there is no "relationship" to speak of.[5] "Customer focus" seems to scramble *means* and *ends:* when you are told that a "corporation cares," you know somebody is kidding. Care is not that sort of thing; it has to be "up-front and personal" in a system that enables such encounters, not a cheesy simulation.

A related fault in market self-regulation is the attribution of the wrong status to "the other guy," particularly through the misapplication of market discipline. Flying at 36,000 feet, I am a trusting and constrained *passenger* dependent on safe systems, not an autonomous *customer* free-to-choose. If university students really were "customers," degrees would be *commodities* and assignments something to be *purchased* on the internet (whereas students are really *learners* who matter in themselves and plagiarism is forbidden). Professors and students who meet as "providers" and "purchasers" risk being overtaken by mutual discomfort. The care-deficits which markets create [7-9] by associating "love and gold" are also implicated in the recent quadrupling of UK prescriptions for anti-depressants

---

[3] Clandestine agents who report on the behavior of front line employees.

[4] Relationship marketing involves sending promotional materials to customers' home addresses, targeted according to their individual shopping patterns. The necessary data is collected via "loyalty card" schemes, so that in return for small discounts, shoppers provide retailers with a complete record of all their purchases. These data can be sold to third-parties so that they can develop similar "relationships."

[5] There isn't space to discuss the links between profit and reform but the C19th evidence is that there is a strong positive link between them. Big owners were happy to hand much of their social authority and "responsibilities" to state regulators of all kinds and this arrangement still thrives in high-tax/high welfare, low inequality/no poverty Nordic countries. These show consistently greater health and happiness, and lower crime than richer countries.

to children, now running at 630,000 per year (1-in-19) and children whose bedrooms will contain an abundance of expensive electronic gifts from their parents.

Like unregulated manufacturing employment, the market cannot be relied on to create good outcomes because many competitors will also be tempted by a "race to the bottom" to cut costs. Budget airlines, fast food, and "Zoo-Television" shows test the limits of existing regulation at the *cheap end*. Others will "race to the top" taking the five-star hotel route to high standards, including the sedate service that is pleasing to wealthy clients. Neither speed-up nor servility is favorable to emotional laborers.

LIVING NIGHTMARES

While emotional labor can be mutually enriching (caring nurses and responsive patients; convincing actors and rapturous audiences; considerate police and quiescent detainees), it also contains the highest potential for abuse; of clients by workers and workers by clients. *Screw-you* ethics are especially poisonous to well-being in asymmetrical power relationships. The more asymmetrical, the more damage, like murdered sex-workers, workplace bullying, child abuse by priests, boot-camp cult-suicides, lynch mobs, "extraordinary rendition," "termination with extreme prejudice," or the marketization of fear through extortion rackets, kidnapping, terrorism, and torture. All are "up-front and emotional" and often make the headlines. These dreadful examples also show how foolish libertarians are to assume that humans do most good if left to themselves and that maximizing individual freedom under conditions of extreme inequality necessarily maximizes happiness.

Provided the institutional "back support" is good, each is better off by being constrained by the other person and if the other person is disadvantaged then back supports matter even more; thus the duties of care and justice are enshrined quite robustly in the UK's Police and Criminal Evidence Act. By comparing client *and* worker testimonies, better conditions can be created in which neither is treated with indifference, used, or devoured.

One intriguing early example of institutional anxiety management is the Catholic confessional. Confession is meant to be good for the soul—preserving the temporal and spiritual well-being of penitents. One of my undergraduate students found that priests are not stressed by hearing what confessors say because of their license to practice. On the authority of "St. Peter's Keys," any advice offered by ordained priests is "validated instantaneously by St. Peter," minimizing fear of doing harm. By comparison, it was found that social work was more stressful because any decision can be disputed. Custody Sergeants are intermediate in terms of stress, because they have *warranted authority* to make *any lawful decision*—decisions which their Chief Constables *are legally bound to uphold*. Like priests, they are equipped to make the right judgment by training in the Law. As long as a licensed decision is defensible, the Chief Constable (like St. Peter!) is bound to uphold it. Thus the "back support" of licensed emotional labor makes a great difference. One can therefore see the case for *licensed* counseling, which is similarly "confessional" and advisory; licensed doorstep security, licensed morticians, and so on.

These cases corroborate the literature that shows "stress" to be a function of the demands of the job and the degree of control exercised by the worker [10], which the Vatican realized early on! How much license to grant can be ascertained by surveys, personal testimonies, and observation, but autonomy, license, and authorization belong together. Ultimately, this is why we need the United Nations for authorized, multi-lateral use of force, instead of private "guns-for-hire."

IMPROVEMENTS CLEAR TO TIME-TRAVELERS: A THOUGHT EXPERIMENT

Although abstract economic, political, social, and even theological theory has accounted for many of the features we are interested in, there are other simpler and less complicated means by which reformers have brought about change in the conditions of emotional labor—approaches which any "reasonable person" can appreciate easily enough. Anglo-American reformers in the nineteenth and early twentieth century's favored "common sense" methods for recording public squalor, bringing awareness of poverty to political consciousness in Britain, then in America. If we look back along this road, we can ask whether continuation along a similar route will lead to improvements in the conditions of emotional labor?

Within the advanced capitalist states, we can say that since the early nineteenth century, our physical well-being and educational development has advanced spectacularly. For a middle-aged *mental laborer,* environmental risk is vanishingly small, despite talk of terrorist threats and climate change. Other mental laborers, such as air traffic controllers who guide planes approaching London Heathrow, maintain fixed separation using conspicuous advances in engineering science since the 1880s.[6] *Manual laborers* who will clear refuse and handle baggage from those planes are protected somewhat by health and safety standards. There will be public health standards, buildings standards, food safety standards, anti-discrimination laws, legislation on unfair dismissal and bullying, and limitations on the working day (weak in the United Kingdom and the United States compared with Continental Europe). The standards apply to mental laborers by default.

Travelers in those planes are looked after by our third type of worker: *emotional laborers,* paid to affect feelings. Cabin crew contain anxieties, distract restless children and crying babies, and indulge business class customers with hospitable smiles and genuflections. They preserve aircraft safety by appeasing or restraining irate or unruly passengers. Flight attendants may also have identified who is the "BOB" passenger (best on board) on whom they'll lavish extra attention just because they want to. Cabin crew are trained to be courageous in a crash-landing.

---

[6] It is the unregulated part of this system that is dangerous: non-taxed aviation fuel converted into CO_2 in the upper atmosphere, accumulating public nuisance on a global scale. It is a standing joke that neo-liberals would welcome the End of the World if it was accomplished fairly.

EMOTIONAL LABOR AND THE PURSUIT OF HAPPINESS / 307

On arrival, travelers encounter straight-faced emotional labor: *passport control, customs clearance,* and possibly *detention.* For many, the next encounter is with a cheery London taxi driver, then a soft-spoken reservation clerk, a proud waiter, possibly a hard-pressed bar worker trying to meet the fast clock-speed of the "drinking shed." If looking for a good time, visitors can buy infectious laughter at the Comedy Store (Oxendon Street). If taken ill, paramedics will be there in minutes. A breathless midnight weather forecaster puts an optimistic gloss on "occasional showers and sunny intervals tomorrow." All emotional labor.

Thought-experiment indicates that manual laborers from the 1830s would prefer the housing, workplace, and built environment of today to 14-hour days in Soho's sewing lofts in the age of cholera. Most mental laborers from the 1830s would make the same swap. Most travelers from the 1830s would be safer traveling now. Few welcome detention, but that too is accomplished in a better-regulated, more just fashion than in the 1830s and with a reducing rate of deaths-in-custody. The prisoner of the 1830s might willingly change places with today's "detained person" who is attended by a Custody Sergeant, a Jailer, and a Forensic Nurse under statutory obligations to uphold care and justice. Most slaves would choose wage labor. All would see the progress made.

It is harder to be sure that the average time-traveler from the past would find present day emotional labor done better today than then. Comedy might be hard to understand because the social circumstances that shape our sense of humor are so changed; they'd find receptionists less deferential. But it is doubtful that nineteenth-century London was more hospitable. The threat of lethal infection and its wild down-river no-go areas should deter the sane from time-traveling backwards. Indeed, there are scores of ways of validating the claim that statutory interventions have worked better than early reformers could have hoped. Likewise, if we work as hard now to improve front-line conditions as public health professionals worked back then, we can ensure that time-travel a century into the future would find happier and more fulfilled individuals than today.

What to do? Reformers recorded thousands of workers' testimonies in obsessive detail and aggregated death rates in each *enumeration district,* enabling both richly qualitative *and* aggregate quantitative comparisons from which causes and effects could be inferred. The epidemiology of the factory system, unwholesome water, cruel habitations, marshy districts, the Metropolis, poor sustenance, moral corruption, and exhaustion became clear. Millions of lives were saved by simple means.

The reform of the conditions of emotional labor also calls for comparative surveys of both sides to each encounter and figuring out what "common decency" suggests for any front-line; not just New Orleans, Abu Graib, Guantanamo, and war zones glimpsed over the reporter's shoulder. It could be about boarding your next bus, what you and the schedule do to the driver [11] and what the driver and the schedule do to you. Customers (passengers) should not insist that they are "always right." Often they are, but likewise ask the emotional laborer what they need in order to do a good job safely and it will typically benefit the customer. Student criticism about their professor often teaches what needs to be put right for professor *and* student; likewise, what the professor has to say about the student.

A COMMISSION ON THE CONDITIONS OF EMOTIONAL LABOR

One of the best proven devices for identifying poor conditions and spreading good practice remains the quasi-judicial Commission and inquiries into the conditions of emotional labor should begin with encounters where the asymmetry between worker and client is greatest. Police custody suites are asymmetrical in terms of officers' powers to detain, but this can be balanced by a detained person's (DP) statutory rights and just judicial systems. Roughly equivalent good practice exists within other branches of emotional labor and one rapid way of spreading it would be through direct dialogue between corresponding groups of emotional laborers and between corresponding client groups, for example, between those working in Custody Suites and in Accident and Emergency Departments and between DPs and patients. The management lessons will show kinship too.

One happy lesson from custody is that, though governed and monitored, individuals still "do it their way" or else clients see through the pretense.[7] Emotional labor cannot be scripted without risk of presenting a robotic impression and destroying the persuasive capability of "deep-acting" [1], therefore *individual* testimony to the Commission matters.

By talking at length with emotional laborers, clients, and managers, a Commission on the Conditions of Emotional Labor might suggest minimum standards in each service, for example, train and station staffing, staff/student ratios, nurse/ patient ratios for each type of clinical settings (standards which already exist), campus counseling provision, standards in mental health nursing, stewarding of large-scale events, and maximum tours of duty. Following the nineteenth-century model, the standards begin as recommendations developed from good practice, but become compulsory as soon as candid inspection allows. It will cost, but we will be happier.

A kind of a start has been made on this in the United Kingdom in the form of public certification schemes which proclaim organizations to be "Investors in People," best-value exercises and valorizing service skills through General National Vocational Qualifications. Why not add "work-life balance" certification and "right clock-speed" certification? The justification for extreme client behavior should lessen much as they do in decent police custody.

---

[7] It was said that if a DP noticed that an officer was mimicking the style of another officer, that was not really his or her own style, then this could be dangerous. DPs see "faking it" as highly provocative and move rapidly to kicking-off, or exploit the Custody Sergeant mercilessly in a "mind-game" where they play the advantage of "being themselves."

UNEXPECTED HAZARD

However, the pursuit of happiness has had peculiar consequences in the regular workplace. Hochschild [8] has already found that "soft" HR management, the Human Relations approach to the workplace, and "flat structures" have succeeded for office workers at "Americo," but at a cost elsewhere. Work is becoming somewhat more hospitable, "like home." But home is becoming "like work," cold and stressful, creating an unexpected imbalance in the distribution of warmth. This "care deficit" is mitigated by "outsourcing" care to migrant maids and nannies—the "global woman," by "befriending agencies" and even by consultants who train fathers in "high leverage activities that will [make] the most of your important relationships" [12-14]. Hochschild's advice to a Commission into the conditions of emotional labor would therefore be, much like nineteenth-century reformers,' *to examine households as well as workplaces and ponder the connections.* Practical recommendations for collecting data in the workplace and for addressing needs identified through such gathered information have been described in detail in recent innovative work [6, 15].

CLIMBING THE *HIERARCHY OF NEEDS:*
THE THIRD INDUSTRIAL REVOLUTION

The architect Frank Lloyd Wright joked, "Give me the luxuries of life and I will willingly do without the necessities."[8] The luxury of being able to express his kind of humor, and of my call for the emancipation of emotion work, presumes that our bodily security and educational development are assured. The expansion of schooling in architecture, accounting, engineering, medicine, sociology, the law, and so on, presumes that childhood, adolescence, and early adulthood was set aside for the "rising middle classes" and it assumed a successful factory system and that public health needs are met as well. Overseas production means that factory inspection is put at risk, but the meeting of what Maslow called "basic (physical) needs" and "hygiene factors," then up his "hierarchy" via "motivating factors" and finally to "self-actualization" at the top, has this "bottom-upwards" tendency. First, reform of the factory system and physical well-being; second, attainment through the education system; third, earthly happiness through front-line work.

English records indicate that in the 1500s life was so numbingly precarious that inter-personal relations were cold, calculating, and instrumental [16]. Bodily, mental, and emotional enhancement seem to have gone in step developments in manual, mental, and then emotional divisions of labor and we are lucky to be living through a Third Industrial Revolution.

Even economists—instinctive free-marketeers—are changing their minds. Frank [17] finds that experiences produce more lasting happiness than consumer durables and argues that working hours should be cut in order to have more experiences, even if it means fewer things. Similarly, Layard [18] points out that happiness has

---

[8] Quoted in his obituary, April 9, 1954.

not risen in line with economic growth. To a point, material improvement and happiness advance together, but beyond $15,000 per head, money makes little difference, while "most studies in most countries show a secular increase in depression." He supports state initiatives to rebalance "work" and "life" and "Well-Being Centers," offering cognitive behavioral therapy [19], any initiative which improves workplace security (including stopping performance-related pay) and fosters social trust. He embraces utilitarianism and taxation [18]. But neither Frank nor Layard comment on the emotional laborer-client relationship in which well-being is the most immediate issue for both. Members of the Commission I'm calling for may be sympathetic to Frank and to Layard's "new science of happiness" [20], but what about the workers? Layard says little or nothing on conditions for the 10,000 Cognitive Behavioral Therapy practitioners he calls for.

The Commissioners are more likely to find the answers among those testifying about their own experience, clients included. There is plenty to be done, but good reason to be cheerful.

REFERENCES

1. Hochschild, A., *The Managed Heart: The Commercialization of Human Feeling*, University of California Press, Berkeley, 1983.
2. Smith, S. L., Theology of Emotion, *Soundings*, 11, pp. 152-158, Spring 1999.
3. Mill, J. S., *Utilitarianism*, Hackett, Indianapolis, 1863/2001.
4. Hand, S. (ed.), *The Levinas Reader*, Blackwell, Oxford, 1989.
5. Menzies-Lyth, I. E. P., A Case Study in the Functioning of a Social System as a Defence against Anxiety, *Human Relations*, 13, pp. 95-121, 1960.
6. Rosskam, E., *Excess Baggage: Leveling the Load and Changing the Workplace*, Baywood, Amityville, NY, 2007.
7. Hochschild, A. R., The Politics of Culture; Traditional, Postmodern, Cold-Modern, and Warm-Modern Ideals of Care, *Social Politics: International Studies in Gender, State, and Society*, 2:2, pp. 331-346, 1995.
8. Hochschild, A., *The Time Bind: When Work Becomes Home and Home Becomes Work*, Metropolitan Books, New York, 1997.
9. Ehrenreich, B. and A. R. Hochschild, *The Global Woman: Nannies, Maids, and Sex Workers in the New Economy*, Metropolitan Books, New York, 2002.
10. Karasek, R. and T. Theorell, *Healthy Work: Stress, Productivity, and the Reconstruction of Working Life*, Basic Books, New York, 1990.
11. ITF, *Urban Transport: A Periodic Bulletin*, 1st March ed, International Transport Workers' Federation, London, UK, 1995.
12. Hochschild, A. R., "Rent a Mom" And Other Services: Markets, Meanings and Emotions, *The International Journal of Work Organization and Emotion*, 1:1, pp. 74-86, 2005.
13. Hochschild, A. R., On the Edge of the Time Bind: Time and Market Culture, *Social Research*, 72:2, pp. 339-354, 2005.
14. Tough, P., The Year in Ideas, *New York Times Magazine*, December 15, 2002.
15. Keith, M., J. Brophy, P. Kirby, and E. Rosskam, *Barefoot Research: A Workers' Manual for Organizing on Work Security*, International Labour Office, Geneva, Switzerland, 2002.

16. Stone, L., *Family, Sex, and Marriage in England 1500-1800,* Penguin Books, London, UK, 1990.
17. Frank, R., *Luxury Fever: Why Money Fails to Satisfy in an Era of Excess,* Free Press, New York, 1999.
18. Layard, R., Happiness: Has Social Science a Clue?, in *Lionel Robbins Memorial Lecture London,* London School of Economics, London, UK, 2003.
19. Layard, R., *The Depression Report: A New Deal for Depression and Anxiety Disorders,* LSE/CEP Mental Health Policy Group, London, UK, 2006.
20. Layard, R., *Happiness: Lessons from a New Science,* Penguin Books, London, UK, 2005.

CHAPTER 18

Measuring the Protection of Workers' Health: A National Work Security Index

Ellen Rosskam

Changes in the conditions of work have come with globalization and economic liberalization and have included inter alia increased automation and the rapid implementation of information technology. Increasingly working people are confronting new organizational structures and processes including downsizing, precarious employment, increased workload, part-time work, temporary and contractual work, homework, and outsourcing. The massive reorganization of production in the global economy has had a negative effect on a wide range of vulnerable groups, such as low skilled or unskilled workers. The size and nature of these changes combined with the difficulties in regulating their impact suggests a new approach is necessary, one that moves beyond traditional definitions of occupational health and safety, toward a view based on fundamental rights and principles of universalism.

Today's "flexible" work structures are characterized by an absence of guaranteed employment, protection of workers' health, benefits, union representation, or a decent living wage. At the same time, the decentralization of collective bargaining and the deregulation of labor relations and working conditions are increasing the ability of employers to increase their competitiveness on the global market at a great cost to workers' security and benefits.

Considerable empirical evidence demonstrates that more flexible labor markets, in particular those characterized by downsizing and sub-contracting, have been associated with a deterioration in working conditions. The amount of time that some people have to work is a major contributing factor to worsening health. Prolonged working weeks and the re-emergence of long "shifts," even among office workers, appears to be on the rise, greatest in the United States, China, and the United Kingdom, but characterizing work in many other countries. Increasingly, workers feel they have to go to work when ill due to fear of job loss or because they have little or no paid sick leave.

More intense work schedules associated with production systems driven by information technology and new management methods, such as "Just-In-Time," "Lean Production," and "Quick Turnaround," reduce worker autonomy and individual control of work so that productivity gains come at the cost of worse health among workers [1, 2]. The epidemic of chronic health problems associated with work stressors and work-related psychosocial stressors such as, "job strain" that results from jobs with high demand and low worker autonomy (see evidence demonstrating the chronic health problems associated with job strain discussed in parts I and II of this book), remains ignored in the United States, while it is expected to "go global" with the spread of new production systems and management methods.

In most countries, the available information on trends in occupational health is limited and often unreliable. This results in a systematic understatement of most occupational diseases and injuries. Even in countries where information is available, typically it does not reflect the work-induced ills occurring among women workers or workers in the informal economy.

A RIGHTS-BASED APPROACH

In response to these changes, an expanded concept is proposed for the way in which "occupational health and safety" is understood and defined. The expanded concept is based on the fundamental *right* of workers to work that does not adversely affect health or well-being and for these rights to be *universally* guaranteed. The concept of "work security" is proposed here as a revised definition of "occupational health and safety," seen as a fundamental right of all working people. This concept attempts to move beyond the traditional engineering, medical, and technocratic definitions of and approaches to occupational health and safety, toward an expanded view, based on a universalistic rights-based approach.

In its most strict definition, work security refers to secure and reasonably safe working conditions, encompassing occupational health, safety, and the working environment. It includes those provisions which are needed to ensure the protection of workers' health and well-being (occupational health and safety) and addresses working time, paid maternity leave, provision of paid vacation, provision of paid sick leave, protection of disabled workers from discrimination, and restrictions on night work, as well as workplace health and safety committees or departments, and the availability and provision of workers' compensation.

In its larger definition, work security is a fundamental right of all working people and includes a number of protections such as: protection against accidents and illness at work through health, safety, and environmental regulations; protection from discrimination based on work-related or other disabilities, and gender, race, religion or ethnicity; protection from violence, harassment, stress, unsociable hours; rights to employment and income security; paid maternity leave, vacation time, sick leave; reasonable work scheduling and work organization; and right to social supports such as access to health care, education, and child care.[1] Viewed within this context, work security is an expansion of Article 7 on working conditions in the United Nation's International Covenant on Economic, Social and Cultural Rights[2] [3].

Following this expanded concept, a system is needed for monitoring performance on the protection of workers' health beyond the level of the individual workplace. The latter is insufficient to the task of monitoring health and safety at the workplace because systems of surveillance typically do not exist at workplace level and workplace level monitoring by itself does not contribute to national level measures of worker protection. In the United States, ideally, monitoring would take place at county, state, and national levels. Effective methods for worker health surveillance should contribute to this more macro-level monitoring system to ensure the collection and provision of information on the level of performance achieved in the protection of workers' health by a national or state level government. Monitoring systems can help in identifying areas of weakness in the protection of workers' health, as well as indicators for how weaknesses might be ameliorated.

A work security index (WSI) has been developed and is presented here. The index is an attempt to create a benchmarking system for identifying how well a country is performing at a national level, relative to others, in providing work security to its employed population.[3] The WSI was derived from information on 95 countries.

WHO CAN USE THE INDEX AND FOR WHAT PURPOSE?

The WSI can be used to learn how the United States is doing in an internationally comparative context. Examining results achieved by countries with similar conditions could provide tips on how similar results might be achieved in the United States, where such results do not already exist. In the United States, the index could be used to enable individual states to evaluate their performance in protecting workers' health, identify areas of strength and weakness, and compare themselves with other states on successes achieved in the provision of work security.[4] Local,

---

[1] Additional work security rights should include: limits on hours of work and on night work; limits on working age; rights to compensation benefits, pension security, absenteeism protection, long-term care; protection through legislation, enforcement, inspections; right to association; right to collective bargaining; right to refuse unsafe work; right to participate through mechanisms such as joint labor-management health and safety committees and other forms of voice representation; right to know about work-related hazards; right to protection for "whistle-blowers."

[2] http://www.unhchr.ch/html/menu3/b/a_cescr.htm

[3] Availability of data for the indicators determined the countries remaining in the index. Two sets of countries—industrialized and industrializing—were used due to large differences in their social and economic structures, and due to differences in availability of data. The indexes for the industrialized country group are more sophisticated and complete, while for the other group a more limited number of indicators were used in addition to proxy measures. At a final stage, these two country sets were combined.

[4] The indicators can be altered according to local, state, or national level needs in the United States.

state, or federal government, as well as other policy-driving groups, could use the WSI to identify how best to target efforts for improving work security. The WSI could be used to help rationalize the use of scarce resources by identifying where their allocation might make the greatest impact. The same type of evaluation could be undertaken on a county-wide basis within a given state. Findings from such an evaluation would be useful for decision-makers at various levels.

Examining the outcomes for countries in the same region with similar conditions could help governments, trade unions, companies, NGOs, and others gain helpful information on how to make significant improvements in their own work security outcomes. It could help to ensure that decisions about the allocation of resources are needs-based, and that such decisions are supported by evidence indicating whether such allocation makes the most sense. An index built on indicators and data from numerous countries could be of great use to countries not able to collect reliable data related to work security, in particular, developing countries. For example, where data are available from one country in a region, countries having similar social and economic conditions in the same region could use the work security index to extrapolate the level of worker protection that they are achieving. It also could help to indicate where countries lacking reliable data and mechanisms for worker protection are likely to make the most impact with their own resources.

The WSI is a pioneering tool, the first to produce a grouping and ranking of countries based on their level of protection of workers' health and safety [4]. An overview of the WSI and its constructions as well as some key results related to the performance of the United States in the index are provided below.[5]

Three key findings from the work security index:

- Of the 95 countries included in the work security index, more than two-thirds have unsatisfactory levels of worker protection.
- The most critical cases include the most economically deprived countries in Africa, Asia, and Eastern Europe.
- Alone, laws and the mechanisms meant to ensure the implementation of worker protection are insufficient to protect workers' health.[6]

---

[5] Development of the WSI and other similar indexes on socio-economic security was endorsed by the International Labour Office and by national affiliates of the International Confederation of Free Trade Unions (ICFTU) from both northern and southern countries. Occupational health and safety experts from ICFTU national affiliates anticipated using the indexes to help guide their work in a more coherent manner than they have been able to do in the absence of such data.

[6] A number of other fundamental elements are essential to ensure the protection of worker health, including collective voice, basic employment security, and some form of basic income security.

METHODOLOGY[7]

Description of the Indicators

Three groups of indicators were identified to create the index. The groups consist of input, process, and outcome indicators. *Input* indicators are the institutional or legal elements necessary for work security, i.e., the basic laws needed to protect workers' health. But laws in and of themselves, while important, do not protect workers—structures and mechanisms are needed to ensure that laws get implemented. Thus, the second group of indicators consists of *process* indicators, which are the mechanisms or structures that need to be put into place to ensure that the laws are implemented and that they function. The third group of indicators consists of *outcomes* indicators. These are the elements that provide a measure of whether the input and process indicators appear to be effective in reality, demonstrating whether effective worker protection is actually taking place in the country. Ultimately, these are the measures that count the most in evaluating how a country performs on its protection of workers' health.

Input Indicators:
Laws and Regulations

The work security index contains 11 input indicators, consisting of relevant International Labor Conventions (which are legally binding instruments once they are ratified by a country's government) and related hazards; ensuring protection for pregnant workers; limiting working time; limiting night work; providing paid leave (vacation time); and protecting disabled workers. Countries are scored according to whether or not the government has ratified the relevant Conventions.

The other four input indicators consist of relevant national laws on: occupational health and safety; laws requiring the establishment of occupational health services (indicative of a more advanced level of worker protection); laws protecting disabled workers from discrimination; laws limiting hours of work (legal limits on working time are a fundamental measure of a civil society and help to protect workers against extreme forms of exploitation); restricting night work (night work is proven to be less healthy than day work); providing maternity protection; and laws guaranteeing paid vacation leave (laws guaranteeing the right to paid leave help to protect workers against overwork). Because international labor standards outline *minimum* prescribed protections, national laws based on such standards often are not as protective as they may need to be. Countries may have national laws on any of the above-mentioned indicators without having ratified the corresponding international Convention.

---

[7] More details on the methodology for calculating the work security index and the six other socio-economic security indexes are provided in [5].

Process Indicators: Mechanisms to Ensure the Laws and Regulations Function

The work security index includes three *process* indicators. They are considered to be essential mechanisms or structures needed to ensure that the basic laws and regulations described above are implemented in a country. One process indicator is the level of government expenditure on workers' compensation. The level of government expenditure on workers' compensation is higher where GDP is higher, although the generosity of benefits per capita and per injury or illness varies greatly among countries. Higher government expenditure on workers' compensation does not necessarily indicate a higher rate of accidents, injuries, illnesses or a weaker or relatively unhealthy population. It is more often indicative of the existence of an operative structure whereby workers can make claims and of a nationally established list of compensable injuries and illnesses. Conversely, a low level of government expenditure on workers' compensation is not usually indicative of a low level of accidents, injuries, and illnesses. It is more indicative of a low level of GDP, which acts as a barrier to the government paying benefits to injured workers. It also may indicate a lack of monitoring, surveillance, reporting, and notification structures. Low expenditure on workers' compensation may further indicate the absence of trade unions or other organizations giving voice to workers, such that workers may not be aware that a compensation system exists, or how to use it. Finally, low government expenditure on workers' compensation also may reflect a preponderance of low-risk activities, such as subsistence farming, in which dangerous machines and chemicals may not be commonly used.

Another indicator is the existence of disability or invalidity benefits provided to workers injured in work-related accidents.[8] The third process indicator is the existence of bipartite (labor and management) or tripartite (labor, management, and government) occupational health and safety boards or committees. Mechanisms are needed to ensure that laws reach employers and workers at the level of the workplace in order to translate into the protection of workers' health. Most often these mechanisms consist of tripartite or bipartite boards or labor-management health and safety committees. Where these mechanisms exist, usually requiring a legal mandate, consultation is used as a means of addressing and solving problems both locally and nationally. Workers have been shown to be healthier when they are able to participate in decision-making. Conversely, when workers are not included in decision-making about how work is organized and carried out, ill health and reduced productivity often result. Joint labor-management or tripartite health and safety mechanisms are an effective means of monitoring the implementation of national laws and regulations.

---

[8] This is a measure of whether or not workers are protected in the event they are injured at work or made ill from their work. The fact that benefits are provided, however, does not indicate whether the benefits are sufficient or even whether they are commensurate with the incident.

Outcome Indicators: Measures of Worker Protection Occurring in Reality

There are five *outcome* indicators in the work security index. They are used to gauge whether a country is actually and effectively implementing the relevant laws and regulations to protect workers and whether the mechanisms and structures function as they should. Ultimately the best way to evaluate a country's performance in protecting workers' health is by examining what *actually* takes place compared to what is *meant* to take place. The first outcome indicator is the work-related fatal injury rate.[9,10] The second outcome indicator consists of a categorical variable with five codes corresponding to estimated levels of fatal injury under-reporting. Under-reporting is a serious issue, especially in countries with large informal economies because they lack the ability to conduct investigations into whether injuries are work-related. Given the large scope for the under-reporting of work-related fatalities, estimates were developed to correct for the expected degree of under-reporting by individual countries. The third outcome indicator is the share of wage employment in a country's total employment, which is used as a proxy for the proportion of the population having guaranteed compensation for occupational injury.[11,12] The fourth indicator consists of the average reported working time.[13] Average working time indicates the degree to which workers are being overworked and exploited. Damage to physical and psychological health is known to occur when work exceeds 45 hours per week [6-8]. The last outcome indicator consists of average annual paid leave (vacation days) in a country corrected by the relative size of wage employment. The average number of paid vacation days to which workers are entitled is a measure of the importance a government gives to workers' physical and psychological well-being. Workers in countries more oriented toward social benefits are entitled to—and take—more paid vacation days to recuperate from the cumulative effects of work.

---

[9] This refers to the number of fatal injuries per 100,000 workers.

[10] Work-related fatality data, as reported by a number of countries, were used. For countries lacking such data, fatal injury rates were estimated based on neighboring countries of a similar size and with similar conditions, in a given region.

[11] "Percent wage employment" was used as a proxy measure for "percent of the population guaranteed coverage by workers' compensation for work injury" due to data limitations. Correlating available data for some countries were used to test the accuracy of using the proxy. Strong relationships assured reliability of the proxy measure.

[12] The more workers' compensation coverage is extended throughout the active labor force in a country, the more protection and security is afforded to workers. This indicator is a measure of the extent of protection extended to society at large in the event such compensation is needed. Non-coverage of significant groups, such as informal economy workers, older workers, and child workers, leaves workers extremely vulnerable if they suffer a work-related incident.

[13] Average working time indicates the degree to which workers are being overworked and exploited. Damage to physical and psychological health is known to occur when work exceeds 45 hours per week [6-8]. (The impact of long work hours on health is discussed in chapters 6, 7, and 8.) A combination of expressions of working time was utilized.

Clustering Countries

The work security index is based on clustering countries according to their degree of performance on the various indicators. This allows for an examination of individual country performance on work security without comparing all countries against each other, given very different levels of development. The performance of an individual country can be better evaluated by clustering according to countries of the same region, some of which will have similar structures, laws, levels of population and development. Clustering also allows the performance of an individual country to be evaluated according to countries with similar levels of industrialization, development and wealth, even if they are not located in the same region. This method also provides a means for countries to set their own targets, identifying other countries particularly within the same region that have achieved more than they have, and setting standards to aim for over time.

Ranking countries according to their work security index scores[14] for international comparability was found to overshadow important differences in input, process, and outcome performance between countries. Examining a country's ranking on the index alone can be misleading as it may not necessarily reflect how well or poorly that country may be performing on individual measures of work security. Identifying groups of countries with similar performance on work security measures provides a means of recognizing the efforts made by countries, even if they rank low in the index. Conversely, a country may rank relatively high in the index while closer examination may reveal that its actual performance in worker protection (reflected by poor outcome performance) is weak. From both an intra- and inter-country perspective, clusters of countries were found to be much more revealing about the conditions of worker protection in any individual country.

Four distinct clusters have been mapped out:

- *Pacesetters:* This cluster includes those countries that were found to perform well on all three groups of indicators. Countries in this cluster can be seen as models in achieving strong protection in the area of worker health and safety.
- *Pragmatists:* This cluster includes those countries that were found to perform well on the outcome indicators but which perform poorly on any of the input (laws) and process (mechanisms) indicators. Countries in this cluster may have weak or non-existent laws and structures to protect workers' health, yet somehow they still manage to provide relatively strong protection to workers in actuality.
- *Conventionals:* This cluster includes those countries that were found to perform poorly on outcome indicators but which perform well on any of the input and process indicators. Countries in this cluster tend to have strong laws, regulations, and structures to protect workers' health, but they tend to be on paper only. In actuality, the protections those laws and mechanisms are meant to ensure do not get translated into practice.

[14] The ranking of the 95 countries in the work security index can be found in [4, p. 418].

• *Much to be Done Group:* This cluster includes those countries that were found to perform poorly on all three groups of indicators. Countries in this cluster (two-thirds of the countries in the index fell into this cluster) lack protective laws, regulations, and structures related to the protection of workers' health and do not have a good record on protection of the country's working population. Countries in this cluster need to take serious measures toward reducing the individual and social burdens resulting from the significant lack of worker health protections.

The various clusters presented by region are shown in Figure 1.

Building the Index

The guiding principles in the building of the work security index were: 1) simplicity, transparency, and those most fundamental elements needed in any society without which workers remain unprotected and which can lead to unemployment, poverty, and chronically high stress; and 2) the availability and reliability of data. The work security index uses a simple additive model (with outcome weighted to equal input + process):

$$WSI = Input + Process + 2x \text{ Outcome}$$

Regardless of how a country performs on input and process indicators, it is ultimately the performance on outcome measures that reveals most about how well a country performs in protecting its workforce.

FINDINGS

The work security index includes data from 95 countries. The performance of these countries in protecting workers' health and well-being is presented in Figure 2. Analysis of the index is based on the hypothesis that industrialized countries provide better work security than non-industrialized countries and economies in transition. A country is considered to provide "good coverage" on work security when the work injuries program of the country covers: 1) the whole population; or 2) the entire working population; or 3) the working population with exceptions. Lesser degrees of coverage are considered as unsatisfactory work security coverage.

The "Pacesetter" cluster is made up entirely of Western European countries—all having strong legislation, effective mechanisms, and good outcome measures. There are no "Pacesetters" in any other region. Luxemburg, Sweden, and Finland are the three countries shown to provide the strongest work security. Common to these countries are strong laws and regulations, effective mechanisms to ensure that the laws are implemented, and good outcome measures. These findings are the result of the high degree of importance attributed to social protection in the Nordic countries and in Luxemburg.

Figure 3 shows how the United States performed in the work security index. Analysis of the performance of the United States revealed a low score on laws and

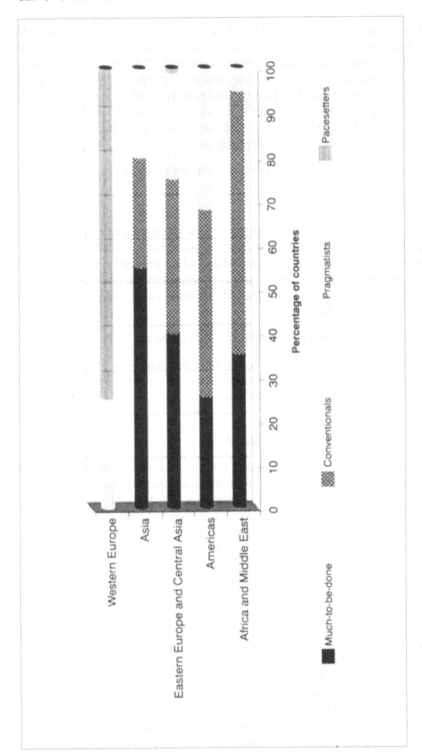

Figure 1. Work security index: clusters by region. **Source**: [4].
© 2004, International Labour Organization. Used with permission.

	High score on Outcome			
	High score on Input/Process		Low score on Input/Process	
	Pacesetters		Pragmatists	
Regions	Countries		Countries	
Africa and Middle East			Israel	
Americas			Argentina Barbados Canada	Chile United States
Asia			Australia Japan	New Zealand
Eastern Europe and Central Asia	Slovenia		Czech Republic Estonia Hungary	Latvia Lithuania Poland Slovakia
Western Europe	Belgium Denmark Spain Finland France Germany Iceland	Italy Luxembourg Netherlands Norway Portugal Switzerland Sweden	Austria Greece	Ireland United Kingdom

	Low score on Outcome			
	High score on Input/Process		Low score on Input/Process	
	Conventionals		Much-to-be-done	
Regions	Countries		Countries	
Africa and Middle East	Algeria Benin Burkina Faso Burundi Congo Côte d'Ivoire Egypt Ethiopia	Ghana Lebanon Madagascar Morocco Nigeria Senegal Sierra Leone	Guinea-Bissau Mauritania Mauritius Rwanda	South Africa Tunisia Turkey Zimbabwe
Americas	Brazil Colombia Costa Rica Ecuador	Mexico Peru Venezuela	Dominican Republic Honduras	Panama Saint Kitts and Nevis
Asia	Bangladesh Korea, Republic of	Pakistan	China India Indonesia Nepal	Philippines Sri Lanka Thailand
Eastern Europe and Central Asia	Azerbaijan Belarus Croatia Kyrgyzstan	Russian Federation Tajikistan Ukraine	Albania Armenia Bulgaria Georgia Kazakhstan	Moldova, Republic of Romania Turkmenistan Uzbekistan
Western Europe				

Figure 2. Work security index for 95 countries. **Source**: [4].
© 2004, International Labour Organization. Used with permission.

Ranking: Countries:	26 Hungary	27 Lithuania	28 Slovakia	29 United States	30 Croatia	31 Latvia	32 Argentina
Work Security Index	0.665	0.665	0.660	0.656	0.646	0.633	0.628
Conv. 1: Restricting hours of work	No	Yes	Yes	No	No	No	Yes
Conv. 103: Maternity Protection	Yes	No	No	No	Yes	No	No
Conv. 132: Annual Holidays with Pay	Yes	No	No	No	Yes	Yes	No
Conv. 155: Existence of OSH law	Yes	Yes	Yes	No	Yes	Yes	No
Conv. 159: No discrimination against disabled workers	Yes	Yes	Yes	No	Yes	No	Yes
Conv. 161: Establishment of OH services	Yes	No	Yes	No	Yes	No	No
Conv. 171: Restricting night work	No	Yes	No	No	No	No	No
Law on OSH	Yes	Yes	Yes	Yes	Yes	Yes	Yes
Law on paid leave	Yes	Yes	Yes	No	Yes	Yes	Yes
Law on disability	Yes	Yes	Yes	Yes	Yes	Yes	Yes
Law on paid maternity leave	Yes	Yes	Yes	No	Yes	Yes	Yes
Government spending on workers' compensation	0.13	0.09	0.12	0.49	0.12	0.09	0.17
OSH board or committee	Yes	Yes	Yes	Yes	Yes	Yes	Yes
Earnings-related cash benefits for injured workers	63.0	80.0	76.0	66.7	85.0	80.0	70.0
Fatal Occupational Injuries – ILO estimates	11.4	6.0	8.4	4.5	9.1	7.4	11.1
Level of injury underreporting	Medium	High	High	Low	High	High	Medium
% Wage workers (proxy of % workers covered for work injury)	84.8	79.2	53.9	92.6	75.2	84.7	72.1
Average paid leave (corrected with % wage empl.)	21.2	15.8	13.5	9.3	13.5	17.0	17.3
Average reported working time	44.0	36.4	36.5	34.5	41.9	41.2	42.2
Input	0.944	0.833	0.888	0.222	0.944	0.805	0.777
Process	0.553	0.599	0.600	0.761	0.635	0.599	0.603
Outcome	0.582	0.614	0.576	0.820	0.503	0.564	0.567

Figure 3. The United States in the work security index.
© 2004, International Labour Organization. Used with permission.

mechanisms, but a medium score on outcomes. The low score on laws and mechanisms for the United States appears to be an artifact to some degree, most likely explained by the lack of ratification of international labor standards while national laws exist in most of the areas listed under input indicators. The United States scored low on process indicators because there is no federally mandated mechanism to ensure the use of health and safety boards or committees.

Performance of the United States on outcome indicators appears relatively low due to the absence of legally mandated minimum paid vacation in the United States. This shortcoming should be redressed, with paid vacation leave federally mandated as a minimum right, similar to those guaranteed rights provided in the Pacesetter countries. Learning from the Pacesetter countries, average working time in the United States needs to be reduced and carefully monitored to aid in the prevention of chronic diseases such as hypertension. An analysis of the performance of the United States in the index reveals a need to make statistical adjustments, or to apply weighting inside groups of indicators, such as within the input group, to avoid "penalizing" countries that have national laws but which do not ratify international labor standards. Without such an adjustment, the United States may appear lower ranked in the index than the reality.

In the area of maternity leave, the United States has no federal law guaranteeing the provision of paid maternity leave—only unpaid maternity leave is guaranteed. The amount of leave that is provided trails behind most west and east European countries where maternity leave is both paid and more generous in leave time.

Overall, the United States ranked 29 out of 95 countries in the index, with 28 countries ranked ahead of the United States in the protection of workers' health. Surely we can do better given the amount of money the United States spends on health care. In general, countries outperforming the United States spend less on health care yet have better outcome measures. It is noteworthy that all of the Pacesetter countries have universal health care systems. In the United States, improving population health outcomes and controlling costs for both government and business would likely require implementing a national health care system with a focus on prevention rather than treatment.

An argument in support of using the WSI for the individual states in the United States is based on the division between the federal and the state-based legal systems. For example, while federal laws exist for certain minimum necessary worker protections, responsibility to ensure that the laws are respected and implemented is left to each individual state. Since there is no national data collection system linking information on work and health from the 50 states, it is difficult to know how well those federal laws are actually implemented across the country. Therefore, WSI data reflecting only the federal level may not make the most sense in the case of the United States.

Eastern Europe and the Americas are the regions with the best performing industrializing or transition economies (countries classified as Pragmatists). These countries have relatively weak legislation related to work security or on mechanisms to ensure the application of the laws but still achieve good results in the outcome measures. By contrast, more than two-thirds of the countries in the index have unsatisfactory levels of work security. The latter are classified as Conventionals or Much-to-be-Done, in almost equal numbers. The Conventionals could be considered as "average" performers in that they have satisfactory laws or regulations and/or satisfactory mechanisms for implementing those laws, but nonetheless perform rather poorly on the outcome measures. The most critical cases are in the category of Much-to-be-Done, which includes the most deprived countries from Africa, Asia, and Eastern Europe. The countries of Central and Eastern Europe and the post-Soviet republics have a history of strong legislation on the various aspects of work security, including nearly 100% trade union membership until the fall of communism. Some of the other countries, particularly those in Asia, have more recently upgraded what were basic factory acts carried over from colonial periods to include other laws on work security. Notwithstanding, the results show that, while laws and mechanisms may exist, alone they are insufficient to protect workers' health.

INDICATORS ELIMINATED AND FUTURE CONSIDERATIONS

A lack of data precluded a number of indicators being included, such as whether health and safety is an important focus of a country's labor inspectorate, as compared with a labor inspectorate that focuses mainly on the implementation of the body of labor laws rather than on prevention and the elimination of workplace hazards. In the United States, the "labor inspectorate" is federal OSHA or individual state occupational safety and health administrations. The number of OSHA inspectors in the United States is extremely low compared with the size of the working population and the number of workplaces across the country. Following decades of reduced funding to federal OSHA, the government adopted an approach of encouraging employers to use "voluntary initiatives" to self-monitor and essentially self-regulate their compliance with OSHA regulations. Concurrent with the "voluntary initiatives" approach, OSHA's compliance—not prevention—focus, and the greatly diminished number of organized workers in the United States, worker health protections have significantly decreased since the 1980s.

Data unavailability also precluded including the level of commitment of a country to ensuring work security demonstrated by the percentage of government expenditure on the prevention of work-related accidents, ill health, and disability. Various positive outcomes are likely to be associated with a high level of expenditure on prevention, while low expenditure should be associated with higher incidence and prevalence of work-related accidents and ill-health, where these are reported and measured. In the United States, a lack of adequate attention paid to prevention seems to have become a widespread social ill, in part due to the focus on treatment rather than prevention that dominates the U.S. health care system. Profits are generated by *treating* ills when they occur—not by *preventing* them, including the ills created by poor work organization.

Data limitations also did not permit including the percentage of insurance paid by firms by high-risk activity (particularly mining, construction, and agriculture). In the United States, one of the most common complaints heard from industry has to do with the high cost of workers' compensation insurance. While insurance costs have skyrocketed in the United States, worker protections have spiraled downward. Challenges related to focusing on the "bottom-line" are discussed in detail elsewhere in this book (see chapter 9).

Problems with data required eliminating a number of other indicators including: the average amount of maternity leave granted under national law to estimate how well paid maternity leave laws are implemented; the percent of disabled workers who return to work each year compared with the total rate of workers with work-related disabilities. In the United States, the percent of disabled workers re-integrated into gainful employment each year would be a useful measure of the overall level of importance attributed to workers' health, and the level of incapacity required in order for a worker to qualify for disability benefits. In the United States, disability benefits are provided only for certain illnesses, and paid for shorter periods of time than in most Western European countries, even if a worker is incapacitated. Considering the extent of disability in the United States induced by psychosocial stressors such as job strain, more attention to work organization is needed.

The percent of workers in mining and construction in each country (two of the three most hazardous work sectors globally) was also eliminated along with working time lost due to work-related accidents, compared with the rate of employment. A high rate of lost work time can be indicative of a low level of worker protection, with significant proportions of workers suffering work-related ill health, accidents, or injuries. As discussed throughout this book, lost work time in the United States is a major concern for business due to the associated costs. Yet there seems to be little understanding that much of America's chronic disease epidemic, resulting in much lost work time, is associated with work factors such as the poor organization of work and resulting psychosocial stressors. Indeed it appears that in the United States, the high rate of lost work time is indicative of a low level of worker protection. Data on lost work time in the United States should be considered as only the tip of the iceberg, since they do not include lost productivity "hidden" in the form of presenteeism.

The percent of male workers working more than 45 hours per week (similar data on female workers would be even scarcer) was also excluded because of lack of reliable data. In the United States, excessive working hours (more than 45 hours per week) constitute a demonstrated health risk. Notwithstanding, the American working population leads the industrialized world in average number of hours worked per year. Future development of the WSI should include excessive working hours as a factor.

CONCLUSION

A rights-based approach for redefining concepts underlying the field of occupational health is proposed herein as a departure from medical, engineering, and technocratic approaches to occupational health. The proposed approach is based on principles of universalism and basic rights due to all citizens. A work security index is presented as a benchmarking system for evaluating how well local, state, or national level governments perform in protecting workers' health, based on a rights-based approach to work and health. A key element in a rights-based approach to work security is universal access to health care.

No system or methodology exists in the United States to allow policy-makers to know how well any individual state is performing in protecting workers' health and well-being. Knowledge about the strengths and weaknesses in the performance of different states could be a powerful tool for both policy-makers and voice groups. Such information is not routinely collected and shared in the United States but could be widely disseminated without much difficulty.

The protection of workers' health and well-being seems far too distant. In the industrializing countries, liberalization, privatization, and other aspects of globalization have brought new challenges that have not been met as yet. In wealthy countries, changes in the nature of work have induced crises of work-induced stress often manifested as depression, burnout, hypertension, and cardiovascular disease. In the poorest areas of the world, poverty and the disasters that people face daily feed into chronic insecurity and chronic stress in work and non-working life.

In identifying areas needing work, a body of knowledge is needed about the effects of work on women's health and about the health consequences of jobs performed by women. The United States could lead the way in this important area. Gender-specific data on issues related to work security, particularly data on women workers, are extremely difficult, if not impossible, to obtain for the majority of countries. In the United States, research and practice in occupational health has been conditioned by the workers' compensation system. Men have from three to ten times more compensated industrial accidents and injuries per worker than women [9]. These statistics are often interpreted to mean that women's jobs are safer than men's, while in reality, the hazards inherent in many jobs performed by women are hidden behind an illusion of "safe" and "clean" work [10]. Yet because there is a lack of research on the majority of jobs performed by women, particularly in relation to work-related health effects, policies are often based on conclusions erroneously drawn from the work performed by men. In most countries of the world, women are concentrated in particular sectors of the economy—in service jobs, in selected areas of manufacturing, and in agriculture. Within each of these areas of work there is a concentration of women in the jobs with the lowest pay and the least status [11]. A consequence is that the impact of waged work on millions of women in both formal and informal economies continues to go unrecorded and unregulated, despite the fact that many jobs performed exclusively or predominantly by women have an important physical component, which can produce pain and even disability.

Many working people lack protection against workplace risks, which are entirely preventable. Effective monitoring and surveillance are needed to prevent the adverse health outcomes associated with work-induced stress and job strain in particular, both barely addressed in the United States. At the same time, well known hazards, such as those from dangerous substances, machinery, tools and manual handling still require a great deal of attention. Most countries in the world could do much better in adhering to strategies that have been even relatively successful in the countries identified as Pacesetters. The application of a empirically-based benchmarking system, such as the work security index, is thus proposed as a measure to help countries identify where their resources might make the greatest impact in protecting the health of their working populations. Considering that sufficient success in this area has not been made to date in most countries around the world, adopting an approach based on fundamental rights and principles of universalism may be the most sensible alternative.

REFERENCES

1. Delbridge, R., P. Turnbull, and B. Wilkinson, Pushing Back the Frontiers: Management Control and Work Intensification under JIT/TQM Factory Regimes, *New Technology, Work and Employment,* 1:2, pp. 97-106, 1995.
2. Parker, M. and J. Slaughter, *Working Smart,* Labor Education and Research Project, Detroit, 1994.
3. Keith, M. I., J. Brophy, P. Kirby, and E. Rosskam, *Barefoot Research: A Workers' Manual for Organizing on Work Security,* International Labour Office, Geneva, Switzerland, 2002.
4. Annycke, P., F. Bonnet, S. Dasgupta, A. Khan, J. Figueiredo, E. Rosskam, G. Standing, and L. Zsoldos, *Economic Security for a Better World.* International Labour Office, Geneva, Switzerland, 2004.
5. Bonnet, F., J. B. Figueiredo, and G. Standing, A Family of Decent Work Indexes, *International Labor Review,* 142:2, pp. 213-238, 2003.
6. Kawakami, N., S. Araki, N. Takatsuka, H. Shimizu, and H. Ishibashi, Overtime, Psychosocial Working Conditions, and Occurrence of Non-Insulin Dependent Diabetes Mellitus in Japanese Men, *Journal of Epidemiology and Community Health,* 53:6, pp. 359-363, 1999.
7. Lee, S., G. A. Colditz, L. F. Berkman, and I. Kawachi, Prospective Study of Job Insecurity and Coronary Heart Disease in US Women, *American Journal of Epidemiology,* 14:1, pp. 24-30, 2004.
8. Kroenke, C. H., D. Spiegelman, J. Manson, E. S. Schernhammer, G. A. Colditz, and I. Kawachi, Work Characteristics and Incidence of Type 2 Diabetes in Women, *American Journal of Epidemiology,* 165:2, pp. 175-183, 2007.
9. Messing, K., *One-Eyed Science: Occupational Health and Women Workers,* Temple University Press, Philadelphia, PA, 1998.
10. Rosskam, E., *Excess Baggage: Leveling the Load and Changing the Workplace,* Baywood, Amityville, NY, 2007.
11. Doyal, L., *What Makes Women Sick?,* Macmillan Press, London, UK, 1995.

CHAPTER 19

Conclusion:
Curing Unhealthy Work

Peter L. Schnall, Marnie Dobson,
Ellen Rosskam, and Paul Landsbergis

The United States is facing its greatest economic crisis since the "great depression" with rising unemployment rates,[1] a large wealth and income gap between the rich and poor, and a fraying social safety net. At the same time, conditions at work are deteriorating for most working people. Numerous news stories have reported on studies and surveys documenting high stress levels among the U.S. workforce and demonstrating the importance of work stress in causing mental and physical illness. In a survey released by the American Psychological Association in October 2007, 74% of Americans acknowledged feeling stressed about work [1].[2] In addition, there has been press coverage of recent research reporting 1) that work stress contributes to depression [2] and 2) that returning to work at a high-stress job (one with chronic high demands and low control, or "job strain") for someone with a previous heart attack places them at greater risk of a repeat heart attack [3, 4], adding to the evidence that work stressors have effects on many common health outcomes.

By the age of 50, most members of the U.S. workforce suffer from at least one, and sometimes more, work-related illnesses including: 1) injuries (e.g., back, neck, and repetitive strain injuries) 2) work-related mental health conditions (including burnout, depression, and anxiety-related disorders) (see chapter 7); or

---

[1] Official unemployment rates in the United States do not reflect the high degree of under-employment or the percent of the population in types of employment that still leave people at poverty level (employment in a minimum wage job means an individual is counted as "employed" but such employment does not mean a person can afford market-rate housing or health insurance). The large number of senior citizens employed in low wage service sector jobs reflects the lack of old age security in the United States.
[2] APA News Release [1].

331

3) cardiovascular heart disease (CVD) of one form or another, including hypertension and coronary artery disease (see chapter 6). The heavy burden of work-related illness impacts employee productivity and health care costs (see chapter 9) and translates into considerable costs to both businesses and society as a whole, in the form of accidents, absenteeism, presenteeism (lowered job performance), and employee turnover, all of which diminish productivity. Add on the direct medical, legal, and insurance costs, workers' compensation payments as well as tort and FELA (Federal Employers Liability Act) judgments and we find that work stress is very costly indeed, with a price tag for U.S. industry estimated at least at $300 billion and perhaps as much as $1 trillion annually when we include the costs to society as a whole (see chapter 9). In addition to the economic costs, work stress has immense social costs on the well-being of families and communities.

In modern industrial society, continuous technological innovations are intertwined with new management practices leading to an ever-changing workplace in which productivity, measured by output per hour, has been increasing at a greater than 2.5% rate per year overall, and at 4% per year in the manufacturing sector, for more than 10 years [5, 6]. These increases in productivity have not been passed on to U.S. workers in the form of higher wages or shorter work weeks. In most other developed countries, especially Western European countries, increased productivity in the workplace has resulted in benefits to working people through a substantial decrease in work hours per week [7]. U.S. workers have not enjoyed such benefits. On the contrary, the United States now leads all industrialized countries (including Japan) in hours worked *per year* [8, 9]. The United States is the *only* western industrialized country which does not have a federal law ensuring all working people have a minimum of paid vacation time.[3] In addition, average hours worked per year hides trends in opposite directions since between 1970-2000 an increasing percent of U.S. men and women were working more than 50 hours per week (26% of men and 11% of women in 2000), while an increasing percent were underemployed and working fewer than 30 hours per week [11]. Furthermore, many women have joined the paid labor force in recent decades leading to dual wage-earner families with the result that total family hours worked has increased dramatically. The average U.S. married-couple family worked 247 more hours in 1996 than in 1989 [12]. The effects of this intensification of work (e.g., work family conflict) [13] may be having lasting negative effects on the well-being of individuals and their families.

Changes at the workplace, in addition to long work hours (see chapters 7 and 8), that are having an adverse impact on health, include psychosocial stressors, such as

---

[3] In the United States, federal law leaves decisions about vacation time up to individual employers. Many employers do not provide workers with paid vacation time or paid sick leave (17% of all U.S. workers have no vacation time). Many employers who do offer workers paid vacation time use what is in essence a basic human right to make themselves attractive as competitive employers, similar to offering health insurance and retirement programs. In contrast, all other western industrialized countries ensure that health care, pensions, and a minimum of 4 weeks paid vacation time (and often more) are provided as part of national social protection programs [10].

excessive demands coupled with inadequate control (i.e., job strain), lack of social support, social isolation, imbalances between effort and reward, lack of social justice, lack of respectful work conditions, and "emotional labor" (see chapters 6 and 7). The latter has been only recently recognized. As the service sector expands in the United States, "Front line" workers, the "smiling faces" of the company (e.g., customer service representatives), are exposed to the stressful conditions of "emotional labor," having to fake emotions to put forward the best face of the company (see chapters 7 and 17). These workplace stressors contribute to unhealthy or "noxious" work environments or "noxious work." Exposing workers to an increasing array of organizational demands and psychosocial exposures, exceeding the human organism's capacity to cope, leads in turn to chronic biological arousal (i.e., higher blood pressure, heart rate, and levels of adrenalin), which ultimately can damage one's health—physically and/or psychologically.

Work has long been divided along the social hierarchies of class, race, and gender (see chapters 3 and 8). For many workers in lower social class jobs, or non-Caucasian or female workers, their life situations are characterized by less power, fewer skills, and fewer opportunities to find fulfilling work. A result of these divisions is that the most socially powerless groups often take the worst jobs and are exposed to more "noxious working" environments, contributing to the different health outcomes between social groups (see chapters 3 and 8). Greater exposures to "noxious" working conditions among workers in low-wage jobs may contribute to the higher risk of heart disease and stroke among lower (vs. higher) socioeconomic groups (see chapter 6).

Given the widespread exposure to stressors in the work environment, it is not surprising to find that a large portion of the workforce complains of "stress at work." Various surveys have found that 40 to 75% of U.S. workers report feeling chronically stressed [1, 14] and many manifest stress-related illnesses. By age 50, 60% of inner city bus drivers in the United States have developed persistently elevated blood pressure (i.e., hypertension) [15], which often leads to cardiovascular disease and a lifetime of treatment. While work stressors are not the sole cause of ill health or of any particular health outcome (most illnesses including work-related ones have many causes), their contribution to the burden of mental and physical ill health in the U.S. workforce is quite substantial. One in six working men and women suffers from burnout or depression at any given moment in time [16, 17], while one in three has hypertension or coronary artery disease [18]. Some studies estimate that job strain alone accounts for at least 70% of burnout [19] and 30% of hypertension among working people [20].

The dominant medical explanation of these epidemics in the United States is that individuals are personally responsible for their life condition, including their health, and conceives of illness as resulting from the unfortunate combination of individual vulnerability (for example, unhealthy genes) or risk-taking behaviors such as cigarette smoking or lack of exercise. This "medical model" of the disease process ignores social causes of disease (sometimes called "upstream causes") [21], for example, social class and working conditions, in favor of individual explanations "downstream causes" such as an unhealthy diet). It is reinforced by a mechanical

334 / UNHEALTHY WORK

view of illness as resulting from a breakdown in self-regulation or homeostasis (the body's ability to return physiological parameters to a predetermined state of equilibrium). This explanation is implausible for chronic health problems such as hypertension which afflict virtually the entire U.S. population by age 60 to 70, but which do not exist in non-industrial cultures and thus cannot be attributed to inherent processes of aging [22]. Chronic illnesses, such as depression, hypertension, and coronary artery disease appear to be "modern epidemics" [23], the consequence of excessive environmental load (such as chronic stressors at work) on the human organism over prolonged periods of time [24, 25].

The stress that work environments can cause workers and the resultant spillover to their personal lives and families is usually ignored by our society and often denied by the individual in the face of the urgency to retain employment and help support one's family. Common expressions about work, such as "just be glad you have a job," implies one should not complain (especially about stress) and sums up both the hopelessness of current work life for many, as well as the attitude of a dominant culture more concerned with productivity than the well-being of its workforce. What we observe is that the nature of work and the social contract underpinning work—that is, the idea that a good-faith effort to work will be met by safe working conditions and some kind of comparable reward and/or employment security—are changing rapidly without debate or vote, undermining our democracy. These changes threaten a key aspect of a "good society"[4] (see chapter 1): that people are entitled to work in conditions that are safe, not harmful to their health, and that they are fairly rewarded for their work.

During the last 25 years, new systems of work organization have been introduced by employers throughout the industrialized world in order to improve productivity, product quality, and profitability, and they have been in part responsible for the increase in job stress. Such efforts have taken a variety of forms and names, including lean production (also called Japanese Production Management (JPM)), total quality management (TQM), quick turnaround, just-in-time, cellular or modular manufacturing, and high performance work organization. These new management practices have been praised by some but frequently criticized by others [26] as quite inadequate reforms of the traditional assembly-line approach to job design (e.g., "Taylorism"). Lean production tends to intensify work. All of these newly emerging management practices affect the organization of work and many generate psychosocial stressors that are as noxious to the health and well-being of workers as unseen chemical toxins. Paradoxically, while these new management practices claim to be far from the principles and practices of Taylorism with its inherent total control over workers, in reality, in most cases, things have changed very little in the degree and types of control that these management practices maintain over working people. The evidence presented in this book suggests that,

---

[4] While a healthy workplace is one aspect of a "good society," there are other elements we believe are crucial including adequate food, clothing, and health care, and the right to life, liberty, and the pursuit of happiness. The subject of what constitutes a "good society" is broad and warrants an essay of its own; herein our focus is on work.

rather than focusing on the individual worker as the primary place to put the blame for ill health *we must consider that working conditions determine the condition of workers.*

As working conditions deteriorate in part due to global competition, so too has the social fabric of supports provided by the government in the United States. Our governments over the last three decades have lacked the political desire or will, despite a clear consensus of U.S. citizens [27] to provide resources to ensure real social protection for all members of society (for example, health insurance for all, paid family leave, assurance of having at least a minimum income to house and feed one's family and to provide for retirement) and it lacks the vision to see how these social supports might improve working life, which in turn might contribute to social well-being, greater health, and a better society.

Stress and its health consequences are not an "individual problem" but a societal one; and specifically a problem related to the workplace. Responsibility for health is a shared social and societal process. A "good society" must pay attention to "upstream" or social causes of ill health rather than being content to leave most of the responsibility for ill health to overburdened individuals and their families. Our society holds that there is a democratic process by which we decide what resources will be devoted to protecting the public's health, including the health of workers, and providing health care to the most vulnerable, especially children, the elderly, and the poor. It is often the case today that politicians and lobbyists ignore the public's wishes and act to shape our laws for private gain, contributing to a breakdown in our democratic system. Today, in many areas of our public and private lives, the interests of the wealthy and powerful and their many supporters have won out over those of the middle-class, working-class, and poor. The lobbyists, politicians, and well-paid pundits who say "just be glad you have a job" often fail to recognize that beyond their short-term interests there are long-term costs to society and business, costs which will continue to mount if not recognized and acted upon.

GLOBALIZATION:
HOW IT CONTRIBUTES TO "NOXIOUS WORK"

A major premise of this book is that the processes of globalization and the changes it is creating in workplaces found in countries around the world are of major significance to U.S. workers because what occurs in distant countries is tied directly to changes in both work and the workplace in the United States. Global economic competition is promoting unhealthy work, in part, by drawing millions of people into unregulated and unprotected industrial labor markets in developing countries, exposing them to noxious work environments, and by inhibiting the kinds of important changes necessary to ensure a healthy work environment for working people throughout the world. As industrialization proceeds rapidly in the countries of South America, Southeast Asia, and more recently in China and India, millions of workers have migrated from rural areas to urban areas to become low-paid industrial wage workers or migrant construction workers in a sector lacking any form of protection (see chapter 2). Corporations with home bases in Western countries continue to rush to these new labor markets seeking ever cheaper labor and unregulated and unacceptable working conditions leading to what has been called a "race to the bottom." These new workers enter the lowest paying jobs where they frequently experience "noxious" working conditions for more hours per day and at far lower levels of pay than their Western counterparts. White-collar office work is also outsourced to developing countries where workers frequently face noxious work environments and a lack of employment security.

Motivated by and complementing the rapid economic changes in Asia and elsewhere are a series of changes in work and working conditions in the United States and in other Western countries that attempt to extend cost-cutting measures to all aspects of the organization of work as part of efforts to enhance productivity and earnings and to compete in the global marketplace. These changes have included:

1. A decline for many in autonomy and skill required for their jobs;
2. The outsourcing of labor to developing countries where the cost of labor is lower and the regulation of working conditions is minimal or nonexistent, with the consequence of a loss from the United States of high quality, well-paid blue-collar work and more recently information-processing service-sector work;
3. The "feminization" of the work force, particularly in low-income occupations, resulting in women being exposed disproportionately to noxious working conditions associated with low-paying jobs;
4. Increases in over- and underemployment and employment insecurity in the United States accompanied by increases in temporary, part-time, and flexible labor ("precarious employment");
5. A sharp increase in recent years in the gap in wealth and income levels between rich and poor.

These changes also reflect the dominance of *neoliberalism*, an economic and political ideology which maintains that free markets and free trade will produce the best outcome not only for economic growth but also for human welfare—and that the role of government needs to be greatly reduced. It is the ideology behind many of the changes brought about by globalization. Globalization is not, as many believe, just about free trade. Neoliberal policies and practices are reflected not only in the changing nature of work but also in the privatization of public services (for example, education, health care, pensions, labor market training services, social care for children and the elderly, prisons). Privatization undermines the social safety net promised by our democratic society founded on principles of equality and citizenship rights and represents another means of transferring wealth and resources from working people to corporate elites.

Neoliberal policies in the United States and worldwide amplify the impact of noxious working environments on our health and bear significant responsibility for the growing social and economic inequalities between rich and poor. Globalization and neoliberalism promote unhealthy work environments because the inherent philosophy and practices contribute to the growth of a "dispensable worker" and a growing imbalance of power between workers and employers.

The Centrality of Control

"Lean production" techniques, introduced in the United States by Toyota Motor Corporation in the 1980s, have been increasingly applied to both blue- and white-collar work leading frequently to unhealthy changes in the way work is organized. Fredrick Taylor, writing 100 years ago, was quite candid about the importance of control over the work process, and his desire to remove the control that skilled workmen had when he said, "The managers, assume . . . the burden of gathering together all of the traditional knowledge which in the past has been possessed by the workmen and then classifying, tabulating, and reducing this knowledge to rules, laws, and formulae . . . " [28]. Tracing the history of Taylor's "scientific management" in the twentieth century, Braverman argues that the scientific management movement has been primarily responsible for the shaping of modern corporations. Workers become virtually interchangeable and have little control over the work process as work becomes about mass-producing goods and services, requiring greater centralization, and the use of science and technology in the machines and procedures of a workplace. In addition, workers have little say over how work is organized except where workers have collective bargaining rights [29].

If workplace stressors are increasing in general (e.g., demands are increasing and control and autonomy at work are declining for many jobs), then the possibility of achieving healthy work is also declining. It is not surprising to find that the psychosocial stress measures described in chapters 6 and 7 tap into a general sense of powerlessness which has resulted from both historical and contemporary transformations of work. Virtually every identified psychosocial stressor that impacts health assesses control at some level of existence from the task level described in the Karasek Job Strain model to the global control over life direction inherent in Siegrist's Effort-Reward Imbalance model [30, 31]. A 1994 U.S. Departments of Labor and Commerce report found that "over 80% of American workers want a say in decisions affecting their jobs and how their work is performed" [32]. When workers have higher levels of autonomy, more control, and more say about their work, they are happier, healthier, and more productive [33]. This observation is well accepted by many managers who attempt to increase variety of skill usage through job rotation.

Collective Struggles for Control

The workplace, along with government and the courts, are the major locations where corporations and management come in active contact with workers and unions. All three social institutions are "contested terrain" where struggles between management and workers for control over work processes persist. As a consequence of these struggles, there is a dynamic ebb and flow of power relationships over the control of work. Sometimes these struggles have resulted in limitations and important exceptions to the intensification of work in the global economy, which suggests that work organization and corporations are therefore more flexible and changeable than some might imagine.

While work environments managed according to principles of workplace democracy, such as the Volvo Uddevalla plant or SEMCO enterprises in Brazil (see chapter 11), offer some possibility for a more autonomous, healthy working environment, the traditional method by which employees have influenced working conditions, including job stressors, is through the establishment of labor unions [34]. This is an example of the exercise of "collective control" [35], a strategy often utilized when prospects for exerting control individually at work are limited. Real differences in interests between management and workers often result in struggles at work. Working conditions at any moment in time reflect the competing needs of business and labor wherein each pursues its own separate agenda at the workplace; the former acts to maximize profitability and extract wealth from working people, while the latter struggles for its fair share and humane conditions at work.

Declining Unionization, Expanding Wealth, and Neoliberalism

In the United States, the proportion of employees who are members of labor unions has declined sharply in the last 40 years. Weakened unions have been unable to prevent employers from implementing aspects of "lean production," such as downsizing, outsourcing to low-wage suppliers, 24-hour operations, compressed work weeks, increased overtime, contract work, and workforce flexibility. Downsizing, excessive overtime, and long working hours can have dramatically negative effects on employee health. Such trends may help to explain increases in "time constraints" and workload demands reported in European and U.S. surveys over the last 30 years. The U.S. labor movement has also been unable to influence the enactment of legislation to improve psychosocial working conditions (i.e., reduce job strain), such as was achieved in Scandinavian countries, nor has it been able to prevent the decline in real income for workers in low socio-economic status categories [36, 37].

As globalization has proceeded, enormous wealth has been created worldwide, much of it concentrated in the hands of the owners of production. In the United States, during the last several decades, an enormous shift of wealth has occurred away from working people toward the wealthiest in America. The top 1% of Americans now control 40% of the wealth while the bottom 40% control less than 1% of the wealth in the United States [38], which is undoubtedly *not* consistent with the principles of the Declaration of Independence and the U.S. Constitution which hold that all men are created equal and are endowed with "inalienable rights . . . among these are life, liberty, and the pursuit of happiness." The increasing inequality of wealth is due in part to recent legal changes that have granted wealthy individuals and corporations enhanced tax savings through more regressive tax rates and favorable tax exemptions. The grossly unequal concentration of wealth into the hands of a very few has been accompanied by further changes in political and social power between classes in America which have, in turn, contributed to negative changes at the workplace and in society (see chapter 3). Observed changes include:

- An increasingly noxious and stressful workplace leading to a variety of mental and physical illnesses;
- An increasing tendency for work to invade private time with a blurring of work/family boundaries;
- Little or no increase in real income (after taking inflation into account) for most working people during the last 20 years;
- Increasing social inequality and poverty (for example, at least 20% of the U.S. population is without any health insurance) as more and more wealth is concentrated in the hands of fewer and fewer while more and more people come to occupy poorly paying and noxious jobs; and
- The imbalance of power between owners and workers is manifested in the fact that social policies are increasingly being influenced by special interest groups and corporations. Not only is there further degradation of work but there is also increasing corruption of our political system by corporate money, leading to weakened social protection and workers' rights, reduced legal rights to unionization, and lessened pension security, job safety and health, and access to health care.

This picture is somewhat reminiscent of America at the beginning of the nineteenth century: high levels of income inequality, political dominance by corporations, sweatshop labor, few unions, and a lack of rights on the job—a period known as the "Gilded Age." However, following the "great depression," many positive changes occurred as a result of the political reforms of the New Deal. Income inequality declined and remained much lower with the wealthy getting a smaller percentage of an increasing "pie" while working Americans saw unprecedented gains, in part due to strong unions, an increasing minimum wage, and a progressive tax system which helped limit inequality [39]. This period culminated in the 1960s with the expansion of higher education, the passage of the Civil Rights Act and Medicare, and finally in 1970 with the passage of OSHA. The period of relative political strength for working people ended in the late 1970s with increasing political conservatism and growing corporate power. Income inequality has now risen to its highest levels since the 1930s, lack of regulation of workplace, consumer, and environmental regulations has become the norm, and unions are at their weakest levels since the 1930s. A victim of these changes is an important aspect of our "good society's" sense of "fairness"—the slow disappearance of the "social contract" between employer and employee which promised a decent job with reasonable wages, a safe and healthy work environment, and employment security.

Much of what is said in the public media about social inequality is shaped by the influence of neoliberalism, the belief that the market is ultimately "good" for all. Recently Michael Yates observed that, "What is never said, because it cannot be said, is that inequality is a normal feature of capitalist economies, and growing inequality is a natural consequence of capitalism . . . " [40]. While the labor movement and its allies achieved many improvements for working people during the 1930s to early 1970s and continues to struggle for the good of working people, since the late 1970s in the United States it has been steadily losing ground. A politically weaker labor movement, as witnessed in the declining number of union members in the United States during the last 50 years, combined with a conservative shift in politics, and the growing influence of neoliberal economic and political policies, has led to a further worsening of working conditions and growing inequality.

In our society, government is supposed to act as a mediator between management and labor to minimize conflict and promote the social good. Laws can have a profound impact on the organization of work, including determining safety rules, staffing minimums, work-hour limits, whether contract bargaining will occur, and the likelihood of union representation. The legal system is empowered to interpret these laws and regulations. Yet in recent decades the laws that determine the form of the workplace in the United States have come to reflect increasingly the neoliberal ideology.

This leads us to a most important conclusion: efforts at reforms of the workplace must be a part of a broader effort to address the current fundamental imbalance of power between groups in society and at the workplace, as well as to challenge the dominance of neoliberalism as a political and economic ideology. Struggles around the workplace need to be in concert with struggles around tax reform (e.g., wealth redistribution), health insurance, the environment (e.g., sustainable development), and social and environmental justice at local, national, and global levels. Workplace change to improve worker health is an important part of broader social and economic struggles.

WHAT CHANGES ARE BEING MADE TO WORKING CONDITIONS AND WORKERS' HEALTH?

A major premise of this book is that globalization and neoliberalism have changed the nature of modern work and are promoting noxious working environments where working people are experiencing work intensification and increasingly precarious employment with little control over their employment situation. Part III of the book offers a snapshot of the kinds of efforts that are being made to improve working conditions. While unionization is declining and neoliberal policies are working against the promotion of legislation to improve psychosocial working conditions, chapters in Part III highlight the efforts (and the obstacles) made by diverse organizations to foster positive changes in the work environment.

A number of issues constitute important obstacles to change at the workplace, such as lack of knowledge about "noxious work," lack of statutory regulation and/or enforcement of existing regulations, and the diminishing influence of unions. In addition, a surprising finding emerged in the course of the research for this book, which was the discovery of a lack of common understanding among the various "stakeholders" (e.g., management, labor representatives, and academic researchers) when it came to the impact of "psychosocial stressors" and "work organization" on the health of workers. A profound lack of dialogue appears to act as a significant brake on change in this area. Deborah Gordon describes how she found that various stakeholders appear to speak the same language while in fact they do not, and that they lack a common understanding of terms (especially regarding job stress), experiences, approaches, and perceptions about the adverse effects of work organization today.

These problems, highlighted in chapter 10, are associated with the political and ideological struggle over the naming and recognition of work-related stress and illnesses, a central premise in the introduction of this book. How scientific knowledge gets taken up by different stakeholder groups, and counted as legitimate or dismissed, is a politically and economically driven process reflecting in part differences in power between labor and business. Business has a vested interest in locating the cause of ill health within individual workers, which may initially appear more cost-effective to deal with than changing business practices. While we encourage improved communication around the meaning of "psychosocial stressors" and "work organization" between the different stakeholder groups (e.g., labor, management, and researchers), we also recognize that structural obstacles (e.g., global competitiveness) may inhibit management from seriously considering improvements to work organization.

So What is Healthy Work?

Similar to the principle of the World Health Organization that *health is more than the absence of disease* is the realization that a healthy workplace and *healthy work will require more than the absence of noxious workplace psychosocial stressors* or shorter work weeks. People need to perceive that their skills are being used on the job, that they have a say in how their job is done, and that the work demands placed upon them are reasonable and fair. But beyond these specific needs regarding job characteristics, the achievement of healthy work requires that working people be treated with respect and not as objects and that their interests and needs are taken into account in decision-making concerning work and the workplace. We all need to treat each other respectfully at work and we need a concept of respectful work, which provides a clear understanding of the role and responsibilities each of us has at work. For workers at any level of a hierarchy not to be involved in and able to influence decision-making is to treat them as children and is disrespectful of workers' knowledge, competencies, and experience [41].

Beyond feeling respected at our job we must also feel reasonably secure and not live in fear that we will be fired without cause or notice. Most importantly, we must believe that our employer takes every reasonable precaution to protect the health and safety of employees and that s/he has a genuine concern for the well-being of employees. Ultimately, in a "good society," we would all feel that our work is valued, has purpose, and contributes to the greater social good.

Are Workplace-Based Interventions Successful?

In approaching the issue of implementation of interventions to improve working conditions, we acknowledge that the vision of healthy work defined above is not shared by all stakeholders. Some employers see worker health as a costly deterrent to maximum productivity and financial profit, while others have a commitment to healthy workers but not necessarily healthy workplaces. Many employers are caught in a contradiction between the need for productivity, which requires healthy working people, and the need for cost-cutting and more efficient work environments, which may negatively impact the health of workers. For people to be healthy, both physically and mentally, they must enjoy job security, decent working conditions with control over work processes and other conditions, all of which are costly to businesses and could mean less opportunity for owners and managers to extract economic value from working people. On the other hand, we recognize that many workers and even some unions place a healthy workplace lower down the list of priorities these days after such issues as job security and wages (see chapter 10).

What progress has there been toward achieving a healthier workplace in the United States? Work organization change interventions have been achieved using varied approaches (see chapter 11). Part III of this book revealed that successful approaches to changing and improving work organization employ three elements: 1) they draw from the existing body of scientific knowledge about the workplace; 2) they rely on the principle of cooperative action—innovative collaborations between unions and researchers allow the collective voice of workers to identify improvements to be made to their work environments and then utilize existing collective bargaining agreements or labor management committees to implement workplace change; and 3) they introduce changes at the workplace designed to improve health and productivity.

Chapters 13 and 14 describe Participatory Action Research (PAR) efforts by unions to mobilize their membership to voice their health and safety concerns and to make changes to working conditions. Researcher-labor collaborations can be an effective and important mechanism to give voice to often invisible issues like psychosocial stressors and work organization and demonstrate how research findings can be combined with union efforts to achieve work organization change. Efforts to improve workplace health and safety can be effective and go well beyond the individual level to the organization of work itself. PAR offers key insights for academic researchers interested in collaborative methodologies to produce scientific knowledge that can "carry" change into the workplace (see chapter 12). The Maintenance Cooperation Trust Fund (MCTF), described by its director Lilia Garcia (see chapter 15), demonstrates another powerful and innovative technique to bring about workplace change by engaging businesses' own self-interests to support improvements in working conditions for janitorial workers. This intervention strategy had participating businesses and the union (SEIU) contributing to a trust fund (created under the Taft-Hartley Act) whose purpose was to "level the playing field" by ensuring that non-signatory companies were held in compliance with fair business practices.

Taking a big picture view, successful interventions have been relatively few and far between, particularly in the United States, and appear to remain workplace-based except where a national or international trade union is involved, or a strong coalition of interests exists, in which case broader policy changes can and have been achieved. Notwithstanding, the need for *both* strong statutory regulation and strong collective voice cannot be over-emphasized.

Reforms take place in a social context and reflect the relative power between social classes and groups within a society. In the United States, with its great imbalance of power between corporations and workers, change is difficult and even laws already on the books go un-enforced. One such example is the 1970 OSH Act, enforcement of which under the Bush administration has become based on "voluntary compliance." While new laws governing workplace hazards are undoubtedly needed, enforcement of the laws we already have is crucial to protect the health of working people.

As pointed out by Deborah Gordon in chapter 10, the vast majority of working people, employers, politicians, and even public health professionals, remain ill-informed about the need for serious changes in the organization of work to maintain and promote workers' health in today's globalized, intensified world of work. Additionally, they are also ill-informed about the types of interventions demonstrated to achieve sustainable results, *and* about the various costs of inaction. Parentetically, we observe that businesses routinely implement changes in work organization intended to enhance the productivity and profitability of their enterprises. Unfortunately, these changes are all too frequently uninformed by knowledge of their health consequences. While the costs involved in changing work organization may affect the "bottom line," the costs of rising health insurance premiums and lost productivity from ill workers may outstrip the costs of changing business practices. As a society, we should not stand by and allow the organization of work to detrimentally affect the health and well-being of our family, friends, and co-workers. In Western Europe, due to stronger labor movements and political parties that represent the interests of working people, research evidence has been translated into national policies aimed at creating healthy work environments by restricting psychosocial stressors, long work hours, and ensuring paid vacation time. Policy-makers in the United States need to follow suit.

A better understanding of the relationship between work and health on the part of all stakeholders is critical to the success of efforts to create healthier work environments. Additionally, a commitment to a healthier workplace will require initial capital expenditures by businesses and our society to improve working conditions which will pay for themselves in the long run in the form of healthier workers, greater productivity, and lower health care costs.

WHAT CAN BE DONE? RESEARCH AND POLICY PRIORITIES TO ACHIEVE A HEALTHY WORKPLACE IN THE TWENTY-FIRST CENTURY

Steps to improve conditions of work require action on several different fronts. First, we need a better understanding of the problem that is "noxious work" and a greater recognition on the part of all stakeholders that all working conditions, including "noxious work," are the results of human planning (or lack thereof) and as such are changeable. This recognition can be accomplished, in part, through further research with particular emphasis on distinguishing between healthy or unhealthy working conditions in collaboration with workers and companies. Research priorities include a need for a better understanding of:

- The specific dimensions of healthy and unhealthy jobs;
- An examination of the productivity of collective work vs. "lean production" systems;
- The effectiveness of interventions at the workplace;
- A clearer understanding of how working conditions and productivity go together and how they produce illness when they are in conflict;
- A clearer understanding of the relationships between social class, gender, and race relative to specific working conditions and especially regarding exposure to physical and psychosocial hazards; and
- The costs of unhealthy working conditions to business and society in general.

Second, we need better identification of the scope of the work-related health problems, which can be accomplished by surveillance at the workplace. Identified workplace exposures (e.g., job strain, effort-reward imbalance, emotional labor, etc.) and negative health outcomes need to be monitored at the workplace. Occupational health experts from Europe, Japan, and the United States called in 1998 in the Tokyo Declaration for a program of "surveillance at individual workplaces and monitoring at national and regional levels in order to identify the extent of work-related stress, health problems, and to provide baselines against which to evaluate efforts at amelioration" [41]. They recommended that "workplaces assess both workplace stressors and health outcomes known to result from such exposures [e.g., hypertension] on an annual basis" [42].

In addition to researchers, businesses and governments must also do their part to carry out surveillance within workplaces and occupations and document the associations between work organization and health. Employers must recognize that these illnesses and their costs are caused by their own business practices and take steps to remedy the root causes. Since many large companies require annual physical exams and collect a great deal of relevant health data, it should be a relatively simple task to enter this information into a database and make it available to those concerned with worker health. Appropriate precautions to protect employee confidentiality must always be observed [43].

Third, we need more and better efforts at workplace change carried out collectively between workers, researchers, and management. Work sites identified through surveillance to be at high risk for burnout, depression, or CVD, for example, could be targeted for interventions using a PAR approach described by Ellen Rosskam in chapter 12. "Primary prevention" interventions would focus on creating a healthy workplace. For example, high strain (high demands and low control) jobs could be redesigned to provide greater levels of employee decision-making authority and skill discretion and workloads that are more realistic, compatible with human capacity, and with the input of workers performing specific jobs. Since the workplace appears to be a "leverage point" with regard to many risk factors for illness, including standard CVD risk factors [18], such interventions could have the additional benefit of lowering these risk factors. Intervention efforts in workplaces need to take seriously the effects of work on the mental health of employees and go beyond simple *secondary* intervention programs of stress management, which locate the solution within the individual, to adjust the way work is organized and to focus on *primary* prevention. Just as the connections between work and health are multiple, so too must be the efforts toward change. Part III of this book presents promising case studies of change in working conditions that point the way to the possibilities and the multiple avenues that can and must be taken.

Fourth, we need social policies that recognize that unhealthy workplaces result, in part, from the current imbalance in power between working people and management. One step toward achieving a greater balance of power would involve the enforcement of the regulations that are already the "law of the land" in an even-handed and fair manner. They would include enforcement of current statutes such as the OSH Act. An OSHA Ergonomics standard that was put into effect in 2000 and repealed in 2001 under the then-new Bush Administration had guidelines for controlling work stressors as a strategy for reducing musculoskeletal disorders. The current California ergonomics regulation states that ". . . employers shall consider engineering controls . . . and administrative controls, such as job rotation, work pacing or work breaks" [44]. It would also be an important step toward balancing power between management and labor if unionization and collective bargaining were encouraged through interpretation and enforcement of current regulations by government agencies such as the National Labor Relations Board (NLRB). As one example, the NLRB has a long history of pro-management decisions impacting on the workplace, evidenced by the 2005 ruling upholding an employer's rule against employees fraternizing with each other—on or off the premises, a ruling seen by labor as an impingement on the right to organize [45].

Fifth, we need new regulations that will discourage the worst forms of work organization and psychosocial stressors. Japan and much of Western Europe have taken the lead in passing legislation making certain forms of work stress illegal and mandating healthy work. An example is the *Swedish Work Environment Act (Act No. 677, amended in 1991)* [46].

Achieving healthy working conditions will require:

1. Legislation to reduce workplace psychosocial hazards and risks to health;
2. Legislation and standards that support equity for women and minority populations;
3. Limits on legal hours of work per week;
4. Workers' compensation boards to sufficiently recognize and compensate repetitive strain injuries, mental health problems related to work stressors, overload, family-work conflicts, and chronic diseases such as hypertension related to exposure to psychosocial stressors; and
5. Provision of mechanisms for the self-employed to attain healthy working conditions.

These regulations need to be international in scope with an enforcement mechanism to protect countries and companies from being victimized by non-compliers, and from a competitive disadvantage if companies try and save costs by moving operations to countries with the lowest wages and worst working conditions. Essentially, we need legal statutes with effective enforcement that require companies to apply the same stringent protections in their practices overseas as required of them in the United States.

Sixth, we need laws and regulations that make employment less precarious and to improve the social safety net so that workers will not feel forced to keep a hazardous job simply because s/he needs the health insurance, or because there is no job security and would fear being fired if they raised any complaints.

Seventh, we need laws and regulations that encourage autonomy and involvement at both work and in the community and which will encourage ordinary citizens to be more active participants in the life of our country. There are many steps needed to encourage active participation by members of society but three in particular would appear most helpful:

1. Laws and regulations that remove the current obstacles to joining unions.
2. Limiting the work week and/or overtime to allow for greater social participation.
3. Election laws that make it easier for people to participate in government (e.g., elections held on a day without work).

Eighth, we need to increase the availability of work, improve the adequacy of income from work, and have work schedules and policies that help workers balance work and their personal or family needs and responsibilities [47].

HEALTHY WORKPLACES AND BEYOND

Reducing the risk that working people will be exposed to "noxious work" begins with the recognition that the organization of work can be changed. The recommendations we have outlined above are only the "front line of defense" against work-induced illness. Identifying and recognizing work-related illness is in itself a political and economic struggle. Associating work-related physical and mental illness with psychosocial stressors in the work organization requires going beyond research studies and the academic world to developing collaborative partnerships with labor and management.

In direct contradiction to building healthier work environments are unregulated economic markets. Unfettered capitalism makes it almost impossible for companies driven to compete in a global economy to truly invest in necessary changes to work practices to alleviate psychosocial stressors, promote healthy work, or to ensure economic security for workers. It is this broader economic perspective that leads us to recommend that change in work organization must be accompanied by broader social and economic changes. It requires recognition by corporations and governments that unregulated globalization is socially destructive and that greater efforts by labor unions working together internationally are necessary to confront the forces of globalization. The latter is already occurring increasingly [48].

While some employers and businesses are paying heed to the call for healthier *workers*, it is apparent that this concern may not extend to healthy *workplaces*. Work organization is still "off the radar screen" of corporate health and safety concerns (see chapter 13) as many companies have yet to realize the importance of "investing" in healthier workplaces. However, some employers, responding to their own economic self-interest, are working with labor to "equalize the playing field." An example is that corporations in the custodial services industry are making economic contributions to support MCTF's efforts to improve working conditions and the economic security of janitors who lack any "collective voice representation" (such as a union). When the "bottom line" is affected, business is more responsive. We strongly encourage employers, businesses, and those in company health and safety to focus on the health of workers by creating healthier workplaces through changes in work organization, and we have demonstrated that it is in their economic interests to do so (see chapter 9).

Efforts to create a healthy workplace must go hand in hand with efforts to reduce social and income inequality that divides working populations and the larger American society by gender, race, and ethnicity. Likewise, international efforts, including labor organizing, need to continue along with and as part of social and environmental justice movements to allow for sustainable development in developing countries and in transitional economies. For these movements to be successful, however—and they must be, both for the health of working people around the world and for the environmental health of the planet—the United States must show a commitment to join with other industrialized countries to enforce its existing national policies and laws, to observe international laws, and to create new legislation that shows its commitment to the development of a "good society."

We recognize, unfortunately, that these steps by themselves do not fully address the need for work environments that are responsive to the human needs for dignity, creativity, and a sense of worth; that go beyond simply limiting "noxious work" to promoting health and well-being [49]. Designing work that promotes health will require the collective participation of workers in improving the work environment and requires at the very least, as a first step, clearer communication and renewed commitment between all stakeholder groups, including labor and management, to promoting the principles of a "good society." Ultimately, a "good" society has greater equality, is a healthier society, one where people feel safer, where there is less fear, where there are fewer threats to well-being, and where human potential can be unleashed to its fullest. Let us not forget, as pointed out by Erich Fromm 50 years ago, that ". . . economy must become the servant for the development of man. Capital must serve labor; things must serve life" [50, p. 8].

REFERENCES

1. APA News Release, Stress a Major Health Problem in the U.S., Warns APA: New Poll Shows Stress on the Rise, Affecting Health, Relationships and Work Americans Say Housing Costs an Added Stressor in 2007, October 24, 2007.

2. Robertson-Blackmore E., S. A. Stansfeld, I. Weller, S. Munce, B. M. Zagorski, and D. E. Stewart, Major Depressive Episodes and Work Stress: Results from a National Population Survey, *American Journal of Public Health,* 97:11, pp. 2088-2093, 2007.

3. Aboa-Eboule, C. E., Strain and Risk of Recurrent Coronary Events, *Journal of the American Medical Association,* 298:14, pp. 1652-1660, 2007.

4. Orth-Gomer, K., Editorial: Job Strain and Risk of Recurrent Coronary Events, *Journal of the American Medical Association,* 298:14, pp. 1693-1694, 2007.

5. Cho, E., Workforce Competitiveness in a Global Economy, in *American and Finnish Chambers of Commerce in Finland, Helsinki, Finland,* Helsinki, Finland, 2007.

6. U.S. Department of Labor, Bureau of the Labor Statistics. Productivity Change in the Manufacturing Sector, 1987-2006, 2007.

7. KILM, *Hours of Work,* International Labor Organization, Geneva, Switzerland, 2007.

8. Workers' Health International, *Workers' Health International Newsletter (WHIN),* January-June:55, 1999.

9. Lee, S., D. Mc Cann, and J. C. Messenger, *Working Time around the World: Trends in Working Hours, Laws, and Policies in a Global Comparative Perspective,* Routledge and ILO, London and Geneva, 2007.

10. Robinson, J., *Work to Live,* Penguin Grove, New York, 2003.

11. Jacobs, J. A., K. Gerson, *The Time Divide,* Harvard University Press, Boston, MA, 2004.

12. Mishel, L. and J. Bernstein, *The State of Working America,* Economic Policy Institute, Washington, DC, 1998.

13. Dones, N. and N. Firestein, Labor's Participation in Work Family Issues: Successes and Obstacles, in *Learning from the Past—Looking to the Future,* Beem, C. and J. Heymann (eds.), The Work, Family and Democracy Project, Racine, WI, 2002.

14. National Institute for Occupational Safety and Health, *Stress . . . At Work,* NIOSH, Cincinnati, OH, 1999.

15. Ragland, D., M. A. Winkelby, J. Schwalbe, et al., Prevalence of Hypertension in Bus Drivers, *International Journal of Epidemiology,* 16, pp. 208-214, 1987.

16. Robins, T., M. Hugentobler, M. Kaminski, and S. Klitzman, Implementation of the Federal Hazard Communication Standard: Does Training Work?, *Journal of Occupational Medicine,* 32:11, pp. 1133-1140, 1990.

17. Columbia University's Mailman School of Public Health, Largest Survey on Depression Suggests Higher Prevalence in *U.S. Science Daily:* Retrieved November 19, 2007, from http://www.sciencedaily.com/releases/2005/10/051027084249.htm, 2005.

18. Schnall, P., K. Belkic, P. A. Landsbergis, and D. Baker, The Workplace and Cardiovascular Disease, in *Occupational Medicine: State-of-the-Art Reviews,* Hanley and Belfus, Philadelphia, PA, 2000.

19. Ahola, K., T. Honkonen, M. Kivimaki, et al., Contribution of Burnout to the Association between Job Strain and Depression: The Health 2000 Study, *Journal of Occupational and Environmental Medicine,* 48:10, pp. 1023-1030, 2006.

20. Landsbergis, P. A., P. Schnall, K. Warren, T. Pickering, and J. Schwartz, *The Effect of Job Strain on Ambulatory Blood Pressure in Men: Does It Vary by Age, Hypertensive Status, Social Support or Socioeconomic Status?,* in Psychosocial Factors at Work Conference 1998, Copenhagen, Denmark.

21. McKinlay, J., A Case for Refocusing Upstream: The Political Economy of Illness, in *Patients, Physicians and Illness: A Sourcebook in Behavioral Science and Health,* Gartley, J. (ed.), Free Press, New York, pp. 9-25, 1979.

22. Waldron, I., M. Nowatarski, M. Freimer, J. P. Henry, N. Post, and C. Witten, Cross-Cultural Variation in Blood Pressure: A Qualitative Analysis of the Relationship of

Blood Pressure to Cultural Characteristics, Salt Consumption and Body Weight, *Social Science and Medicine,* 16, pp. 419-430, 1982.

23. Schnall, P. L. and R. Kern, Hypertension in American Society: An Introduction to Historical Materialist Epidemiology, in *The Sociology of Health and Illness: Critical Perspectives,* Conrad, P. and R. Kern (eds.), St. Martin's Press, New York, pp. 97-122, 1981.

24. Sterling, P., *Principles of Allostasis: Optimal Design, Predictive Regulation, Pathophysiology, and Rational Therapeutic,* Schulkin, J. (ed.), Cambridge University Press, Massachusetts, 2004.

25. McEwen, B. S., Protective and Damaging Effects of Stress Mediators, *The New England Journal of Medicine,* 338:3, pp. 171-179, 1998.

26. Parker, M. and J. Slaughter, *Working Smart,* Labor Education and Research Project, Detroit, MI, 1994.

27. The Pew Research Center, *Trends in Political Values and Core Attitudes: 1987-2007,* Pew Institute, Washington, DC, 2007.

28. Taylor, F., *The Principles of Scientific Management,* Private Printing, Harper Bros., New York, 1911.

29. Braverman, H., *Labor and Monopoly Capital: The Degradation of Work in the Twentieth Century,* Monthly Review Press, New York, 1998.

30. Siegrist, J., Sociological Concepts in the Etiology of Chronic Disease: The Case of Ischemic Heart Disease, *Social Science & Medicine,* 22:2, pp. 247-253, 1986.

31. Siegrist, J., D. Klein, and K. H. Voigt, Linking Sociological with Physiological Data: The Model of Effort-Reward Imbalance at Work, *Acta Physiologica Scandinavica,* 161, pp. 112-116, 1997.

32. U.S. Departments of Labor and Commerce, *Fact Finding Report. Commission on the Future of Worker-Management Relations,* US Departments of Labor and Commerce, Washington, DC, pp. 37, 50, 52, 1994.

33. Freeman, R. B. and J. Rogers, *What Workers Want,* ILR Press, Ithaca, NY, 2006.

34. Landsbergis, P. A. and J. Cahill, Labor Union Programs to Reduce or Prevent Occupational Stress in the United States, *International Journal of Health Services,* 24, pp. 105-129, 1994.

35. Johnson, J. V., Collective Control: Strategies for Survival in the Workplace, *International Journal of Health Services,* 19:3, pp. 469-480, 1989.

36. Weinberg, D., *A Brief Look at Postwar U.S. Income Inequality,* U.S. Census Bureau, Current Population Reports, Washington, DC, 1996.

37. Wolff, E., *Top Heavy: A Study of Wealth Inequality in America,* Twentieth Century Fund Press, New York, 1995.

38. Davies, J. B., S. Sandstrom, and A. Shorrocks, *The World Distribution of Household Wealth,* Department of Economics University of Western Ontario, London, Canada, 2006.

39. Krugman, P., *Conscience of a Liberal,* W. W. Norton and Company, Inc., New York, January 2009.

40. Yates, M., More Unequal: Aspects of Class in the U.S., in *Monthly Review,* 59:6, New York, 2007.

41. Rosskam, E., *Excess Baggage: Leveling the Load and Changing the Workplace,* Baywood, Amityville, NY, 2007.

42. The Tokyo Declaration, *Journal of the Tokyo Medical University,* 56:6, pp. 760-767, 1998.

43. Stokols, D., K. R. Pelletier, and J. E. Fielding, Integration of Medical Care and Worksite Health Promotion, *Journal of the American Medical Association,* 273:14, pp. 1136-1142, 1995. Available at: hr.blr.com.news.aspx?id=16351

44. California Government, *California Code of Regulations, Title 8, Section 1510. Repetitive Motion Injuries*, in *8, Section 1510*, http://www.dir.ca.gov/title8/5110.html
45. Guardsmark LLC, *344 NLRB No. 97 (2005)*, National Labour Relations Board, 2005, available from: http://hr.blr.com/news.aspx?id=16351
46. Swedish Working Environment Act, *Amending the Working Environment Act (No. 1160 of 1977)*, in *1160 of 1977* (Svensk författningssamling, 17 June 1991, No. 677, p. 115.) Sweden, 1991.
47. Polanyi, M., Employment and Working Conditions: A Response, in *presentation given at The Social Determinants of Health Across the Life-Span Conference*, Toronto, 2002.
48. Bronfenbrenner, K., *Global Unions: Challenging Transnational Capital through Cross-Border Campaigns (Frank W. Pierce Memorial Lectureship and Conference Series)*, Cornell University, New York, 2007.
49. Schnall, P., K. Belkic, P. A. Landsbergis, and D. Baker, Why the Workplace and Cardiovascular Disease? *Occupational Medicine: State of the Art Reviews*, 15:1, pp. 1-5, 2000.
50. Fromm, E., Freedom in the Work Situation, in *Labor in a Free Society*, Harrington M. and P. Jacobs (eds.), University of California Press, Berkeley and Los Angeles, 1959.

Contributors

Ray Antonio is a former bus driver who began his career with the San Francisco MUNI and was first hired as a bus driver in January of 1974. Subsequently, he became a full-time union representative, recording secretary, executive Vice President, and finally President of the Transport Workers' Union Local 250A which represents bus drivers in San Francisco retiring as president in 2002. Ray played an active role in developing the SF Bus Driver Project and actively encouraged collaboration between the TWU and the SF MTA.

Dr. Dean Baker is a Professor of Clinical Medicine and the Director of the Center for Occupational and Environmental Health at U.C. Irvine. He is also the Director of the Preventive Medicine-Occupational Medicine Residency Program. He has been actively involved in research on occupational stressors for 30 years including collaborative research with Dr. Robert Karasek and colleagues at Columbia University in 1980 on job strain and CVD. He is a co-editor of *Workplace and Cardiovascular Disease* (Hanley and Belfus, 2000) and has published numerous papers on work stress and health outcomes.

Mike Casey was elected President of the Hotel Employees & Restaurant Employees Union, Local 2 in May 1994. He was elected in 2001 as an H.E.R.E. International Vice President. Mr. Casey previously worked for Local 2 as a Union Representative and Director of Organizing for 8 years. He formerly served as a Union Representative and Organizer for the Communications Workers of America, Farm Labor Organizing Committee, and the California School Employees Association. Mike is also a former member of the Newspaper Guild and the Irish Transport and General Workers Union.

Dr. Marnie Dobson is a Research Associate in the Center for Occupational and Environmental Health at the University of California, Irvine and Associate Director of the Center for Social Epidemiology in Venice, California. She received her Ph.D. in Social Science from the Department of Sociology at the University of California, Irvine. Her research interests are gender and work, emotional labor, and work organization/psychosocial stressors and mental health outcomes. She has published in a number of peer-reviewed interdisciplinary journals bridging qualitative, ethnographic methods, and quantitative survey methods and is currently

351

collaborating with colleagues Dr. Peter Schnall, Dr. Paul Landsbergis, and Dr. Deborah Gordon and Dr. Maritza Jauregui on a number of ongoing projects, including this book.

Dr. June Fisher is a Clinical Professor of Medicine in the University of California Division of Occupational and Environmental Medicine. She has played a prominent role in establishing the importance of work stress as a risk factor for hypertension among bus drivers having conducted research for 30 years as director of the SF MUNI Bus Driver Project. In collaboration with SF Municipal Bus Drivers and the SF Municipal Transit Authority (MTA) she has led in developing innovative interventions for reducing occupational stress among bus drivers including the Ambassador Program.

Dr. John Frank was a Scholar (beginning in 1987), and then a Fellow (since 1991) with the Canadian Institute for Advanced Research Population Health Program, and is a Professor at the University of Toronto Department of Public Health Sciences. As a physician-epidemiologist, with special expertise in prevention, his main area of interest is the biopsychosocial determinants of health status at the population level. He was the founding Director of Research at the Institute for Work & Health in Toronto from 1991 until 1997, and is currently a Senior Scientist there. In December 2000, he was appointed Inaugural Scientific Director of the Canadian Institutes of Health Research (CIHR)—Institute of Population and Public Health (IPPH), located at the University of Toronto. As one of 13 CIHR Institutes across the country, IPPH's mandate is to study the full range of determinants of health, and systematically apply that knowledge to improve population health status, both in Canada and globally.

Lilia García is the executive director of the Maintenance Cooperation Trust Fund (MCTF), a janitorial watchdog organization that investigates janitorial contractors for employment law violations. Under Lilia's leadership the young organization has grown, establishing offices in Los Angeles, Orange County, and San Diego. Lilia was born and raised in unincorporated East Los Angeles, she is the fourth daughter of Guillermina Corrales Garcia and Manuel Flores García. Her family settled in East Los Angeles from northern Mexico in 1956. Coming from a working class immigrant family, Lilia has a personal passion for strengthening workplace protections.

Deborah R. Gordon is a medical anthropologist who has conducted anthropological research in health care settings since 1970, in the United States, Israel, and since 1984, in Italy. Trained in anthropology and medical anthropology at UC Berkeley and UCSF, she is currently an adjunct professor in the Department of Anthropology, History, and Medicine at UC San Francisco teaching courses in medical anthropology at UC Berkeley and UCSF. In 2001, Dr. Gordon began ethnographic research on hospital workers as part of a larger study of gradients of health. In 2002, she was awarded a grant from the NIH Human Genome Institute to conduct "community engagement" process in a Tuscan town in Italy for the International Haplotype Map project. In 2003 she began research with Professor Peter Schnall at the Center for Occupational and Environmental Health at UC Irvine and the Center for Social Epidemiology with opinion leaders around work and health

n California, which lead to the organization of a California Forum on "The Way
We Work and Its Impact on our Health" and this volume.

Dr. Maritza Jauregui is an Assistant Professor of Public Health at Richard
Stockton College of New Jersey. She received her Ph.D. from the University of
California Irvine. Her research and teaching interests are in environmental health,
occupational health, health disparities, wellness, and traditional healing systems.
Dr. Jauregui was an original presenter and organizer at the California Forum
"The Way We Work and Its Impact on our Health" and she has published
numerous publications with colleagues Dr. Peter Schnall, Dr. Paul Landsbergis,
and Dr. Mamie Dobson.

Dr. Paul Landsbergis is Associate Professor in the Department of Community
and Preventive Medicine, Mount Sinai School of Medicine, New York. He is
the co-editor of the textbook *The Workplace and Cardiovascular Disease,* and a
co-author of recent review articles on job strain and cardiovascular disease, and
on interventions to reduce job stress and improve health. Dr. Landsbergis was a
member of the National Research Council's Committee on the Health and Safety
Needs of Older Workers and the National Institute for Occupational Safety and
Health Intervention Effectiveness Research Team.

Dr. Chrisy Moutsatsos is an Assistant Professor in Anthropology and Women's
Studies at Iowa State University. She teaches and publishes on the topics of
gender, consumption, and globalization. She is currently working on a manuscript
entitled, "Global Gaze, Local Bodies: An Ethnographic Account of Consumption
and Femininity in Urban Greece," to be published by Duke University Press.

Dr. Ellen Rosskam is a Policy Scholar at the Woodrow Wilson International
Center for Scholars, Visiting Senior Fellow at the University of Surrey, European
Institute of Health and Medical Sciences and Visiting Professor at the University of
Massachusetts, Lowell, Work Environment Department. She is a public health and
social protection specialist. Her latest book, *Excess Baggage: Leveling the Load
and Changing the Workplace* (2007), is available from Baywood, Amityville, New
York. Contact: eerosskam@yahoo.com

Dr. Peter L. Schnall is an active researcher and expert on the role of occupational
stress in causing hypertension and cardiovascular disease. He is a Clinical Professor
of Medicine at the UC Irvine Division of Occupational and Environmental Medicine
where he directs the Center's program in work organization and cardiovascular
disease. Dr. Schnall is the lead editor of *The Workplace and Cardiovascular Disease*
(Hanley and Belfus, 2000) the standard textbook in this field. Dr. Schnall is also
the Director of a non-profit foundation, the Center for Social Epidemiology, based
in Venice, California whose purpose is to educate the public about the health
consequences of work stress.

Dr. Peter Smith is a researcher at the Institute for Work & Health in Toronto,
Canada. His major research interests are in the changing nature of work in Canada
and other developed countries and the impact of these changes on the health
of workers. In particular he is interested in how these changes affect particular
sub-groups of labor force participants (e.g., particular occupational groups, women,
and recent immigrants).

Dr. Stephen Smith is a member of Brunel University's Business School in the United Kingdom, of the Centre for Research in Emotion Work (CREW) and of the Working with Emotions Network (EMNET), which has convened several conferences and workshops in emotions subject-matter. He edits the *International Journal of Work Organisation and Emotion*. At present he is conducting an evaluation of a placement scheme for probationary police officers (for Kent Constabulary); exploring the links between emotion and local authority as found across a range of public/private forums made up of local officials, politicians, citizen-groups, and economic notables, and collaborating with Dr. Rosskam and the ITF to explore conditions of labor among air transport workers.

Dr. Haiou Yang is an Associate Specialist in the Center for Occupational and Environmental Health, University of California Irvine. She received her doctoral degree in sociology from the University of Hawaii. Her research covers a wide range of areas, including work stress and cardiovascular health, racial and ethnic health disparities, children's environmental health, risk communications for infectious diseases, health status of people exposed to pesticides, disability and rehabilitation, and population dynamics and political cultures of China. She has published her work in various journals, such as *Hypertension, Social Biology, American Journal of Public Health, Journal of Disability Policy Studies,* and *Journal of Cross-Cultural Gerontology*.

Dr. Edward Yelin is a Professor of Medicine and Health Policy at the University of California, San Francisco. His research is concerned with the impact of changes in work and in the economy at large on employment among persons with chronic disease and disability. Dr. Yelin is the author of over 200 articles, editorials, and books and is an elected member of the National Academy of Social Insurance.

Index

358 / UNHEALTHY WORK

Delta Airlines, 27
Demand, job. *See* Job strain
Demand-control model, 43-46, 123
Democracy in the workplace/worker
ownership, 200-201
Denmark, 47, 74, 175, 202-203, 292
Depersonalization, 115
Depression, 101, 114-116, 120-121, 331
See also Mental health, impact of work
on
Deregulation of health and safety, 92
Diabetes. *See* Race/ethnicity and
work/health in California
Disability, worker, 5-6, 156-160
Disease etiology,
political/economic/cultural dimensions
of work-related, 9-11
See also Cardiovascular disease;
Interventions to reduce stress and
improve work organization/worker
health; Mental health, impact of
work on
Dispossession, accumulation by, 50-51
Dobson, Marnie, 87, 171, 351-352
Downsizing, 1, 27, 92, 95, 125, 154,
201, 251, 338

Eastman Kodak, 27
Economic Security for a Better World, 24
Educational level of labor force, 68-69
Effort-reward imbalance (ERI)
adverse impact on health, 333
blood pressure, 98
cardiovascular disease, 2, 94, 95, 100
control, the centrality of, 337
defining terms, 8
hotel workers' injuries,
organizing/collaborating to reduce,
258
hypertension, 7
mental health, impact of work on,
121-122, 126
social class and work/health inequalities,
46, 47
surveillance, workplace, 344
United Kingdom, 120
workplace characteristics *vs.* employee
emotions, 174-175

Elder abuse, 301
Emotional labor
commission on the conditions of, 308
common interest between client and
provider, 301-305
co-presence, 300-301
defining terms, 117
happiness and experiences *vs.* consumer
durables, 309-310
home-work connections, 309
job and employee focused, 123
mental health, impact of work on,
122-124, 127
overview, 299-300
prejudice both parties, conditions which,
301
rebalancing work and life, 309-310
screw-you ethics, 305
service sector, 127, 333
support, institutional back, 305-306
thought experiment: improvements clear
to time-travelers, 306-308
workplace characteristics *vs.* employee
emotions, 174-175
Emotions as responses to power/status
differentials, 100
Employee Assistance Programs (EAPs),
126, 183
Employee ownership, 200-201
Employee stock option plans (ESOPs), 200
Employment insecurity, 5
Energy efficient technologies, 25
Environmental Health and Safety (EHS)
managers, 182-183
Ergonomics, 193-194, 345
Essential hypertension, 90
Ethnic minority groups. *See* Race/ethnicity
and work/health in California
Europe
cardiovascular disease, 101
hours, work, 86
individual worker vulnerabilities *vs.*
systemic workplace characteristics,
175
legislative/policy interventions, 195
measurement of changes in psychosocial
working conditions, 74
national policies, healthy work
environment, 292
new world of work, 5

International Conference on Occupational
Health, 175
International Finance Corporation (IFC), 21
International Labor Organization (ILO), 24,
223-224
International Monetary Fund (IMF), 21
International Transport Workers'
Federation (ITF), 218, 223, 225-226,
241
Interventions to reduce stress and improve
work organization/worker health
action research, 196-197
collectively bargained approaches, 197
democracy in the workplace/worker
ownership, 200-201
downsizing, 201
employer/organizational interventions,
194, 195
ergonomics, 193-194
evaluations of work redesign and organizational interventions, 203-204
health promotion/stress management,
201-202
integrated health promotion-occupational
health programs, 202-203, 292
new systems of work organization,
198-200
overview, 169-172
policy/legislative interventions, 193-195
prevention, primary/secondary/tertiary,
193, 194, 344-345
redesign, job, 197-198
summary/conclusions, 204
surveillance, workplace, 195-196
See also Curing unhealthy work;
Emotional labor; Hotel workers'
injuries, organizing/collaborating to
reduce; Maintenance Cooperation
Trust Fund; MUNI Health and
Safety Project; Occupational and
environmental medicine; Participatory Action Research; Stakeholder
perspectives on work/stress; Work
Security Index
Ireland, 30, 224
Italy, 26, 30

JACE study, 44, 45
Janitorial industry. *See* Maintenance
Cooperation Trust Fund

Japan
blood pressure, 97
cardiovascular disease, 94, 101
energy efficient technologies, 25
hours, work, 86, 125
individual worker vulnerabilities *vs.*
systemic workplace characteristics,
175
lean production, 198, 199
manufacturing jobs, 26
new world of work, 5
occupational and environmental
medicine, 293-294
regulations, governmental, 345
surveillance, workplace, 195-196, 344
World War II and U.S. rebuilding
war-destroyed economy of, 25
Jauregui, Maritza, 88, 170, 353
J.C. Penney, 23
Job strain
adverse impact on health, 333
assembly-line approach to job design,
90
blood pressure, 2, 96-98
cardiovascular disease, 8, 90, 92, 94-95,
99, 331
control, collective struggles for,
337-338
control, the centrality of, 337
hotel workers' injuries,
organizing/collaborating to reduce,
258
hypertension, 7
janitorial industry, 277-278
mental health, impact of work on, 114,
118-121, 126
occupational and environmental
medicine, 287
reduced workforce, increased work
demands on a, 5
social class and work/health inequalities,
42-46
workplace characteristics *vs.* employee
emotions, 174-175
See also Interventions to reduce stress
and improve work
organization/worker health
Johnson, Jeffrey, 18, 88
Justice, organizational, 125
Just-In-Time (JIT), 314

[Work Security Index (WSI)]
summary/conclusions, 327-329
who can use index and for what purpose,
315-316
Work Site Blood Pressure Study (WSBPS),
New York City, 98, 99, 124, 198
World Bank, 21
World Health Organization, 341
World Trade Organization (WTO), 21

World War II and U.S. rebuilding Europe's
war-destroyed economies, 25
Wright, E. O., 40-42
Wright, Frank L., 309
Wyoming, 156

Yang, Haiou, 88, 354
Yates, Michael, 339
Yelin, Edward, 19, 354